CONFLICTED ANTIQUITIES

Conflicted Antiquities

EGYPTOLOGY, EGYPTOMANIA,

EGYPTIAN MODERNITY

Elliott Colla

Duke University Press

Durham and London

2007

© 2007 Duke University Press
All rights reserved
Printed in the United States of America on acid-free paper ∞
Designed by C. H. Westmoreland
Typeset in Warnock Pro by Achorn International
Library of Congress Cataloging-in-Publication Data appear
on the last printed page of this book.

Duke University Press gratefully acknowledges the support
of Brown University, which provided funds toward the
production of this book.

To Josephine, who sent me,
and Dele, who welcomed me home.
And always, to Nadia, who'd rather
come along.

Contents

ACKNOWLEDGMENTS ix

Introduction: The Egyptian Sculpture Room 1

1 The Artifaction of the Memnon Head 24

Ozymandias 67

2 Conflicted Antiquities: Islam's Pharaoh
and Emergent Egyptology 72

The Antiqakhana 116

3 Pharaonic Selves 121

Two Pharaohs 166

4 The Discovery of Tutankhamen's Tomb:
Archaeology, Politics, Literature 172

Nahdat Misr 227

5 Pharaonism after Pharaonism:
Mahfouz and Qutb 234

Conclusion 273

NOTES 279

BIBLIOGRAPHY 311

INDEX 329

Acknowledgments

This book did not come into being by itself, nor was it produced single-handedly. In conducting my research for the book I was fortunate to be assisted by the able team of Ghenwa Hayek and Ben Kamber in Providence, Kouross Esmaeli in New York, and Reham Shams El-Dean in Cairo. Likewise invaluable was the assistance of the staffs at Dar al-Kutub, Dar al-Watha'iq, the British Library, the British Museum, and the Ministère des Affaires Étrangères. Charles Auger and Carol Wilson-Allen provided continuous and patient assistance throughout. My research was also supported by a variety of generous institutions, including SSRC, the Townsend Center for the Humanities at UC Berkeley, the Wriston and Solomon Fellowships at Brown, and, finally, the Andew W. Mellon Foundation. Without the mentorship and encouragement of Gaber Asfour and Sayyid Bahrawi in Cairo, I would have been lost many years ago—thank you.

I have also benefited greatly from the comments, critiques, and friendship of many colleagues who read drafts of chapters. Special—and admittedly tardy—gratitude is owed to those around Berkeley who read the fragments of a dissertation and encouraged me to make it more: Abdul JanMohamed, Priya Joshi, Margaret Larkin, Michael Lucey, James Monroe, Stefania Pandolfo, Tony Brown, Jeff Fort, Carolina Gonzalez, Leah Middlebrook, Nancy Reynolds, and Jonathan Zatlin. The entire manuscript benefited greatly from continuous and generous feedback from many colleagues in New York, including most especially Lila Abu-Lughod, Ammiel Alcalay, Shiva Balaghi, Samera Esmeir, Khaled Fahmy, Ilana Feldman, Phil Kennedy, Zach Lockman, Muhsin al-Musawi, Kamran Rastegar, Everett K. Rowson, and Nader Uthman. Thanks to Timothy Mitchell, Fred Cooper, Jane Burbank, Allan Hunter, Kate Zaloom, and the 2004–05 ICAS group for pushing chapter 1 in new directions during my time at NYU. The intervention of Joel Gordon and Ted Swedenburg was crucial for refining chapter 5 into what it has become. Clary Bencomo, Gamal Eid, Ahmad Hassan, Sonallah Ibrahim, Salima Ikram, Richard Jacquemond, Samia Mehrez, Muhammad al-Sharqawi, and Nicholas Warner are part of the reason Cairo has always felt so much like home. Fawzi Mohammadein, labor organizer and friend, did not live to see this book completed, but much of my thinking on the subject of ancient and modern Egypt comes from our conversations: I hope I have done his memory justice. The process of writing would have been lonely without friends like Tim Bewes, Rob Blecher, Susan Bernstein, Marilyn Booth, Fulvio Domini, Michael Friedenberg, Lara Harb, Ken Haynes, Ray Huling, Vickie Langohr, Maud Mandel, Shira Robinson, Kathie Schmid, and Chris Toensing. Special thanks also to Patrick Heller, Jo Lee, Little Nadia, Floppers, and Bald Dolly for their hospitality. At home at Brown, I received a necessary push from my colleague Rey Chow, who stayed up nights to make sure this got done. Arnold Weinstein and Ed Ahearn also provided me the backing one needs to write. Rumee Ahmed, Sherine Hamdy, Ian Straughn, Amy Vegari, and Thérèse Shere provided keen aid during the last days of manuscript revision. Dore Levy and Jim Trilling gave me enough aid, food, and drink to make this project mine—they know how much this book is also theirs. I cannot express my gratitude to Joel Beinin, who has witnessed and prodded this project for over a decade now. Rabbina ya'awwiku! Finally, to my family: many thanks for your support and curiosity.

Readers are travelers; they move across lands belonging to someone else, like nomads poaching their way across fields they did not write, despoiling the wealth of Egypt to enjoy it themselves.

—MICHEL DE CERTEAU

No one can look at these wonders without their eyes and breasts filling with wonder, and no one can attempt to describe them without realizing that it is beyond his power to do so.

—DIYA' AL-DIN IBN AL-ATHIR
(d. 1239 CE)

Figure 1. The head of the Younger Memnon installed in the Egyptian Sculpture Room of the Townley Gallery. Engraving by C. Heath after F. Mackenzie, for *Views of London* (1825). © Copyright the Trustees of The British Museum.

The Egyptian Sculpture Room

The image shown here, from 1825, is of the colossal bust of the Younger Memnon in the Egyptian Sculpture Room, part of the Townley Gallery in the original buildings of the British Museum.[1] Raised on a pedestal, the bust sits among other antiquities of Egyptian provenance. While the Egyptian Sculpture Room contains only stone objects, other sorts of objects such as wooden artifacts, papyri, and mummies are displayed in other rooms, alongside similar kinds of objects. The colossal bust rests between two elevated windows, the only sources of light in the gallery. The engraving shown here frames the Egyptian Sculpture Room between columns that support a pediment of unmistakably Greek form. On the far side of the room, a well-dressed gentleman and lady study the display. We are looking at a picture of large antiquities in the gallery of a famous museum. What else is there to say? The kind of room portrayed in this image has become so familiar that it seems not to need explanation. Yet a cursory survey of the quality of the space represented in this image shows that quite a bit is happening.

Most obviously, the gallery depicted here is a space of visual exhibition. The structure of the museum display privileges one particular sensory faculty (sight) while prohibiting others (such as touch). Organized as spectacle, the gallery creates a palpable sense of separation between the viewer and the objects. One might understand this separation as an instance of what Martin Heidegger once described in terms of "the world picture," meaning not "a picture of the world, but the world grasped as picture."[2] The image of the Egyptian Sculpture Room is a threefold illustration of this insight. First, the "world grasped as picture" offers a kind of human subjectivity constituted in relation to nonhuman objects. Heidegger's critique begins from his reading of the German word for "representation," *Vorstellung* (lit. "setting forth"). In Heidegger's reading, the language by which such an act of representation is conceived betrays its tautological quality: "This objectification of beings is accomplished in a setting-before, a representing [*Vor-stellen*], aimed at bringing each being before it in such a way that the man who calculates can be sure—and that means certain—of the being."[3] The subjectivity offered here is problematic since it posits that the being of objects—such as those collected, displayed, visited, and discussed within museums—is reducible to the human understanding of them. The subjectivities it offers (the curator, the museum-goer, the critic) depend on a fragile relationship to objects of its own making. Put this way, the mode of relationship created by the museum exhibit is one that is contingent, even precarious. This brings me to a second point in Heidegger's critique, that the subjectivity offered by the "world as picture" is not just tautological, but also an essay of control:

> That the world becomes picture is one and the same process whereby, in the midst of beings, man becomes subject. . . . The interweaving of these two processes (that the world becomes picture and man the subject), which is decisive for the essence of modernity, illuminates the founding process of modern history, a process that, at first sight, seems almost nonsensical. The process, namely, whereby the more completely and comprehensively the world, as conquered, stands at man's disposal, and the more objectively the object appears, all the more subjectively (i.e., peremptorily) does the *subiectum* rise up, and all the more inexorably, too, do observations and teachings about the world transform themselves into a doctrine of man, into an anthropology.[4]

In the museum, the "world as picture" means that human subjects stand not only separate from but also opposed to the objects on display. In the Egyptian Sculpture Room, this suggests that even if their bodies are dwarfed by the objects on display, the museum-goers stand against (and over) them, since they are offered for their gaze, their edification. Heidegger's third observation is that the "world as picture" involves another order of confusion: the inability to see that the separation created between subjects and objects is not intrinsic, but rather the product of human imagination and labor. This critique certainly holds true in the Egyptian Sculpture Room: the arrangement of objects in the room is presented not as humanly imposed but rather as deriving naturally from the being of the objects. The "world as picture" illustrated by the museum gallery thus involves a disavowal of its own epistemological grounds: "Beings as a whole are now taken in such a way that a being is first and only in being insofar as it is set in place by representing-producing [*vorstellendherstellenden*] humanity."[5]

In *Colonising Egypt*, Timothy Mitchell famously applied the Heideggerian critique of representation to nineteenth-century exhibitions of Egypt.[6] In Mitchell's reading, the exhibition presents objects as if they were faithful copies of original objects whose existence is separate from the act of representation. Mitchell draws out the significance of this in two directions. He emphasizes that the exhibition is foremost a productive institution, creating presence-effects which may or may not have previously existed. In this way, Mitchell shows that the exhibition in Paris in 1889 of "an Egyptian alley" did not so much copy an actual place as constitute a new one. The second line of critique in Mitchell's analysis stems from the observation that the exhibition creates a separation between representations and the world of real things. This point is central to understanding the power of the exhibition in modern history and suggests that the act of representation embodied in the exhibition of an Egyptian alley in Paris involves more than the construction of a new material object like an alley. The production of separation means that one could also generate a concept of the thing represented and create from it typologies and taxonomies. Thus the exhibit in Paris is not merely of *an* Egyptian alley, but rather *the* typical Egyptian alley. As Mitchell points out, the epistemology of separation was crucial to the formulation of abstract concepts (such as tradition and backwardness) which framed Egypt as an object to be worked upon, the target of an overarching plan whose slogans were modernity, reform, and development. In this way, the epistemology of the exhibition is one that follows the logic of instrumentality—"the world as picture" looks for and produces projects of making and transformation.

Large plans may not have been so evident in the exhibit of the Egyptian Sculpture Room in 1825, but the pedagogical mission of the British Museum certainly did present its objects as instruments. The antiquities on display were conceived of as instruments for the edification of museum-goers. Following Heidegger, Max Horkheimer and Theodor Adorno theorized that such instrumentalization was more than an epistemological mistake. It was also the source of potential violence. Describing the kind of knowledge and subjectivity that are based on the objectification of the world, they write, "The awakening of the self is paid for by acknowledge-ment of power as the principle of all relations. . . . Enlightenment behaves toward things as a dictator toward men. He knows them in so far as he can manipulate them. The man of science knows things in so far as he can make them. In this way their potentiality is turned to his ends."[7] For Horkheimer and Adorno, as for Heidegger, founding human subjectivity on an essential opposition toward the world may have produced pow-erful forms of knowledge that treat the world as an object to be made, undone, and remade. But this means that knowledge becomes conceived of chiefly in terms of its use, and its use measured by the standards of ef-ficacy, power, and control. To read the Egyptian Sculpture Room in light of such critiques is to recognize that it is a space able to create subjects who conceive of themselves as separate from and superior to the objects of their study. In this reading, the Egyptian Sculpture Room socializes its subjects into seeing Egypt, already in 1825, as being under the power of their civilized gaze.

The Heideggerian critique of the "world grasped as picture" suggests that the relation obtained in the museum display is one of domination and control. Although this critique is compelling, it does not correspond to ac-counts of travelers and museum-goers who described their experience of viewing Egyptian antiquities not in these terms, but in ones of familiarity and closeness. Rarely did individuals who viewed these objects, both in Egypt and in the British Museum, talk about their immediate experience in terms of domination. On the contrary, they tended to emphasize the fact that they felt awe, marvel, even humility. They describe the experience of being moved by the huge scale of many Egyptian antiquities. In sum, they routinely describe the objects as the site of an experience in which objects are bearers of their own meaning and active participants in the event. In this reading, the Egyptian artifacts appear to run the show, subjecting Brit-ish museum-goers to the image of Egyptian grandeur they embody. What this suggests is that by itself the "world as picture" model does not explain everything that is happening in this museum display, or that, if the "world as picture" model is to hold, we need to understand the paradoxical way in which it disavows its form of power. While it is significant that the objects on display in the Egyptian Sculpture Room were concrete reminders of the power held by those who gazed at them, it is no less significant that they—and not those who looked at them—were thought to be the primary bearers of that power. The ambiguous form of power associated with, but also unacknowledged by, the explicit structure of Egyptological exhibitions from this period would have lasting effects. I will leave for the moment the questions about objects raised (but not fully answered) by this line of thought to address other aspects of the Egyptian Sculpture Room.

The Egyptian Sculpture Room depicted here is a national space, part of the National Repository (as the British Museum was called), funded publicly by act of Parliament,[8] and expressly designed to promote patriotic sensibilities.[9] Like other rooms in the gallery, this room displays an arrangement that attests to the cultural refinement of the English nation and to the reach of the British Empire. The various galleries of the museum present an array of concrete objects from around the world. As an assemblage, these objects form an abstract image of the globe with London at its center. This room is thus also a pedagogical space, creating for metropolitan audiences a material inventory of the stuff of empire and its abstract concept.

Besides representing aspects of nation and empire, the room presents lessons in aesthetic taste and historical appreciation that serve as "civilizing rituals" for museum visitors.[10] One part of this ritual is bound up in the notion of direct aesthetic experience. Unlike the descriptions of Egyptian objects in travel accounts and unlike the famous visual images of Egyptian monuments in books like the *Description de l'Égypte*, the Egyptian Sculpture Room offers the appearance of an unmediated sensation of the objects themselves. In this sense, "the museum is more than a location . . . it is a script" directing aesthetic experience.[11] Beyond being a site for the cultivation of (certain kinds of) corporeal experience and taste, the museum offers other sorts of lessons as well. On the one hand, there is the synchronic lesson of taxonomy and order. This is realized by the placement of like objects with one another or by the division of arts, mediums, and national traditions from one another in the space of the museum.[12] On the other hand, there are the diachronic lessons of art history, development, and progress. In this way, the material objects mark events within the plot of the universal survey museum:[13] the forward march of human civilization from its classical origins in Greece and Rome, through Renaissance Italy, to modern-day London.[14]

The space of the Egyptian Sculpture Room is organized around both kinds of scripts. We can certainly interpret the objects in this room taxonomically insofar as we find only sculpture of a certain provenance (Egypt), scale (monumental), and material (stone). Other kinds of Egyptian objects—smaller stone objects and objects made of wood, metal, papyrus, and human flesh (mummy)—are displayed in other places in the British Museum. Moreover, the Egyptian Sculpture Room is located at the end of the long hall of the Townley Gallery, which houses only stone sculptures of ancient Mediterranean provenance. At the same time, we are encouraged to read these objects as part of a historical narrative. The location of the Egyptian Sculpture Room nestles its objects within a broader survey of fine art. Indeed, the lesson about Egyptian art and culture that emerges from this arrangement is itself situated against (and in the engraving is literally framed by) classical Greek styles whose aesthetic and historical values were taken to be axiomatic.

Overarching these wider lessons in history and taste is arguably the most important, though most abstract, value concretized in the museum room: conservation. Like air, this value permeates the Egyptian Sculpture Room but is impossible to see in itself. Its effects, however, are everywhere—from the cleanliness of the floor and lack of dust on the sculptures to the neatness of the displays and care with which the objects are treated. Conservation implies not just the act of preserving the objects from material decay, but also the cultivation of good administration as a virtue in itself. The clean, well-structured look of the Egyptian Sculpture Room attests to its conscientious management and gives rise to an ethical discourse surrounding the treatment of museum pieces by the curatorial staff.[15] The moral value of rational management cannot therefore be underestimated: it is fundamental to the museum belief that the objects rightfully belong where they are because that is where they are best cared for. Far from clarifying our understanding of the gallery's meaning, however, the theme of conservation introduces a tension between competing notions of temporality. Just as the museum organizes its objects to suggest a developmental narrative of history writ large, the gallery space itself is static and designed to insulate objects from the ravages of history. The capacity to stop time, to preserve, is what enables the presentation of objects as diachronic history.

Less obviously to us now, this room is an emergent space. In 1825, the Townley Gallery (completed in 1808) was a relatively recent addition to the older museum building (Montagu House), which had, by 1805, become too small to adequately display the rapidly growing collection of antique statuary. Many of the objects in the collection—like the colossal bust of the Younger Memnon—were themselves very recent additions. Thus, the placement of these objects in relation to one another was also fairly new. Indeed, when the Memnon head arrived in 1819, the curator of the Townley Gallery had to rearrange the entire space drastically to make room for it. At the same time, this room is a temporary space. By the late 1820s, Montagu House had been torn down to make way for the much grander galleries designed by Robert Smirke that remain to this day. Within another few years, the Townley Gallery too would be demolished to make way for the new building. By 1834, the Memnon head would be relocated to the Egyptian Sculpture Gallery in the new wing of the museum.

The space of this room is also a socially exclusive space, as intimated by the fine dress of the museum-goers in the image: in 1825 one still had to apply and be recognized as a proper visitor in order to be admitted. For this reason it is also a space of conflicts: not only did many of those excluded from the room contest the legitimacy of the museum as a public institution, but within the room itself, curators doubted whether the objects belonged in a museum at all. For all the above reasons, this particular room was an ambiguous space. The ambiguity was related to, but also far more pervasive than, the fact that while the Memnon bust was duly catalogued and displayed as a discrete piece, little was known about it other than its material composition and general location of modern acquisition. Nothing beyond classical myth was known about its origins or original use, not to mention the ruler depicted in the sculpture. Indeed, such basic information as this was lacking for most of the pieces in the Egyptian Sculpture Room. Given that deficit, it is difficult to say what the lesson of the exhibition hall could be, let alone how it was supposed to fit into the larger nineteenth-century debates about taste and the history of fine art. This ambiguity does not mean the Egyptian Sculpture Room had no meaning, but rather that at this point its sense had more to do with the emergence of the British Museum than with the Egyptian past. It might be objected that the ambiguity was itself temporary, since by the 1830s, following widespread acceptance of Jean-François Champollion's theories about the hieroglyphic language, curators and museum-goers had access to increasingly certain historical information about the Pharaonic past and the significance of its objects. Yet it is precisely at this moment—before such knowledge was produced—that one should begin to study it.

The 1825 setting of the Egyptian Sculpture Room is central to the story of this book. The story is not just about a room, however, or just about the objects it contained. It is about the broad array of discourses and institutions made possible by the existence of such rooms and objects and by the kinds of people who worked in the rooms, who passed through them, and who thought about their social and cultural meanings.

Nevertheless, objects—and the Memnon head especially—are a good place to enter these discourses. Though the Memnon bust was an old object, in many senses its status as an artifact was a new avatar. The modern sense of an art object as an artifact in a museum was being invented at the same time the Memnon bust was arriving in London. While I will soon have more to say about the subject, let me signal what I mean by "artifact," since my usage deviates slightly from convention. Usually, the term is associated with the emergence of new methods of treating material culture during the early nineteenth century. In particular, the term is linked to the work of the Danish archaeologist Christian Jürgensen Thomsen, whose innovations in the study of the palaeolithic past stressed the context and arrangements in which objects were found. Instead of using material culture to confirm already known chronologies, Thomsen looked to deduce information about prehistoric periods from the objects themselves. Key to Thomsen's method were a number of practices: the treatment of excavation sites as self-contained units, that is as evidence that spoke to the significance of the objects found within them; the study of objects' material composition, their usage, patterns of style and decoration, and their relation to other objects found in their proximity. Notably, this method bracketed considerations of taste—what was sought was data, not art. Likewise, considerations of Biblical or classical history were no longer automatically assumed as relevant. As a consequence, an artifact was not considered as a unique piece, but rather as part of a class of objects arranged within an emerging taxonomical grid. In conventional accounts of archaeology, this shift in the treatment of material culture marks the change from eighteenth-century antiquarianism to the modern science of archaeology. As these accounts point out, Egyptology was quite slow to make a shift in the direction of "true science," and the advent of a "self-contained and systematic study . . . as distinguished from the antiquarianism of earlier times" does not occur until the career of William Matthews Flinders Petrie in the late nineteenth century.[16]

In this study, I do not seek to redefine the term "artifact" so much as to explore its conceptual roots and the institutions of its birth. Admittedly, my use of the term with reference to the reception of Pharaonic antiquities during the 1820s may strike some as anachronistic. Indeed, during this period, the meaning of Egyptian antiquities was still very much tied to debates about taste and Biblical history. Similarly, it would be many decades before the scientific methods employed by Thomsen and his students gained a foothold in Egyptology. Still, there are important reasons for starting a study of the concept at this moment, for the term was deployed with reference to ancient Egyptian objects long before the period that is described as "scientific" by the histories of archaeology. Critically, the emergence of the new treatment of Egyptian antiquities was itself rooted in the long process of separating *naturalia* and *artificialia* within the early modern museum collections of Europe. As Stephanie Moser has pointed out, during the eighteenth century Egyptian antiquities were regularly treated as both natural and as man-made (artificial) objects.[17] The term "artifact," a nominalization derived from the latter category, sought to redefine such ambiguities by establishing two things: on the one hand, the human rather than natural origin of an object; and on the other, its status as the product of an act of making. Most especially, its concept seeks to separate factual questions of what it means to have been made by human labor from questions of value. The birth of the artifact is thus embedded in the history of how the museum (as a "public" place of study) emerged from the curiosity cabinet, and how the modern "scientific" disciplines of the ancient past (such as archaeology and Egyptology) emerged from older traditions of antiquarianism.

The invention of the Egyptian artifact in the context of spaces like the Townley Gallery was to have many consequences (see chapter 1). First, it produced a new understanding of the material of the ancient Egyptian past, without which Egyptology could not have come into being. At the same time, the artifact brought into being a new relation to the material world of modern Egypt and its inhabitants. This aspect was not lost on travelers, politicians, and archaeologists of the period, who recognized that to know ancient Egypt, one needed to gain control of as many artifacts as possible. To reach this end, they might need to control modern Egypt. The possibility was already a matter of discussion as the Memnon head was being removed from Egypt. As Richard Robertson, traveling in Egypt during this time, put it, "Let us not complain of the want of information respecting ancient Egypt, till we have made ourselves thoroughly masters of all that remains in the country."[18] Thus, the artifact was becoming not just a crucial object for producing solid knowledge about the ancient past, but also an instrument of colonial intervention sixty years before the start of direct British rule in Egypt. Much of this book is dedicated to exploring these links between museum collecting, Egyptology, and colonial rule, while also showing how the conflict over Pharaonic material culture became both a source of nationalist culture and a central issue in Egyptian contestations of European hegemony.

EGYPTOLOGY'S HISTORIES

The first years of the history of Pharaonic artifacts reveal much about the emergence of museum acquisition in Egypt, the forms of knowledge— like Egyptology—it helped create, and the forms of colonial power that emerged in tandem with them. Not surprisingly, the 1810s feature prominently in the standard histories of Egyptology, though in an uneasy way. In these accounts, the decade marks a turning point in the history of understanding ancient Egypt and its objects, and thus the beginning of a new set of social relations and cultural practices made possible by the new acquisitions and the new institution of the Egyptian artifact. Yet, whether the histories present this period as an unfortunate (but forgivable) prehistory or condemn its protagonists for their excesses, they sharply distinguish the 1810s from a later moment of enlightenment in which the values of true science and responsible administration prevail. In other words, the dominant story told in all these histories is actually concerned with the advent of modern Egyptology, which is a triumphalist history of "us moderns." It is time to reconnect our history with the events that put the Memnon head on display in the Egyptian Sculpture Room if we want to see just where our sense of modernity comes from and what sensibilities its emergence precluded. Conversely, if we want to say that the 1810s represent an era of ignorance and a detachable prehistory of Egyptology, then we are obliged to consider how this era and its traditions shaped what we take to be professional, that is, disinterested, science. If we hope to understand the power of Egyptology we need to explore at more length what precedes it and consider the ways in which earlier discourses and practices contributed to the emergence of this modern science. Far from emerging sui generis, Egyptology is built upon the practices against which it sought to distinguish itself. Far from being successfully purged, these older practices and concepts are embedded in the customs that govern the reception of antiquities to this day, whether in the field or in the museum.

My discussion of the Egyptian Sculpture Room to this point has been framed in terms of the contingent and conflicted understanding of the European reception of its objects. The sense of conflict becomes even more acute when the place of modern Egypt within this history is taken into account. The emergence of Egyptology in Europe was as consequential for modern Egyptians as it was for Europeans. Starting in the late eighteenth century, excavation sites and museum exhibitions were very often the terrain where the contradictions and struggles of Egyptian modernity were most sharply revealed. On the level of colonial rivalries, the French and British often clashed at these sites; however, the larger picture delineates antagonisms between Europeans and the Egyptians themselves. These conflicts intensified during the twentieth century when excavation sites and museums became the scene of struggles between many Egyptian national groups: urban elites and rural peasants, secularists and Islamists, proponents of pan-Arabism and territorial nationalists, and so on.

Until very recently, the history of colonial archaeology in Egypt has been restricted to a very narrow range of account, one that might be called the colonial enlightenment narrative. This body of writing tends to reproduce (consciously or otherwise) one of the central colonial assumptions of early European antiquity collectors, namely, that ancient Egypt and its treasures were the rightful patrimony of the West.[19] Key in this body of writing is the ideology of conservation, itself an important component of nineteenth-century museum formation and archaeological research and an operative term in texts composed by European explorers, excavators, tourists, and administrators in Egypt.[20] Later writers of the colonial enlightenment version of this history tend to reproduce the assumptions contained in their primary sources, composed by such European explorers and archaeologists. They argue the legitimacy of colonial archaeology and artifact acquisition in terms of conserving objects which, if left in situ, would surely have been lost or destroyed. These are narratives in which great men—from Champollion and Karl Richard Lepsius to Gaston Maspero and Howard Carter—figure large, saving monuments from throngs of fellaheen and deciphering their secrets back home in London, Paris, and Berlin. While these accounts of Egyptology often admit unfortunate commercial abuses that occurred in this history of acquisitions (such as those surrounding the Memnon head), they usually stress that the necessity and benefit of acquisition outweighed all harm.[21] Though the terms of the colonial enlightenment narrative belong to their nineteenth-century progenitors, they remain to this day dominant in popular writing and even in much of the scholarship on Egyptology's history.

During the 1970s, a revisionist history of colonial archaeology in Egypt began to appear. This new narrative, produced mostly in the West, criticized European acquisition projects while characterizing them as haphazard pillage and organized theft.[22] This body of writing might be called the colonial rape narrative, since the infelicitous trope of sexual violation recurs often in them. These accounts cover more or less the same events as the older histories and only rarely seek out new primary sources. As narratives, they also tell the same story of Europeans discovering artifacts in the wilderness of Egypt. However, they display a greater degree of skepticism toward the colonial rhetorics of scientific disinterest and altruistic curiosity. Another body of literature on Egyptology that is especially attuned to its familiar pattern of material dispossession has been associated with Afrocentrism. Most famously among these, Martin Bernal's *Black Athena* theorized the broader consequences that colonial excavation and acquisition had for the science of Egyptology.[23] As others besides Bernal have pointed out, since the issue of historical interpretation is closely tied to the question of control, the significance of colonialism goes beyond the issue of material dispossession.[24] Indeed, because material custody was a necessary condition for scientific and historical interpretation, colonized peoples were effectively barred from interpreting their own past. Bernal's argument goes beyond this, of course, to explore the ways in which nineteenth-century Egyptology incorporated racist assumptions about the nature of civilization and in the process effectively "whitened" the Pharaonic phenotype. While there is much to doubt in his positive claims about the (black) African identity of ancient Egyptians,[25] Bernal does convincingly show how

Europeans had often made claims on the Pharaohs that were no less racial than his. Moreover, Bernal succeeded in putting the issue of colonial epistemology on the table, even if others have been tardy in continuing his critique of the epistemology of Egyptology.

The most obvious fault in both the revisionist accounts (including Afrocentric accounts) and the colonial enlightenment narrative is that modern Egyptians simply do not figure in the story. For instance, scholars of European Egyptomania,[26] even those attuned to its postcolonial critique, have been largely unaware of the fact that a comparable cultural phenomenon occurred in Egypt during the 1920s and 1930s as Egyptian intellectuals and artists studied ancient Egypt and considered it the source of modern Egyptian identity.[27] Likewise, while revisionist accounts speak against injustices against Egypt, they tend to represent Egyptians merely as victims or bystanders, not participants, in the history of Egyptology. The reason is simple: both kinds of accounts were written by scholars who did not consult the extensive Arabic-language archives on the subject. Predictably, by ignoring Egyptian sources these historians came to think that colonial archaeology in Egypt was a conversation that took place only among European travelers, explorers, tourists, administrators, and archaeologists. In such accounts, the backdrop of modern Egypt is incidental, sometimes tragic, and, most of all, obscure. As a consequence of this style of writing, conventional histories of Egyptology stress the infamous Anglo-Franco rivalry in nineteenth-century museum acquisitions and in Egyptology itself. While no doubt worthy of the attention it has received, the focus has obscured the existence of other actors and other lines of antagonism.

This shortcoming has been addressed in a third body of writing on colonial Egyptology that might be called the national enlightenment narrative. Drawing on primary sources within the Egyptian archives (and also on a minor tradition within Egyptian historiography), the national enlightenment narrative foregrounds the place of ancient Egypt in nineteenth- and twentieth-century Egyptian culture and sketches the formation of national museums, the academic study of the ancient past, and the popular dissemination of images and stories that take ancient Egypt as a theme and contemporary issue.[28] In many ways, the national enlightenment narrative diverges from the traditional colonial narrative: the colonial argues that Egyptians were indifferent to antiquities and thus lacking in culture, while the national argues that modern Egyptians have a more legitimate claim to Egyptian antiquities than do Europeans; the colonial claims that the best home for Pharaonic artifacts is in London or Paris, while the national argues they belong in Cairo; the colonial asserts that the ancient Egyptians were the indirect progenitors of Western civilization, while the national claims them as the direct ancestors of modern Egyptians.[29] But, importantly, the two versions share at least one attitude: like the colonial enlightenment narrative, the national enlightenment narrative argues that Egyptian peasants were the chief threat to ancient monuments.[30] In both narratives, the values of preservation and acquisition serve as unambiguous, desirable indices of modernity and civilization.

A fourth, more diffuse style of writing this history may be thought of in terms of agnostic narrative, since it highlights the constructed, contingent, and contested character of archaeological practices and of the civilizational narratives that are built upon them. All told, this body of writing on colonial and postindependence archaeology in Egypt underscores the fact that its practices are constructed and that its accomplishments are more ambiguous than previously acknowledged. Agnostic narratives recognize the contingency of archaeological knowledge and also of its application in narratives and images designed to legitimate contemporary identities, be they Egyptian, European, or African. The writers in this body of work display a deep ambivalence toward positivist claims on artifacts and history, whether composed by apologists of empire, of the nation, or of Afrocentrism. In all versions of this style of historiography, the term "conservation" does not have the stable, privileged place it has in the other narratives of colonial archaeology in Egypt. For instance, Jacques Tagher's singular account of antiquities collection illustrates that there was no clean break between the rapacious practices of the early nineteenth century and the allegedly more legitimate forms of museum acquisition later in the century.[31] Similarly, the groundbreaking but underappreciated work of Antoine Khater on Egyptian antiquities law and its inconsistent application went far to illustrate a deep ambivalence toward conservation ideology even among those figures who appear as heroes within the national enlightenment narrative.[32] In his researches, Neil Asher Silberman has described how the relationship between the Egyptian present and its antiquity is constructed, ever shifting, and informed by a range of conflicting social and political pressures.[33] Likewise, in their work Israel Gershoni and James Jankowski have shown how the political identification between ancient and modern Egypt sometimes encouraged by secularist national elites during the 1930s—Pharaonism—was one that was tenuous and intensely debated.[34] Jan Assmann's work problematizes the relation between material evidence and narrative claims on ancient Egypt in other directions.[35] Recently, Lynn Meskell has submitted the methods and categories of Egyptology to questions raised by contemporary science studies.[36] Meskell does not merely show that the claims of Egyptology are affected by the political context around them, but rather that the very structures and methods of the most professional and competent archaeological science contain their own kind of politics.[37] In this sense, the political aspects of Egyptology's history cannot be explained away as instances of bad, impure, or unobjective science.[38] Writing also in this vein, Timothy Mitchell has demonstrated how Egyptology has functioned as one administrative institution among others specially authorized, under the banner of technical expertise, to manage Egypt's wealth, resources, and, most important, population. As Mitchell shows, these forms of expert knowledge have constituted their own special mode of power.[39]

ANTIQUITIES AND CONFLICT

To give some sense of how the work of Egyptology takes place amidst sets of conflicts, one could not do better than start with a brief consideration of the most exemplary kind of Egyptological institution: the excavation site. While they are in the field, Egyptologists seek as much as they can to create laboratory conditions.[40] To do this, they cordon off their site as much as possible from the social, political, and cultural contexts around it, effectively creating an interior ("the dig," where scientists work to create conditions of objective research) separated from what is around it, which becomes a place of "externalities." The standards, practices, and technical ability to achieve this end may have changed dramatically over Egyptology's history, but the ideal of clinical separation has remained a theoretical constant from very early on. Yet, insofar as the typical method of separation has historically entailed the wholesale appropriation of land and expulsion of local peasant communities by colonial authorities (and later by Egyptian state officials), by no means can one say that even the best Egyptological science has ever been nonpolitical. As the history of the southern

Egyptian village of Gurna indicates, for example, Egyptological interest and concern have long been (and continue to be) key mechanisms of regular and often violent state intervention in the lives of modern Egyptians.[41]

The recent engagement between scholars of Egyptology and science studies is welcome because it recharts the multiple and significant intersections linking archaeology and the European museum to the history of modern Egypt. In this way, it indicates how one might move beyond the history of ideas model that has tended to dominate the colonial and national enlightenment narratives of Egyptology. In this model, the relation between archaeological discovery and Egyptological knowledge is often portrayed as mechanical: discovery leads to breakthroughs in understanding, which are then applied in making new discoveries; this process repeats and improves upon itself, and thus knowledge accumulates. Accordingly, Egyptology's development appears to move in a smooth upward fashion, without regard for (or serious disturbance by) the fact that most of the relevant events took place in, or in relation to, modern Egypt, a country whose experience of colonial modernity has been anything but smooth and uneventful. In contrast, science studies encourages Egyptologists to rethink how knowledge is actually produced by inquiring into the relation between Egyptology's interior—its knowledge—and those factors it usually declares to be mere externalities. Inspired by this critique, this book asks a number of questions usually not considered to be relevant to Egyptology—questions about location and practice, object and representation. Briefly, I will argue that it matters that most of Egyptology's work has taken place in modern Egypt; it matters that the practice of Egyptological inquiry has rested as much on political and legal arrangements (and experimentation based on local knowledge) as it has on scientific methods; it matters that Egyptologists, like other modern scientists and scholars, needed to invent the class of objects (artifacts) on which they would work and over which they would have unique authority; and it matters that Egyptological claims were not pure concepts, but representations that took place in and around long-standing traditions, not to mention emerging semantic fields. Finally, it matters that these practices, objects, and representations—themselves ambiguous—were the site where significant social and cultural conflicts found expression.

One of the first arguments of this book is that Egyptology's object, the artifact, came into being somewhere between Egypt and London, and that this ushered in a new form of power linking archaeology, Egyptology, print culture, literature, and the arts with colonial and national politics. It should not be startling to assume that innovations in the formation of agency might have first emerged in the colonies, since, as scholars have routinely observed, the colonies of Europe were often quite explicitly constructed as laboratories for developing social and political technologies that might be used in the metropole.[42] And despite the Eurocentric focus that still predominates in Egyptology's autobiography, it is difficult to imagine that the discipline's center of gravity has ever been securely located in Europe. Indeed, the actual work of Egyptology has never strayed far from the Egyptian countryside. Egyptology has always been partly situated in Egypt, even if there has always been a sharp line drawn between the field and the museum.

There is nothing remarkably new in these observations. Yet much said here will be rebuffed by those for whom Egyptology seems nothing more than the scholarly, disinterested study of the ancient past of Egypt carried out by uniquely qualified experts. When Martin Bernal attempted, twenty years ago, to illustrate the ways in which European Egyptology was colored by its own traditions of racism and colonialism, his claims were rejected as nonsense by Egyptologists and classicists alike. Readers will note in the following chapters that, unlike Bernal, for the most part I remain agnostic about the veracity of the particular claims Egyptology makes about the ancient past. It is the relevance of Egyptology in modern Egypt, not what it says about ancient Egypt, that most concerns me. In this way, I will insist that Egyptology needs to be understood as a particular institution of colonial power and later nationalist power in Egypt.

Thus, this study begins with, and returns to, the simple idea that acquisitionsts, Egyptologists, and curators have always been situated. They do not study ancient objects in a distanced and acontextual way but are actively engaged in remaking those objects, and remaking them within the horizons in which they labor. The objects they have made, artifacts, are more than mere instruments by which colonial knowledge and power are created. That is because artifacts are not just products of human agency but also constitutive of it. They are not merely inert or detachable from the kind of knowledge and power which comes into being through the interaction of scientists and their objects of study. To employ a useful, oft-cited phrase, artifacts are "entangled" with the sciences that take them to be their objects.[43]

Likewise, Egyptologists work within contexts that are informed by disputes and conflicts. Though their scholarship may always be about the ancient past, their claims have always touched upon issues—Islam, peasants, nationalist claims to cultural patrimony—that are thoroughly modern. This is as true in today's Egyptology as it was in that of the 1800s. Like other modern sciences, Egyptological study involves acts of intervention into the material composition of its objects even as it strives to observe them dispassionately. In this sense, it is always a productive, not merely a reflective, practice and has, since the 1810s, transformed the Egyptian countryside in radical ways. Likewise, the knowledge Egyptologists produce, like other orders of knowledge, has always articulated a form of power: sometimes it has been marshaled to justify explicitly colonial ends, other times it has served to contest colonial rule, and it has almost always been used to discipline the peasantry of Upper Egypt.

The significance of these dynamics extends beyond the reach of Egyptology. Indeed, the struggle over the administration of ancient Egyptian objects is central to understanding Egyptian nationalist culture during the colonial period. This is because, for one thing, the debate over the ownership of Pharaonic Egypt did not simply pit Egyptian nationalists against European colonial administrators. Just as colonial administrators routinely relied upon preservationist ideology to justify their expropriation of Pharaonic antiquities, so Egyptian elites found it useful for exerting new forms of control over rural populations. Thus concepts such as appreciation and preservation implied much more than a way of thinking aesthetically and historically about objects—they also had vast implications for developing new forms of political governance. Moreover, the appropriation of Pharaonic art and culture was controversial as the basis for a national imaginary within Egypt itself. In particular, cultural Pharaonism reflected the taste and ideology of a narrow elite and took little account of the Muslim culture that had prevailed in Egypt for more than twelve hundred years.

My argument here explores these various conflicts by situating expressive culture in the institutions of material culture. Textual representations of Egyptian antiquities and fictional narratives on Pharaonic themes were not simply posterior reflections of material practice. On the contrary, archaeology and museum culture anticipated, as much as they proceeded from, the cultural imaginary of Egyptomania and Pharaonism. Similarly, it is not the case that Egyptian and European travelers and writers encountered Egyptian antiquities unmediated. Indeed, even their most personal encounters were never purely individual. The experience of the Egyptian antique was shaped by the exhibitionary institutions that framed the experience of monuments abroad and museums at home, just as it was conditioned by books and images consumed before leaving. In this sense, even the most subjective aspects of material culture are socially constructed. But it is time to move beyond the now routine observation that cultural objects are constructed by human subjects to argue that antiquities were not merely passive objects in history. As nonhuman objects, they were entangled in the social life of human actors and played an active role in the formation of power relations, whether in the British Empire or in the Egyptian nation-state.[44] This is to echo a fundamental precept of science studies: there is no sharp separation between material objects and the concepts and human capacities they enable.[45] This is a call not to return to traditional materialism, but rather to notice that humans, Egyptian antiquities, and the representations of artifacts formed part of a sprawling network of agents and *actants*.[46] One indicator of this fact is that even though the processes of artifaction and figuration attempted to construct antiquities as inert matter, the stuff itself often did not obey this command. The proliferation of mummy fictions in English and French literatures attests to the anxieties that attended this. Moreover, while Egyptian antiquities were an important "object site" for the articulation of struggles among human subjects, the ground of this site was itself in motion. The consequences of this thoroughly conditioned the various cultural formations that emanated from the science of Egyptology, from museums to tourism, from pop Egyptomania in Europe to literary and political Pharaonism in Egypt. The Egyptian Sculpture Room may not have been the origin of this process, but it was a crucial node in the network of artifacts—the assemblage of political and cultural *agencements*—which began to emerge in the 1810s and which remains to this day so powerful that its power is never noticed.

A brief word on the organization of this book. Chapter 1 fleshes out the process by which antiquities were excavated and transported from Egypt and then received at their museum destination. The experiment pursued in this chapter is the tracing of a moment in a single object's biography as recorded by travelers, collectors, diplomats, officers, curators, and so on. I sought to gather as many documents of its provenance as possible, and in so doing narrate the story of a thing as it was transformed into an object of travelers' interest, and then into an artifact acquired and put on display in the British Museum. If I have erred in the way of length and detail in this account, it has been to stress one of the primary facts of the new mode of antiquities collecting—namely, that the transformation of thing into artifact would be unthinkable without this archive of descriptive claims. This process—the creation of an artifact—is of primary significance for the wider narratives of the book, since it laid the foundation for a new way of thinking about Egyptian antiquities that would soon have consequences well beyond Egyptology. Chapter 2 charts the emergence of a set of ideas about the governance of modern Egypt that was made possible by the new artifact discourse while also situating this emergence against older local and regional traditions of thinking about ancient Egyptian monuments. Chapter 3 traces one consequence that Egyptological knowledge would have for modern Egyptians, since it became the source of a new sense of individual and collective identity. This chapter explores how motifs, themes, and narratives of modern Egyptian interest in ancient Egypt resonated deeply with others from the *Nahda*, the Arab modernist project of the nineteenth century and early twentieth. Chapter 4 revisits the institutional practices of Egyptology by way of the example of the discovery of King Tutankhamen's tomb in 1922. Here we find that the science of the discovery was hopelessly entangled with contemporary nationalist politics and literary culture, and that this entanglement cannot be dismissed as mere externality to the practice of archaeological science. Chapter 5 describes the limits of Pharaonism, the Egyptian literary and political school of the 1920s and 1930s that was based on interest in Egyptological discovery. This chapter presents readings in Naguib Mahfouz's early Pharaonist literary works alongside readings in the work of the contemporary Islamists Hassan al-Banna and Sayyid Qutb. The resulting juxtaposition illuminates the degree to which literary Pharaonism was founded on assumptions that were always deeply contested.

The organization of the book is historical, though not strictly so. Rather, each chapter develops its own thematic argument even as it presents a discrete historical moment or series of moments. Moreover, while the order of the chapters is roughly chronological, starting in the 1810s and ending in the 1940s, the broader themes of the book are concerned with the emergence and development of colonial and nationalist cultures in modern Egypt.

While conducting my research, I was constantly reminded of the fact that ancient Egypt and its material culture have meant so many things to so many people over the years. Consider in this regard the following list of attitudes about, representations of, and claims on Pharaonic Egypt. For Neoplatonists, Rosicrucians, Freemasons (and in their way, new-age pagans), ancient Egypt has long been associated with Hermes Trismegistus and the origins of magic and alchemy, rationality and spiritualism. For Jews, the annual observance of Passover is a reminder that ancient Egypt was a place of bondage—and yet readers of the story of Joseph would not be mistaken to think that Egypt might also figure as a place of refuge. For rising empires, both ancient and modern, Egypt has always been a symbol of ancient sovereignty whose power might be grasped through the acquisition (or reproduction) of its monumental objects—hence the conspicuous placement of obelisks in Rome, London, Paris, New York, and Washington. During the first years of the French Revolution, ancient Egypt served as inspiration for a secular symbolic order designed to replace the church. For the nineteenth-century English surgeon-showman, Thomas "Mummy" Pettigrew, ancient Egypt was a fount of anatomical curiosity; for Joseph Smith, his contemporary in the United States, it was a source of divine revelation. Throughout the nineteenth century, Christian scholars studied ancient Egypt, looking for scientific evidence of the literal truth of Biblical narrative. In modern opera, to take one example of modern expressive culture, Egyptian themes figured centrally, as in Verdi's *Aïda* and Mozart's *Die Zauberflöte*. Later, the image of ancient Egypt would loom large in pulp genres of writing, from mystery to fantasy to science fiction. In Hollywood, Egyptian antiquities have always meant the adventure of discovery and the danger of the supernatural. In African American thought and culture, Egypt has appeared as a place of origin and proof of the sophistication and age of African civilization. We could add to this list the rich and diverse ways of thinking about ancient Egypt that appear within the textual tradition of orthodox Islam and the popular practices of Egyptian peasants—from the melancholic contemplation of ancient ruins to the seeking of fertility totems within ancient temple sites, and from the use of mummy detritus as fertilizer to the pragmatic use of pyramids as rock quarries. Finally, Egypt's Coptic community has long had an intimate, though fraught, relationship to their pre-Christian past—as both direct descendents and apostates from the ancient civilization, they have at times rejected their association with Pharaonic Egypt, and at others championed it.

The above is a just a partial list of the possible topics one could study while exploring the modern image of ancient Egypt. The list also sheds light on a basic problem: the body of cultural representations of ancient Egypt is not just massive, it is also heterogeneous and contradictory. Admittedly, most of the items on this list are not given any consideration in this book. Instead I have chosen to focus on just a fraction of the modern cultural production inspired by the Pharaonic past, a sliver that until the present has not been sufficiently studied—the relationship between the ancient past and modern Egyptian culture during the colonial period, with a special emphasis on the ties between Egyptology and literary culture. Despite this narrow focus, I found no lack of heterogeneity, tension, and contradiction within and between the modern Egyptian traditions of representing the ancient past. These antagonisms and ambiguities are the underlying theme of this book, and I have attempted to leave them as they are rather than iron them out or fold them into a single, smooth story.

To accomplish this, I have arranged between each chapter brief contrapuntal readings that highlight the contested, conflicted, and ambiguous character of each text and cultural formation. For example, between chapters 3 and 4, I describe the way that the figure of Pharaoh re-emerges during the colonial period as writers like Ya'qub Sanu' and Ahmad Shawqi sought to critique the despotic character of contemporary political rule. Importantly, their use of the figure of Pharaoh was not exactly the negative one received from the Bible or the Quran, nor the positive one derived from Egyptian Egyptology. Their figuration of Pharaoh speaks *with* and also *against* these other traditions, which are described in earlier chapters—and serves as a lucid example of what I mean by counterpoint. It made little sense to delete them from this study or to try to make them fit where they do not belong. The counterpoints in this book are arranged to indicate the degree to which the texts and themes of the preceding chapter become complicated or undermined when other representations enter the picture.

Part of my motivation for organizing these counterpoints is due to my conviction, following Edward Said's powerful study *Culture and Imperialism*, that the analysis of colonial culture must be attuned to the dialogical character of colonial and anti-colonial power relations, which are themselves composed of back-and-forth movements between brutal violence and inspired creativity, bloody struggle and human conversation. I have attempted to signal this dynamic in the title of the book: the antiquities under discussion here are not only things over which (and because of which) conflicts have arisen, but their very matter is itself conflicted—that is, fraught, ambiguous, and wholly contested. Indeed, the cultural history charted here illustrates the degree to which the modern Egyptian consideration of ancient artifacts is composed (in an almost impossibly unified manner) of elements drawn from a long history of colonial dispossession, a longer tradition of classical Arabo-Islamic literary expression, the class chauvinism of enlightenment nationalist culture, and the revisionist critique of political Islamism.

1

The Artifaction of the Memnon Head

According to the curator's report, the head of the statue of the younger Memnon was elevated onto its pedestal in the Egyptian Sculpture Room in early January 1819.[1] Perhaps, by the end of this day, when it was set among other Egyptian antiquities in the British Museum, the Memnon head had become that special kind of modern object known as an artifact. Yet it is highly doubtful whether the act of elevation in and of itself transformed the object into the museum artifact. More reasonably, one might recognize it as merely one event in a long chain of events in the biography of the object. Fortunately, much of this narrative is available by way of travel accounts and the correspondence between the collectors in Egypt, the officers of the British Museum, and their go-betweens in the navy and the diplomatic corps. Thus the Memnon head's movements can be traced with surprising precision. In late July 1816, a work team removed the head from its location in the complex of ancient Theban ruins called at the time the Memnonium. On August 12, 1816, it arrived on the west bank of the Nile, opposite the town of Luxor.[2] On November 21, it was loaded onto a flat-bottomed river barge. It arrived in Cairo on December 15,[3] and in Rosetta on January 10, 1817. Four days later, British military engineers unloaded it at the pasha's warehouse in the port of Alexandria.[4] By this time, the museum trustees had been notified many times over by travelers and diplomatic agents that the colossal statue was on its way to London. The head then waited in Alexandria[5] as the British Museum and the Foreign Office arranged transportation with the British Admiralty. In October 1817, it was loaded onto the British naval transport *Minerva* bound for Malta,[6] and in December 1817 it was transferred at Malta to the storeship *Weymouth*.[7] In March 1818, the Admiralty and the Foreign Office announced its arrival in England.[8] On April 10, the Memnon head and the other antiquities which accompanied it arrived at the customs

Figure 2. Installation of Head of the Younger Memnon, January 9, 1819. Watercolor, inscribed "Wm. Alexander fac.," 1819. © Copyright the Trustees of The British Museum.

office, which deemed them, as gifts for the British Museum, free from import taxes;[9] on April 17, the British Museum asked to use the Office of Ordnance's crane for unloading the Memnon head at London's Tower Wharf.[10] Throughout the period the head was en route, announcements of its "discovery" and imminent arrival appeared in the European press.[11] Inspired by the news, the poets Percy Bysshe Shelley and Horace Smith competed with one another in composing sonnets on the theme of the colossal statue.[12]

What does this paper trail reveal? First, it illustrates that the act of installing the Memnon head in the Egyptian Sculpture Room was but the culmination of a long, deliberate process involving many sets of actors acting in various capacities. In this way, the dates and locations of the object's transshipment not only indicate events in the life of the Memnon head, but also mark nodes in a network of actors and organizations. As we shall see, in itself, the first task—moving the colossal statue fragment from its original site to the banks of the Nile—involved complicated and tense labor as well as diplomatic and imperial negotiations. The collectors, working as agents of the British consul, contracted local peasants, interacted with regional and local officials of the nascent Egyptian state, and competed with antiquities collectors working for the French government. Transporting the Memnon head down the Nile, exporting it through customs, and unloading it in London involved equally complex sets of relationships and more dispersed organizational networks, including the port authority of Alexandria, the British Foreign Office, the Admiralty, customs officials, and finally the trustees and officers of the British Museum.

Besides mapping the networks of the actors involved, however, the paper trail is itself a segment of the process by which the Memnon head became a museum artifact. This is part of the significance of the travel accounts, the letters, and the curators' reports that have always been attached to the statue during its museum life. Together, these documents form the Memnon head's provenance, the story of its movements from the field to the museum. The provenance is not just a record of the events that occurred during the transport of the Memnon head *ex situ* to the place where it became a museum piece. The provenance certainly chronicles these processes. But the creation of a textual record of the object's biography was fundamental to the very process of artifaction itself. Indeed, many of the actors involved in collecting the Memnon head made a conscious effort to create and organize an archive of their work. Likewise, for their part, the officers who installed the head in the museum and who cared for it afterward collected and preserved these texts because their existence was understood to be vital to the meaning of the object. Because of their efforts, we are able to read about the journey of the Memnon head in the same detail—particular names, dates, and places—we find in the accounts of human travelers from the same period. The paperwork attached to the Memnon head thus performs two functions: on one hand, it tells the story of how the Memnon head became a museum artifact; on the other, as an archive attached to the object, it plays a central role in the process by which the Memnon head became an artifact.

The invention of the Pharaonic artifact, of which the Memnon bust is most exemplary, marks a turning point in the modern European view of Egypt. Part of the novelty was that the agents who helped bring the Memnon bust to London were acquiring objects not for private collections but for the young national museum of Great Britain. The new form of the museum entailed new modes of collecting, such as collecting antiquities as unique pieces rather than as more or less interchangeable objects. Moreover, they sought them out on a scale never before attempted and marshaled unprecedented levels of private and public resources to accomplish their goals. This innovation was not of their own invention, however, but rather a result of new arrangements between Mehmed 'Ali, the pasha of Egypt, and the European powers concerning excavation in Egypt. At the same time that the rules discouraged individual Europeans from undertaking excavations around antiquities sites, they granted consular agents unprecedented freedom to pursue collection activities.[13] The arrangement that emerged by the mid-1810s was that the diplomatic representatives of the European powers with the closest ties to the Egyptian state—the French and Austrian consuls—had a near total monopoly in the antiquities commerce. If we are to trust the accounts of European travelers at the time, their only competition was the Upper Egyptian village of Gurna, which, given its location and organization, had long been a powerful player in the commerce of sculpture, papyrus, and mummy.[14]

The collectors who removed the Memnon head from Egypt were acting in the name of the new British consul. Moreover, they claimed that they sought that object neither for personal gain nor for political profit. But this is not the whole story: while it is true that the Memnon head was collected as a gift for the British Museum, it is also true that the other antiquities collected during the same expedition were meant to be sold to the highest bidder. Yet it was the Memnon head's value as a museum piece, not as a commodity, that motivated the activities and rhetoric of the collectors who brought the colossal bust to London. It was this rhetoric also that informed its reception into the museum. To be clear: the new set of values did not change the basic patterns by which antiquities were removed from Egypt. Indeed, the traffic continued apace and even increased. However, the *meaning* of that traffic changed with the emergence of artifact discourse. Excavation and transport now took place in the name of disinterested management and study, that is, "acquisition." This new way of speaking about and treating Pharaonic antiquities enabled Europeans to gain control over antiquities sites throughout the nineteenth century, and its logic expanded British and French power and profit even as it disavowed both. Once generalized, the discourse of the artifact gave both shape and substance to later forms of colonial discourse about managing *all* the resources of modern Egypt.

This chapter traces the artifaction of the Memnon head as a set of processes. In speaking of artifaction as a process, I am employing terms and concepts not usually associated with this period of antiquities collection in Egypt. To clarify: the normative sense of the artifact refers to a particular scientific method divorced from most of the aesthetic and historical debates described in this chapter. My point in widening the concept of the artifact is to show that the moment in which the Memnon head was collected marks the beginning of a new era of treating Egyptian antiquities, one deviating significantly from older antiquarian habits, even if it does not fully resemble the kind of scientific archaeology normally associated with the term "artifact." In this regard, one might ask, At what point did the colossal antiquity become that modern object peculiar to the institutions of art history and archaeological sciences? Did its life as an artifact begin the moment it was elevated on a pedestal at the museum? When it was excavated? Or was it already an artifact in its ancient resting place? The answer to these questions is that there is no originary moment, but rather a series of events in an ongoing process. Moreover, the truths of these events depend on the perspective from which they are viewed. Thus the story of artifaction may well convey a sense of how an object becomes an artifact, but it does not begin to explain the unique significance such objects have once their status as artifacts is obtained. This last point is the focus of this chapter's conclusion, where I argue that it is most precise to define the artifact not in terms of its intrinsic qualities, but rather by way of the tensions and contradictions which permeate and link it to intense political, social, and cultural conflicts.

EXCAVATION AND REMOVAL

The great head of Memnon will please, and when you contemplate its grandeur, recollect that Thebes has at present the remains of thirty-seven statues of equal dimensions: many greater.—CHARLES LEONARD IRBY AND JAMES MANGLES, *Travels in Egypt*

In 1816, Henry Salt, the British consul in Egypt, contracted the services of the Paduan Giovanni Belzoni "for the purpose of raising the head of the statue of the younger Memnon, and carrying it down the Nile."[15] Salt had more than one reason compelling him to acquire the Memnon head. He had read about the colossal bust in numerous travel accounts[16] and had also received direct reports from colleagues such as John Lewis Burckhardt. More immediately perhaps, Salt had only recently arrived at his post in Cairo and began to realize that his official salary was seriously deficient.[17] Looking to supplement his income, he did what other European consuls in Egypt did at the time: he engaged in the commerce of antiquities.

As for the Memnon head, it was part of a complex of ruins that had long been a pilgrimage site for Western explorers, tourists, and writers. Diodorus Siculus had identified the site as belonging to Ozymandias, a corruption of "User-maat-Re," one of Ramses II's names. Diodorus's description of the site and citation of the inscription ("King of Kings am I, Ozymandyas. If any would know how great I am and where I lie, let him surpass one of my works") would be echoed in Shelley's poem "Ozymandias."[18] An earlier traveler, Strabo, had referred to the site as the Memnonium, after Memnon, the Egyptian king said to have joined in the siege of Troy.[19] In modern times, travelers visited the site and compared what they saw to how the places were described by the ancients. In the process, they replaced a long-standing deference to the accounts of the ancients with a new style of travel writing based on empirical experience.

The English traveler Richard Pococke visited the site in 1737. His description of the Memnonium follows Diodorus but also notes that ages had passed since the ancient traveler visited the place.[20] His narrative includes a number of images of the Memnonium ruins, including one that appears to have been of the statue of which the Memnon head was a part. That same year, the Danish traveler Frederick Lewis Norden visited the site, described what he saw, and produced drawings considered the most accurate until the turn of the nineteenth century.[21] James Bruce visited the site in the late 1760s, commenting on the Memnon head in glowing terms.[22] During their short occupation of the country at the end of the eighteenth century, the French referred to the site as the Memnonium and studied it at length. Vivant Denon's account of his travels in Upper Egypt during the occupation even further fixed the Memnonium—and Ozymandias—as one of the most prominent monuments in this literary and pictorial tradition of describing Egypt.[23] Published in 1802, *Voyages dans la basse et la haute Égypte* went through forty editions during the next century and was not just an essential component of libraries but effectively functioned as a guidebook for European tourists until the twentieth century. At the same time, the encyclopedic *Description de l'Égypte* (1809–20), composed by Napoléon Bonaparte's savants, depicts the Memnonium in massive plates that were considered the most accurate even after the invention of photography.[24]

These depictions only encouraged more visits, and more depictions. William Hamilton's oft-cited *Aegyptiaca* (1809) lingers at the Memnonium and declares it "the most beautiful and perfect piece of Egyptian sculpture that can be seen throughout the whole country."[25] Hamilton noted that the French had apparently used explosives in an attempt to move the colossal head. Local villagers repeated this claim to the Swiss-Anglo traveler John Lewis Burckhardt. Burckhardt, known as Sheikh Ibrahim because he traveled through Upper Egypt in 1813 in the guise of a Muslim cleric from Hindustan, was told that years earlier the French had failed to move the Memnon head but had drilled a hole in it while trying.[26] In 1814, Henry Light, traveling through Egypt and the Red Sea, visited the Memnonium and commented that the colossal head could be moved if one could employ the labor of local villagers.[27] In 1815, a wealthy English traveler, William John Bankes, took ropes and pulleys to the site in the hope of moving it but was unsuccessful.[28] That same year, Burckhardt attempted to persuade Mehmed ʿAli to send the colossal head as a present to the prince regent in England, but the pasha did not consider stone an appropriate gift.[29] Meanwhile, in England, the study of hieroglyphics continued among antiquarians, who were as anxious as ever for more texts on which to practice their linguistic theories.[30] By 1816, Hamilton was secretary of the Africa Association as well as undersecretary of state at the Foreign Office. In a memorandum from the previous year, the Foreign Office had urged its diplomatic agents to collect for the British Museum, promising recompense no matter the outcome: "Whatever the expense of the undertaking, whether successful or otherwise, it would be most cheerfully supported by an enlightened nation, eager to anticipate its Rivals in the prosecution of the best interests of science and literature."[31] The British Museum had good cause to worry about the activities of rival acquisitionists, especially in Egypt, where the French consul, Bernardino Drovetti, had been using his position to corner the market in antiquities ever since he had been installed in 1802.[32] Apprised of the importance of Egyptian antiquities that could be brought to England, the most active trustee of the British Museum, Joseph Banks, advised the newly appointed Consul Salt to use his diplomatic position for the museum's benefit. Likewise, Salt's former patron, Lord Mountnorris, requested Salt to collect Egyptian antiquities on his behalf.[33]

By the time Salt was installed as British consul in 1816 there was thus a wide array of influences leading him not only to seek out antiquities, but also to take a particular interest in the Memnon head: a classical and modern tradition of celebrating the monuments of Upper Egypt, and the Memnonium in particular; a strong personal interest in Egyptian antiquities among key individuals at the British Foreign Office, the Africa Association, and the British Museum; and an ever-growing scholarly interest in ancient Egypt and its writing systems. Additional factors were the personal economic distress of a recently appointed consul, the existence of a vibrant market in antiquities, and the practical experience of travelers who knew what it would take to move the Memnon head.

Giovanni Belzoni, who was contracted, as noted, to collect the Memnon head, had met the British consul by way of Burckhardt, and it was Burckhardt who together with Salt commissioned Belzoni's journey to Upper Egypt.[34] Belzoni was an unlikely person to be hired to undertake such difficult work, considering he had not lived very long in Cairo and had never visited Upper Egypt. At the time, Belzoni's reputation was largely associated with the fact that he had performed for years in London as a circus strongman called the Patagonian Sampson.[35] Belzoni had, however, learned water mechanics while producing scale reproductions of famous naval battles for the stage at Sadler's Wells. On the basis of his practical knowledge of hydraulics, Belzoni was recruited by an agent of Mehmed ʿAli, who was looking for European engineers to aid in the development of Egypt's water resources. Hired to produce a new kind of waterwheel, Belzoni eventually found himself out of work when what he built failed to impress the pasha. Thus, suddenly unemployed in the summer of 1816, Belzoni approached his friend Burckhardt, knowing he was interested in delivering the Memnon head to London.

Besides detailing how Belzoni should prepare for the expedition, Salt's contract elaborates how to communicate the British consul's authority through the domains of various Ottoman officials in Upper Egypt.[36] This was to be done by way of letters that extended the pasha's protection and aid to their bearer. Salt had acquired the letters from the pasha and consigned copies of them to Belzoni for the duration of his trip. Belzoni was expected to use this kind of document—a *firman*—to announce his presence to high officials as he journeyed through the provinces of Upper Egypt.[37] His first political negotiation would thus be accomplished by presenting his letters from Mehmed ʿAli, the pasha of Cairo, to his son Ibrahim, pasha of Upper Egypt at the time. The contract next stipulates in great detail where the desired object was located and sets further conditions on the mission, stating that should the task prove too difficult Belzoni should cease his operations. It requests that Belzoni maintain records of his expenses, which would be reimbursed. Finally, it emphasizes that, once the statue was on board, the boat should proceed directly to Alexandria, stopping only at Bulaq for further directions. As Belzoni wryly notes in his account, the contract does not stipulate the matter of his payment. The dispute over whether Belzoni was Salt's partner in the enterprise or merely his employee was to have real significance for all parties concerned.

Supplied with a line of credit and a small amount of cash, Belzoni left Cairo accompanied by his household and a hired interpreter, Giovanni d'Athanasi, who had long served as dragoman at the British consulate.[38] In the town of Manfalut, the group met Ibrahim Pasha, who happened to be en route to Cairo. Ibrahim requested that Belzoni present his papers to the official he had left in charge. Ibrahim was traveling with the French consul Drovetti, who was himself accompanying a shipment of antiquities he had collected in Upper Egypt. Much to Belzoni's annoyance, the French consul informed him that "the Arabs would not work at Thebes."[39] Belzoni's party arrived in Assyut (Siout), and Belzoni, as Salt had requested, met with Dr. Scotto, Ibrahim Pasha's personal physician.[40] When Scotto heard of Belzoni's plan to remove the Memnon head he replied that there were "many difficulties: first, about obtaining permission to have the necessary workmen; then there were no boats to be had; and next, the bust was a mass of stone not worth the carriage; at last, he plainly recommended to me not to meddle in this business, for I should meet with many disagreeable things, and have many obstacles to encounter."[41] Belzoni later presented the firman Salt had obtained from Mehmed 'Ali Pasha, and the official provided him with orders to the provincial officials and local officials where Belzoni intended to work. In Assyut, Belzoni hired a Greek carpenter, and they proceeded farther south. A week later, the party arrived at Luxor, whose sight greatly impressed Belzoni. He writes,

> I beg the reader to observe, that but very imperfect ideas can be formed of the extensive ruins of Thebes, even from the accounts of the most skilful and accurate travellers. It is absolutely impossible to imagine the scene displayed, without seeing it. The most sublime ideas, that can be formed from the most magnificent specimens of our present architecture, would give a very incorrect picture of these ruins; for such is the difference, not only in magnitude, but in form, proportion, and construction, that even the pencil can convey but a faint idea of the whole.[42]

Belzoni's astonishment echoed that of the accounts of modern Western travelers to Egypt.[43] But this language of aesthetic experience was relatively recent in Belzoni's day. Western travelers may have long marveled at the ancient monuments of Thebes, but the attribute of beauty was not often applied to antiquities in Egypt until the 1780s. In fact, when travelers in the late eighteenth century began to describe Egyptian monuments in terms of beauty and sublimity, they were engaged in a polemic about expanding the standard of beauty beyond the classical measure of proportion derived from Greek sculpture, architecture, and music.[44] Part of this shift away from proportional standards of beauty involved the attempt to expand the history of fine art beyond its traditional Greek origins to include Egypt.[45] But part was also linked to the rise of empirical experience as a value in itself.[46] Thus, Belzoni's comments belong to an Enlightenment aesthetic tradition (including Edmund Burke, Immanuel Kant, Friedrich von Schiller, and the English romantics), in which beauty was said to be a product of experience and perception. In this account of aesthetics, beauty was not some property intrinsic in objects, but rather belonged to the feelings aroused within the subjects who regarded them. The significance of this is not just that Belzoni's travel experience, like that of his contemporaries, resonated with the themes and dispositions of romantic poets.[47] It is also that the new sensibility established a relation between subjects and objects—a claim on them—that was directly sensory and emotional but moral as well.

Belzoni's depiction of his arrival at Thebes is also noteworthy for what it says about the place as a collection of ruins: "It appeared to me like entering a city of giants who after a long conflict were all destroyed, leaving the ruins of their various temples as the only proofs of their former existence . . . who will not fail to wonder how a nation, which was once so great as to erect these stupendous edifices, could so far fall into oblivion that even their language and writing are totally unknown to us."[48] As Alois Riegl pointed out, the ruin is a particularly modern kind of antique object.[49] Not merely a dilapidated building or a structure whose form has been completely obliterated, the ruin exists somewhere in between—as a liminal space providing the particular aesthetic pleasure associated with the picturesque.[50] More than a pile of rubble but less than a monument whose original use has been preserved, the ruin evokes a peculiar sense of historical time, namely, that there is an absolute break between the ancient past and the modern present. What matters in the aesthetic experience of ruins is the meeting between the modern and the ancient. All else is distraction. The rise of this romantic sensibility would have had few consequences if not for the fact that, since the period of their original construction until the modern period, Pharaonic monuments usually had served many functions (including habitation) and held many meanings for the people who lived in and around them. According to the new aesthetic norms, indications that the ruins had an abiding local meaning that was not purely ancient were to be ignored and obliterated. In this way, the discourse of the ruin created a particular kind of ethnographic relationship between the traveler and the natives who live in and around ancient monuments.[51] As we shall see, the romantic discourse of ruins was crucial for developing the notion that the monuments of ancient Egypt should be sharply separated from forms of modern Egyptian life, since these detracted from their proper meaning as ancient objects.

Belzoni, aware that he would have to take advantage of the rising river if he hoped to move the statue, got to work:

> As I entered these ruins, my first thought was to examine the colossal bust I had to take away. I found it near the remains of its body and chair, with its face upwards, and apparently smiling on me, at the thought of being taken to England. I must say that my expectations were exceeded by its beauty, but not by its size. I observed that it must have been absolutely the same statue as is mentioned by Norden, lying in his time with its face downwards, which must have been the cause of its preservation. I will not venture to assert who separated the bust from the rest of the body by an explosion, or by whom the bust has been turned face upwards.

As a description of Belzoni's first encounter with the Memnon head, this passage is richly suggestive. Like travelers before, Belzoni compares his own direct perception of the object to impressions gathered from the accounts of others. This is not a moment of pure discovery. The tropes of this passage reverse the agency of what is about to happen. It is the bust that seems to have expected Belzoni's arrival, and it is the bust, not Belzoni, that seems most pleased Belzoni has come to remove it. The prosopopoeic figure—the nonobject that beckons the collector—recurs throughout this account and others of the time.

At this point, Belzoni's party set up camp in the Memnonium and unloaded the rudimentary tools they had brought to transport the colossal bust to the river's edge: fourteen thick wooden beams, four lengths of palm rope, and four logs for rolling. On July 24, Belzoni presented himself to the provincial official, the *kashif* (district governor), in Erments in order to obtain permission to employ eighty Egyptians from the village of Gurna. Belzoni notes that the kashif received him with the deceptive "politeness which is peculiar to the Turks, even when they do not mean in the slightest degree to comply with your wishes."[52] According to Belzoni, after he presented the firman he had obtained from the official in Asyut, the kashif gave a number of contradictory reasons why the request was impossible: the peasants were too busy to want to work for him; it was too much to ask people to undertake such an arduous task during Ramadan, the month of fasting; the peasants' labor could not be spared since it was badly needed at the moment by the pasha. Angrily, Belzoni replied that he would go the next morning to Gurna to engage his workers. The kashif replied that tomorrow they would see to it. The next day, no workers arrived. Belzoni visited the kashif again, presenting him with a gift of coffee and tobacco and hinting that there would be more such presents if his request were granted. Belzoni visited the *qa'im-maqam* (local administrator) of Gurna, only to learn that the man was a close business associate of his rival Drovetti, the French consul and antiquities collector. Again the answer was "tomorrow, perhaps." Again, the next day no workforce materialized, even though Belzoni was convinced the peasants wanted the opportunity to work for him. Finally, on the third day, a number of men appeared, and Belzoni hired them at thirty paras per day, which, according to Belzoni, was substantially more than they earned working in the fields. The work itself was straightforward:

> The mode I adopted to place [the head] on the car was very simple, for work of no other description could be executed by these people as their utmost sagacity reaches only to pulling a rope, or sitting on the extremity of a lever as a counterpoise. By means of four levers I raised the bust, so as to leave a vacancy under it, to introduce the car; and after it was slowly lodged on this, I had the car raised in the front, with the bust on it, so as to get one of the rollers underneath. I then had the same operation performed at the back, and the colossus was ready to be pulled up. I caused it to be well secured on the car, and the ropes so placed that the power might be divided. I stationed men with levers at each side of the car, to assist occasionally if the colossus should be inclined to turn to either side. In this manner I kept it safe from falling. Lastly, I placed men in the front, distributing them equally at the four ropes, while others were ready to change the rollers alternately. Thus I succeeded in getting it removed the distance of several yards from its original place. According to my instructions, I sent an Arab to Cairo with the intelligence that the bust had begun its journey towards England.[53]

Belzoni's description of the movement of the Memnon head deserves comment. The first-person voice of the passage makes it clear that the agent behind this effort is Belzoni himself; he is literally the subject of the actions performed. Additionally, he directs the action and organizes the bodies of the natives, who perform subordinate and passive forms of work. There is something curious about the presence of the Gurna natives in this passage: they are present, but it is as if they are not actors in the scene. In this scene, Belzoni seems to be distinguishing two kinds of labor: his own effort, which is purposive and human, and the labor of the Gurna peasants, which, lacking intent, is not fully active, not fully human. In this regard consider the following image, taken from Belzoni's narrative, which represents the labor of the Gurna villagers as collective, undifferentiated, and, in comparison with the Memnon head, puny.

The following day, Belzoni, by his own account, had to "break the bases of two columns" in the Memnonium in order to make room for the car carrying the Memnon head, and by that evening the bust had been transported fifty yards. Over the next week, work proceeded apace, and the Memnon bust was brought closer to a point of land where it might be safely loaded on a boat during the inundation. On August 6, someone ordered the Gurna peasants to stop working for Belzoni. The situation was precarious, seeing that, unless the statue was moved to higher ground quickly, the rising river waters would cover it. Belzoni accosted the qa'im-maqam of Gurna that day, holding him at gunpoint while his bodyguard disarmed the official. After thrashing the man, Belzoni learned that the stoppage order originated with the kashif of Erments. Later, Belzoni would learn that it was Drovetti who had given the official the idea. The theme of rivalry with the French consul recurs throughout Belzoni's account.

That evening, Belzoni visited the kashif, dining with the official's entourage as they broke their fast. Belzoni made a present of his pistols to the kashif, at which point the kashif redrafted a new firman authorizing Belzoni to hire the peasants at Gurna. On August 12, 1816, the Memnon head arrived at a suitable place for loading. Belzoni paid his workers "bakshis" [sic] of one piastre each, noting, for the only time, that they had performed labor for him: "They well deserved their reward, after an exertion to which no labour can be compared. The hard task they had, to track such a weight, the heavy poles they were obliged to carry to use as levers, and the continual replacing the rollers [sic] with the extreme heat and dust were more than any European could have withstood; but here is what is more remarkable, during all the days of this exertion, it being

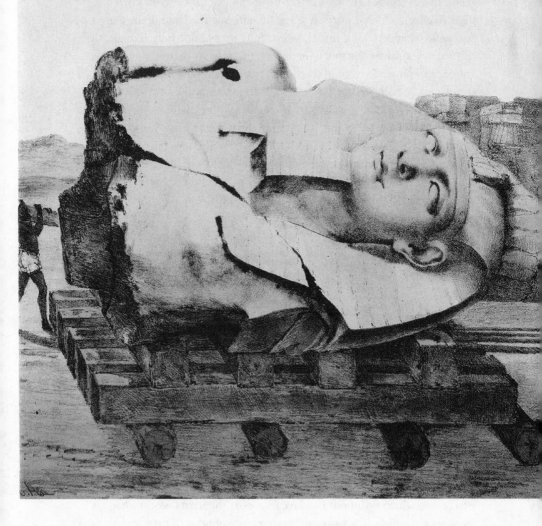

Figure 3. Giovanni Belzoni, "Mode in Which the Young Memnon Head Now in the British Museum was Removed," from *Plates Illustrative of the Researches and Operations of G. Belzoni in Egypt and Nubia* (London: John Murray, 1820). Image by permission of The Beinecke Rare Book and Manuscript Library of Yale University.

Ramadan, they never ate or drank till after sunset."[54] At this point, Belzoni wrote to Salt requesting a boat be sent from Cairo, as there were no boats available in Luxor. In the meantime, Belzoni would make use of his time by traveling south in search of other antiquities to bring to the consul. Before leaving Luxor, Belzoni built an earthen bulwark around the bust to protect it from the elements and from his French rivals.

Belzoni's subsequent journey south is well known.[55] He traveled through Upper Egypt and through Nubia and was one of the first Europeans to describe the Pharaonic antiquities beyond the second cataract. Famously, he is the first to have excavated the base of the Abu Simbel colossi and the first to have penetrated their interior temple. A number of themes from this segment of his account bear upon the story of the removal of the Memnon head.

On more than one occasion, Belzoni comments on what he saw as a disparity between the beauty of ancient Egyptian monuments and the ugliness of modern Egypt. Much of the town of Edfu, for instance, was built into an ancient temple at the time.[56] He notes that the town was

> inhabited by people of a different religion from those who built the temple. The pronaos is very wide and is the only one to be seen in Egypt in such perfection, though completely encumbered with Arab huts. The portico is also magnificent; but unfortunately above three-fourths of it is covered with rubbish. . . . The fellahs have built part of their village on the top of it, as well as stables for cattle, &c. . . . On looking at an edifice of such magnitude, workmanship, and antiquity, inhabited by a half savage people whose huts are stuck against it not unlike wasps' nests, and to contrast their filthy clothes with these sacred images that were once so highly venerated makes one strongly feel the difference between the ancient and modern state of Egypt.[57]

The juxtaposition of the modern and the ancient—a recurring feature in the discourse on ruins—caused Belzoni much consternation. In describing the difference between the modern and the ancient in terms of "rubbish" versus "magnificence" and "savagery" versus "perfection" he was not alone. From the moment in the late eighteenth century when Europeans began to seek aesthetic experiences around Egyptian monuments, the fact that the monuments were inhabited was a problem. European travelers and, later, tourists were dismayed to find their view of ancient monuments encumbered by modern habitations and their immediate experience of the (sublime) past interrupted by encounters with the (squalid) present. Belzoni's discourse on ruins expresses an emerging desire to separate the objects of the past from their present context and to protect antiquities from the threat posed by peasants.

At Abu Simbel, Belzoni needed a small army of laborers to pursue his excavation, an undertaking far more considerable and complicated than the removal of the Memnon head had been. As at Gurna, Belzoni encountered resistance from local officials, who, being much farther removed from Cairo, were under little obligation to regard the firman Belzoni presented them. As at Gurna, Belzoni used a mixture of bribes and force to convince local notables to help him marshal a force of day laborers. There was at least one difference, however: whereas wage labor was a known practice in Gurna, at Abu Simbel this apparently was not the case. Indeed, according to Belzoni, the local officials told him that goods were exchanged through barter in the region and that his Cairene coins were of no value. This not only complicated Belzoni's negotiations over labor tremendously, but thoroughly confused his discussion of the value of the antiquities as well.

When Belzoni first met with the kashif, he refused to believe that Belzoni was interested in the antiquities themselves. Like the villagers of Gurna, he assumed that Belzoni was seeking the gold that frequently was found among ruins. According to the kashif, only a short time earlier another European (Drovetti) had carried away such gold from the region. Why, the kashif asked, would Belzoni come so far in search of *stones*: "What had [Belzoni] to do with stones if it were not that [he] was able to procure gold from them?" Belzoni answers, "The stones I wished to take away were broken pieces belonging to an old Pharaoh people; and that by these pieces we were in hopes of learning whether our ancestors came from that country, which was the reason of my coming in search of stones."[58] A few months later, Belzoni was accused of this same charge of treasure seeking among the ruins.[59] The distinction struck between stones and gold is intriguing because it articulates a collision between two systems of value—one economic, one apparently not—taking place in the material of the objects at stake. In this sense, the distinction between stones and gold most clearly and genuinely expresses the peculiar set of noncommercial values motivating Belzoni's expedition.

Still, to pursue his disinterested acquisitions, Belzoni first had to produce a sense of economic interest in the project among others. To convince the suspicious kashif that Egyptian currency might have value, Belzoni staged a performance of monetary economy. First, he arranged with the captain of his boat that if someone were to approach with money, he was to exchange it for its worth in grain. Then, while negotiating with the kashif about wages, he displayed a piastre coin, handing it to a man in the audience and telling him to go to the boat to see what it might buy. It was only after this man returned with the story of how he had exchanged the money for grain that the kashif agreed to Belzoni's scheme, though he stipulated a daily wage of two piastres, many times over what Belzoni had paid his workers at Gurna. Yet, it was one thing to reach an agreement over hypothetical wages and another to obtain political permission for the excavation. Belzoni went farther south in search of another kashif whose support was now necessary. This official, like the other, was convinced that Belzoni was a treasure seeker pursuing gold. Belzoni promised "that if I found the temple full of gold, I should give him half. . . . if I found only stones, they should be all my own property."[60] Since the kashif cared little for stones, he assented. Now, it only remained for Belzoni to raise a labor force. Again, Belzoni depicts those who would work for him as "complete savages . . . entirely unacquainted with any kind of labour" and ignorant of the value of money.[61]

Here, Belzoni encountered a different order of problem: he wanted only thirty men, but the nearby village demanded he hire one hundred; later, they would demand to be paid collectively, regardless of the actual labor of the individuals involved. More bribes, confrontations, and gifts followed, and eventually work began. There were stoppages and obstacles again. In order to keep up the momentum, Belzoni found it advantageous not to correct what he saw as the avaricious superstitions of his savage laborers: "As it was the first day of our enterprise, they went on better than I expected, and all their thought and talk were on the quantity of gold, pearls, and jewels, we should find in the place. I did not discourage them in their supposition as I considered it to be the best stimulus they could have to proceed."[62] In time, it becomes clear that Belzoni's avowed motivations diverged sharply from those of his workforce and the local officials:

[The two kashifs] gave me to understand plainly that all that was there was their own property and that the treasure should be for themselves. Even the savages began to lay their account in the division of the spoil. I assured them that I expected to find nothing but stones and wanted no treasure. They still persisted that, if I took away the stones, the treasure was in them; and that if I could make a drawing or likeness of them, I could extract the treasure from them also, without their perceiving it. Some proposed that if there were any figure discovered, it should be broken before I carried it away to see the inside of it.[63]

What is striking about Belzoni's account of the work at Abu Simbel is how much of it revolves around the confusion between commercial and noncommercial systems of value. Nevertheless, if there was confusion, much of it stemmed from the contradictory messages about acquisition that Belzoni brought into Nubia. On the one hand, he attempts to communicate that his desire to collect antiquities was not driven by riches and that his motivation was one of scholarly disinterest. On the other hand, to accomplish this goal, he not only introduces the notion of the wage and the workings of a monetary economy, but also encourages his laborers and their political bosses to entertain the notion that the value of the antiquities lies in the gold (supposedly) found in or near them. In Belzoni's own words, antiquities represent a source of material wealth even as their true value is said to be nonmaterial; nevertheless, even as he claims they have no value, that they are mere stones, the undertaking of acquisition inextricably links the antiquities to networks of power and motives of profit and exchange.

In the fall, Belzoni halted his Abu Simbel excavation, leaving what remained to be done for the following year. At this point, he was pressed for time to return to Luxor before the Nile receded. On arriving at Luxor, Belzoni heard disparaging remarks made by some of Drovetti's agents, who claimed that the colossal head was not worth the effort of moving so far. These same agents had returned to Gurna and, with the qa'im-maqam's support, insisted that no more work be done for British collectors. Belzoni also began to seek a boat to transport the Memnon head. At this point he encountered great resistance among the boat captains of the town, who told him that if, as Belzoni claimed, the Memnon head did not contain gold, it was not worth the risk and expense to load it onto the barge. Belzoni finally negotiated with a boat owner who was on his way upstream to return to Luxor. To secure the agreement, Belzoni paid an extravagant sum. While waiting for the boat to return, Belzoni explored Luxor, Karnak, and the Valley of the Kings, collecting an array of smaller statues that he would also ship to the consul. In November, the boat Belzoni had hired returned from Aswan, though it was now unexpectedly filled with dates. Belzoni learned that the owner had reconsidered the deal and wanted to return the deposit. The change of heart, as Belzoni learned, was due to Drovetti's agents. At the same time, Belzoni heard reports that the same agents mutilated a number of other statues he had left in Philae until he could arrange their transport. It was at this low point, according to Belzoni, that he found a door open onto the favor of the kashif of Erments. Belzoni learned that Drovetti's latest gifts from Cairo—recompense for the kashif's support during that season of antiquities collection—had been far from generous. Belzoni pounced on the opportunity, and announced that the British consul would be very grateful for any aid the kashif might show its agents. The kashif interceded on Belzoni's behalf and ordered the boat owner to honor his prior agreement with Belzoni. For his efforts, the kashif was promised a brace of pistols from Cairo. On November 15, 1816, Belzoni writes, "[We] collected, though not without trouble, a hundred and thirty men; and I began to make a causeway by which to convey the head down to the river side, for the bank was more than fifteen feet above the level of the water which had retired at least a hundred feet from it."[64] The following day, Belzoni was told he did not have to pay the peasants, since the kashif intended to make "a present of their labour." Belzoni refused, saying "it was not my custom to have the labour of men for nothing nor would the consul of England accept such a present."[65] On November 17, the head was successfully loaded onto the boat. Belzoni's account of the event again depicts him as the chief force driving the event:

> I succeeded in my attempt and the head of the younger Memnon was actually embarked. I cannot help observing that it was no easy undertaking to put a piece of granite of such bulk and weight on board a boat that, if it received the weight on one side, would immediately upset. . . . The causeway I had made gradually sloped to the edge of the water close

to the boat, and with the four poles I formed a bridge from the bank into the centre of the boat so that when the weight bore on the bridge, it pressed only on the centre of the boat. The bridge rested partly on the causeway, partly on the side of the boat, and partly on this centre of it. On the opposite side of the boat I put some mats well filled with straw. I necessarily stationed a few Arabs in the boat, and some at each side, with a lever of palm wood, as I had nothing else. At the middle of the bridge I put a sack filled with sand that, if the colossus should run too fast into the boat, it might be stopped. In the ground behind the colossus I had a piece of a palm tree firmly planted, round which a rope was twisted and then fastened to its car to let it descend gradually. I set a lever at work on each side, and at the same time that the men in the boat were pulling, others were slackening ropes, and others shifting the rollers as the colossus advanced.[66]

The next day, the boat sailed for Cairo, then Rosetta. Leaving the Nile, the boat sailed to the port of Alexandria, where, with the help of the crew of a British transport that was equipped with tackle, it was unloaded on the pier.

RECEPTION

We saw here the great head of Memorandum; and I'm sure I shall never forget him. Some say he was King of the Abiders, which I think likely, from his size: others say he was King of the Thieves, in Upper Egypt. At any rate, it's a great lump of stone, and must be the best lot the Government thought.
—THE SATIRIST, August 18, 1833

While there was much confusion during the removal of the Memnon head about the source of its value, the mixed welcome it received at the British Museum only added to the ambiguities of its acquisition. Though the piece was popular with museum patrons, it was far less so with the men officially entrusted with its care. Taylor Combe, head of the Department of Antiquities, acknowledged the installation of the Memnon head in a single terse sentence appended to an otherwise enthusiastic report about medieval numismatic acquisitions from the British Isles.[67] Combe's subsequent report describes the installation of the piece solely in terms of the problems it caused to the aesthetic composition of the display in the Townley Gallery.[68] Again, after noting coin acquisitions, Combe writes, "[I] made a new arrangement of the articles in the Egyptian Room; in which arrangement it has been his aim to preserve the same line of objects, as in the other compartments of the Gallery, and to produce as much symmetry as was compatible with the situation on one side of the room, of so large an object as the colossal head."[69] The reaction of the museum's trustees to the gift was tempered.[70] At the very moment the Memnon head was being installed, Joseph Banks, the director of the British Museum, wrote to Salt, "Though in truth we are here much satisfied with the Memnon, and consider it as a *chef-d'oeuvre* of Egyptian sculpture, yet we have not placed that statue among the works of *Fine Art*. It stands in the Egyptian Rooms. Whether any statue that has been found in Egypt can be brought into competition with the grand works of the Townley Gallery remains to be proved unless however they really are so, the prices you have set upon your acquisitions are very unlikely to be realized in Europe."[71] These were sharp words from the man who had earlier so encouraged Salt to use his consular office to collect antiquities. Yet Banks's ambivalence about the aesthetic value of the Memnon head was actually not so remarkable, being simply the expression of an old aesthetic tradition that drew a sharp line between the Egyptian sculpture and fine art.[72]

Banks's reference to price raises another issue. Though the Memnon head had been sent as a gift to the British Museum, Salt was pressing the museum to purchase other antiquities he and his agents (including Belzoni) had collected. This last point drew the rebuke of Banks, who went on to censure Salt for abandoning his "original intention" of placing the matter of antiquities collection "in the hands of the public."[73] Here, an aspect of the 1816 expedition that is partly submerged in Belzoni's account is relevant: though Belzoni was certain that his acquisitions were "disinterested,"[74] he also knew Salt was funding the expedition as a for-profit venture. The mixture of the categories of public/private and commercial/noncommercial may have been what troubled the museum trustees.[75] More likely, however, it was the recent public uproar caused by the extravagant purchase of the Parthenon friezes from Lord Elgin that led the trustees to insist that acquisitions from Egypt be gifts, a point to which I will return shortly. Banks was not alone in his sharp response to Salt's attempt to sell the museum the other pieces that arrived with the Memnon head. Hamilton, the man whose glowing description of the Memnon head had led Salt to acquire the piece, wrote similarly discouraging words.[76] In a third letter, Salt's former patron, Lord Mountnorris, joined Banks and Hamilton in admonishing Salt for trying to sell antiquities to the museum. Together, these sharp responses to Salt's gift indicate two lines of resistance to the reception of Egyptian antiquities at the British Museum in 1819: the first had to do with the *Egyptian* character of the antiquities; the second, with the *commercial* character of such acquisitions.

While Egyptian antiquities had been included in the collection of the British Museum from its inception, in 1819 they were not considered part of its fine art collection, of which Greek and Roman statues held pride of place. There were at least two reasons for this: a long-standing scholarly tradition that placed Athens and Rome at the origin of European art and world civilization, and a lack of basic knowledge about ancient Egyptian language, history, and culture. In light of this, it is not difficult to understand the response of curators who had been mandated to build a collection in order to inculcate a clear art-history narrative to the public. They were at a loss as to what to do with Egyptian pieces, whose aesthetic style was contrary to the Greco-Roman standard of beauty and whose origins and meaning were unknown. Given these factors, how could they have assimilated the Egyptian antiquities into the existing standards of beauty and narratives of art history? Even though British travelers had been vociferously asserting the beauty of the art they saw in Egypt, their claims had little resonance at the British Museum.

The uncertain reception of the Memnon head has very much to do with philosophical shifts taking place within the British Museum during the early nineteenth century. Ian Jenkins has aptly described this as a conscious shift in thinking about the meaning of the museum itself, a shift from the paradigm of the *Wunderkammer* to that of the *Kunstkammer*, that is, from the royal curiosity cabinet to the public art museum that offers a universal survey of aesthetic history.[77] These changes were themselves instantiated in the increasing tendency toward administrative division and specialization within the museum's collections. From its inception in 1756 until 1807, the museum had only three departments—Manuscripts, Printed Books, and Natural History. The capture of celebrated Egyptian antiquities from Bonaparte's army in 1801 and the purchase in 1805 of a large private collection of Greek and Roman sculptures from Charles Townley massively increased the museum's holdings of antiquities. With this large addition, the old administrative categories, which placed statuary under the care of librarians, no longer made much sense, and in 1807 the Department of Antiquities was formed along with a subdepartment of Prints and Drawings.[78] These divisions did more than solve organizational problems; they also expressed an emerging consensus that the department's holdings should be a finely crafted collection that formed a systematic survey of art, not a conglomeration of wonders, oddities, and curiosities. The construction of the Townley Sculpture Gallery in 1808 gave architectural form to these new ideas. Originally, curators arranged the pieces thematically around the concept of the picturesque, though they soon moved to a more strictly chronological arrangements of objects.[79]

The shift from the appreciation of static classical forms to a historical understanding of art bore greatly upon the meaning of Egyptian antiquities. In the eighteenth century, in the work of the influential aesthetician Johann Winckelmann most particularly, Egypt had offered the antithesis of the aesthetic values embodied in classical Greek and Roman statuary. Paraphrasing Winckelmann, a museum guidebook from 1832 states, "It is generally assumed that all Egyptian figures are stiff, ugly, and devoid of grace which Winckelmann, going a step further . . . attributes to the general want of beauty in the nation."[80] Winckelmann urged scholars to concentrate on the purest Greek forms rather than "waste . . . thoughts on trifles" and occupy oneself "with low ideas."[81] Moreover, he provided a method of study, beginning with the details of individual pieces and moving to the deeper unities underlying different eras of classical statuary. Winckelmann's hermeneutic—a study of parts, synthesized into more abstract wholes, brought to bear again upon the study of parts—would provide the logic for the modern scholarly study of fine art. By the early 1800s this relatively static taxonomy would be supplemented by another notion—that art's history was one of progress.[82] In this model, "the chain of art" began in Egypt, then continued through the more familiar history of Greece and Rome. Nevertheless, Egypt did not figure here as part of the history of progress, but as the lifeless ground from which civilizational progress—a uniquely Greek invention—rose.[83] These concepts imbued the curatorial attitudes toward statues and the rooms which held them alike. In the Townley Gallery, curators paid the same attention to the values of balance and proportion in their display as to such attributes in the objects themselves. The arrangement of objects on display was an amplification of the kinds of patterns found in art. Hence, one can begin to understand Combe's frustration when he was given the impossible task of fitting the Memnon head into a space ruled by the proportions and scale of classical humanism. As a non-classical piece, it had no easy place in the collection, a problem magnified by the enormous size of the piece itself.

The sense that art had a history was crucial for understanding the place of Egyptian antiquities within the department's collection in 1819. Egyptian objects, while apparently popular with patrons, served as a primitive and rough example when set against the higher, more dynamic forms of beauty found in the Greek and Roman statues. By this logic, the Memnon head would be installed in the Egyptian Sculpture Room even as it failed to reach the higher standards of classical statuary. In this regard, the 1832 guidebook remarks,

> The stranger who visits the Gallery of Sculpture, in the British Museum, cannot fail to be struck with the curious collection of objects in the room of Egyptian Antiquities. Passing from the contemplation of the almost faultless representations of the human form in marble, the triumph of Grecian art, he comes to figures more remarkable, at first sight, for their singular forms and colossal size, than for their beauty. Though the contrast between what he has just left and the new scene to which he is introduced, creates at first no pleasing impression, feelings of curiosity and admiration soon arise from a more careful examination of what is around him.[84]

The welcome Egyptian antiquities had was thus complicated: though they were not fine art, their meaning had some relation to aesthetic values. They were not beautiful objects but aroused curiosity instead.

The category of the curiosity opens upon another set of ambiguities in the reception of the Memnon head. Not all Egyptian antiquities were included in the antiquities collection. Some were displayed as curiosities alongside wonders of the natural world. As the museum transformed from the model of the curiosity cabinet to the nineteenth-century pedagogical public museum, the category of the artificial curiosity became increasingly problematic. An earlier series of incidents involving Egyptian curiosities is telling in this regard. Even before the formation of the

Department of Antiquities, museum officers were rethinking the rationale of the collection and the fitness of articles on display. In 1806, a directive was issued to create order among the collections and to label the items on display. As Edward Miller notes, "The following year an even more drastic reorganisation took place. Certain objects, most of a medical or anatomical nature, were declared unfit to be preserved in the museum and were ordered to be disposed of to the Hunterian Museum, which, as a professional medical collection, was considered a more suitable home to them."[85] At the top of the list of items the director of the museum asked to be removed from display were Egyptian mummies, along with other such "artificial curiosities, many of which are of a very trifling nature and by no means fit to be exhibited in such a Repository as the Museum."[86] These mummies may be the same that appear in a housecleaning report from 1809, which was likewise directed at scouring up the basement rooms of Montagu House, the original, now-dilapidated building of the British Museum. The author of this report referred to the threat to the objects posed by water in dire terms and recommended removing objects like mummies from the collection rather than "suffering them to decay and be consumed in the damp apartments they are now deposited."[87] Years later, the problem of rotting lumber, rubbish, and unwanted curios remained. Combe inherited this problem in 1811, reporting that "4 mummies . . . in a state of decay on the ground floor of the New Buildings . . . are a harbour for dirt, and are only fit to be destroyed."[88] Not long after, Combe found a solution by donating the mummies to the Royal Academy of Surgeons.[89] It was easier to clean the basement than to transform antique curiosities into suitable objects for the museum's galleries of art.

Long before the Memnon head was on its way to London, most of the museum reorganization had already taken place, and most of the curios had been effectively purged from the Department of Antiquities. Nevertheless, one of the first notices the trustees received about the imminent arrival of the piece praised Egyptian antiquities for being exactly this, "curiosities" and "ornaments."[90] Thus, on its arrival, the Memnon head that appeared was something of an artificial curiosity, the very category of object which the museum was attempting to purge from its collection. The shifting semantic field of the term *artificial curiosity* is critical to understanding how the Memnon head was received. The word *curiosity* took on a pejorative meaning and came to mean an object of wonder and mystery more fitting for a natural history exhibition—or carnival show—than a place where scholars studied the art of human civilization. In contrast, the word *artificial*, meaning "*man-made*," did not bother curators. In fact, the appropriateness of this term increased as the museum focused its attention on the study of human rather than natural history. The persistent value of the concept of man-madeness is arguably what provoked the transformation of the adjective *artificial* into the substantive noun *artifact*, a neologism of the moment.[91]

It was not a simple matter to transform the Memnon head from a curiosity into a piece fit for inclusion within the art-history paradigm of the Department of Antiquities, especially when so little was known about its original historical context. Much hinged on developments that took place outside of the museum, particularly those linked to recent linguistic theories concerning hieroglyphic writing. Throughout the reports he filed until his death in 1825, Combe's reception of Egyptian antiquities remained skeptical, even hostile. Keeper of the Antiquities Richard Westmacott was warmer, although he continued to relegate Egyptian statuary to a lesser place.

In contrast, the museum catalogues and guides from the period indicate a subtle change occurring in attitudes toward Egyptian antiquities. A museum guidebook from 1821 describes the contents of the Egyptian Sculpture Room as follows: "Many of the articles contained in this Room were collected by the French in different parts of Egypt, and came into the possession of the English army, in consequence of the capitulation of Alexandria, in the month of September, 1801. They were brought to England in February, 1802, under the care of General Turner, and were sent, by order of His Late Majesty, to the British Museum."[92] The description is not so much of the objects' composition or meaning as of the history of their acquisition. The entry for the Memnon head follows this pattern in that it has more to say about the feat of removing it than it does about the piece as an object of study in itself.[93] This fact is not so surprising considering how little besides its contemporary history was known about the piece at the time.

Soon after the head's arrival, G. H. Noeden, a sublibrarian assigned to assist Combe, studied the Memnon head and published his findings in 1822.[94] Noeden's study marks the first attempt to remake the Memnon head into an object fit for inclusion in the institution as an *object of study* rather than as curiosity or pretense for narrating the heroic deeds of con-temporary collectors. Central to Noeden's effort was the task of measur-ing the piece. Exact figures for height (8′ 9″), circumference (15′ 3″ at top of breast, 14′ 7″ below), and weight (between 10 and 12 tons) appear in a table as crucial facts in themselves. Other measurements of various segments of the statue suggest that Noeden was searching for ratios that might at-test to an association between Egyptian and Greco-Roman standards of beauty. In Noeden's account a new kind of description is at work, one which, by means of measurement, establishes both its material factuality and its aesthetic status in relation to known standards of beauty. Arguably in these lines the beginnings of artifact discourse on the Memnon head are discernible.

The 1832 guidebook on the Egyptian antiquities in the museum's col-lection (published by the Society for the Diffusion of Useful Knowledge) was perhaps the first to state openly another assumption about how an artifact, as opposed to a curiosity, might be received. Though he concedes that aesthetic appreciation of Egyptian pieces could only follow historical knowledge, the author asserts that Egyptian antiquities deserved more attention than mere curiosity. While such knowledge was more or less lacking at the time, the author of the guidebook makes clear that Egyptian antiquities belong in the same collection as classical antiquities because they too are art. To make this conceptual shift, the author argues, one needs to absorb the context from which Egyptian antiquities were taken.[95] This guidebook devotes most of its discussion of the Memnon head to narrating at great length the history of its acquisition and citing the story of French vandalism alongside descriptions that appeared in *Description de l'Égypte*, Denon, and Norden. It also includes Noeden's table of mea-sures and presents a close reading of Egyptian statues as pieces of art. The author's comments on the Memnon head's racial features are striking in this regard. He writes that the nose of the

Memnon may be called beautiful, though it has not the European form; it is far from being so round and thick as that of his colossal neighbour opposite. Indeed the nostrils of the Memnon are, in our opinion, the fin-est pair in all the Museum, if we compare them with those of statues in perfect repose, and it is only with such that any comparison can be fairly made. . . . The lips of the granite figure opposite the Memnon are the thickest specimen the Museum offers, and the whole character of this face is much rounder and more massy than any other which we have seen. Though it is not the negro face, we cannot help feeling, as we look upon it, that its features recall to our minds that kind of outline which we understand by the term African, a word that means, in ordinary acceptation, something of the negro cast of face.[96]

Racialized aesthetic analysis may not have persuaded many curators. In fact, locating Egyptian art in Africa would have had wholly negative associations in contemporary models of aesthetics (such as G. W. F. Hegel's). Nevertheless, it does signal a new framework by which one could study the Egyptian antiquities in the collection as pieces of art. And in the end, it was this imperative—to study Egyptian antiquities as if one were studying examples of classical art—that mattered most.

By the early 1830s, following growing acceptance of Champollion's theories, there was widespread skepticism toward earlier traditions of interpreting Egyptian antiquities. With regard to the Memnon head, it was at this time confidently pointed out that there was no reason to call the colossal bust by the name of Memnon.[97] This skepticism would be replaced by a more positivist confidence in the 1840s as scholars began to read the primary sources of Egyptian history and the now-legible names written on the museum pieces. The consequences of this knowledge were wide: it was possible to read not only Egyptian history, but also the history of the objects in the collection. The name of Memnon was corrected to Ramses II during these years, and the place of Egyptian art in the antiquities collection transformed. An introduction to a museum guidebook from 1842 reads as follows:

The object of the present work is to publish a Selection of the Choisest [sic] Monuments existing in the National Collection of this country. It commences with those of Egypt, from the high authenticated antiquity of many of them, and from their being the source from which the arts of Sculpture and of Painting, and perhaps even the Sciences, were handed to the Greeks—from the Greeks to us. *They are the Alpha of the history of Art.* The collection of the British Museum is so rich in this newly opened mine of antiquity, of which so little has been edited, that no apology is necessary in commencing with this branch.[98]

Not only had Egypt been allowed into the same aesthetic narrative as classical art, but it had now become the *origin* of that history. Within roughly twenty years, the place of Egyptian antiquities, including the Memnon head, shifted from the margins of the museum's art collection to its center. Moreover, there had accrued by this time enough information about the origins, uses, and meaning of Egyptian antiquities that they were no longer interpreted solely through the old lens of Greece and Rome:

> Attached to every object will be found a succinct description of its use, application, locality, and relations; such as will, it is hoped, suffice the general reader and offer to the Archaeologist the broad outline of the subject. In treating each Branch, a preference will, of course, be given to the first authorities; thus, Egyptian Antiquities will be illustrated from the monuments and Hieroglyphics of Egypt, not from the second-hand information of the Greeks which the present state of hieroglyphical knowledge refutes or challenges. Hellenic remains will also be judged by Hellenism, and the labours of Continental Antiquaries brought before the British Public.[99]

Furthermore, these guidebooks suggest that the accumulation of knowledge about ancient Egypt generally led to an increase in the ability of curators and connoisseurs to arrange Egyptian antiquities into a coherent historical narrative and to appreciate objects as discrete items worthy of individual study. Gone were the days in which the principle of balance and symmetry determined the style of arrangement, replaced by a taxonomic logic and historical arcs. Subsequent guidebooks built on these principles, and by the 1850s museum visitors would be given increasingly comprehensive historical lessons about ancient Egypt, the purpose of which was to increase their ability to appreciate Egyptian antiquities as art:

> Before we proceed to the separate description of the Monuments which have been procured from Egypt, and which now enrich the National Collection at the British Museum, we propose briefly to lay before our readers an outline of the nature of the celebrated country in which these, the earliest remains of ancient art, have been discovered, with some account of its most celebrated cities and buildings now wholly ruined. It seems, indeed, hardly possible thoroughly to appreciate the remains of ancient art without some knowledge of the peculiarities of the lands which they

once adorned and illustrated. Thus a knowledge of the religious creed of a nation or a race, the language they spoke, the ordinary life they led, are almost essential requisites in tracing out the course of their artistic history.[100]

These institutional and philosophical changes obtained in the spaces of the museum displays themselves. In 1832, the museum opened a permanent gallery built especially for the Elgin marbles. Since their installment in 1817, the Elgin marbles had been consigned to a hastily built room off the Townley Gallery. Now, they had an expensive new gallery, with top lighting, in the new wings being constructed by Robert Smirke. With the completion of a new Egyptian Sculpture Gallery in 1833, it was proposed that the Memnon head be immediately relocated to fill the larger space. The task of moving the head was daunting. Westmacott wrote at the time,

> I am in some difficulty and quite at a standstill with the head of the Memnon. There is no private source on which I can rely for its removal with safety either to the men or to the object itself. I calculate the weight at about 14 tons, but this could be effected with care by the Government tackle and three or four of their men.[101]

The Office of Ordnance was contacted again, and a detachment of gunners was sent to the museum. In order to accomplish their task, the military engineers were compelled to reinforce floors. In June 1834, the Memnon head was installed in the new, much larger space.

Unlike the gallery built for the Elgin marbles, however, the new Egyptian Sculpture Gallery, like the old Egyptian Sculpture Room, was designed for side lighting rather than top lighting. This detail was itself a consequence of the aesthetic judgment that Egyptian sculptures, being of inferior quality, did not deserve the special lighting reserved for higher Greek and Roman forms. James Fergusson, writing in the 1840s, would spell out the logic of this arrangement, arguing that "the light is sufficient and sufficiently diffused, and for Egyptian sculpture it is of very little consequence how or in what direction the light falls. The artists on the banks of the Nile never aimed at aesthetic beauty of form, so that the sculptural products of their art scarcely depend more on their shadows than architectural members do."[102] In sum, even as the Memnon head was finally admitted into the

Figure 4. Gunners installing Memnon head in Egyptian Sculpture Gallery. Drawing by E. W. Cooke, signed June 2, 1834. © Copyright the Trustees of The British Museum.

British Museum's realm of art, its place was still behind that of classical Greco-Roman art. Moreover, as knowledge about Pharaonic political dynasties accumulated in the years thereafter, the treatment of the Memnon head and other such objects began to change in curators' descriptions. This shift is slight but perceptible, away from questions of the compositional or mimetic aspects of individual pieces, and toward issues of material composition, ornament, patterning, and use. If, during the 1820s, questions of taste and experience dominated the description of Egyptian antiquities, in later decades this was supplemented by debates about how such objects might be studied to learn about ancient history itself.

The slow but steady warming in the aesthetic reception of the Memnon head was only one factor in the development of its significance as a museum artifact. The other was tied to anxieties about the museum's public financing. Part of this had to do with the fallout from the purchase of the Parthenon friezes in 1816.[103] There is no doubt the friezes revolutionized English painting and literature and encouraged artists and poets to discard the derivative beau ideal style for direct experience with the original. The museum trustees, pressing their case for purchase with public funds, were confident, stressing that Elgin should be recompensed not only for offering the friezes to the country, but for saving them from either sure destruction at the hands of the Ottomans or certain acquisition at the hands of the French.[104] A royal act authorized the purchase, invested Elgin and his heirs as trustees to the museum, and stipulated that the pieces "be preserved and kept together in the . . . British Museum whole and entire, and distinguished by the name or appellation of 'the Elgin Collection.'"[105] Thus, the Parthenon friezes were rebaptized as the Elgin marbles.

Almost forgotten in this story is that the huge cost of the marbles (thirty-five thousand pounds, roughly equivalent to 3.5 million dollars in today's currency) to the British government was seen as excessive by many, especially given that the country was still reeling from recent war expenditures. The response of the trustees was consistent: since the purchase was invested in a public institution (the museum), its benefits accrued to the public. Yet claims about the public character of the museum only intensified the debate. From the outset in 1753, the founders of the museum insisted that the collections were meant "for the use and benefit of the publick, who may have free access to view and peruse the same."[106] Likewise, from this early time, the trustees won public funds to support the foundation, expansion, and maintenance of the institution. Also from the outset, however, there were serious questions about whether public funds should go to support the collection of "knick knackeries" donated by wealthy travelers.[107] With regard to admission, the museum's effective definition of *public* was one that, until midcentury and beyond, excluded the vast majority of the working- and middle-class British public.[108] The museum was referred to disparagingly as "a place intended only for the amusement of the curious and rich," useless for the nation at large.[109] Throughout this period, arguments arose within the museum administration first about whether (and later about how) to make the definition of the public more inclusive. But the officers did not proceed quickly enough. As one angry critic put it in 1836, "The baneful spirit of aristocratic monopoly interferes even with our national institutions, and operates, in a great degree, to the exclusion of the working classes from the enjoyment of the blessings bequeathed for public good, by a generous benevolence. These prefatory remarks are especially applicable to the British Museum, which, even on the cautious admissions of its own officers, is characterized by inefficient management, and a very narrow accessibility as regards the great body of the people."[110] Hence, rather than mollifying critics, the key term ("the public") in the trustees' response to criticism of the Elgin purchase only increased demands that admission to the museum be opened up to a wider spectrum of society.

With regard to the use of public funds for acquisition, the trustees of 1819 were not willing to expend any of their budget on Egyptian antiquities. By the mid-1820s, however, they were negotiating to purchase small groups of pieces collected by Salt and even Drovetti. Still, the figures involved in the purchase of Egyptian antiquities were a fraction of those paid for Greco-Roman statuary. Nonetheless, the rising costs of acquisition, the upkeep of Montagu House, and later the new construction meant that the issue of the museum's funding and its public character would be raised by those who were outraged by the institution's exclusionary practices. Striking in this account from a debate in 1823 in the Supply Committee of the House of Commons is how aesthetic questions about Egyptian antiquities are woven into a basic fiscal point:

[The trustees] imported taste from a country which was said indeed to have been once the land of arts and sciences; they brought and imported from Egypt a head of Memnon; and having got it safely home, they discovered that it stood rather higher than their ceiling. Then they wanted a place to hold the head, and two other huge Egyptian relics of a singular shape; so they built a double cube, which was the continuation of the aforesaid parallelogram. Unfortunately, it turned out that this head of Memnon was a dev'lish long head, insomuch that they were obliged to raise the ceiling of his closet somewhat higher, so that the roof of the closet which held the Townley [statue of] Venus was at one elevation, and the roof of the closet which enclosed the Memnon's head was at another. The arrangement of these different closets was so odd, the closets themselves were so dissimilar the one from the other, that they were, as Shakespeare said, "Each monstrous, till its fellow came to match it."[111]

After praising the "disinterestedness" of the trustees, the member of Parliament cites their inept management as a waste of public funds. Banks, representing the museum, attempted to correct the record by pointing out that this account of the Memnon head in Montagu House was patently untrue. Nonetheless, the criticism stuck. Through this period, criticism of the public character of the museum expanded to cover the procedures of admission, the affordability of museum guides, and the costs of antiquities acquisition.

Although the gift of the Memnon head in 1819 might have been eagerly received by the trustees of the British Museum, it was not, and the reasons for this were not just aesthetic. In contrast to the acquisition of the Elgin marbles, the colossal head involved little expense to the museum. Still, coming on the heels of the sharp debate about the worthiness of public spending on other Mediterranean rocks, the Memnon head could not be easily championed at the museum. In that the statue's value could not be easily assimilated into the art-history order which privileged Greek and Roman art, and in that its historical significance was a cipher, the Memnon head was as much a burden as it was a blessing for the museum in 1819. Indeed, for a long time it was clearly easier for the trustees to continue their pursuit of expensive acquisitions in Greco-Roman statuary than it was to receive Egyptian antiquities free of charge. Arguably, what eventually changed the trustees' attitude toward Egyptian antiquities was probably not aesthetic debates or even the accumulation of solid historical information about the past. Rather, it was French success in the field of collecting Egyptian monuments. Anglo-French rivalry in collecting was, during this period, fairly lopsided—acquisition agents, including both the French consul, Bernardino Drovetti, and the British consul, Henry Salt, found the Louvre much more eager to purchase what they collected, and it paid handsomely. In other words, the desire not to be left behind in the imperial rush of collection was likely the decisive pressure that changed the place of Egypt in the British Museum's collection.

THE MEMNON HEAD AS ARTIFACT

The story of the Memnon head speaks volumes about the cultural institution of the artifact at the moment of its emergence. It illustrates that the artifact is a product of a history of making and remaking, and that each of these moments of creation is itself expressive of social conflicts and cultural emergences. The story also suggests there is an abiding normative quality to artifacts. That is, they circulate in specific institutions and in doing so embody the rules and regulations of those institutions. The artifact can thus be said to articulate a matrix of social and cultural forces. That is, the artifact both joins and separates a number of fields of activity, the most obvious of which are the commercial and noncommercial aspects of the colonial enterprise emerging simultaneously in Egypt, England, and elsewhere. As the account of the Memnon head suggests, it may make more sense to define the artifact not in a positive sense, but rather in terms of interlocking tensions: it is sacralized as an object understood to be complete in itself (a work) and also the fragment of something larger (a piece);[112] it is both an instrument (of pedagogy) and an end (to be appreciated) in itself; it is sometimes a good for sale and most often a noncommodity;[113] it is an object both found and made; it belongs to both private and public interest; it is both a fact and a value;[114] and finally, impossibly, it is something both alienable and socially entangled.[115]

The concept of the artifact has had a special meaning in the disciplines of archaeology, museum studies, and art history: a product of human thought and labor, as distinct from objects taken from the realm of natural history. In labeling such objects artifacts, the art historian or archaeologist seeks not to evaluate them according to the aesthetic or cultural prejudices of the present, but, as much as possible, to understand the values and uses they may have had in their original context. For modern disciplines that study the material culture of the ancient past, *artifact* is both a useful label for classifying proper objects of study and a powerful concept that helps to move the horizon of interpretation beyond that of the immediate present. For archaeologists, to speak of artifacts may only involve two acts: to refer to a specific kind of material object, and to think according to the given theoretical concepts of the sciences whose objects of study are artifacts. For students of archaeology's history, however, it involves at least a third act: to employ the term "artifact" that belongs to a specialized discipline, ascribes its unique authority, and excludes others.

Distinguishing between these aspects of the discourse of artifacts allows one to recognize some of its peculiarities. Theoretically, the label of the artifact might be applied universally to all objects created by human culture. In practice, however, not all such objects are treated as artifacts for the simple reason that not every product of human civilization is put into a museum or studied as an example of material culture. This is an obvious but critical observation: there are specific disciplinary practices associated with the word *artifact*; and those objects known as artifacts exist as artifacts only insofar as they have been brought within the modern institutions of archaeology, museums, art history, and so on.[116] Thus the term *artifact*, despite the careful neutrality of its common disciplinary usage, is value laden in more than one sense.[117] Most important, the concept of the artifact has a rhetorical function in the traditional histories of Egyptology, such as in this recent account:

> The exploits of Salt and Drovetti sometimes make sad reading these days. An archaeologist, or anyone who cares about the past, resents grave robbers and artifact hunters, for these people do irreparable damage to the remains of the past. It seems tragic that for more than a century the Nile Valley was subjected to the depredations of people like Salt and Drovetti, their hired plunderers, and others more destructive. This, however, was the prearchaeological age. Many professional collectors were well-intentioned people who thought they were performing a useful service to scholarship while making money. . . . There is some consolation in the fact that many of the antiquities that were taken from Egypt during the nineteenth century eventually found their way to museums where they could be protected and appreciated—indeed, many artifacts

were probably saved by being removed from Egypt—but even in those cases there was a loss that could never be made good.[118]

Indeed, traditional histories of Egyptology commonly assert that part of what distinguished the kind of intellectual work done by the first Egyptologists from the kind of work done by those antiquarians who came before was that Egyptologists worked on artifacts. In this way, the invention of the artifact was critical for legitimating Egyptology as a science and distinguishing it from its prehistory in the amateurism of antiquarian hobbyists and gentlemen excavators. With this in mind, one might reframe the distinction that was so crucial to Egyptology's self-making: while the word *artifact* may be used to denote objects of study, at the same time it connotes a range of values and practices associated with the institutions of modern science. Moreover, inasmuch as the emergence of Egyptological science was predicated on the invention of this new class of objects, it helped create a new class of experts whose knowledge granted them privileged access and authority over regions where antiquities were found.[119] Whether the treatment of the Memnon head I have traced here fully matches up to later, normative definitions of the scientific object known as the artifact is doubtful. For one thing, the head was intentionally collected as a unique piece, and its significance was initially debated in terms of aesthetics. For another, many of the methods associated with scientific archaeology—the attention to material composition, patterning, and the closed site—entered the field of Egyptology much later, during the last decades of the nineteenth century. Nonetheless, in nascent form, many of the key elements of artifact discourse were at work in the new treatment of the Memnon head, and as its treatment changed over the course of the early nineteenth century, they developed too. For this reason, it is a useful case for exploring the processes of how antiquarian treatments gave way to new practices, how pre-science became science.

More than merely describing a set of objects, the language of the artifact—which emerged at the same time as the acquisition of the Memnon head—organized its objects within a new form of knowledge and claimed them for new institutions of interpretative power. As a language for laying claim to objects, the discourse of the artifact is peculiarly normative, since it both implies and disavows claims of ownership. In the Memnon head's paper trail, appropriation and possession are major themes, yet the notion that the artifact belongs to those collecting it is so taken for granted that it is seldom articulated. Moreover, at no point do any of the agents—the travelers, the acquisitionists, the consul, the trustees—involved in collecting and transporting the Memnon head to London lay claim to the object for themselves. Similarly, while the Memnon head may have come into the possession of the British Museum, it was not claimed as property either by anyone there or by anyone involved in the acts that effected its transport to England. In this sense, there is no deed that definitively establishes the object as the property of the British Museum. Its provenance attempts to explain why the object rightly belongs where it sits but succeeds only in telling how it got there. Thus one of the fundamental paradoxes of the artifact as a cultural object: it may be in the custody of those who proclaim themselves to be the best parties to conserve and study it, but it is not their property. According to artifact discourse, if the Memnon head must belong to someone, it belongs to civilization or humanity in the abstract. In this rendition, the British Museum claims to be not the owner of the piece but merely its custodian.

The story of the removal of the Memnon bust from Egypt narrates the movement of an object through time and space and also the emergence of new institutional practices of culture based on the artifact form. Still, an obvious question dogs this account of the Memnon head: was the process of artifaction not also an act of theft?

It is tempting to call the acquisition a kind of theft at least insofar as those involved in acquiring the Memnon head knew (or supposed) that the natives did not appreciate its true value and thus could be prevailed upon to surrender it without fair compensation. The facts of the transaction seem to fit the textbook definition of the crime of larceny. But how is it that even though the story I have told is well known (as it is), there has never been a consensus that (let alone serious consideration whether) the act was done in bad faith, or was criminal in nature? The lack of consensus is not because this acquisition was exceptional compared to what came after. On the contrary, the artifaction style by which the Memnon head was removed became the rule of acquisitions, and its example was repeated, with variations of course, throughout the nineteenth century.

Condemnations have always been raised against this kind of antiquities acquisition, both by Europeans writing at the time and in more recent decades.[120] Because those individuals raising the criticism have been work-ing at a distance from the centers of Egyptological and museum authority, however, their voices have been largely ignored. Similarly, for reasons I will discuss in subsequent chapters, there has never been a serious at-tempt on the part of Egyptians or Egyptian governments to repatriate ob-jects collected in the nineteenth century, nor should we expect them to.[121] This apparent Egyptian indifference toward the transgressions of antiqui-ties acquisition functions crucially in traditional accounts of Egyptology and has gone far to support the claim that the acquisition of Pharaonic antiquities could not have been theft. A key part of that argument, which has been rehashed from the 1810s until the present, is that Egyptians are more than indifferent in their attitudes toward Pharaonic antiquities: as Muslim iconoclasts and ignorant peasants, they pose a grave threat to the objects' survival. In this narrative, European acquisitions appear as acts of redemption, not dispossession. Once the objects were relocated to Europe, the language of conservation extended this line of thought and helped fuel the notion that the remedy for bad local government (in places like Egypt) is always European intervention. As we shall see, the notion that Egyptians did not care or could not manage their antiquities had its roots in a deliberate misrecognition of alternative Egyptian and Muslim traditions of thinking about and appreciating Pharaonic antiquities. In other words, fears about Islamic iconoclasm and peasant ignorance have had an important conceptual function in claims for colonial intervention. Because acquisition was represented as an act of conservation offsetting the kind of destruction to which antiquities were doomed if they were left in place, it was seen—and continues to be seen—as more or less legiti-mate. In the light cast by conservation discourse, the issue of acquisition is rarely described as illicit.

So, was the artifaction of the Memnon head a form of theft? Those who describe this history of antiquities acquisition in terms of theft have largely restricted their critique to claims about property rights.[122] I would argue, though, that such claims fail to grasp the particular modus operandi of acquisition carried on under the banner of the artifact and founded on the persistence of two not entirely incorrect impressions: on the one hand, the legal and commercial transactions that took place around antiquities collection were quite ambiguous; and on the other, acquisition was an act of preservation. Here one begins to see how the discourse of the artifact did not obscure claims about property rights concerning antiquities but rather effectively shifted the field of claim and contestation altogether. Before the 1810s, Europeans had been taking antiquities from Egypt without ever speaking about preservation or calling their activities anything other than what they were: commercial exchanges among local, state, and diplomatic agents. There are many indications that this commerce was large and formed a substantial part of the off-season economic activities of portions of Upper Egypt.[123] Though the removal of the Memnon head relied on this commerce, the style of its acquisition was new in that it sought a moral grounding for its actions and sought to legitimate itself as noncommercial and disinterested. The peculiar form of moral discourse surrounding the acquisition of the Memnon head—the discourse of the artifact—combined elements of salvationism, altruism, and scientism. Taken together, these elements of artifact discourse illustrate why the act of acquisition, so often criticized, has rarely been associated with theft. More than that, however, the powerful and persistent capacities of artifact discourse also suggest that any serious critique of acquisition cannot be confined to claims about discrete acts of theft, since what was at stake was the emergence of a new, more diffuse form of power—a network joining material objects and human subjects, powerful states and shifting aesthetic sensibilities, scientific fieldwork and museum pleasures. If this issue were considered with regard to restitutive justice, it would become apparent immediately how the claim of theft fails to grasp fully the broader context of colonial power: while one might imagine a successful legal campaign to repatriate individual objects like the Memnon head, this would still not undo the history of colonial domination that artifact discourse helped produce.

These last insights are clearly reflected in the official accounts of the removal of the Memnon head, which, though indifferent toward discrete property rights, are deeply concerned with shifting power relations. In fact, the primary sources describing the Memnon head's removal are saturated with the description of imperial power and its effects, rules, and ambiguities. One might say that the story of the Memnon head's artifaction tells also of the intersection of four imperial powers. Most obviously, the acquisition of the Memnon head took place in the context of competition between the French and British empires. Quite literally, the acquisition agents saw their competition as one over spaces and objects, territories which either empire might dominate. Acquisition concerns were not distinct from the diplomatic activities of each empire; moreover, the military capacities of each were marshaled to accomplish the task. These competitions in Egypt were then consciously reproduced in the museum collections of each empire's metropole. At the same time, British–French competition for antiquities took place in the territories of a third empire. The Ottoman Empire's grasp on North Africa was already tenuous by the 1810s, although Egypt would remain under Ottoman sovereignty, and later under nominal Ottoman suzerainty, for another hundred years. Although Belzoni's account tells the story of how British power might be projected into Upper Egypt and Nubia, the fact of Ottoman governance infuses its every page. Although Belzoni's depiction of Ottoman rule may have been motivated by the fact he had to negotiate with regional and local officials throughout his travels, the centrality of Ottoman rule in his account goes beyond the merely descriptive. For Belzoni and Salt, each empire implied a set of particular moral values. If these authors assumed the British Empire to be dynamic, fair-minded, efficient, and rational, they saw the Ottoman Empire as stagnant, tyrannical, corrupt, and ignorant. There was little new about this kind of Orientalist moralism save for the mediating role played by the specter of a fourth empire in Belzoni's account—Pharaonic Egypt. In many senses, it was the shadow of ancient empire that motivated acquisition in the first place.[124] Undoubtedly, a substantial share of the aesthetic and historical value that accrued in objects like the Memnon head derived from their association with one of the most powerful empires of the ancient world. And, as we shall see in the next chapter, the imperial character of Pharaonic antiquities could rub off on those powerful enough to hold them in their grasp.

Ozymandias

I met a traveller from an antique land
Who said:—"Two vast and trunkless legs of stone
Stand in the desert. Near them on the sand,
Half sunk, a shatter'd visage lies, whose frown
And wrinkled lip and sneer of cold command
Tell that its sculptor well those passions read
Which yet survive, stamp'd on these lifeless things,
The hand that mock'd them and the heart that fed.
And on the pedestal these words appear:
'My name is Ozymandias, king of kings:
Look on my works, ye mighty, and despair!'
Nothing beside remains: round the decay
Of that colossal wreck, boundless and bare,
The lone and level sands stretch far away."
—SHELLEY, "Ozymandias"

My account of the artifaction of the Memnon head has foregrounded the material aspects of the process of artifaction. For the most part, I have read sources indexically, as references to actual events, actual people, and an actual object. Of course, each source is also a representation. To observe this is to emphasize a point made earlier about the performance played by the paper trail of the provenance itself. That is, the archives did not merely tell the story of how the Memnon head became an artifact; they were also gathered to guarantee that very outcome. To underscore the substantive role played by representations in the artifaction process I want to briefly consider Shelley's sonnet "Ozymandias" since it too belongs to this body of texts bundled with the Memnon head. Much might be said about the poem, but I will consider only three points: the first has to do with how it frames the object as a ruin; the second, with its use of prosopopoeia (personification); the third, with how it performs within the network of artifaction.

Of the various representations attached to the Memnon head, Shelley's poem is undoubtedly the most famous. It was composed in the context of a friendly literary competition with Horace Smith, as both men, like much of the London lettered class, followed reports of the head's imminent arrival.[1] The poem's literary power results from how it explores monumentalization as an uncertain act of signification.[2] It accomplishes this effect by conceptually linking the crafts of the sculptor and the poet, each of whom (in his own way) creates works of art intended to last beyond the historical moment in which they are made. At the same time, however, "Ozymandias" injects real ambiguity into the question of the meaning-making art since each artist—the sculptor who "mocks" and the poet who ironizes—creates a work that has, in a sense, a life of its own, one that cannot be reduced to the intent of the humans making it. Shelley's poem is a study of the gesture of monumentalization insofar as it explores this theme both in its depiction of the sculptor and in its own form as a poem.[3]

As critics have pointed out, Shelley relied heavily on the accounts of travelers like Diodorus Siculus, Pococke, and Denon who visited the Memnonium.[4] Indeed, the poem signals this fact at the beginning: "I met a traveler from an antique land / Who said . . ." It is not especially surprising that Shelley would seek inspiration for his poem in the extensive body of travel writing on Egypt. Yet it is striking that the central image of the poem—the "colossal wreck"—would be framed in such a way as to emphasize its received, citational quality. In so doing, the poem gestures toward the authority of experience in travel writing of the period. What has not been fully appreciated is how Shelley imagined the place—a "desert" of "lone and level sands"—as being outside of human society. While the Memnonium may not have been as populated as other Egyptian temples and tombs during this period, it is abundantly clear in the accounts of Belzoni and others that the place was far from uninhabited. Of course, it is beside the point to fault Shelley's lack of realism because his poem depopulates the Memnonium. It is, however, salient to observe how much his image corresponds to the view—expressed by Belzoni and others—that the antiquities of Egypt ought to be separated from the modern inhabitants. In order to produce the illusion that the ancient past is immediately available, "Ozymandias" necessarily removes the object from its social context. This act of rendition mirrors in essence the radical recontextualization that Egyptian antiquities underwent as they were brought under the sign of the artifact.

Still, the poem does more than this. The act of citation puts a double distance between any place called here and the scene described. The ruin lies far away across space and time; the expanse is extended again by the fact that it appears as received speech. Yet, for all the distance marked by geography, antiquity, and irony, the poem performs a close examination of the statue. In the sense that it is a study of an object, the poem telescopes us directly into the presence of the ruin. Here, we are with the postantiquarian scholar of art who closely studies the individual piece of work as a totality in itself, though one that opens up onto other hermeneutical scenes. This intimate study of the face quickly leads to a consideration of the relation between the sculpture's artist and his subject, the tyrant Pharaoh. The poem suggests that the sculpture of the king is not an unambiguous one, since the very gestures which indicate the subject's power ("wrinkled lip and sneer of cold command") also attest to the control of the artist, whose "heart" created the statue and whose "hand" appears to have mocked his subject. Critics have focused on this description of the relationship between artist and king in order to argue that Shelley is here asserting the power of the creative arts over politics. But, more germane to thinking about the Memnon head as an artifact, we might recognize Shelley's effort—in pure imagination—to read for an original context (the relation between patron and artist) through which one might interpret subtle, even ironic, aspects within a work of Egyptian art. In other words, the "study" enacted in the poem was precisely one that art historians could not yet perform. In this sense, the poem prefigures a later moment when the Memnon head would become a historical artifact, just as it anticipates the historian's eye studying it.

A larger irony lingers, however, in the juxtaposition of the sculpture's inscription ("Look on my works, ye mighty, and despair!") and its current state of ruin and neglect. One function of this writing is to lend voice and words to the inanimate object. The image on which the poem ends is like that of a colossal statue speaking with no one to heed his words save the modern traveler or reader of inscriptions. What is the significance of representing this object as sneering and communicating? Similarly, Belzoni portrayed the Memnon head as a living thing when he described it as smiling at him at the thought of being taken away. To call this kind of figure personification is correct, but that observation does not flesh out the full meaning. What Shelley's poem describes in figurative terms is thus more or less what the statue actually is: the product of human labor; a representation of a human form that has a relation to human life; a representation that has an association with human power. By imagining the lively aspect of the statue, Shelley's poem reactivates the human aspects of the object that were congealed in the stone.

The personified figurative language of literary descriptions—in Belzoni, in Shelley, and elsewhere—is a useful correction to the impression that artifacts are the passive objects of actions and processes performed by human actors. It becomes a dominant theme in much European (and later Egyptian) literature about Pharaonic antiquities (especially that about mummies). This tradition of prosopopoeia suggests that there might be traces of the human in the object itself, or at least qualities in the artifact, like agency, that one normally associates with human life. Indeed, the literary description of the object often returns to this point in order to reveal something that the other forms of discourse do not: namely, that its existence is entangled with the lives of the humans around it and in that sense it might be said to have a life. In this way, Shelley's poem compels us to ask, What if artifacts are not inert? What if they are not just the instruments or consequences of history making, but rather agents within it? This second question may appear strange, since it runs contrary to the common assumption that agency is a uniquely human attribute. Yet it may be that the prosopopoeic literary descriptions capture this aspect of the artifact more accurately than prosaic accounts.

The point might be made differently: the artifaction of the Memnon head entailed catching it in networks of concepts, writing, sciences, and practices normally associated exclusively with humans. Artifacts brought into such networks, and assimilated into such institutions, helped those who controlled them produce claims that were not just about the ancient past, but also about the modern present. These claims had, as we shall see, profound implications for how Egypt's modern rulers—colonial and nationalist—would legitimate their power. Just as the knowledge and power produced in relation to artifacts must become entangled with their matter, so too must human agency, when it is constructed in relation to objects, share some life with them. In this regard, the personified artifact resonates with the notion of the *actant*, since it too describes how power might obtain in the matter of an object when it is part of an assemblage of social and political relations.[5] Shelley's sonnet thus suggests that the artifact is a prosthesis in the performance of human power relations and a material site within a network of forces that encompasses humans and nonhumans alike.

A final point with regard to the poem's association with the Memnon head artifact and the issue of entanglement. Recall that Shelley's poem derives from a long tradition of travel writing on Pharaonic antiquities and in that sense might be said to be a secondary (or tertiary) artifact in relation to the object itself. However, the poem's publication predated the arrival of the Memnon head in London, and its light no doubt helped illuminate the object itself. We know also that John Keats visited the Egyptian collection at the British Museum during the early months of the Memnon head's arrival, and was inspired to write at least seven poems on ancient Egyptian themes as a result. Is it accurate to say that the meaning of "Ozymandias" derives from the object it is said to represent or that the image created by the poem is what informs the museum-goer's experience of the artifact? To frame the relationship between artifact and representation in terms of the familiar conundrum raised by the original and the copy misses what was likely a more crucial aspect, namely, that when joined together, poem and statue (or artifact and provenance, or object and representation) formed a network of concepts, images, and material facts powerful enough to make it seem natural and inevitable that the Memnon head would now reside in London for the contemplation of the British public. In this way, Shelley's poem does more than describe an Egyptian monument or problematize the gesture of artistic monumentalization. In monumentalizing the alienability of objects found in Egypt, the poem is part of the wider set of networks that together effected the Memnon head's artifaction. "Ozymandias" is thus more than a poem about an object. It is an instance of how in the emergent institutions of Egyptology and Egyptomania there was "no important difference between stories and materials."[6]

2

Conflicted Antiquities:
Islam's Pharaoh and the Emergent Egyptology

Among the marvels (*'aja'ib*) of construction are the pyramids in Egypt, the height of each of which is four hundred cubits. . . . Himyaritic characters are written on them by the hand of the King. This writing is filled with every magic and wonder (*'ajib*) of medicine and astrology. It is said, though God knows best, that they were constructed by Ptolemaeus Claudius, the King. It is also said that the following challenge is inscribed upon them: "I am the one who built these Pyramids. Let he who claims to be strong in his dominion try to tear them down, for surely it is easier to destroy than to build!" All the riches of the world could not pay the cost of razing these pyramids.
—IBN KHURRADADHBIH (d. 911 CE), *al-Masalik wa-l-mamalik*

Belzoni's and Salt's efforts to acquire Pharaonic antiquities did not go unnoticed by Egyptians. Consider the following account by Egypt's chief chronicler of the early nineteenth century, 'Abd al-Rahman al-Jabarti (1753–1826):

> Finally, [among the events of this month, Dhu-l–Hijja 1232 (October 12–November 10, 1817)] the activities of a group of English Europeans who wanted to investigate the famous pyramids at Giza, west of Fustat. By nature and desire they like to study curious objects and inquire into trivial details, especially monuments [*athar*] and wonders [*'aja'ib*] of the land, paintings and statues found in tombs and ancient temples in Upper Egypt and elsewhere. Some of these Englishmen travel all over the world for such purposes, spending great sums of money for their supplies and hired attendants.[1]

The European taste for Pharaonic antiquities is admittedly not a central focus of Jabarti's writing and rarely noted in his chronicles of Egypt.[2] But when the historian does mention European antiquarianism, he adopts a skeptical tone. He witnessed the arrival of the Memnon bust in the port of Cairo:

> These English Europeans also brought back the head of a large idol [*sanam*]. This they transported in a ship they hired for 16 purses, or 320,000 silver paras. They sent the objects to their homeland to sell at many times the amount they had spent on them, these being for them a type of curio merchandise. When I heard about these figures I went . . . to see them in the consul's house. . . . There I saw those things as I have described them, and we admired their craftsmanship and evenness, and how the bright sheen of their surfaces has endured through centuries whose number is unknown save by the Knower of the beyond.[3]

Jabarti was an astute observer of European behavior. During the French occupation (1798–1801), he avidly participated in the research institute established by Bonaparte's savants, a collaboration for which he paid after the French evacuation. The impassive tone of Jabarti's observations about Pharaonic antiquities becomes significant in light of his deep familiarity with Frankish habits. Though one might assume that Jabarti was exposed to European discussions of the historical and aesthetic value of the objects, the focus of his interest is more on the activities of the collectors than on the things themselves. For him, the European acquisition of antiquities is a form of strange commerce.

In comparison with those of European travelers, Jabarti's descriptions of Egyptian antiquities are cursory. The objects are never named. However, the historian's account is by no means indifferent. His language bespeaks an interest in the objects, though it does not quite intersect with that of Europeans. Jabarti's tone toward the activities of the Englishmen is deprecating, even scornful. Their research in tombs and temples is not real knowledge but mere trivia, their expenses extravagant. Most important, what was a cultural treasure for Belzoni and Salt has religious significance for the Egyptian historian: it is an idol (*sanam*). The term *sanam*—a statue formed for the purpose of worship—is in no small part pejorative, associated with idolatry (*taghut*) and polytheism (*shirk*).[4] In this sense, the word's appearance marks a distinction from contemporary European accounts of antiquities, which were neutral, if not indifferent, toward the pagan implications of Pharaonic antiquities. From the normative aesthetic or historical standpoint of European antiquarians, whether in the field or the museum, the original religious significance of such objects was not as important as what they might say about the civilization which produced them. But Jabarti's reference to the ancient statue as an idol shows that, from his standpoint, it mattered that the civilization that produced them was pagan. Jabarti does express an appreciation of the objects, but it is rather an appreciation for them as signs of God's transcendence. He considers the objects from at least three perspectives: he implicitly foregrounds their association with the pagan past, then admires (*ta'ajjaba*) the quality of their artifice (*sina'a*), and then appreciates them again as material signs that point unambiguously to the existence of a larger, metaphysical realm.

By no means do Jabarti's comments mark the beginning of the relationship between Egyptians and Pharaonic antiquities. For centuries, the Pharaonic past had a prominent, though often ambiguous, position in the monotheistic traditions of Egypt. Within Jewish and Coptic traditions, the image of Pharaoh was associated with unholy tyranny. For Muslims, this figure connoted the pre-Islamic period of ignorance, heedlessness, polytheism, and tribalism. Insofar as they were associated with an era of unrestrained opulence, objects from the Pharaonic past were thought of alternately as hidden treasure, products of slave labor, and talismans with magical properties. At the same time, the objects evoked important theological issues: on the one hand, their antiquity gestured beyond normal human scales of time and toward the eternal and divine; on the other hand, their pagan origin and ruined state suggested the vanity of human endeavor in this world. Clustered around these signs were the concepts of *'ibar* and *'aja'ib*, or "lessons" and "wonders." Thus, Jabarti's complex mix of skepticism about and appreciation for the ancient objects was not novel. Rather he gestures toward a tradition of contemplation of Pharaonic antiquities that appears in the work of earlier generations of Muslim historians, philosophers, and travelers.

Jabarti's account should be read nonetheless as uniquely modern in that it portends a confrontation between this Islamic tradition surrounding Pharaonic antiquity and the emergent European discourse on antiquities.

It would be wrong to say that the second discourse erased the first, for religious discourses on Pharaonic antiquity remained a powerful source for dissident, especially Islamist thinking in Egypt throughout the twentieth century, as we shall see later. Yet the new European institutions of archaeological preservation and appreciation were undeniably in the ascendant at the time Jabarti commented on Belzoni and Salt. By the 1830s, these institutions had developed to the point where they began to push religious discourse to the margins of the larger cultural conversations about the significance of ancient objects in Egypt. Jabarti's text marks a turning point, located between an old tradition on Pharaonic antiquity and the soon-to-be dominant Frankish attitudes and practices the author so clearly dismisses.

The first section of this chapter begins by surveying the Arabo-Islamic tradition of writing on Pharaonic antiquities in Egypt that is implicit in the above passage. The image of ancient Egypt is complex within Islamic teaching: it is associated with Pharaoh, a uniquely arrogant, sinful figure in the Qur'an; yet its remnants—the products of an ancient, learned civilization—are also signs and wonders that invite closer study. By Jabarti's day, there was a long tradition of legends about Pharaonic antiquities in Arabic letters, some absorbed from ancient Greek and Roman sources, others developed in conversation with religious teaching and the thoughts of Muslim travelers, and still others developed more locally.[5] In the 1810s, this tradition was undoubtedly as compelling as any of the contemporary European theories about the Pharaonic past.

The second section of this chapter contrasts the Arabo-Islamic tradition with the emergence of Egyptology in Europe. In chapter 1, I outlined the acquisition of Pharaonic antiquities at a moment when their historical significance was still mostly the object of speculation. Moral claims for the legitimacy of European acquisition were based not on superior knowledge of the past, but rather on superior technologies of representation and preservation. With Champollion's decipherment of hieroglyphs in the 1820s, the balance shifted. In time, it became possible to make positive assertions about the ancient Egyptian past. The science of Egyptology began to replace the enthusiasm of antiquarianism. In the previous chapter I discussed how control of Pharaonic objects was wrested from Egyptians in the 1810s. In this chapter I investigate how control over the objects led to increasingly accurate methods of interpreting them in the

1820s and beyond. The best example, of course, is the Rosetta stone, taken from Egypt by a British warship following the French evacuation in 1801. In a very real sense, if European scholars had not secured material possession of the original object (placed in the British Museum) and copies (in the Louvre), it is doubtful whether they would have deciphered the ancient Egyptian language when they did. Yet it was never in doubt from the moment the stone was found that it "belonged" rightfully to Europeans rather than Egyptians. Not only did the control of objects lead to breakthroughs in interpretation, but these breakthroughs provided further moral ammunition to arguments about the control of antiquities. In this light, it is impossible to disentangle the conceptual field of Egyptology from the material objects it studied or the social and political fields in which claims of possession were articulated and contested. Here, some of the wider consequences of the discourse of artifacts become visible: it created not only a new form of knowledge, Egyptology, but also new ways of understanding the imperial power relations underwriting this European science, perhaps the first academic discipline whose fortune wholly depended on colonial domination. In fact, the new science provided a confidence in interpretation that was not just limited to ancient artifacts: arguments about the superiority of European sciences of interpretation were crucial in developing a wider, colonial sensibility that it was Europeans, not Egyptians, who knew Egypt best. To expand knowledge about ancient Egypt was to bolster European claims for governing modern Egypt, an argument that is developed in the third section of this chapter.

PHARAOH

The warnings came to the people of Pharaoh. They rejected each one of Our signs. So We seized them with the grip of one mighty and powerful.
—AL-QUR'AN, 54: 41–42

There is perhaps no narrative so often recalled in the Qur'an as the confrontation between Moses and Pharaoh.[6] Given the prominent place of this incident, there is a rich exegetical tradition on the figure of Pharaoh in Islam.[7] The text suggests two slightly different contexts for interpreting

Pharaoh, neither of them favorable. There are many passages in the Qur'an which focus on Pharaoh's confrontation with Moses and, by extension, with God. Throughout, Pharaoh exemplifies a historical and uniquely Egyptian example of the arrogance of rejecting God's sovereignty. In the many retellings of this confrontation, Pharaoh is described as arrogant (*mustakbir*), a transgressor (*musrif*), a corrupter (*mufsid*), and a rebellious tyrant (*taghiy*).

Arguably, however, it is his haughtiness (*'uluww*) that is the source of his moral corruption.[8] When confronted by Moses, Pharaoh dismisses the signs of God as mere magic and sorcery. Insisting on his own divinity, Pharaoh exclaims, "I am not aware of any other lord of yours but myself."[9] After witnessing the miracles wrought by Moses, Pharaoh's son and thousands of Egyptian magicians convert to Moses' religion, but for all their righteousness they remain a minority. Even after God afflicts Egypt with famine, floods, locusts, and frogs, Pharaoh remains stubbornly defiant. It is not that Pharaoh and the Egyptians fail to see the plagues as signs of the power of the Israelites' God. Each time they challenge Moses, and each time God shows his power in response, they come to recognize the truth of Moses' mission. But in the wake of each trial, Pharaoh forgets the lesson God has taught. It is for this reason that there is probably no better example of disbelief (*kufr*) in the Qur'an than the figure of Pharaoh.[10] Although the Qur'an depicts some individual ancient Egyptians as being righteous—most notably the Pharaoh of Jacob's narrative—it portrays the figure of Moses' Pharaoh as uniquely villainous.[11]

The figure of this Pharaoh also occurs as part of a longer chain of ancient peoples who reject God's message, as, for instance, in the opening verses of Sura 69:

What is the concrete reality? What do you comprehend by the concrete reality? The Thamud and 'Ad denied the consequential calamity. So the Thamud were destroyed by a storm of thunder and lightning. And the 'Ad were destroyed by the furious cold blast of roaring wind. . . . Then came Pharaoh, and those before him whose habitations were overthrown while they were committing crimes. When they disobeyed the apostle of their Lord He seized them with an overwhelming punishment . . . in order to make it a warning for you, so that the ear might retain its lesson.[12]

Pharaoh appears here not as a specific individual who denied God's power, but rather as a symbol of ancient Egypt more generally, which is itself only one among other pagan civilizations, like Thamud and 'Ad, named in the Qur'an.[13] This list of ancient civilizations is crucial to another main theme in the text, namely, that throughout history God has periodically revealed his truth to peoples who have rejected or remained indifferent toward it. For such peoples, there is special punishment: destruction. The ruins of the ancient civilizations stand as concrete proof of this.

At the same time, for centuries ancient Egyptian monuments, especially the pyramids, had a prominent place in the writings of Muslim philosophers, historians, and geographers. In this tradition their significance is linked (though not reducible) to the narratives of Pharaoh's arrogance. Rather, the ruins of ancient civilizations point to the vanity of human efforts to transcend time. Likewise, ruins confirm a central tenet of Islam, namely, God's transcendence over the created world.[14] In this light, the physical remains of Pharaoh's destruction, like that of Thamud and 'Ad, signify (negatively) as warning to those who would reject God's message and (positively) as encouragement to the faith of believers: "We have been sending word to them that they may take warning. Those to whom We gave the Book before this do believe in it; and when it is read out to them, say: 'We believe in it. It's the truth from our Lord. We had committed ourselves before it came.'"[15] The word glossed above as "taking warning" might be more literally translated as "striving to remember." Remembrance (*tadhakkur*) is a central theme in these passages, just as it is throughout the Qur'an. It is tied to a pessimistic assertion that humans tend to forget, and to forget in particular God's generosity and mercy. Most prominent among the examples of forgetfulness in the Qur'an is that of the Jewish people, who, no sooner liberated from Pharaoh's bondage, forget who saved them and return to worshiping the Golden Calf. In this account, forgetfulness is a sign not merely of innate human weakness, but also of a failure of faith. This kind of failure lies at the core of the concept of *kufr*, which is not just a matter of disbelief, but also an act of disacknowledging God's mercy that is fundamentally ungrateful.[16] Throughout the Qur'an there are examples of God's reminding believers not to forget—in this way, *tadhkir* (reminding, warning) is one of the central themes of the text. Memory in this account refers not simply to a mental faculty, but also to an intentional action, a moral striving to remember despite the innate human tendency to forget. For these reasons, ruins have a special double role: they function as both physical evidence of the pagan history recounted in the Qur'an and as material reminders not to forget the significance of these past events.

While there has long been a common assumption that Islamic culture is at heart iconoclastic, a large body of literature on the subject suggests that Muslim piety did not direct itself at pre-Islamic monuments and artifacts in any consistent pattern.[17] On the contrary, many classical authors asserted that the ruins of ancient civilizations (*athar*, "monuments," lit., "traces" and "reminders") were warnings for Muslims to consider.[18] This is especially true of those travelers and historians who researched the subject of Pharaonic monuments.

For instance, in the classical genre of *fada'il* literature, where the "merits" of a country are listed exhaustively, Pharaonic monuments figure large precisely because they serve as lessons of history (*'ibar*) for consideration or contemplation (*i'tibar*).[19] In the body of writing on Pharaonic monuments in classical Arabic literature, the point of their lesson recurs often in titles.[20] Encompassing geography, science, and history, this literature strives to synthesize all that was known of ancient Egypt during the medieval period, which derived from Greek sources and the best classical Muslim histories. Of the many titles, three stand out for the detail and extent of their comments on Pharaonic monuments: *Lights of the Highest Celestial Bodies in Revealing the Secrets of the Pyramids* by Jamal al-Din al-Idrisi (d. 1251 CE); *The Book of Benefit and the Consideration of Lessons*, the travel account of the Abbasid physician 'Abd al-Latif ibn Yusuf al-Baghdadi (d. 1231 CE); and the "Treatise on the Pyramids" by Jalal al-Din al-Suyuti (d. 1505CE).[21] Though different in style and genre, these accounts offer a coherent, if somewhat tautological, message: the ruins of ancient Egypt are to be contemplated for the crucial lessons they offer.

The message announced in the invocation of Idrisi's treatise on the pyramids reads, "Praise be to God who made those imposing signs, those standards for measuring curiosities and monuments [*athar*], into pages that, even if silent, speak with the worthiest lessons [*'ibar*] for consideration [*i'tibar*]."[22] In Idrisi's account, "The pyramids are among the monuments [*athar*] the sight of which compels contemplation [*i'tibar*]." The first chapter of Idrisi's treatise develops the idea of monuments as lessons (*'ibar*) that called on believers to consider the fate of those who did not accept God's message. In the opening passages, he quotes, among other Qur'anic verses, the exhortation to "travel the Earth and see what happened to those who disbelieved."[23] Idrisi goes on at length to list the moral benefits of visits to monuments, whose lessons range from history and science to issues of faith and metaphysical truths. The author refers to the story of the Moroccan pilgrim to Mecca who, upon returning home, is asked by his Sufi master, "Tell me about what you saw of the Pyramids of Egypt." Replying that he had not seen them, he is upbraided harshly by his teacher. Humiliated, the story ends with the man returning to Cairo to make amends for his failure.[24] So normative is this exhortation in Idrisi's account that it poses an almost legal obligation to visit and contemplate the monuments.[25]

RUINS AND WONDER

When you pass by the pyramids, say: 'How many are the lessons they have for the intelligent one who would gaze at them!'—AHMAD IBN MUHAMMAD (d. 1482 CE), as quoted in Jalal al-Din al-Suyuti, *Hasan al-Muhadara*

The ruins of Egypt were thus first and foremost tied to the idea of historical lessons (*'ibar*) that, by encouraging the practice of contemplation (*i'tibar*), might mitigate the effects of forgetful and disbelieving human nature. But while it is true that the practice of contemplating Pharaonic monuments was enjoined as a religious duty in the writings of Muslim philosophers and historians, it also dovetailed with a much older Arabic literary figure, that of ruins or "the abandoned encampment" (*al-atlal*). In countless classical odes, ruins serve as a motivating trope: the persona of the poet stops at the material traces of a past habitation which recall for him events and people associated with that time and place. Like other pre-Islamic odes, that of the poet Labid ibn Rabi'a (c. 600 CE), begins with such an image:

> The habitations in Minan have been obliterated, both the overnight sites and the spring campgrounds. Both Ghawl and Rijam have been taken over by beasts.
> The traces of the flood channels of al-Rayyan have been stripped bare, worn smooth, like writing on rocks . . .

The flash floods uncovered the ruins (*tulul*) as though they were writings
   whose text is revived by pens.
Or as though they were a tattooed lady whose lines were restored by rubbing indigo over them.[26]

In the oral, nomadic culture of pre-Islamic Arabia, ruins serve as the figures of memory, writing, and the possibility of culture.[27]

The importance of ruins in this tradition cannot be exaggerated: without writing, knowledge has no life outside of human memory.[28] Classical
Arabic poems are not only structured around recurring mnemonic de-
vices, but are also filled with concrete figures of the reminder.[29] The figure
of ruins signals an intractable problem of culture, namely, the interdepen-
dence of memory and forgetfulness, writing and erasing. The ruins index
the most concrete monuments of culture in the nomadic landscape (camp
making) and turn these referents into the motivating trope of literary figuration. By placing the figure of ruins at its beginning, this poetic tradition
foregrounds a struggle between time and culture. Ruins in this tradition
not only signify remembrance and the possibility of culture, but also gesture toward the inevitability of forgetting, to the moment when the poetic
figure, like its referent, would be obliterated by the ravages of time.

Hence, it is no accident that the poetic tradition of ruins (*atlal*) would
inform the discussion of Pharaonic monuments (*athar*) whenever the latter appear in classical poetry. The tone is often bleak, mirroring that of the
pre-Islamic ode (*qasida*), as in these lines where the poet al-Mutanabbi
(915–65 CE) reflects on the vanity of human efforts to create:

Where is he among whose structures the pyramids belong? Who were his
   folk? When did he live? And what brought him down?
These moments have survived their inhabitants, though only for a while.
   For when annihilation seizes them, they too will surely follow.[30]

Even if the pyramids have outlasted the civilization which built them, they
too will crumble and fade. In the classical tradition, the figure of Pharaonic ruins serves to express loss itself: their present form might gesture
toward an original inhabited structure, but their difference from their
original shape—their decay—points to the passage of time and the inevitable process of entropy.[31] The melancholic tone of the poetic figure is also

that of history lessons (*'ibar*). Another passage from Idrisi's account reads as follows: "Let the empty courtyards of the ruins / monuments (*athar*) be quenched with a copious pouring of tears flooding from the rain clouds of his eyelashes. Let him wake up from sleep to these clear signs, these sobering stirrings. Let him pass mindfully among places and quarters whose time of habitation has passed. As the Speaker of Truth said, 'How many gardens and fountains did they leave behind.'"[32] Although the concluding words of the passage reveal its religious tenor, and although it is composed in prose, the themes and figures—the empty courtyards, the pouring of tears from rain cloud eyes—are derived from classical poetry. Thus, what was once a crucial figure for understanding (and staving off) loss in pre-Islamic culture becomes, in classical Arabic literature on Pharaonic monuments, a supplement to the religious practice of contemplation and heeding lessons.

Alongside this exhortation to consider ruins in a melancholic key is an overlapping call encouraging Muslims to marvel at (*ta'ajjub*) Pharaonic monuments and to appreciate them as wonders (*'aja'ib*). Arabic literature inherited discourse on the wonders of the classical world, where it appeared in geographical descriptions. *'Aja'ib* literature from the classical period described in great detail the wonders of God's creation, often indulging in speculative descriptions about the oddities of nature in far-off regions. In countless works of cosmography, geography, the descriptions of "ways and kingdoms" (*masalik wa-mamalik*), and biographical accounts of travel, writers reported on the strange and the marvelous, including long lists of unusual flora and fauna, the customs of foreign peoples, the habits of jinn and other supernatural beings. Importantly, they rarely fail to include descriptions of the wonders of the world, especially Egyptian monuments.[33] The wonder, *al-'ajiba*, derives from the verb *'ajaba* which means "to wonder at, to consider extraordinary or strange." In this register, "to wonder" refers equally to an immediate experience, a disposition, and also an activity one cultivates and practices. Wonder connotes both perception and a more reflective, deliberate form of cognition. Critically, it has a strong connection to the practice of one's religious faith.

At what does the discourse on *'aja'ib* encourage us to wonder? There are tautologies at work here. The thing of wonder (*al-'ajiba*) is thus the object in relationship to which the activity of wonder happens (*'ajaba*), the object without which the activity could not take place. Importantly, to marvel at things in the world is to marvel at their status as creations. In this sense, the concept of marvel cannot be separated from a consideration of the divine act of creation, which necessarily appears to human eyes as strange and incomprehensible. This is most obviously true in the case of natural wonders and curiosities the very existence of which presents the enigma of a phenomenon whose cause is unknowable. This, in many accounts, is the very essence of wonder's definition.[34] Man-made wonders from the ancient world generate a similar effect. By contemplating the unknown—and ostensibly unknowable—circumstances of their making, one might learn, by analogy, something about the mystery of divine creation. The marvel is thus foremost a concrete sign of creative agencies whose causes and workings lie beyond the pale of human reckoning. The contemplation of marvel is therefore paradoxical: on the one hand it reminds the human subject of his limited powers to grasp creation, let alone create; on the other hand, the act of contemplation draws the mind toward an understanding of the Creator's divinity, and in so doing, ennobles the contemplating subject.

Insofar as wondrous monuments, such as the pyramids, trigger the sensual experience of wonder and the cultivation of a sense of wonder (ta'ajjub), they provoke meditation, on both the objects of the created world and on the intellect which contemplates the world. In this way, the concept of wonder (ta'ajjub) figures as a philosophical imperative within many of the descriptions of Pharaonic antiquities. For example, in his treatise on the pyramids, Idrisi states, "To marvel at the marvelous (al-ta'ajjub min al-'ajba) indicates the fit disposition of a sentient human mind and the healthy structure of an astute intellect. That a human might not marvel at the marvelous, that a human might not desire to contemplate the splendid and the pure object of contemplation, is a sign of a defective disposition whose possessor needs treatment."[35] The 'Abbasid traveler 'Abd al-Latif al-Baghdadi similarly writes of a sense of awe in his account of viewing Pharaonic monuments:

In spite of the attempts of various nations to annihilate even its most minute traces by transporting to other parts the different stones and materials of which it was constructed, by demolishing its buildings and mutilating the figures with which they were adorned; and finally, in spite of the ravages of time during upwards of four thousand years, its ruins yet present to the spectator a combination of wonders which confound the understanding, and which, to describe, the most eloquent would attempt in vain. The more the collection is considered, the greater admiration it inspires; and every additional glance at the ruins is a source of fresh delight. Scarcely do they give birth in the mind of the beholder to one idea before this originates another still more admirable; this instant he prides himself on his perfect comprehension of them, and again another instant his pride is lowered by the staring conviction of the inadequacy of his conceptions.[36]

In poetry, we also find the theme of wonder, as in these lines from 'Ali ibn Muhammad ibn al-Sa'ati (d. 1207 CE):

There are many marvels too delicate for the words of prattlers or for going on and on about.

Among them are the twin pyramids. In their presence, time grows pyramidically old. The days slip away, though each one only increases the beauty of the Pyramids' youth.

My God!—what timelessness in a structure! It covets the heavens—a pavilion erected with the longest of tent ropes!

It stands as if in the posture of humility, mourning over days and centuries gone by.

It conceals the contents of its discourse from all men's hearing even as it directs its address into men's hearts.[37]

The marvel and wonder surrounding man-made monuments were closely associated with the idea that the sciences and arts of antiquity were superior to those of the present. Despite negative portrayals of Pharaonic civilization in religious tradition, there was an understanding that the ancient Egyptians were particularly advanced in the sciences and technology. Nowhere was their advanced learning more clearly evidenced than in the architecture they left behind. Again, the pyramids were identified as incontestable examples of the perfection of Egyptian science, even if the civilization that produced it was heathen. Baghdadi writes,

The reflecting man, contemplating these vestiges of antiquity, feels inclined to excuse the error of the vulgar, who believed that mortals in those distant ages in which they were constructed, lived to a more advanced period than is usual in our days; that they were of gigantic stature, or that, by striking a stone with a wand, they caused it to obey their orders and to transport itself to wherever their will dictated. In fact, one is seized with a kind of stupor on picturing to oneself the great resources of genius, the profound knowledge of geometry, the resolution and patience requisite for the completion of similar works.[38]

The sentiment is echoed by the Andalusian traveler Abu al-Salt (d. 1134 CE), who is quoted in Idrisi's account: "It is clear that among the ancient Egyptians there was a group possessing understanding and sciences, especially knowledge of engineering and astronomy. What points to this is what they left behind in the way of miraculous, marvelous creations like the pyramids and ancient temples. Truly, these are among the ruins which have confounded the most perceptive, rational minds and showed the limits of weighty ideas, and left for intellects the arduous work of marveling [ta'ajjub] at them and thinking about them."[39]

While wonder (ta'ajjub) and the kind of contemplation (i'tibar) inspired by the lessons of history ('ibar) are rightly understood as ethical dispositions, classical Arabic literature was also interested in other aspects of Pharaonic antiquities. For instance, there are long, speculative histories, cobbled from ancient sources, on the builders of the pyramids.[40] Many commentators in these accounts link the medieval Arabic name of the Pharaoh who built the Great Pyramid (Akhenukh) with that of the prophet Idris from the Islamic tradition, and also with the figure of Hermes Trismegistus, who is said to have given the pyramids their name (haram) in Arabic.[41] Likewise, in these accounts there are many attempts to measure the objects as precisely as possible.[42] Finally, there are hagiographic references to the early Muslims who visited Pharaonic monuments, such as in this story Idrisi recounts: "How happy was the ground of the pyramids when it was honored to receive the footsteps of those generous prophets and whose surfaces were trod upon by the hooves of the steed of those holy warriors among the companions of the Prophet. How many foreheads touched those empty grounds while praying prostrate before God? How many tender voices whose echoes were heard while in worship and reciting loudly, 'There is no god but God!' "[43] Other accounts assert that, despite both implicit and explicit encouragement of iconoclasm in Islamic teaching, early Muslim rulers sought to let the monuments stand. Such accounts do not mark an effort to Islamicize Pharaonic objects so much as to Islamicize an appreciation of them.

ICONOCLASM AND ADMIRATION

The good men of Egypt were the greatest people in terms of knowledge and the most advanced in terms of their skill in soothsaying. The wisest Greeks swore by how advanced the Egyptians were in such matters. They would say, "No sooner do the wise men of Egypt inform us about something than we benefit from them in that very matter. They claimed it was the heavenly bodies that advanced their sciences and informed them about metaphysical essences. They said it was the stars that taught them the secrets of the nature of things, and that guided them to the sciences of the occult. They understood well the eminent talismans and sublime laws. They begat children who spoke at birth. They created pictures that moved and wonders for all to see. Their wisdom is undeniable."—ABU ʿUBAYD AL-BAKRI (d. 1094), *al-Masalik wa-l-mamalik*

While there were attacks on pre-Islamic art by Muslims in Egypt, for the most part they were directed at Christian symbols, in particular the cross.[44] In this respect, Baghdadi's comments on idols (*asnam*) are especially informative. As a physician, Baghdadi was interested in Pharaonic statues for their depiction of the human body: "As for the idols found among these ruins, whether their number or extraordinary size be considered, they surpass description: nor can even a conception of them be formed; but most worthy of admiration is the nicety observed in their forms, their exact proportions, and their resemblance to nature."[45] Using Galen to frame his discussion of medicine, the author notes the usefulness of the statues for the study of the body; using Aristotle to frame his comments on the artifice of the statues, he finds them admirable for the exactness of their proportions. Finally, he turns to the pagan context of their creation:

At the period these statues were formed, the worship of idols was universally spread over the earth and reigned among all nations. . . . The people of Israel, having witnessed the homage paid by the Egyptians to these idols, the profound veneration they manifested for them, and the zeal they showed in the worship of them, accustomed, moreover, by their long residence among these people to witness those superstitious practices, and meeting in Syria with nations similarly addicted to the worship of idols, requested Moses to give them gods like other people. This occasioned Moses (peace be on him) to use this reproof: "You are a nation of idolaters." Most of the Christians, being either Copts or Sabaeans, continued to preserve a great predilection for the worship of the nation from which they drew their origin, and suffered themselves to be readily drawn over to the customs of their fathers.[46]

Baghdadi goes on to link the prevalence of icons in Christian churches with belief in the Trinity, a doctrine often criticized by Muslim theologians as a form of polytheism (*shirk*). He almost implies that Muslims are immune to the addiction that ancient peoples, and their contemporary descendents, have to idolatry. The physician's ease around idols suggests a complicated attitude: a simultaneous recognition of their pagan origin, their usefulness to medical science, and also their beauty as likenesses of the human form.

These attitudes—allowing the object to remain or actively encouraging contemplation of the object—are repeated throughout accounts on the Pharaonic monuments of Egypt. For instance, Idrisi (like others) notes that, on more than one occasion, modern Muslim rulers had attempted to destroy, deface, or quarry Pharaonic monuments. One early Muslim ruler of Egypt, Ibn Tulun, is said to have failed in his attempts to penetrate the interior of the pyramids. More famous is the account of the 'Abbasid caliph al-Ma'mun who commissioned a party to open the largest pyramid. According to the story, when the tomb was opened, they found a jar containing one thousand dinars—the exact amount the caliph had expended in his excavation efforts. Baghdadi's account tells also of the foolish attempts of Salah al-Din's son, al-'Aziz, who, as governor of Egypt, attempted to demolish pyramids:

> [The] Sultan dispatched drillers, stonecutters, and ropers under the conduct of some of the principal officers and Amirs of his court, with orders for its destruction. Accordingly they pitched their camp near the pyramid, where they collected from every quarter a vast number of workmen

who were maintained at a prodigious expense. Here they remained for the space of eight months, with their horses, occupied wholly in putting into effect the commission with which they were entrusted, removing every day, after oppressive labour and almost utter exhaustion of the strength of those employed, at most but one or two stones. . . . After remaining long encamped on this spot, and expending all their pecuniary means, as their toil and fatigue continually increased, while on the contrary their resolution diminished daily and their strength became exhausted, those of the commission were forced, shamed and censured, to abandon their undertaking. So far from obtaining the promised success and accomplishing their design, all they did was to spoil the pyramid and exhibit a manifest proof of their inability and failure.[47]

Other narratives of attempts to destroy monuments, notably Salah al-Din's use of the pyramids as a quarry to build the walls of medieval Cairo, are met with the author's disapprobation.[48]

In these accounts, the message is clear: it is not only vain to attempt to destroy Pharaonic monuments but also arrogant. By analogy, it is also morally wrong, since it is not unlike Pharaoh's challenges to God. On the subject of the destruction of monuments, Idrisi recounts a narrative, cited from al-Mas'udi, of an earlier Muslim traveler in Upper Egypt who witnessed locals quarrying stone from Theban ruins. He writes,

My father said, "Look, son, what the Pharaohs built and how it is being destroyed by these idiots. Nothing is more tragic and sad than the loss of what these ruins offer to those who would regard them and consider their lessons. If I had my say in the matter, I would prevent these ignoramuses from destroying them. What sort of wisdom preaches that these ruins should be removed from the face of the Earth? On this very ground trod the stallions of the Prophet's Companions, God Bless Them, as they headed to conquer Nubia after taking Egypt. These people saw these buildings but their hands did not stretch out to ruin them. Rather, they left them as a sign to teach a lesson to those who would consider, and a reminder to every seeker of knowledge."[49]

Another passage from the same source describes the author walking near Cairo:

We were in the ruins of the city of 'Ayn Shams [ancient Heliopolis], wandering around its pastures and meadows. The order had been issued giving its stones to quarriers, just as it had been issued for the ancient ruins of Upper Egypt. The following lines of the poet al-Ma'arri sang out to me . . .

I passed by a quarter of evil men, and was horrified by the song of the stones
    under the pickaxe
A thick arm seized the stones, [so violently it was] as if Fate itself had
    brought on a lion's war between them.
O you who would destroy, may your right arm be paralyzed! Leave these
    ruins for the seeker of knowledge, the one who would regard them, the
    one who would learn their lessons.
The ruined dwellings of a people have addressed us with their speech, and I
    know of no speech sweeter than these dwellings![50]

The point in contemplating Pharaonic monuments in these accounts is not to situate the objects within a historical grid that fixes their meanings, or within an exhibitionary frame that transforms the objects into the possessions of those who gaze at them. Rather, the kind of appreciation offered in this medieval Muslim plea to preserve the objects is more ambiguous—perhaps because it is a melancholic mode of appreciation. To contemplate Pharaonic monuments in this way offers, at best, an understanding that human existence is small in comparison with historical time, and that human endeavors to build civilization are vain when compared to the act of divine creation. These ruins, like those of the pre-Islamic ode, mark a triple challenge: to the past they say, "Your efforts to transcend time have failed"; to the present they say, "You may never build edifices as great as those of the ancient world"; to humans, they say, "And how much greater are the works of the Creator." In all these ways, these ruins present a model of culture at whose core is the contemplation of loss.

Baghdadi contrasts the stupidity of contemporary (that is, thirteenth-century) iconoclasts with the wisdom of the makers of the monuments:

The different rulers were careful at all times of preserving these valuable relics of antiquity, and though avowed enemies of the people by whom these statues were erected, would not allow of their being damaged, or destroyed at pleasure. Many advantages presented by these monuments dictated this line of conduct. In the first place, they regarded them as a species of annals which recalled the memory of past ages; secondly, they stood as witnesses of the truth of the books of revelation; for mention is made, as well of these idols as the people who adored them, in [the Qur'an]. Thus the sight of what remains of them adds the testimony of proof to that authority, and confirms the verity of tradition. These monuments, moreover, are admonitions of futurity, by calling attention to the lot reserved for things of this world. Besides, they present a sketch of the history and conduct of the ancient inhabitants of the earth; we learn, in studying them, to what eminence they had attained in the sciences, what the extent of their genius, and other similar circumstances.[51]

The point, in Baghdadi's account as in Idrisi's, is twofold: the objects should be preserved in their present state both for the information they offer about the ancient past and for what they say about the present. In this sense, these accounts present an extraordinarily dynamic model for reckoning time. It is significant that the kind of appreciation offered in Idrisi's and Baghdadi's accounts is not one that subordinates the objects of the past to the judgment of the present. Neither do they suggest a kind of preservation that would intervene in the natural life of the objects by preserving them in their present form or by trying to re-create their original form. If anything, the meaning of the monuments in these accounts is not the positive knowledge they offer about the past, but rather the lessons they offer about the passing of time. Like ruins in classical odes, Pharaonic monuments figure as physical markers by which time itself might be grasped, its lessons heeded, and its contemplators humbled in the process.

Despite the richness of these accounts, researchers lack sufficient information about their institutional life to say whether they formed a sustained line of scholarship, let alone an intellectual tradition systematically passed down over generations. Indeed, while one can admire the thoughtfulness of these writings, it would be a mistake to think of them as forming a corpus of positive knowledge about the ancient past, especially since the issue of hieroglyphic writing remained more or less a cipher. In fact, these accounts tended to repeat the accounts of ancients while adding little to them in terms of new information or practical application. Moreover, we do not know to what degree their claims were disseminated, collected, or institutionalized, which is to say, we know little of their significance except as a constellation of textual representations. In contrast, there is evidence of long-standing local practices that suggests the philosophic pose evinced in this body of writing was always contested and perhaps only marginal. For one thing, as even these accounts acknowledge, the practice of monument quarrying and inhabitation was widespread and regular over the centuries. For another, the philosophic regard for Pharaonic antiquities existed alongside (and in tension with) the apparently popular institution of treasure seeking (*mutalib*). As treasure-seeking treatises and the export figures on mummy indicate, there is no denying that tomb raiding (which had been practiced in ancient Egypt as well) was a lucrative trade throughout the medieval period and remained so for much of the nineteenth century. Alongside this, there were the popular religious practices, among Muslims and Copts alike, which associated Pharaonic sites and objects with fertility, magic, and divination. One might also consider in this regard the ways in which monuments figured into the lived environment, both as spaces of continuous inhabitation and as sources of solid building materials and decoration. These practices, ranging from the heterodox to the pragmatic and banal, are nearly absent from the traditions of representation considered here. In sum, while the attitudes presented by Muslim travelers such as Baghdadi and Egyptian historians such as Suyuti formed a textual rather than popular tradition, it was one that resonated with larger themes within Arabo-Islamic civilization. Moreover, as Jabarti's account indicates, elements of this tradition were still quite alive in the nineteenth century.

READING AND KNOWING

Many of the sculptures [in the British Museum] were collected by the French in different parts of Egypt, and afterwards came into possession of the British army. The most curious and interesting of the whole of these is the Rosetta stone. . . . It is the principal key we possess to the translation of the hieroglyphics on the monuments of Egypt; for as the inscriptions are evidently the same, if the Greek is understood, it will to a certain extent assist us in deciphering the other portions of the sculpture.—*The Pictorial Times*, April 1, 1843

As long as there was no solid historical information about the culture which produced Pharaonic monuments, European acquisitionists had little intellectual advantage over local Egyptians and cosmopolitan Muslim intellectuals when it came to interpreting them. True, Europeans had captured the ear of the pasha, who granted them excavation firmans with increasing regularity. True, they were developing, in the language of science, a doctrine of preservationism, no matter how inconsistently it was practiced. Yet however much European travelers of the early nineteenth century would continue to claim a superior appreciation of Pharaonic antiquities, neither they nor even the most learned of museum curators had much to say about the historical value of the objects they were visiting, purchasing, collecting, displaying, destroying, and trying to conserve.

During the 1810s, the issue had everything to do with writing. Or rather, it had to do with a modern lack of understanding about the ancient language of the Egyptians. Hieroglyphics were readily recognized as writing, but a kind of writing which could not be read. For centuries, Egyptian hieroglyphics had symbolized signification that was inaccessible.[52] As one traveler in Egypt during the 1810s would put it, hieroglyphs might be appreciated for their aesthetic appearance but certainly not as intelligible signs:

> The hieroglyphic is the only unknown alphabet that a person entirely ignorant of the subject it is employed to unfold, can contemplate with pleasure and advantage; for its elementary parts consist of such an assemblage of objects, both animate and inanimate, of familiar occurrence, grouped together in such a way, either in whole or in part, that it is almost as impossible to refrain from casting the eye over a page of hieroglyphics, as it is from perusing an inscription in any known language; and it is impossible not to attach some meaning to many of the various groups that, in this pictorial language, address themselves to the eye. So the mind of the spectator is entertained with the writing, although the real meaning of it is unknown.[53]

Even by the time this traveler's account was published, however, Jean-François Champollion had published a compelling theory for deciphering the language. Not surprisingly, the process of interpretation undertaken by Champollion depended heavily on the control of an ancient object found in modern Egypt: the Rosetta stone.

Since the story is well known, I will only sketch it here.[54] It begins with a stele discovered by a French engineering officer during efforts to reinforce Fort Julien at the Mediterranean port city of Rashid, or Rosetta, in 1799. Because this stone had three systems of writing on it—Greek, demotic, and hieroglyphic—it was separated from the other stones being heaped onto the battlements. Soon after, the savants of the expedition brought it back to their scientific headquarters in Cairo, *l'Institut de l'Égypte*, housed in the expropriated palace of the Mameluke notable Hassan Kashif. There, they translated the Greek text and started to work on the other scripts.[55] Following the defeat and evacuation of the French forces in 1801, French scientists were forced to surrender many of the items they had collected during their occupation of the country, though they managed to keep their notes. Among the artifacts confiscated, the stele was immediately recognized by the British as uniquely valuable for the study of ancient Egyptian writing.[56] The piece was soon transported back to London, where it was delivered to the British Museum. From the moment it arrived, the stone was the focus of research by linguists and classicists. At the same time, a rubbing of the stone had been delivered to Paris, where it was also studied. The 1810s witnessed the first real fruits of this study. In England, Thomas Young had come to the conclusion that ancient Egyptian writing was both pictographic and phonetic in nature. In France, Bonaparte's savants began publishing the encyclopedic *Description de l'Égypte* in 1809, while others, like Silvestre de Sacy and Johann David Åkerblad, studied the stone, poring over the savants' notes on ancient Egyptian monuments and establishing correspondences between its Greek and demotic characters. After studying Semitic languages, Coptic, and Chinese, Champollion spent the better part of the 1810s working from notes, deciphering fragments of cartouches, gradually distinguishing the letters of the hieroglyphic alphabet, and eventually theorizing the function of the determinative. In 1824, Champollion published his *Précis du système hiéroglyphique des anciens Égyptiens*, arguing that "hieroglyphic writing is a complex system, a script simultaneously figurative, symbolic, and phonetic, in one and the same text, in one and the same sentence, and, I should say, almost in one and the same word."[57]

It was not until Champollion had already spent two decades working on Pharaonic artifacts that, in 1828, he followed in the footsteps of others who had traveled to Egypt. His letters from Egypt show the profound transformation his discovery had made, not just in terms of what he was learning by copying and translating hieroglyphs in tombs and temples, but also in terms of the experience of travel itself. Now the experience of Pharaonic monuments could be one of reading. Gone was the sense of obscure mystery that hieroglyphic writing had once produced, replaced by a growing sense of transparency and confidence. The theme of confirmation dominates his travel account. Each object he encounters serves to corroborate his lexicography: "I am proud, now that I have followed the course of the Nile from its mouth to the second cataract, to be able to tell you that there is nothing that needs modification in our *Lettre sur l'alphabet des hiéroglyphes*. Our alphabet is right: it has been applied with equal success, first to Egyptian monuments from the time of the Romans and the Ptolemaic rulers, then, and this is far more interesting, to the inscriptions in all the temples, palaces and tombs of the Pharaonic epochs."[58] A particular sort of relationship thus opens up between reading, writing, and the European traveler in Egypt. In Champollion, the experience of Egypt works to correct what the European imagined of Egypt before traveling: "[Having] been for six months among the monuments of Egypt, I am startled by what I am reading fluently, rather than what my imagination is able to come up with."[59]

The knowledge Champollion brought to Egypt redrew the landscape as a legible text. Previously, Egyptian artifacts were, at best, the object of aesthetic or philosophic speculation. Now, they appeared not just as works whose aesthetic values could be judged, but also as historical archives. The Egyptologist Auguste Mariette commented on this shift in his guidebook designed for visitors coming to Egypt to celebrate the opening of the Suez Canal in 1869:

> To appreciate the true beauty of Egyptian monuments, one needs to engage in a preliminary study, a kind of initiation. Before Champollion had recovered the long-lost key to the hieroglyphs, one could study an Egyptian monument as one might study a Greek one, not asking from it more than what its exterior form revealed. But the perfectly legible texts under our eyes today have shifted the question.... [The monuments] that cover

the banks of the Nile are, for Egypt, testimonies to its past grandeur, and like parchment pedigrees of its ancient nobility. For foreigners, they represent pages taken from the archives of one of the most glorious peoples of the world.[60]

Throughout his letters, Champollion critiques the errors made by previous generations of travelers, for whom hieroglyphics were but ciphers. As the first literate person to visit Pharaonic monuments in centuries, Champollion could read, unlike travelers before him, that they were covered with the names of the kings who built them, descriptions of the historical events they were built to commemorate, and prayers to the gods to whom they were consecrated. If the French expedition's main product, *Description de l'Égypte*, presented Egypt as a text to be read in Europe, Champollion's voyage effectively revised the text of the original itself. Egyptian monuments were more than things to be reproduced in a book: all of Egypt was now a book for those who could read. Reading the texts of the monuments involved a process of rewriting, since often Champollion found errors in the modern names of the ancient places. It was he who authoritatively showed why the names of Ozymandias and Memnon needed to be revised to Ramses.[61]

As we saw in chapter 1, it was one thing for Champollion to assert his theory, it was another for others to accept it. Throughout the following decade many challenged Champollion's model, especially since so much remained to be explained, deciphered, and translated. While for Champollion and a few others, Egyptian antiquities immediately became a vast, transparent library, it took some time before his theory was widely applied. Champollion's theory and findings (or readings) in Egypt continued to be resisted by scholars, especially in England. Even ten years after the publication of Champollion's discovery, the official guide to the British Museum continued to treat the museum's Egyptian pieces as curiosities precisely because, it claimed, their hieroglyphics remained a mystery:

> The stranger who visits the Gallery of Sculpture, in the British Museum, cannot fail to be struck with the curious collection of objects in the room of Egyptian Antiquities. Passing from the contemplation of the almost faultless representations of the human form in marble, the triumph of Grecian art, he comes to figures more remarkable, at first sight, for their singular forms and colossal size, than for their beauty. . . . When he is told

that these are but a few samples of the wonderful works that still exist in Egypt . . . that the ancient tombs and temples of that country still furnish inexhaustible materials to enrich our Museums and gratify the curiosity of the antiquary, he will at once perceive that a mere knowledge of the names assigned to these pieces of stone would convey no information at all, and that any description of them must be unintelligible, if it does not connect them with the country from which they came and the monuments of which they are but a part.[62]

As objects without a classical provenance, Pharaonic antiquities could be little more than curious objects about whose history one could only speculate. As such, they continued to have an insecure place in the universal survey narrative offered by the museum.

But the significance of Champollion's findings did eventually produce a shift in museum attitudes toward Pharaonic monuments because they made it possible to read what the artifacts had to say about themselves, their makers, and the context in which they were made. They could be arranged and displayed so as to develop narratives of civilizational progress and political dynasties. This transformation—begun by Champollion's theory and ending with its adoption by curators and scholars in the 1840s—effectively ended the long tradition of aesthetic thought in which ancient Egypt had figured as outside and opposed to the narrative of European civilization. Champollion's discoveries, once accepted in key institutions and put into practice in the field, replaced speculative assertion with positive forms of knowledge. These discoveries were themselves based in those networks of acquistion, transportation, and interpretation apparent in the story of the Memnon head. This new knowledge, the knowledge of the artifact, was more empirical than philosophical and changed how European visitors looked at the objects in Egypt. The changes also radically transformed how modern Europeans and modern Egyptians looked at one another, for the balance of interpretive power now definitively shifted between Europeans and Egyptians. Increasingly, the ability to interpret ancient Egypt was understood, certainly by Europeans, as further indication of their superior moral right to be the primary caretakers of Pharaonic artifacts and monuments. In this way, the new discourse of the artifact extended beyond historical claims about Egypt's past and became a prominent component within a new form of intervention into Egypt's present.

The development was not merely one of ideas, but of nascent institutions and policies. A key moment in this history came when Champollion, at the completion of his tour of Egypt, raised the issue of antiquities preservation with Mehmed ʿAli. The pasha had a famous interest in strong historical leaders, including, alongside Napoleon, the Pharaoh Ramses, whose name was a recent discovery.[63] When the pasha commissioned Champollion to write a brief history of ancient Egypt, the author decided to supplement the text with recommendations for the conservation of antiquities. Champollion's summary of ancient history is fascinating, in no small part because it told a story of a country that had been so often invaded by outsiders that it was difficult to say who the natives of Egypt were. Such an idea must have seemed welcome to the Albanian-born Ottoman pasha: "The first tribes which populated Egypt, that is, the Nile Valley between Aswan and the Mediterranean, came from Abyssinia or Senar. It is impossible to assign the date of the first migration since it happened so long ago. The ancient Egyptians belong to a race of men who completely resemble . . . the inhabitants of Nubia. One finds none of the traits of the ancient population among the Copts. The Copts are the product of a mixing made up of all the nations who have successively ruled over Egypt."[64] Although Champollion's history focuses exclusively on the ancient past, it clearly aims to deliver a message of reform for the present. Throughout his description of the civilizational accomplishments of the Pharaohs, Champollion urges the pasha to follow their example by building canals and encouraging industry. Describing Ramses' reign, Champollion writes,

> This illustrious conqueror, known throughout history as Sesostris, was at one and the same time the bravest of warriors and the best of princes. All the riches extracted from the nations under his submission and the tributes received he put to use in building immense public utility works. He founded new cities, tried to raise the lands of other ones, and surrounded a group of others with fortified embankments to protect them from the inundation of the Nile. He dug a number of canals . . . and covered Egypt with magnificent buildings of which a great number still remain.[65]

It is hard to imagine that Mehmed ʿAli Pasha, then engaged both in military campaigns throughout the region and in extensive hydraulic and urbanization projects throughout the Egyptian countryside, would have missed the rosy analogy between his efforts and those of Ramses. Champollion also urged grand political reforms: "[Ramses], not content with embellishing Egypt with such sumptuous monuments, wanted to ensure the happiness of his population. He published new laws, the most important of which gave his subjects of all classes the right to own property. . . . It is under the rule of Ramses the Great, or Sesostris, that Egypt rose to the pinnacle of its political power and internal splendor."[66] Champollion then lists the number of countries conquered by Ramses, many of which, like Nubia, Senar, Syria, and Arabia were also places associated with Mehmed 'Ali's own campaigns in the region. Champollion's account argues that there had to be a balance between Egypt's power as a regional empire and its internal welfare. Concluding with remarks on the conquest of Egypt by the Persians, Champollion asserts, in terms that would not have been mistaken by the pasha, that too much emphasis on foreign expeditions ended the period of "Egypt's national independence" under the Pharaohs.

In his account of ancient history, Champollion refers often to the surviving monuments. They figure as concrete signs of the failure of past rulers, political lessons which the pasha might learn. Champollion's account is remarkable because perhaps for the first time it offered the history of ancient Egypt as allegory to a ruler of Egypt since antiquity. It is unclear what, if any, effects Champollion's allegory had on the pasha's thinking, since it would be years before Pharaonic antiquity had a prominent place in Egyptian state rhetoric, let alone in its policies. Yet along with the history lesson, Champollion attached a note which described the recent destruction of Pharaonic monuments and urged the pasha to take steps to preserve Egyptian antiquities:

It is in Egypt's greatest interest that Your Highness' Government attend to the whole preservation of its ancient buildings and monuments, the object and principal goal of the travels undertaken, as if it were a contest, by flocks of Europeans belonging to the most distinguished classes of society. The regret [of these travelers] is matched by that of intellectual Europe, which bitterly deplores the total destruction of countless ancient monuments, demolished without a trace during the last few years. Certainly, these barbaric demolitions have taken place—against the clear policies and well-known intentions of Your Highness—by agents incapable of appreciating the damages that they unknowingly wreak upon the country in this manner. Such monuments are lost beyond all hope and their loss arouses, among the educated classes, a sense of unease and merited concern for the fate of the monuments which still exist. . . .

It is therefore imperative the conservation policies of Your Highness be well-known among your agents, that they follow them and execute them to the letter. All Europe will recognize the active measures that Your Majesty will take to insure the preservation of the temples, palaces, tombs and all the types of monuments which still bear witness to the power and glory of ancient Egypt and which are, at the same time, the most beautiful ornaments of modern Egypt. With this goal in mind, Your Majesty could order:

1. That no one, under any pretext, be allowed to remove a single rock or stone, sculpted or otherwise, from the ancient structures and monuments which remain in Egypt and Nubia . . .

2. . . . . [That] in the future, no one wrecks those tombs where peasants [*fellahs*] destroy sculptures and frescoes, either by taking up lodging in them with their animals or by removing small pieces of the sculptures to sell to the travelers, ruining, in the process, the entire tomb chambers. . . . It is among monuments of this sort that the largest devastations take place daily. They are committed by peasants, either for their own sake or for the sake of the antiquities dealers whose money the peasants chase after. . . . In sum, the clear interest of science does not demand that excavation be halted . . . but rather that those performing excavations submit to a rule so that the preservation of those tombs discovered now and in the future, would be insured, that there be a strong guarantee against the attacks of ignorance or blind greed.[67]

Champollion's appeal to rule and order is often cited as the source of antiquities policies that began to appear in 1835, an issue to which I will turn later. However, the terms of Champollion's appeal demand some unpacking on their own. Significantly, Champollion's appeal imagines Egypt as a nation among nations, or rather, a nation under the watchful eye of Europe. Despite the allegorical address of the history quoted earlier in which the relics of ancient Egypt might be read by the rulers of modern Egypt, here Champollion asks that Pharaonic antiquities be protected largely for the enjoyment and contemplation of European travelers and scholars. The underlying assumption—that ancient Egypt should be readily available to the "educated" and "distinguished classes of European society"—is paired with concern about the "barbaric destruction" taking place largely at the hands of the peasants of Upper Egypt. While here and elsewhere Champollion expresses outrage about the damage done by European travelers and acquisitionists, it is Egyptian peasants who figure as the chief villains in the narrative. Acting for themselves, or as "incapable agents" of others, they wreak devastation on monuments while greedily chasing after European money.

Champollion's reference to the "well-known conservation policies" of Mehmed 'Ali most likely refers to the informal arrangements adopted by the Egyptian state, largely in response to French and British diplomatic pressure, that effectively divided the territory of Egypt into two zones of collection activity.[68] Although the government at this time took an active interest in the activities of collectors, there was no such thing as a coherent policy toward antiquities. Rather, the kinds of activities described in the previous chapter continued with little change: excavators traveled through the Egyptian provinces armed with official concessions from Cairo whose authority had to be constantly renegotiated by regional governors, local officials, and village chieftains.

STATE MANAGEMENT, FOREIGN INTERVENTION

You are admiring the miracles of ancient Egypt, we scrutinize the infinite abominations of modern Egypt! Oh! How far one is removed from the other! The more I think about it the more I am astonished by the antiquity of Egypt, its wisdom, genius, knowledge, power. And the more I see, the more I am convinced that modern-day Egypt should be placed at the centre of the type of nations that one should mistrust and flee from.—LETTER FROM PARISET TO CHAMPOLLION, January 1829, in *Egyptian Diaries*

European knowledge of Egypt, especially of ancient Egypt, played a crucial role in legitimizing, indeed, in articulating the need for foreign intervention in Egyptian governance. There is perhaps no better example of how such claims worked than a House of Commons address by Lord Arthur

Balfour in 1910, cited prominently in Edward W. Said's *Orientalism*. Balfour's address claimed that British rule in Egypt, which had begun nearly thirty years earlier, was not about the "superiority or inferiority" of one nation over the other. Rather, Balfour asserts, "We know the civilization of Egypt better than we know the civilization of any other country, we know it further back; we know it more intimately; we know more about it."[69] Said limns the passage this way: "Knowledge to Balfour means surveying a civilization from its origins to its prime to its decline—and of course it means *being able to do that*." Said's reading of the passage is rich, since he insists that representation and knowledge be connected to the material conditions—in this case, military occupation—in which knowledge is obtained. Moreover, Said points out that the force of Balfour's speech lies in the way it constructs a "we" set off from an object of study, "Egypt." The colonial constitution of the country as an object, rather than a subject, of knowledge was especially true when it came to thinking about ancient Egypt: never was there a consideration that local traditions, let alone the extensive Islamic literature on the Pharaonic past, might have something serious to contribute to an understanding of the relation between ancient and modern Egypt. On the contrary, Egyptology, founded on the methodical interpretation of hieroglyphics, very self-consciously defined itself in opposition to the "legends and superstitions" Muslims held about the past. In this way, this science opened a breach between "modern Egypt" and "ancient Egypt," opposing them in a familiar orientalist binarism of East and West. This opposition was important, not only for thinking about antiquities, but also for thinking about wider issues of governance in nineteenth-century Egypt. For just as preservation and civilizational patrimony were themes of European writing on antiquities, so too were antiquities a critical figure in European writing on modern government in Egypt. Crucial to how these two discourses worked together was the notion that there was a radical break between the history of ancient Egypt and that of modern Egypt.

The document commonly cited as the first piece of antiquities "legislation" in Egypt is instructive in this regard. Echoing Champollion's letter to Mehmed 'Ali, this ordinance of 1835 spoke in the language of protection and conservation. If Champollion had implied that antiquities rightfully belonged to Europeans, the ordinance was quite explicit about it:

Although the remarkable structures and admirable monuments of art and antiquity of Upper Egypt . . . ceaselessly lure numerous European travelers to those lands, we have to admit however that during the last years the taste for, and passionate pursuit of all objects they call by the name of antiquities has resulted in a undeniable devastation of the ancient monuments of Egypt. Such has been the state of things until this day that we fear, with good reason, to watch these monuments—the pride of the passing centuries—disappear before too long from the Egyptian sun, along with their statues and all the precious objects they contain, in order to enrich, until the end, foreign countries.

However, it is well recognized that the Europeans are not the only ones to prohibit the export, by any means, of such objects from their countries. [On the contrary,] whenever antiquities are found, they rush to dispatch connoisseurs who are authorized to collect them and almost always, easing their acquisition by satisfying the greed of ignorant owners for meager sums of money. Much later, these statues, ornamented stones and all objects of the same nature are collected and arranged in order in a building decorated and designed for this purpose, where they are exhibited for the eyes of the public of all nations and contribute powerfully to the glory of the country that possesses them. It is also by an intense study of the inscriptions and the hieroglyphic figures traced on the monuments and objects of antiquity that European intellectuals have, in the last few years, added considerably to the domain of their knowledge.[70]

This decree, which goes on to describe the organization and procedures of the new administration, has often been hailed as the beginning of enlightened state policy on antiquities. But there are reasons to doubt how the document was interpreted in policy, let alone in actual practice.[71] First, as Antoine Khater pointed out, the decree was interpreted as being nonretroactive, which meant that, on the one hand, claims were not made against existing museum collections in Europe, and on the other, currently valid concessions were able to continue for years afterward. Moreover, it failed to define a number of crucial terms—including "excavation," "exploration" and, most important, "antiquity"—all of which became the basis for subsequent disputes.[72] Finally, the text contains ambiguities with regard to grants, property rights, punishments, and the relationship between this new antiquities administration and the other departments of state. To take only one example: state gifting was so common that the "museum" created by the decree closed during the 1850s when the khedive bestowed what few objects remained in it to a minor European royal who briefly toured Egypt.

Given the way the ordinance so explicitly links antiquarianism to Europe, one might miss another key assumption buried in its discourse: that Egyptian antiquities belong to a human civilization. On the surface, the universalism of the claim might seem simple and benign. Undoubtedly, Champollion's breakthrough did enable scholars, tourists, and now even members of Mehmed 'Ali's court to see Pharaonic history as part of a wider history of ancient civilization. As concrete embodiments of this history, Pharaonic antiquities took on a significance that had previously been reserved for artifacts from Greece and Rome, and indeed were finally admitted into art-history surveys alongside Greek and Roman objects. And insofar as Europeans were interested in preserving the artifacts of ancient Egypt, they were motivated, according to the terms of artifact discourse, by their concern for the patrimony of world civilization.

Nonetheless, the kind of survey offered in such histories and museum collections was one that, despite all claims of universalism, remained a form of European particularism. By privileging the place of classical, Renaissance, and especially modern Europe, the new histories that claimed ancient Egypt as part of human civilization were circumscribing it within a narrative whose unambiguous telos was European modernity.[73] In doing so, the new narratives about ancient Egypt effectively put into doubt the relationship between ancient Egypt and other relevant historical and cultural traditions, especially those of Islam and modern Egypt, which, as part of "the Orient," were not only non-Western by definition, but also antithetical to the West's conception of itself. Thus emerged within the discourse on Pharaonic antiquities in modern Egypt a series of distinctions that framed time and place in terms of sharp orientalist oppositions: whereas the past of Egypt was part (or even the origin) of the West, present-day Egypt was construed as part of the Muslim world, that is, the East.

To read the orientalizing tenor of the discourse on ancient Egypt, one needs to begin by recognizing that the ordinance of 1835 did not end European assertions that Europeans had a superior moral right to collect and export Pharaonic artifacts. If anything, the law only refocused the terms of the claim to Pharaonic patrimony. Before, Europeans had claimed that Egyptians were merely indifferent toward the ancient ruins in their country. Now, in the immediate wake of Mehmed 'Ali's first legal efforts to preserve antiquities, Europeans complained about mismanagement, malfeasance, and corruption, saying, in short, that Egyptians were unfit as caretakers of Pharaonic antiquities. The shift, as we shall see, was subtle but powerful, for now the claim on Egypt could be made in terms of a disinterested concern about objects.

The shift is evidenced in the accounts of travelers from the 1830s and 1840s. Most striking in this regard are the lithographs of the Scottish artist David Roberts, who traveled extensively throughout Egypt in 1838–39. While there was a long tradition of depicting Pharaonic ruins in travel accounts, Roberts was perhaps the first accomplished artist who was able to benefit from the new hard Egyptological knowledge provided by Champollion's discoveries.[74] Though he drew on a visual idiom provided by earlier generations of artists (most notably, Vivant Denon, one of the principal compilers of the *Description de l'Égypte*), Roberts's illustrations benefited from technological advances that allowed him to print his images in rich color tints. His lithographs, published in series throughout the 1840s, remain the most familiar images of Pharaonic ruins composed in the nineteenth century. One element that stands out in Roberts's oeuvre is the way it regularly depicts a particular relationship between modern Egyptians and ancient ruins. In many images, modern Egyptians wander through antiquities landscapes, their figures set in the middle ground or background of the scene. In others, the Egyptians are foregrounded, while ruins appear behind them. No matter the focus of the image, however, Egyptians usually appear in ragtag dress, lounging distractedly, staring off into the distance or appearing to converse or conduct business. They sit on fallen columns, climb on colossal statues, lean on walls covered by hieroglyphs, or simply pass by. But they rarely if ever appear to be studying the monuments or indeed noticing their presence at all. One might argue that the figure of the native in Roberts's images is only secondary, that it appears only to give some human scale to the structures which figure so prominently in Roberts's work. However, given the regularity of the native's appearance and the uniformity of his poses, he is clearly there to communicate indifference and neglect.

One of Roberts's images, for example, ostensibly the depiction of a temple, also offers a rich allegory of modern Egyptian society. Taking up the

Figure 5. David Roberts, "Entrance of the Temple of Amun at Thebes," from *The Holy Land: Syria, Idumea, Arabia, Egypt and Nubia* (London: F. G. Moon, 1849). Image by permission of the John Hay Library of Brown University.

Figure 6. David Roberts, "Grand Entrance to the Temple of Luxor," from *The Holy Land: Syria, Idumea, Arabia, Egypt and Nubia* (London: F. G. Moon, 1849). Image by permission of the John Hay Library of Brown University.

center of the picture is a group of Egyptians composed of peasants and Bedouins who huddle on the ground to the right. Sitting and standing opposite and above them are an Egyptian notable and three Ottomans. To the left, a barefoot, veiled Bedouin woman carries water under the curious gaze of an Ottoman adult and child. In the foreground stands a water pipe, around which lie other clay pipes. This is the focal point of the image. It is where the disapproving glare of the bearded notable is directed, as if he has caught the Egyptians engaged in an illicit activity. The Egyptian notable's hands rest still on the pipe's hose, his eyes half closed, apparently in a drug-induced stupor. As a tableau of Egyptian society, the image suggests lethargy and poverty, which only makes the looming presence of the ruins behind more significant. Spatially, the ruins separate the Egyptians from the wider prospect that appears through the portal. More important, however, the ruins are ignored by the subjects in the foreground. The effect is ironic: the banal misery of the present contrasted with the solemn remnants of the civilized past. By juxtaposing ancient and modern Egypt in this way, Roberts suggests that the two are not just separate but even opposed to one another.

In other portraits, Roberts breaks with the custom of European artists who tended to avoid painting the peasants who for much of the nineteenth century still inhabited many Pharaonic temples. This is especially clear in *Grand Entrance to the Temple of Luxor*, where Roberts includes the peasant village built into the monument in order to highlight an antagonism between Pharaonic and Islamic Egypt. In terms of architecture, the sturdy walls of the ancient temple tower over the foreground, dwarfing the squat mud-brick walls that encroach upon and cover parts of the ruins. Inside the temple stands an arrangement of elegant columns and a graceful obelisk. To the side are rudimentary dovecots and, almost completely hidden by the temple, a primitive minaret. The contrasting representations of ancient and modern human subjects redoubles this theme. On the right-hand temple wall relief are the outlines of a Pharaonic king seated on a throne, while in the foreground modern peasants sit in the dirt. On the left-hand is the clear image of a stern royal warrior riding a chariot; in the foreground lounge Bedouins armed with spears. Again, the image conveys more than just a separation between the modern people who inhabit the Egyptian countryside and the ancient monuments there. Not only are the glories of the past shamed by the degradation of the present, they are threatened by it. Admittedly, Roberts was a visual artist, not an Egyptologist. Yet his images are vivid examples of how the emerging science might not simply interpret ancient Egypt, but also redraw the relationship between ancient and modern Egypt in terms of essential oppositions. More than this, they show the threat that modern Egyptians pose to the works of ancient Egyptians. Taken together, these images of threat created a conceptual platform from which to regard intervention.

The rhetorical opposition of modern and ancient Egypt was not limited to aesthetic portrayals of Egypt. It was especially prominent in studies of Egypt's political economy. For instance, in his influential *Report on Egypt and Candia*, presented to the Houses of Lords and Commons in 1838, John Bowring constantly ties the preservation of ancient monuments to a consideration of the political and economic health of modern Egypt. His address opens as follows:

> The interest which has hitherto attached to Egypt has mainly reposed upon those sublime remains of the most remote antiquity of which she is still the depository. Ancient to the ancients themselves, and preserving even to the present hour the monuments which the father of history regards as the oldest existing mementos of the human race, she has afforded a vast field for questionings and speculation, and presented materials alike to recompense the researches of the learned, and to awaken the inquiries of the curious. Compared with the attractions of the past, the investigations as to the present and the future have appeared of little moment.[75]

For the benefit of potential investors, Bowring's report enumerates the social, industrial, and commercial climate of Egypt under Mehmed 'Ali's rule, with numerical charts, import-export figures, budget costs, and extensive lists of government resources and institutions. Crucially, Bowring returns to the subject of Pharaonic antiquities, describing, for instance, the destruction of temples whose stones were used to manufacture lime in the pasha's modern factories.[76] At one point, Bowring suggests a way for the Egyptian state to intervene to protect monuments:

> Among the desiderata to which I had occasion to call the attention of the Egyptian government, was the establishment of some board which should have charge of the ancient public monuments of Egypt. The devastation of these wonderful and most interesting memorials, both by na-

tive authorities and by European visitors, is most deplorable; and it is almost to be regretted that so many vestiges of antiquity should have been laid open to curiosity, as they have been, for the most part, handed over to destruction. On recommending the subject to the attention of the pacha, I pointed out to his highness that these remains were among the most precious possessions of his country; and he did me the honour to request I would draw up a project for the preservation of such public monuments as existed, and for carrying out further researches.[77]

Bowring's recommendations (establishment of administrative agency, museum, prohibition on exports) follow, almost point by point, those of the ordinance of 1835. By placing Pharaonic antiquities (along with slavery, conscription, taxes, and land distribution) at the heart of the most pressing issues of state governance, Bowring fashions their destruction as a key sign of state neglect and their preservation evidence of wise administration. In this way, antiquities figure as more than objects of study in Bowring's account: they are also indicators for evaluating the efficacy and legitimacy of Egyptian government. In contrast to the plans outlined in the 1835 law, which place Egyptian antiquities under the authority of Egyptian state agencies, Bowring's report recommended a commission composed of Egyptian officials and the "Consul-Generals of the four great powers." This international commission, unlike an Egyptian agency, "would become a means of communication and connexion with the civilized world."[78] Whereas in most of his report Bowring aims to describe the modern state of Egypt with an eye to specifically British commercial and political interests, his discussions of Egyptian antiquities are always couched in terms of the interests of civilization more broadly. In other words, he makes his recommendations not in the name of British aims and goals, but rather, more vaguely, in the name of those of the "civilized world." Disavowal of national interest, which, as we saw, was a central element of artifact discourse, became a cornerstone of European antiquities interventionism and explains to a large degree Bowring's hostility toward Cairo's efforts to bring the antiquities under the exclusive control of the pasha.

George Gliddon, U.S. consul in Cairo in the 1830s, also closely tied the state of antiquities in Egypt to the state of the Egyptian state, even if he was not so diplomatic in his assessment of how they were being managed. He begins by drawing a sharp division between modern and ancient Egypt: "Amongst the varied objects that urge the traveller towards the Valley of the Nile; that excite in the minds of the European learned profound and universal interest; and of which, neither transient contemplation, nor investigating study, will disappoint the enthusiast's expectations, or dispel the halo with which ardent imaginations encompass those stupendous and mysterious ruins, they are none equaling in importance, the Monuments of Egypt and of Nubia."[79] The sharpness of Gliddon's tone only increases as he goes on, though his argument remains constant: Egypt's value, whether in the past, present, or future, always lies in the monuments of its past; those antiquities are now, under the pasha's rule, threatened with complete destruction. Gliddon singles out Mehmed 'Ali and his advisors for ridicule and scorn, which only helps to draw a sharp distinction between a glorious ancient Egypt and a modern Egypt populated by lazy, weak natives ruled by corrupt Turks: "Were the existence of the Monuments to cease, Egypt . . . would lose the noblest of her attractions. . . . [Were] the Temples overthrown; the Pyramids demolished; the paintings in the tombs obliterated; and the Sculptures, which record the glories of the Pharaonic epochs, destroyed; all the romance which now attends the wandering footsteps of the intellectual visitor would vanish, with the charm that still lingers round those lonely remains."[80] Though Gliddon was not the only one to claim that Pharaonic monuments were disappearing rapidly from the Egyptian countryside, he was perhaps the first to offer a systematic survey of the destruction that had taken place since antiquarians had begun collecting on a mass scale.[81] His method was to use the *Description de l'Égypte* as his guidebook and to compare that text to what he found in the field: in the almost four decades following the evacuation of French forces, significant portions of Hermopolis Magna, Apollinopolis Parva, and Antæopolis along with substantial portions of Karnac and Thebes had all been destroyed by "the pickaxe and the hammer, the crow-bar and the lever."[82] His account is unique in that it is perhaps the only description of Egypt which represents it chiefly in terms of absences: "Others have had the gratification of delineating, describing, and expounding, what the Monuments of Egypt were, at the period of their respective visits; be mine the more humble task of recording what, where, and why, they are not."[83] Unlike Bowring, Gliddon does mention Mehmed 'Ali's conservation policies, though with thorough skepticism— indeed, his appeal should be read as a wholesale dismissal of the Egyptian state's management of antiquities. Gliddon describes at length the Egyptian government's failure to prevent vandalism, graffiti, and unauthorized excavations. More serious than charges of mere negligence, Gliddon also accuses the state of playing an active role in the destruction of monuments, both by employing temple limestone in its construction projects and by using *sibakh* (humus, rich in nitrates, composed of mummy and buried fragments) in the pasha's gunpowder factories. He refers to antiquities inspectors not as protectors of the antiquities they watch over, but as their "angels of death." In sum, he writes, "in destroying the Ancient Monuments of Egypt, the present government of that country has been influenced by avarice, wantonness and negligence, and has not replaced [the ancient monuments with] any substitutes of [the] modern era worthy of being taken in extenuation of their barbarian desecrations."[84]

Gliddon's account is by no means a generous (or particularly fair) attempt to assess Mehmed 'Ali's policy changes toward Egyptian antiquities, but its criticism is a useful corrective for the rosier histories of preservationism that claim the 1835 ordinance as a watershed event. In Gliddon's judgment, there is no reason to believe that the pasha would ever be committed to saving Pharaonic antiquities from perdition.

The theme of threat dovetails with the implied theme of intervention. Throughout his account Gliddon, like Bowring and others, reads the condition of antiquities in order to interpret the condition of Egyptian government. Gliddon conceptually links the condition of Egyptian antiquities to the state management of antiquities and then to the health of the Egyptian state. At this point, Gliddon's formulation begs the question of sovereignty: since Pharaonic monuments belong to a civilization that is universal, no individual state (and certainly not the Egyptian state) may rightfully claim to be their sole owner or caretaker. Here it is only a slight step to urging an active, interventionist policy toward Pharaonic antiquities. While in practice, this interventionist policy might have shared many elements with earlier stages of colonial European antiquities acquisition in Egypt, semantically the game had shifted considerably: no longer were collectors acting for the glory of individual nations, but rather to uphold the values of civilization itself.

Antiquities intervention differed from other forms of colonial intrusion in Egypt since it was explicitly uncoupled from the concept of national interest and tied instead to concepts like humanity, civilization, and disinterest. Moreover, to intervene in a legitimate fashion, it was not enough to charge mismanagement on the part of the Egyptian government, since that might be reformable. Rather, it was important to argue an essential antipathy between the modern Egyptians and the relics of their ancient past. Gliddon's account of the significance Pharaonic antiquities have for the Muslims of Egypt exemplifies such thinking:

> From time immemorial, augmented in violence as the introduction of Christianity, and the subsequent rise of Mahommedanism, converted the reverential awe with which the people once regarded the Monuments of Egypt's glory, first into bigotted hatred, and then into indifference, has the destruction of Antiquities in that country progressed. . . . The edicts of the Eastern Emperors gave full scope and authority to the Iconoclast in his work of demolition. . . . Later again, the mandates of a "Khaleefah" [Muslim ruler] were issued for the two-fold purpose of obliterating the vestiges of the "Kafirs" [apostates] and of building "Musr el-Qaherah" [Cairo].[85]

Gliddon's argument is simple (though in fact unsupportable): because Islamic tradition is both hostile and indifferent toward Pharaonic antiquities, Muslims pose a unique threat to their survival. Add to this threat the ravages of time and the ignorance of tourists, and there is little hope that antiquities will survive if left in place. Admitting that European collectors were not above criticism, Gliddon nonetheless claims that any harm done was outweighed by the service they performed in removing antiquities from sure destruction in Egypt:

> With respect to Egyptian antiquities, although it is painful that so many have been abstracted . . . had they remained in Egypt during the development of modern "régénération," it is probable that but a few of them would, at the present hour, have been in existence. To those therefore, who have caused their transfer from a Country wherein had they remained, they would have perished, thanks are due. . . . To those Governments or individuals whose munificence, whose discrimination and whose desire to preserve in European security those precious vestiges of early knowledge, induced them to bring these interesting remains "out of the house of bondage," every praise, every gratitude is due.[86]

In sum, he urges a mission to rescue mementos from the civilized (Western) past from destruction at the hands of modern (Oriental) barbarians.

The agents of salvation are, appropriately, "the Antiquaries of Europe," who should now "see the urgent necessity there is for taking these Ruins under their own protection."[87] The "house of bondage" reference to the book of Exodus is a hyperbolic, though recurring, trope: Europe is to Pharaonic antiquities as Moses was to the Israelites.

Insofar as he articulates a narrative in which self-appointed guardians of civilization battle against its destroyers and in which the acquisition of objects in foreign lands is understood to be the disinterested practice of universal humanism, Gliddon anticipated later European policies in other areas of governance. In particular, arguments over the stewardship of Egypt's cultural patrimony prefigured by decades explicitly colonial arguments over the management of Egypt's economy. This is particularly true of the writings of Evelyn Baring (later, Lord Cromer), who played a major role in managing Egypt's debt during the crisis of 1878–79 and who became British consul general during the first twenty-five years of Egypt's occupation. He writes of British intervention precisely in terms of stewardship. Referring to the political crisis of 1882, for instance, Cromer emphasizes Egypt's inability to govern itself. On the face of it, this may have been a sober assessment, but Cromer's rhetoric is compelling because it tacitly assumes, even while disavowing British agency or interest, that only England could be the agent of reform: "What Egypt most of all required was order and good government. Perhaps . . . liberty would follow. No one but a dreamy theorist could imagine that the natural order of things could be reversed, and that liberty could first be accorded to the poor ignorant representatives of the Egyptian people, that the latter would then be able to evolve order out of chaos."[88] What is striking in such arguments is the systematic disavowal that interest or design might have played a role in the intervention, or indeed that intervention was an act carried out by the British. Moreover, in arguing for the legitimacy of British rule in Egypt, Cromer often invokes comparisons between the governance of ancient and modern Egypt. Referring to irrigation, Cromer asserts that

> in the early days of Egyptian civilization, [Man] made great and creditable efforts to turn [Egypt's water resources] to account. "It is certain," says Colonel Ross, "that in old days, there must have been native engineering talent of the very highest order, and when we read of such and such a King restoring public works in a long and glorious reign, there must have

existed a continuous supply of good engineering talent which had carte blanche from the ruler of the day." The Pharaohs, it would thus appear, used their talent according to the best of their lights. The Turks, who ultimately succeeded them, hid theirs in a napkin, with the result that Nature, indignant at the treatment accorded her, minimised the value of her gifts and exacted penalties for the neglect of her laws. In later Mohammedan times, no serious efforts were made to avert drought or inundation.[89]

Ancient Egypt figures importantly in this discourse of governance because it helps to establish the narrative that Muslim rule marked a precipitous decline from the glorious past. Just as Muslims are depicted as being unable to appreciate the value of Pharaonic antiquities, so here they are unable to appreciate their own irrigation system. The reasoning is simple: Egypt's local rulers, incapable of safeguarding the value of either antiquities or the Nile, deserve to be replaced by more competent administrators. Describing how British engineers rescued Egypt from the agricultural crisis brought on by Egyptian mismanagement, Cromer boasts,

> Here was a grand opportunity for the Englishman, and nobly did he avail himself of it. . . . New canals were dug. A variety of useful works were executed in Upper Egypt to guard against the effects of a low Nile. Drainage went hand in hand with irrigation. Before the British engineers had been at work ten years, the cotton crop was trebled, the sugar crop more than trebled, and the country was being gradually covered with a network of light railways and agricultural roads in order to enable the produce to be brought to market. Much, however, as the British engineer had done for Egypt, his work is not yet complete.[90]

Cromer's description of the feats of British engineers serves well as a condensation of his main theme of disinterested British stewardship and superior British science and governance: "The British engineer . . . justified Western methods to Eastern minds. He inculcated, in a manner which arrested and captivated even the blurred intellect and wayward imagination of the poor ignorant Egyptian fellah, the lesson that the usurer and the retailer of adulterated drinks are not the sole products of European civilisation; and inasmuch as he achieved this object, he deserves the gratitude not only of all intelligent Asiatics, but also of all Europeans."[91] The implied reasoning of these assertions is subtle and powerful: Egypt was once great; Egypt under Muslim rule has declined; Egypt does not know how to care for its national patrimony, indeed, modern Egyptians threaten this patrimony; with outside intervention, ancient Egypt could be protected from modern Egyptians; with outside intervention, modern Egypt could be governed wisely and have its greatness restored to it.

Jabarti's text only hints at the antagonism that was to emerge between the Arabo-Islamic tradition on the Pharaonic past and the new science of Egyptology. In Jabarti's time, who would have thought that during the course of the nineteenth century scientific practices of archaeology would come to dominate conversations about ancient Egypt, let alone modern Egypt? Who could have known that the classical Muslim literary tradition on ancient Egypt would be largely forgotten by the end of the century? This fundamental shift in cultural vision among Europeans took place not only because Egyptology had more things to say about the past and more accuracy in its claims, but also because it produced a cultural discourse that resounded with political forces interested in transforming, even wresting, the government of modern Egypt. It may be an exaggeration to say it was the discourse of the artifact that gave rise to the specific form of colonial interventionism by which Britain would come to rule Egypt in 1882. But it is striking that the core claims of artifact discourse (disinterest, preservation, and rational appreciation) were so often mobilized whenever colonial power sought legitimacy in expert knowledge.

Admittedly, the story of this chapter on its own is far from complete because it does not yet consider how Egyptians were absorbing the new discourse of Egyptology and developing it, alongside the Arabo-Islamic tradition, to create new ways of thinking about the Pharaonic past. In the next chapter, we will see how Egyptians turned these conceptual linkages between ancient and modern Egypt around in order to contest the claims Europeans had been making on ancient and modern Egypt alike.

The Antiqakhana (1835–55)

The relics of the past, the dignity of the present.
—EDMÉ JOMARD, commenting on the *Antiqakhana*,
in *Coup-d'oeil impartial sur l'état présent de l'Égypte*

While Europeans interpreted hieroglyphs and claimed a superior knowledge of Egypt, past and present, a new generation of Egyptian intellectuals was becoming aware of the analytical and moral power of Egyptology. For nineteenth-century Egyptians, knowledge of ancient Egypt was part of a science that was European not just in its method and practice, but also in its cultural orientation. At the same time, the first generation of Egyptians to study in Europe was exposed there to the new science of Egyptology and began to adopt the concepts and practices of the European institutions. This development was not linear but rather one of fits and starts. No wonder, for the cultural field in which it took place was characterized by irresolvable conflicts and ongoing struggles: from tensions *within* traditions (as in the ambivalent image of Pharaonic antiquity within classical Arabic literature) to ones *between* discourses (such as that between Islamic traditions concerning ancient Egypt and the new Egyptology); from conflicts between particular institutional actors (such as foreign museums and Egyptian government agencies) to the deeper, agonistic structures engendered by European colonial encroachment across North Africa.

Nothing better exemplifies the tensions and uncertainties of these forces than the legacy of the 1835 ordinance. For all its shortcomings, the document attempted to establish new ways of relating to Egyptian antiquities. Part of the address of the ordinance was explicitly negative, prohibiting and restricting certain kinds of activities, from unauthorized excavation, sales, and transportation of antiquities to the inhabitation of monuments and their use as sources of building material. The decree also attempted to invent a productive relationship between modern Egyptians and Pharaonic artifacts by creating new institutions (such as the museum), new governmental positions (such as those of the antiquities inspectors), and new modes of appreciation (such as tourism). These two tendencies—the prohibitory and the productive—appear clearly in the language of the ordinance:

> Considering then the importance that the Europeans attach to the ancient monuments and the advantages that the study of antiquity brings them, considering further the abundant riches which Egypt, that marvel of the centuries, contains in its breast, the Counsel of the Egyptian Government has thought it proper to decree:
>
> 1. That the future export of antiquities of all kinds be strictly prohibited.
> 2. That all such objects which the government possesses or shall come to possess through future excavations and exploration, be deposited in a special place in Cairo where they can be preserved and conveniently arranged for public exhibition, particularly for travelers and foreigners who arrive daily to view them throughout the country.
> 3. That not only is it expressly forbidden to destroy the ancient monuments of Upper Egypt but the government should take measures to insure their preservation everywhere.
>
> This wise measure would have the double effect of forever preserving the integrity of the monuments for travelers and insure, at all times and in the heart of Egypt itself, the permanent existence of a rich collection of antiquities, truly meriting attention.[1]

Although the ordinance should not be confused with policy (much less implementation), it did establish a new kind of language, one based in preservationist principles, that much later became official law and common practice. Part of the cause of the delay between decree and policy is signaled in the language of the ordinance itself and how it acknowledges that the value of preserving the artifacts has to do with foreign, not local, Egyptian, interest.

With respect to the productive aspects of Egyptian antiquities direc-
tives, the museum had an especially privileged place and thus provides
a view into the scope, the conflicts, and the limitations of the new state
attitude toward antiquities management. The ordinance formally established a special space for the storage and exhibition of antiquities (*al-
Antiqakhana*) in the School of Translation (*Madrasat al-Alsun*), located
in the Western-oriented quarter of Ezbekiyya. The Antiqakhana could
not have asked for a director who was abler, or who enjoyed more state
support, than Rifa'a Rafi' al-Tahtawi (1801–73). As a member of the first
Egyptian educational mission to France (1826–31), Tahtawi was a natural
choice for the job and had studied under the orientalist de Sacy and other
scholars of ancient languages and cultures. Though the two may not have
met, at one point, Champollion wrote one of the reports on Tahtawi's
progress that were sent to Mehmed 'Ali.[2] As we shall see, in the course of
his career, Tahtawi developed an innovative, complex understanding of
ancient Egypt, much of it stemming from his studies in Paris.

As Donald Malcolm Reid has pointed out, the life of Tahtawi's museum
was short and obscure. Only a few years after its establishment, Gliddon
visited the place. His evaluation of the museum was typically harsh:

A National Museum of Egyptian Antiquities. Sublime and felicitous
conception! Echoed by the *Semaphor de Marseilles*, as a new evidence,
"que ce sublime Vieillard ne rêve qu'à la prosperité, et à la régénération
de l'Égypte"—re-echoed by Societies in Europe, as another proof of the
progress of science under the enlightened Mohammed Ali! But with respect to the Museum, seeing that it was a subject exciting too general
an interest to be accepted on the mere faith of a promise, some steps
were required to make the seriousness of the intention apparent. In consequence, an old Lumberroom, or Gallery, in the palace situated in the
Esbekeeyah . . . was swept out, and whitewashed; and its Key, with the
protection of this so-called Museum, was placed under the guardianship
of the "Ministère d'Instruction Publique" [Tahtawi]. . . . Years have rolled
away, and there is no museum, but that identical empty corridor at Cairo,
for I cannot regard the half-dozen valueless stones there placed as even
the nucleus of a collection.[3]

It is tempting to discount Gliddon's description of the museum in light of
his dismissive attitude toward all the projects undertaken by Mehmed 'Ali.

Yet his description confirms the account of another traveler, the noted Egyptologist John Gardner Wilkinson, who was (in contrast to Gliddon) enthusiastic about the pasha's endeavors.[4] Wilkinson describes first the private collection of antiquities in the palace of the pasha's son:

> Ibrahim Pasha has also begun a collection of Egyptian antiquities; and a veto being put to the removal of antiquities from Egypt, great hopes have been entertained of the success of his museum. It is now about ten or eleven years since this collection has been commenced, and in 1831 a Turk was employed at Thebes in excavating, and preventing all access to the underground treasures not sanctioned by government authority. I therefore expected, on my return to Egypt in 1841, to find many objects of interest at the palace, where they are now deposited. My surprise and disappointment were therefore great, when on entering the passage and room where they are kept, I found nothing but a confused mass of broken mummies and cases, some imperfect tablets, and various fragments, which, had they been capable of being spoilt, would have been rendered valueless by the damp of the place; and I can safely say that there was nothing which, had it been given me, I should have thought worth the trouble of taking back to Cairo.[5]

Ironically, only a few years before one might have lodged the same complaint of neglect against the British Museum's treatment of its basement of Egyptian antiquities. But Wilkinson's bleakest assessment of Egyptian antiquarianism is reserved for the official Antiqakhana:

> There is also a collection of antiquities belonging to Mohammed Ali, which is occasionally increased by those seized at the Custom-house, in the possession of persons unauthorised by special favour to take them out of the country. It was to have formed part of a museum to be erected in the Uzbekeeh; but the formation of a museum in Egypt is purely Utopian; and while the impediments raised against the removal of antiquities from Egypt does an injury to the world, Egypt is not a gainer. The excavations are made without knowledge or energy, the Pasha is cheated by those who work, and no one there takes any interest in a museum; and it would not be too much to predict that, after all the vexatious impediments thrown in the way of Europeans, no such institution will ever be formed by the Pasha of Egypt.[6]

From here, the Antiqakhana seems to have only deteriorated. As Donald Reid has pointed out,

> After Muhammad Ali, Abbas I paid sporadic attention to antiquities, ordering two engineers to inspect Upper Egypt and the director of education to report on sites near Cairo. According to Gaston Maspero, Abbas moved the Ezbekiyya collection to the citadel in 1851, but another source asserts that in October 1849 Abbas ordered the School of Languages transferred to Nasriyya. . . . For want of space there, the antiquities were moved to the School of Engineering in Bulaq. In any case, Abbas drew on the collection for a gift to Sultan Abdulaziz, and Said [his successor] presented the remainder to Archduke Maximilian in 1855.[7]

The short, ignominious history of the Antiqakhana illustrates the degree to which formal declarations, like the 1835 ordinance, might remain mere words on the page. So too might the ideas behind them—like preservationism or national patrimony—exist only on the level of concept. By 1855, the collection of Egypt's first indigenous antiquities museum had dissolved. It would be some time before there would be serious state investment to regulate the continuing commercial traffic of antiquities. Effective laws governing the use of antiquities would come even later.

Nonetheless, the false start of the Egyptian state museum is a salient event because it illustrates the real ambiguity toward antiquities among mid-nineteenth-century Egyptians and the ruling Ottoman-Egyptian elite. It is not the case that Egyptians were indifferent toward Pharaonic artifacts, or that they were slow to take up the new science concerning ancient Egypt. Indeed, the Egyptian state's initial formulation of antiquities norms and its movement to form a museum dedicated to the collection and preservation of artifacts express a scholarly attitude toward Pharaonic antiquities that in some ways was ahead of that of some curators at the British Museum. At the same time, whatever new ideas were forming about the ancient past would have little if any life without public institutions to nurture them. For this reason, the example of the Antiqakhana indicates both how quickly a new discourse on Egyptian artifacts might emerge in Cairo and what work would need to be done if was to take hold.

3

Pharaonic Selves

In his account of student life in Paris, Rifa'a Rafi' al-Tahtawi mentions ancient Egypt only in a few places and always in association with European scholarship.[1] The association between knowledge about ancient Egypt and European sciences was predictable. Tahtawi's Paris curriculum had been designed by scholars whose careers were central to the emergence of Egyptology: he was directed on the one hand by Silvestre de Sacy, who had made critical contributions to the decipherment of the hieroglyphs, and on the other by one of Bonaparte's former savants, Edmé-François Jomard, whose monumental work *Description de l'Égypte* fueled public interest in Pharaonic antiquities for decades.

Tahtawi's remarks on Egyptology are remarkable not least because they show he was a quick study. He absorbed the most recent discoveries of the new science even while commenting critically on the acquisition regime underwriting it. At the same time, he began the process of translating the new science into terms that might be legible in Cairo. For example, in his inventory of the sciences and arts among the "Franks," Tahtawi lists the Société Archéologique:

> The Society for the Preservation of Relics of the Ancients is an organization dedicated to searching for, and preserving all the amazing relics of the ancients—buildings, mummies, garments and the like—in order to study the customs of those people. In that place, there are many precious items taken from the land of Egypt, such as the Dendera zodiac bas-relief. The French use it to understand the astronomy of the ancient Egyptians. The French take things like this without [paying] any compensation. They know well their value, and preserve them, and extract from them assorted conclusions and general benefits.[2]

Tahtawi's description is noteworthy in that it links an appreciation of European science with an appraisal of the (immoral) political economy supporting it. It is true, he argues, that the Europeans have taken what does not belong to them. But, he concedes, they have made great use of the material. This argument resonates with the perspective of European contemporaries who lamented the abuses—and acknowledged the resemblance to theft—of museum acquisitions in Egypt even as they extolled its virtues. Later, on his journey home, Tahtawi again mentions the impressive knowledge the French had of ancient Egypt. Visiting a memorial that had been vandalized during the Revolution of 1830, Tahtawi compares the modern French culture of monument building to Pharaonic Egypt: "Inscriptions are a custom among the Europeans, who took their cue from the ancient Egyptians and others. Look at how the Egyptians erected temples and the Pyramids of Giza. They built them as monuments to be seen by those who would come after. We should mention the opinion that Europeans have of them after studying them thoroughly, so that you might compare the truth of what they say to what the fantasies [*awham*] of the [Arab] historians say about them."[3] Tahtawi continues with a brief summary of the most recent European theories of the history of the pyramids:

> In brief, the Europeans say that it was the kings of Egypt who built the pyramids and temples. They differ among themselves as to the time of their construction: some claim they were built 3000 years ago, and that their builder was a king called "Khufu." Others say the king who built them was called "Khamis" or "Cheops." It is very clear that its stones were quarried in Upper Egypt, not in Giza. . . . They say these pyramids go back to one of the Pharaoh kings, that he prepared the great one to hold his corpse and the other two to bury his wife and daughter, but that he was not buried in it. . . . This is what the Europeans say about the pyramids.

The point is clear: the French know more about ancient Egypt than Arab historians. Yet there is something peculiar in Tahtawi's account: while the name Cheops is derived from modern Egyptological sources, the detail about the king and his family comes from old Arabic sources, most likely that of Ibn al-Nadim.[4] In short, Tahtawi leavens his account of "European knowledge" with significant amounts of the Arabic textual tradition.

What does it mean that Tahtawi would present a citation of Islamic tradition within his report of European science? If nothing else, it suggests the continuing relevance of Arabo-Islamic sources, even if their authority had been eclipsed by European sources. However, at times Tahtawi also cites Arab sources. Immediately after this passage, for instance, he cites lines ascribed to the classical poet 'Umara al-Yamani (d. 1175 CE):

> O my companions, do you know of any structures under heaven whose perfection resembles that of Egypt's pyramids?
> All on the face of Earth dread time's oblivion, yet this is a structure that terrifies times itself.
> My glance delights in the guile of its construction, even as my thinking fails to grasp their intention.

Like their medieval source, these lines gesture toward the same philosophical tradition on Pharaonic antiquities that Tahtawi dismisses elsewhere as fiction.

Though Tahtawi was willing to concede the intellectual advancement of European Egyptologists, he insisted that this advantage did not translate into a superior moral right to treat Pharaonic monuments as European property. On the contrary, if Egyptian modernity was to be developed in relation to Pharaonic antiquity, Egyptians had to be able to control Pharaonic antiquities: "It is my opinion that just as Egypt is now emulating the civilization and instruction of European countries, it is more entitled to those things of beauty and craft left by its ancestors. Reasonable people consider their stripping away piece after piece to be like adorning oneself with jewelry taken from others. It is tantamount to theft!"[6] The question of what should be done with the antiquities of Egypt had been raised by earlier generations of European travelers. As described in chapter 2, Europeans had long asserted that modern Egyptians were indifferent toward Pharaonic antiquities and that the objects were threatened by the neglect and greed of Egyptian peasants. Now Egyptians were asserting the same thing about Europeans.

In a way, these passages in Tahtawi mark a turning point in Egyptian thought on the Pharaonic past: on the one hand, the author describes the new Egyptology and emphatically associates it with European learning;

on the other hand, he blends this science with old literary and historio-graphical tradition, sometimes with explicit citations, sometimes without. Moreover, in Tahtawi's account one sees, perhaps for the first time, a new connection between the ancient Egyptian past and the Egyptian present or, more precisely, the creation of an Egyptian modernity. In the old model, vestiges of the ancient past were a lesson for the present to consider. But the content of the Pharaonic past, insofar as its values had been abrogated by the advent of Islam, offered little in terms of positive guidance for the conduct of Muslims in the present. In contrast, the new attitude, com-plete though not self-conscious in Tahtawi's account, shifted focus from the consideration of time in the abstract to the consideration of specific historical periods arranged in a developmental sequence. In this account, ancient history is not disconnected from the present. Moreover, Tahtawi presents increasingly confident assertions about the manners and cus-toms of the ancient Egyptians without moral evaluation. Thus the shape of ideas that became readily accepted among later generations of Egyptian intellectuals: that Islam's relationship to the pagan past might be renegoti-ated; that by absorbing the knowledge of modern European Egyptology, Egyptians would learn about an ancient past that belongs rightly to them; and that only by learning about their ancient past could Egyptians become truly modern and authentically Egyptian.

It is impossible to exaggerate the place of Tahtawi in the development of a self-conscious cultural modernism in Egypt. Arguably, what Tahtawi did best of all was translate, not only concepts, but also institutional structures. On his return to Cairo from Paris, Tahtawi was employed by his patron, Mehmed 'Ali, to serve as editor in chief of Egypt's first news gazette, *al-Waqa'i' al-Misriyya*, director of schools, and state translator, not to mention director of the first Egyptian antiquities museum. When Mehmed 'Ali's grandson, 'Abbas I, took power in 1850, he exiled Tahtawi to Sudan. There, Tahtawi founded a school and continued to write and translate. Upon his return to Cairo in 1854, Tahtawi again took up his activities as educational deputy, was made editor in chief of a new journal, *Rawdat al-Madaris*, and continued to translate. Paid a commission (in land) for each book he translated into Arabic, Tahtawi bequeathed his family a large fortune when he died. Translation of the Pharaonic past played a critical role in his articulation of Egyptian modernity.

This chapter outlines three distinct moments in the history of the absorption of Egyptological thinking into Egyptian letters. What links them is that each moment attempted to connect the discoveries of Egyptology with the formulation of a modern, Egyptian national identity. The first is a syncretic moment along the lines one sees in the work of nineteenth-century intellectuals like Tahtawi and 'Ali Mubarak, who also studied in Paris. Like Tahtawi, Mubarak synthesized aspects of older traditions of ancient Egypt with European Egyptology. While the source of modern Egyptology was European, the lessons offered by the Egyptian intellectuals rechanneled it toward other ends. Tahtawi, for example, was adamant that Pharaonic artifacts, part of Egypt's patrimony, should remain in the country. For his part, Mubarak was not so concerned with the material possession of artifacts as with making the history of ancient Egypt an example for modern Egyptians. Together, Tahtawi's and Mubarak's writings reveal a powerful cluster of concepts and themes coupling ancient and modern Egypt: a new history that retains religious narratives about the past while adding to them information garnered from Egyptological discoveries about Pharaonic antiquity; new concepts of place, space, and community that subtly uncouple Egypt from the Islamic and regional traditions of cultural identity; the image of a bounded territory inhabited by a single people sharing a unified, transhistorical experience; and new practices, like preservation and sightseeing. These concepts and themes, made concrete in the material of antiquities and housed in the single institution of the museum, came to pose a tangible reality, one as immediate as it was timeless. The flexible, simultaneously abstract and concrete character of this new perspective on Pharaonic civilization contributed greatly to its rhetorical potential and explains why, many decades later, it would play a prominent role in the nationalist movement of the 1920s.

The second moment, marked by the dissemination of Egyptological history into Egyptian state schools, created a new generation of intellectuals who were much less interested in the Islamic tradition than they were in European knowledge and the culture of appreciation. Crucially, this moment of absorption, though located in Cairo rather than Paris, was less syncretic than that of Tahtawi. Drawing on elements from 'Ali Mubarak and contemporary Egyptology, this generation talked about the ancient past in a new way: asserting, for instance, that Pharaonic culture was originally monotheistic, that Egypt's ancient empire should inspire modern Egyptian political ambitions, and that Egyptian intellectuals should feel ashamed of the supposed indifference and ignorance of most Egyptians toward the Pharaonic past. Significantly, this moment occurred as Egyptian elites first began to engage in domestic tourism.

The third moment was that of a new literary culture identified positively with the Pharaonic past in ways the Islamic tradition and the science of Egyptology never were. Egyptian intellectuals from the late nineteenth century and the early twentieth described the culture and politics of their day as *al-Nahda*, or "the Awakening" (or "Renaissance"). The word underscores the enlightenment response to the ruptures posed by the advent of modernity in the Arab world and describes the image of intellectual mobilization against Ottoman rule and Western colonialism.[7] It also found strong echoes in the theme of the afterlife in ancient narratives like the Osiris myth, which inspired the Pharaonist literary school in Egypt. In this section, I focus on two representative texts, Tawfiq al-Hakim's novel *Awdat al-ruh* (*Return of the Spirit*) (1932) and Ahmad Husayn's memoir, *Imani* (*My Faith*) (1936), both of which present themes of national resurrection through an appreciation of the ancient past. In many ways, these two authors represent extreme poles of the nationalist movement. Hakim, a humanist educated in France, was associated with the most liberal elements of the Wafd Party, which dominated Egyptian parliamentary politics throughout the 1920s and 1930s. By contrast, Husayn modeled his small party, *Misr al-Fatat* (Young Egypt), on the Italian Fascists. Together, these two texts embrace the wide range of nationalist ideologies that made thematic use of ancient Egypt and demonstrate the flexibility of Pharaonist discourse and nationalism more generally.

THE SECOND ANTIQAKHANA

There is perhaps no better way to see how the new science and old tradition were synthesized than to look at how the second Egyptological museum in Cairo was presented to the public. After the demise of the Ezbekiyya Antiqakhana, the French Egyptologist Auguste Mariette (1821–81) convinced Sa'id Pasha (who had succeeded 'Abbas I as ruler) of the urgency of preserving Egypt's antiquities and creating a state museum for them. In 1858, Mariette was appointed director of a new state agency, the Antiquities Service (*Maslahat al-Athar*). The agreed-upon formula would last until after formal independence in 1952: the Antiquities Service was organized as an Egyptian state agency under European management.

Despite wavering support from the uncertain patrons Sa'id (r. 1854–63) and Isma'il (r. 1863–79), Mariette enjoyed a long tenure as director of the service and ensured the success of the infant governmental agency. In many ways, the agency's existence was closely tied to the fortunes of its director, since Mariette was invested with unique powers, becoming "a bey, second class, with exclusive excavation rights throughout the country, a steamboat, and authorization to levy corvée labor."[8] In 1863, he opened the second Antiqakhana in Bulaq at great expense both to the state and to his own fortune.[9] Crucially, Mariette wanted his museum to serve the interests of Egyptians:

> The Museum of Cairo is not only intended for European travelers. It is the Viceroy's intention that it should be above all accessible to the natives, to whom the Museum is entrusted in order to teach them the history of their country. I would not be maligning the civilization introduced to the banks of the Nile by the dynasty of Mehmed 'Ali if I were to assert that Egypt is still too young in the new life which she has just received to have a public easily impressed in matters of archaeology and art. Not long ago, Egypt destroyed its monuments; today, it respects them; tomorrow it shall love them.[10]

Egyptian enthusiasts of the museum presented Pharaonic culture in syncretic terms. Consider the rhetoric of the translation of his guidebook, which sought to introduce Egyptian readers to the museum and to the Pharaonic past more broadly. The first Arabic-language guide begins as follows:

> We praise You, God, You who are called a hidden treasure. And You answered that You would be known. So You created humankind and shared material blessing, so that they would know You and come to understand You. Thus reality became clear and apparent to all. We ask that God bless Muhammad and grant peace upon him, Your servant and prophet, whom You took to be a pure companion. He was loyal and beloved of You. He commanded people gently, and spread sincere truth among them. He

became renowned and raised up his family as the most deserving of the beautiful reminders [*athar*], along with his companions, those of noble accounts [of the Prophet's life], in which is a lesson [*'ibra*] to those who would consider and a piece of knowledge for him who would transmit it.[11]

The invocation of *Furjat al-mutafarraj* (The Viewer's Pleasure) is admittedly not the work of its author, but of its translator, 'Abdallah Abu al-Su'ud, Mariette's protégé. Its opening passages give some indication of how nineteenth-century Egyptian translators might adapt Egyptology and the museum to the sensibilities of the reading public in urban centers. In the prologue to Mariette's description of the contents of the museum, Abu al-Su'ud engages an idiom of Muslim lessons and reminders. The point is not rote piety, but rather a self-conscious effort to combine two divergent nineteenth-century cultural visions within a uniquely modern Egyptian discourse. His use of the word *athar* is especially revealing. By the late 1850s, *athar* had come to have the technical meaning of "antiquities," as signaled in the Arabic name of the new Antiquities Service (*Maslahat al-Athar*). However, Abu al-Su'ud also plays with connotations that evoke the earlier semantic context.

Another aspect of Abu al-Su'ud's register is equally instructive. He writes that the guidebook is meant "to teach the sons of Egypt [*abna' Misr*] and inform the people of this era about how their ancient forefathers lived." In asserting a line of continuity between the past and the present, Abu al-Su'ud's language deviates from the orthodox register which distinguished between the pagan past and the monotheistic present. Likewise, whereas orientalist discourse sought to separate ancient Egypt from the lives of modern Egyptians, Abu al-Su'ud in contrast asserts a patrilineal relation between past "fathers" and present "sons." Abu al-Su'ud goes on to suggest that there is no antagonism between Islamic culture and ancient Egypt, since

the ancestors of the people of Egypt believed in the existence of a single God [*ilah wahid*], seeing but unseen, worshipped as absolute [*samad*], ancient, eternal, with no beginning and no end. They considered Him holy, revering His sublime blessing and graciousness. They worshipped Him for the loveliness of His beautiful signs [*athar*], and drew close to Him by doing good deeds and avoiding sin. . . . It is known that the Egyptians were advanced in the matter of divinity to the utmost. No other people were more developed in this regard than they.[12]

Abu al-Su'ud's lexicon recalls lines of Sura 112 that express the basic elements of monotheism in Islam. His essay no doubt is one of the first attempts to assert a compatibility between Pharaonic religion and Islamic theology. Abu al-Su'ud also describes at length those aspects of the ancient Egyptian religion—from belief in the afterlife to the importance of burial—which most resemble Muslim faith and practice. By emphasizing the place of the god Amun within Pharaonic religion and by understating its polytheism, Abu al-Su'ud's prologue describes ancient Egypt as an non-pagan, if not proto-Islamic form of monotheism. Abu al-Su'ud's introduction to Mariette's guidebook for the Bulaq Museum is remarkable because it reveals how the cultural significance of the antiquities collection was translated into an Egyptian idiom. The resulting discourse rendered an understanding of ancient Egypt that was neither quite that of Muslim tradition nor quite that of European Egyptology.

NEW HISTORY, NEW GEOGRAPHY, NEW COMMUNITY

The real patriot (*watani*) is justified when filling his heart with patriotism (*hubb al-watan*), for he has become one of its members.
—TAHTAWI, *al-Murshid al-Amin li-l-banat wa-l-banin*

Every lover of the beauty of civilization [*'umran*], every one who smells the bouquet of this age's wine, delights with happiness, his heart filling with joy, when he sees with a loving eye that Egypt's ancient greatness has returned!
—TAHTAWI, *Manahij al-albab al-Misriyya fi-mabahij al-adab al-'asriyya*

For thinking through the connections between the ancient past and the modern present, the most subtle but powerful development in Tahtawi's thought was perhaps his introduction, by way of French orientalists like de Sacy, to the historiography of Ibn Khaldun (d. 1406 CE). Ibn Khaldun's *Muqaddima* does not so much write a history of human civilization as attempt to discover the rules underlying history itself.[13] Moreover, the book is not a study of historical events, but rather a preface (*muqaddima*) to his universal history *Kitab al-'ibar* (*Book of Instructive Lessons*). Ibn Khaldun's writing is a response to Muslim historiography, a tradition that was highly developed. Since the life of the Prophet Muhammad is the model for many aspects of Muslim practice, accurate knowledge of his biography has always been paramount to faith itself. The *Muqaddima* critiques this tradition of Islamic historiography by scrutinizing its method of placing as much emphasis on the reliability of transmitters of reports about the past as it does on the content of the reports themselves. Ibn Khaldun suggests that historians (as opposed to chroniclers) should look for patterns within the occurrence of events, and not just the forms by which news of events are transmitted to the present. Part of what Ibn Khaldun suggests is that one can read effectively for worldly patterns in the unfolding of history. Just as the history of the Prophet is instructive for living as a Muslim, so too might the history of cultural and political change be instructive.

Ibn Khaldun's argument, in brief, is that society is composed of antagonistic factions, one sedentary, the other nomadic. Civilization (*'umran*) is the product of the various ways of life—crafts, professions, habits—that make up a given society. It is not the case, in Ibn Khaldun's model, that sedentary society is naturally superior or that by itself it marks an advancement over nomadic society. That is because nomadic society enjoys an especially developed sense of group solidarity (*'assabiyya*), a civil virtue that becomes weakened by the more luxurious circumstances of the sedentary mode of existence. Over time, the sedentary segments of society tend to decay unless reinvigorated by this sense of group solidarity. Ibn Khaldun's model of society remains as radical as it is powerful: conflict, being society's engine, is natural and productive; civilization is a dialectical project without prescribed telos; the history of civilization moves in cycles of advancement, decline, and renewal.

Tahtawi's interest in Ibn Khaldun led him to supervise the first edition of the *Muqaddima* published in Egypt, effectively introducing the philosopher to Arabic readers in the Levant for the first time in centuries. But while Tahtawi's model of history incorporated elements of Ibn Khaldun's thought (such as the idea of different stages of civilization), he emphatically excluded some of the philosopher's most radical arguments, such as the notion that civilization moves within a dialectic without telos. Like the opening chapters of Ibn Khaldun's *Muqaddima*,

Tahtawi's first chapter discusses the civilizations of the world, ranking them by stage:

> [We] can divide humanity into a number of stages. The first stage consists of savages. The second, of rough barbarians. The third, of the people who have reached the utmost of culture, refinement, sedentarism, civilization and urbanity. An example of the first stage are the savages of the Lands of the Blacks who are like the roaming herds of animals. . . . An example of the second are Bedouins of the desert who have a kind of human sociability . . . and who know right from wrong. . . . An example of the third stage are the countries of Egypt, Syria, Yemen, Byzantium, Persia, Europe, the Maghrib.[14]

Tahtawi continues in this vein, comparing the civilizational accomplishments of Europe (science and technology) with those of the Muslim world (law and linguistics).

Another element of Ibn Khaldun's history that is apparent in Tahtawi's thought is the insistence on reading the events of world history as occurrences whose causes are of a worldly rather than divine origin. Like Ibn Khaldun, Tahtawi divides the study of history into two parts: the first, the history of world events as narrated in the sacred texts of the monotheistic religions; the second, the history of the world as narrated in the best textual sources, regardless of origin. It is the latter form of history with which Tahtawi concerned himself in his final years, especially when he wrote accounts for popular audiences and school curricula. The following categorization of history appears in *Anwar Tawfiq al-Jalil*:

> Egypt's general history, from the ancient age to our present one, can be divided into two essential categories. The first period being what came before Islam; the second, what came after. The first period can be separated into two branches: the first being the pre-Islamic period [*al-Jahiliyya*]; the second, the propagation of the Christian religion by the official decree of the Roman Caesar, Theodosius. Pre-Islamic was essentially the time when Egypt was addicted to the worship of idols [*awthan wa-asnam*]. After that it adhered to Christianity.[15]

By separating the study of the ancient past from sources whose message contained a kind of moralism, Tahtawi opened up a new way of thinking about ancient Egypt. True, in Tahtawi's account the pagan character of

Pharaonic Egypt was indelible, but at the same time its civilizational accomplishments could be discussed on their own terms. Thus, despite its pagan character, he would boast, "Egypt contended with the ancients of the nations, and they conceded that, next to Egypt, they were less important. None surpassed her in the matter of civilization [*tamadduniyya*], and in the field of legislation and executing civil justice, no nation [*umma*] or community [*milla*] rejected the blessing of borrowing from Egypt's sciences. No state or kingdom failed to seek the light of Egypt's lamp."[16]

Welding the Khaldunian historiographical theme of decline and renewal to new developments in the Egyptological accounts of ancient Egyptian history, Tahtawi arrived at a new understanding of the Pharaonic past. The point of appreciating the scientific and engineering accomplishments of ancient Egypt and its political and military strength was thus not merely a lesson about the past, but an image of glory to which the present should aspire. He asserts, for instance, that "in the time of the Pharaohs, Egypt was the mother of the world's nations [*umam al-dunya*] and the barb of its weapon was strong."[17] At the same time, his assessment of more recent history was explicitly bleak: for him, Egypt in modern times was clearly in decline. How did Egypt lose "the virtues and prosperity of ancient times"? On this, the great historian of the modern Middle East, Albert Hourani, wrote, "It was, Tahtawi maintains, because of the historical accident of foreign rule: the rule of the Mamelukes in the later Middle Ages and then, after a brief revival under the early Ottoman sultans, the long misrule of the Circassians. In saying this he echoed the proclamations of Bonaparte."[18] In appearance, Tahtawi's argument about the decline of the present resembles colonial discourse on modern Egypt. Yet, being also informed by Ibn Khaldun's cyclical model, Tahtawi's understanding of decline is charged with the opportunity for renewal of past greatness. Here the image of ancient Egypt becomes quite powerful, suggesting that current decline is not the essential state of Egyptian civilization, but rather a moment to be followed by renewal. In more than one instance, Tahtawi makes this point explicitly, arguing that with Mehmed 'Ali's rule, "Egypt's ancient grandeur had returned."[19] In such arguments lie the beginnings of a new way of conceiving Egyptian modernity: as a return of the distant past.

At the same time Tahtawi was creating a new historical model for Egypt, he and others were linking the new history to new concepts of place and community. For instance, in his introduction to the museum guidebook, Abu al-Su'ud insists that a unique connection exists between ancient and modern Egyptians. Abu al-Su'ud's privileged term "the people of Egypt" (*ahl Misr*) does not distinguish between ancients and moderns but suggests that together they form a continuous whole. The historical distance between modern and ancient Egyptians might suggest differences between them, but such differences are, in Abu al-Su'ud's account, not essential. What joins the people of Egypt together is the shared experience of living within "the Egyptian territories" (*al-diyar al-Misriyya*). This conceptual link between community and territory is especially keen in Tahtawi. In *Manahij al-albab al-Misriyya fi-mabahij al-adab al-'asriyya* (*The Paths of Egyptian Hearts in the Splendors of Contemporary Morals*) Tahtawi builds on the classical *fada'il* genre by developing the concept of merits. In terms derived from French political economy, he discusses public benefit (*al-manafi' al-'umumiyya*)—commerce, industry, and agriculture—with special emphasis on land as a source of wealth. In doing so, he develops a concept that links land and community: *al-watan* (homeland, *patrie*).[20] In Tahtawi's account, the connection Egyptians feel for the land and for each other is innate, though not passive. True, the land of Egypt has its natural advantages (*fada'il*), enjoyed by all those who inhabit it. At the same time, Tahtawi urges his readers to cultivate an active sense of attachment to their country—in short, patriotism, or "love of homeland" (*hubb al-watan*). The concept shares much with Ibn Khaldun's notion of "group solidarity" (*'asabiyya*) in that it describes a kind of sociability that is inherited, but whose existence needs to be actively expressed: if taken for granted and unpracticed, this kind of solidarity weakens in time. Unlike Ibn Khaldun's concept, however, with its emphasis on tribal bonds, Tahtawi's sense of solidarity exists in relation to a particular geographical territory. The patriot (*watani*) is a member of the national community because he loves the land (*watan*). The semantic shift is significant in that it marks a new way of describing Egyptian sociability that is distinct from the more sedimented concepts of religious, sectarian, and ethnic community (*umma, milla,* and *qawm*).

Moreover, the new concept of *watan* was one whose significance, though historical, was nearly timeless. On this point, the link to the changing perception of Pharaonic Egypt is essential. The rediscovery of the historical sources of Pharaonic Egypt provided Tahtawi with another way to formulate a concept of "modern Egypt" that was not broken into discon-nected religious sects or historical periods. As a concept of territory, Egypt in this account extended naturally from the Mediterranean to well below the second cataract, in present-day Sudan. Paradoxically, the discovery of ancient Egyptian history allowed for the creation of a concept of Egyptian national identity that transcended history itself, since, as Tahtawi argued, "the physical constitution of the people of these times is exactly that of the peoples of times past, and their disposition is one and the same."[21] Again, Hourani's comments on Tahtawi are enlightening:

> What is this natural community, this *watan* to which Tahtawi refers? It is Egyptian and not Arab. In his thought there is indeed some shadowy idea of Arabism, but it belongs to the old rather than the new element in it. He praises and defends the part played by the Arabs in the history of Islam; when he talks of patriotism, however, he does not mean the feeling shared by all those who speak Arabic, but that shared by those who live in the land of Egypt. Egypt for him is something distinct, and also some-thing historically continuous. Modern Egypt is the legitimate descendent of the land of the Pharaohs.[22]

The shift in the vocabulary of community was one of the most produc-tive consequences of the shift in perception toward the ancient past. For Tahtawi and Abu al-Su'ud, as opposed to Muslim writers before them, Pharaonic history was not cut off from the present by the advent of Islam, but made part of a history that was continuous and accretive. Moreover, insofar as Pharaonic civilization appeared as the most advanced and de-veloped of the ancient world, its image could represent a potential future just as it portrayed the fact of Egypt's past. For contemporary European writers, ancient Egypt was increasingly understood as an origin of West-ern civilization, even while its geographic location outside of Europe complicated this notion. In contrast, for Egyptian intellectuals, Pharaonic civilization was now becoming inextricably linked to the land of Egypt and seen as the unique product of its geography. This shift, from under-standing Pharaonic Egypt as a distinct historical period to conceiving it as a shared experience of place, was crucial for reaching across time and for creating a new sense of national patrimony.

The issue of national patrimony looms large in Tahtawi's writings, and Pharaonic objects function as the material proof of his categories of history, community, and place. In this regard, his reflections on the Bulaq Antiqakhana, published at the same time as the guidebook in which Abu al-Su'ud's introduction first appeared, are instructive:

> These ancient monuments [*athar*] are called "antiquities" [*antika*]. Mehmed 'Ali issued orders . . . to preserve them; that whatever was excavated from their site would be kept in the Antiquities [Museum] in Cairo; that nothing would be allowed to be taken from [the collection] for export abroad. For these antiquities [*antikat*] are the ornament of Egypt, and it should not be allowed that Egypt be stripped of its finery by sightseers [*mutafarrajin*] from any country in the world. There is still a special, well-ordered antiquities storehouse in Bulaq. But foreigners still take whatever they can get their hands on, by buying images and mummies, i.e., preserved, embalmed body parts. . . . These monuments [*athar*] remain a history awakening all to the past ages, and a witness to the books of revelation. The Qur'an mentions them and their people. To see these monuments is to experience a report from the Prophet's time, it is to confirm Islamic tradition. Another advantage to preserving the monuments is that they tell us something of the condition of those who lived before, and they present their sciences and the purity of their thought. [23]

In these last sentences, we see Tahtawi balancing the two measures of history, divine revelation versus the worldly. Tahtawi's vocabulary attests to this split: his use of the classical term *athar* carries within it the classical sense of monuments as reminders, whereas the neologism *antika* carries the stamp of Egyptology's origins in antiquarianism. Again, Tahtawi did not oppose these two ways of understanding the past, but rather developed them in tandem as part of a single modern Egyptian attitude toward Pharaonic civilization, one that was simultaneously Muslim and Egyptological. Besides elaborating these two models of history, this passage defends the state's preservationist policies, an argument Tahtawi would extend elsewhere. In Tahtawi's later writings, one finds the beginning of a formidable tautology: the Egyptian nation is composed of a people sharing the experience of living in the land of Egypt; Pharaonic monuments are material signs of transhistorical character of the Egyptian nation (*watan*); by protecting Pharaonic monuments, the Egyptian state preserves the identity of the nation; individuals who work to preserve the monuments are engaging in a form of patriotism (*hubb al-watan*).

ANCIENT LAND, NEW ORDER

We have found no one among the sons of Egypt who can . . . guide us aright in understanding the country's notable monuments. We look upon these works but do not know the circumstances of their creation, we wander through them but do not know who made them. . . . But it is our duty to know these things, for it is not fitting for us to remain in ignorance of our country or to neglect the monuments of our ancestors. They are a moral lesson to the reflective mind, a memorial to the thoughtful soul. . . . For what our ancestors have left behind stirs in us the desire to follow in their footsteps, and to produce for our times what they produced in theirs.
—'ALI MUBARAK, as quoted by Michael J. Reimer

Like Tahtawi, 'Ali Mubarak (1823–93) had been sent to study in Paris (1844–49) and was employed by the state upon his return. As minister of education, Mubarak founded schools (including the teachers' college, Dar al-'Ulum) and the first national library (later *Dar al-Kutub*). Appointed minister of public works after visiting Paris in 1868, Mubarak set out to re-create Cairo and the Egyptian countryside. By this time, Egypt was already a vital agricultural and transportation center of the global economy: the railroad linking Alexandria and Cairo was opened in 1856 (Mubarak served also as director-general of state railways); by the 1870s, the entire Nile Valley, from Alexandria and Port Said to Aswan and beyond, would be traversed by rail. Steamship lines linked Egypt ever more directly with Europe and, after the completion of the Suez Canal in 1869, with points east. Telegraph lines connected Cairo to the Egyptian countryside by 1883.

At the same time, the very geography of the cities and the countryside was targeted for rapid change. With inspiration from Georges-Eugène Haussmann's Paris and backing from Isma'il, Mubarak supervised the construction of modern Cairo. In his description of Mubarak's development projects, in some ways the continuation of efforts started under the rule of Mehmed 'Ali, Timothy Mitchell has emphasized the visual character of the new order, or *tanzim* (literally: "ordering"), and its deep links with the nineteenth-century cultural phenomenon of the exhibition. Noting the intensely visual character of the many nineteenth-century European descriptions of Egypt—maps, charts, drawings, paintings, photographs as well as panoramas, museum exhibitions, and world expositions—Mitchell elaborates on how they framed Egypt as an object to be looked at and also positioned the European viewing subject opposite the object of the exhibitionary gaze. Mitchell notes that for Mubarak it was crucial that "the world was something to be constructed and ordered according to an equivalent distinction between physical 'things' and their non-material structure,"[24] since that meant one could apply the conceptual separation so as to ignore, transform, destroy, or replace the physical realm of Egypt. By all accounts, Mubarak's modernization plans, which not only constructed new roads and quarters but destroyed old ones in the process, were based on a long series of conceptual oppositions: the modern versus the old; progress versus stagnation; order versus chaos. In reshaping the city of Cairo, for instance, his intention was to create a rational topography, "an appearance of order" clearer and more hygienic than the older quarters, whose layout was now associated with all that was backward about Egypt. Mitchell writes,

There followed the greatest period of construction and demolition in the city since the growth of Mameluke Cairo in the 1300s. A new structure was laid out between the northern and western edges of the existing city and its new gateway from Alexandria and Europe, the railway station, with plots made available to anyone who would construct a building with a European façade. "The transformation of the city of Cairo from an aesthetic point of view . . ." required "the filling in and leveling of the waste land around the city, the opening up of main streets and new arteries, the creation of squares and open places, the planting of trees, the surfacing of roads, the construction of drains, and regular cleaning and watering." From Khedive Isma'il's new palace of 'Abdin . . . the Boulevard Muhammad Ali was ploughed diagonally through the old city. It was two kilometers long, and in its path stood almost four hundred large houses, three hundred smaller ones, and a great number of mosques, mills, bakeries and bath-houses. These were all destroyed, or cut in half and left standing like dolls' houses with no outer wall, so that when the road was completed the scene resembled "a city that has recently been shelled—houses in all stages of dilapidation, though still inhabited, giving most odd views of domestic interiors, frowning down upon you."[25]

At the same time Mubarak was reordering Egypt, he was busy depicting its geography in his monumental work *al-Khitat al-Tawfiqiyya*. It is perhaps more accurate to say he was preserving a representation of the very geography he was transforming. The title of Mubarak's geography is a citation of Taqiy al-Din al-Maqrizi's fifteenth-century compendium on Egypt, but it also signals the central place that plans (*khitat*) had in Mubarak's thinking.

Antiquities figure significantly in the text and shed light on the issue of the new order simply because they are relegated to a place beyond the scope of the binaries of modernity/tradition, progress/stagnation, and order/chaos that structure Mubarak's presentation. Volume 16 of the work contains a long discourse on the Pyramids of Giza in which the author synthesizes contemporary and ancient Western accounts with Islamic tradition. Citing Herodotus directly, Mubarak states that "Egyptians had an intense hatred for the kings" Cheops and Chephren, builders of the two large pyramids, "so much so that they avoided mentioning their names." But, he adds, "what Mariette Bey has to say about the matter contradicts this assertion. He says that the monuments that remain from their time until the present suggest that the kings Cheops and Shifra [Chephren] enjoyed a special sacred status with the people."[26] In this way, Mubarak reproduces many of the Islamic legends surrounding the history of the pyramids but juxtaposes them with accounts from modern antiquarians, orientalists, and Egyptologists, from de Sacy and Belzoni to Champollion and others. As Darrell Dykstra observes, the one subject where Mubarak rejects the accounts of Arabs and the ancients in favor of those of modern Europeans is measurement: the precision of the Europeans is not just indisputable, it is unsynthesizable with incorrect measurements.[27] The sum effect is a syncretic account that mixes the best modern scholarship, drawn from the contemporary study of hieroglyphs, with ancient authorities, both those from Europe (Herodotus and Strabo are on equal footing here with Champollion and Mariette) and those from the Arab world. The resulting portrayal of Pharaonic Egypt is richly ambiguous, since

Mubarak does not privilege either source of knowledge but rather brings them together in a single assemblage.

In contrast, Mubarak's lengthy fictional work *'Alam al-Din* presents a different version of the interpretation of ancient Egypt and of the issue of order. Whereas *al-Khitat al-Tawfiqiyya* follows the generic contours of the medieval compendium, *'Alam al-Din* is structured around conversations (*musamarat*). In Mubarak's story, the Egyptian protagonist 'Alam al-Din is an al-Azhar graduate hired to aid an Englishman who is editing an edition of the great lexicon of the Arabic language, *Lisan al-'Arab*. As part of their agreement 'Alam al-Din agrees to travel to Europe with his patron. The bulk of the plot follows the travels of the Englishman, 'Alam al-Din, and 'Alam's son, Burhan al-Din, as they go West. The small group first travels through Egypt to Alexandria, and then, on their voyage to Marseilles, they are joined by an English sailor, James. The rest of the book charts their journey to Paris and their adventures and informal discussions in that city. The work is structured as an ongoing conversation and a series of cultural and scientific comparisons: a comparison of West to East, then East to West, and so on.[28]

The primary concern voiced in *'Alam al-Din* is a practical one: its lessons are not for the sake of knowledge itself, but rather about their application to the development of Egypt. Much of the text is dedicated to explaining projects to build Egypt's economic infrastructure. In particular, the conversations return often to the theme of developing Egypt's industrial and water resources. But it is the theme of terrain, the land of Egypt, expressed through a variety of terms (such as *qatr Misr* and *ard Misr*), that is the real focus of discussions, many of which return to topics like land reclamation, irrigation, and repopulation. Land in this fiction connotes not merely place, but also people and their special tie to the country. In this respect, the term *watan* plays as important role in Mubarak's writing as it does in Tahtawi's. In his introduction, Mubarak writes often of Egypt in terms of *watan*, and the term implies not only a form of community tied to a territory, but also, more important, a community with an ethical duty both to develop its own social capacity and the capacity of the land. He draws an analogy between the Egyptian who would seek to benefit the land of Egypt and a landowner (*sahib al-ard*) by whose care and actions the land would be improved.[29] Importantly, it is ancient Egyptians who provide the best model for how modern Egyptians should care for the lands of their country.

To make this point, the work stages a series of lessons in which modern Egyptians learn to recognize the extent of the Pharaonic legacy. For instance, while traveling to Alexandria, the group stops in the town of Tanta, where the famous saint's festival takes place. The British orientalist uses the occasion to educate 'Alam al-Din as to the Pharaonic origins of the name of the town. As the Azhari sheikh explains the Muslim origins of the saint and of saints' festivals more widely, the Englishman corrects him, arguing that they derive from Coptic festivals that in turn derive from ancient celebrations related, perhaps, to the Osiris myth. In Paris, the discussions of ancient Egypt intensify. During one session 'Alam al-Din meets an Englishman at the Société Orientale, who impresses him with his knowledge of Oriental languages and his experiences traveling in the East. The Englishman then lectures on ancient Egypt: "All the useful sciences in our countries [of Europe] come from Egypt, by way of the Romans and others. The progress about which we brag in our countries has its origin in Egypt. For that reason, Egypt has a privileged place with us, indeed, with all the inhabitants of the world. All that we enjoy of progress and wealth is due to the Egyptians. . . . If not for the Egyptians, we would be until today drowning in a sea of ignorance, wandering lost in the valleys of error."[30]

In the course of his speech, which covers topics ancient and modern, the Englishman reproduces descriptions taken straight from al-Maqrizi and Jalal al-Din al-Suyuti as well as vocabulary (such as *al-i'tibar*) from the Islamic tradition. Through these conversations, there is no attempt to resolve the contradictions between modern European accounts and those of medieval Muslims—and in that sense the text shares in the syncretism of Tahtawi's writings. Moreover, the consideration of ancient Egypt is never abstract but related to the development of the modern country. In one conversation, the Englishman and the Azhari sheikh converse about the population of Egypt and its arable lands: "You know well that what happened in the land of Egypt after the demise of the Pharaohs, when it was taken over by foreign rulers. This is one of the causes of its backwardness, its lack of order. This led to the abandonment of the land, its neglect, and the flight of its people, so that much of the country was in ruin."[31] The contours of this narrative should be familiar because they replicate the logic of colonial accounts that described present-day Egypt in terms of decline. In truth, the new knowledge provided by Egyptology may have lent some validity to such comparisons between the state of the country in ancient and in modern times. Comparing statistics compiled in ancient, medieval, and modern times, the Englishman tells the sheikh, "Based on our calculations, the arable land in ancient times was close to 700,000 feddans. By the time of the French occupation, only about half of that was being cultivated."[32] When the sheikh exclaims that development projects launched by Mehmed 'Ali had begun to reclaim lost lands and irrigate others, the Englishman answers optimistically, "Accomplishing development in Egypt is a certainty. The land of Egypt can be cultivated twice as much as it is at present, and more. If the land is taken care of, it is possible that it could be farmed as it once was, and that the land of Egypt could return to its ancient affluence."[33] As in colonial accounts, ancient Egypt functions as a point of comparison for judging the governance of modern Egypt, and again, the comparison hinges upon the question of land use. However, in Mubarak's account the land in question belongs unquestionably to Egyptians who, when they learn from the example of their ancient ancestors, promise to restore it to its full potential. In this model, to modernize the use of land in Egypt, to give it order, is not an innovation, but a return to the country's ancient level of civilization.

The differences between Mubarak's representation of Pharaonic culture and those that came before are apparent. Within the earlier tradition of writing on ancient Egypt, the remnants of the past were a lesson encouraging one to consider one's place with respect to the world and its Creator. Even when considered wondrous, they were an inextricable part of the contemporary landscape of Muslim Egypt and indeed one of its defining features and merits (*fada'il*). Tahtawi sought to bring Pharaonic history into conversation with the present in order to forge a national identity based on the shared experience of living in the land of Egypt. In this sense, the past was not a model that existed apart from how people lived in the present. Importantly, the image of the past was not a plan that Egyptians could emulate, let alone apply. Rather, it was organically part of what living as Egyptians meant. For Tahtawi, the discussion of ancient Egypt was colored by his reading of Ibn Khaldun, for whom the concept of civilization (*al-'umran*) was never separate from the particularities of a given culture. This point is crucial for recognizing the novel significance Pharaonic civilization had for 'Ali Mubarak: no less than the designs drawn up to reorganize the modern city of Cairo, the features of ancient Egyptian civilization had become a *plan* to organize modernity.

PHARAONIC PEDAGOGY

Why isn't Egyptology studied in Egypt the way it is in England? Every educated Egyptian stands before Egyptian monuments knowing nothing more about them but what any ordinary, uneducated person would.
—AHMAD LUTFI AL-SAYYID, "al-Athar al-qadima," *al-Jarida* 1744 (December 8, 1912) in *Taʾammulat fi-l-falsafa*

The truth is that we know less of the value and glory of our country than the tourists do!—AHMAD LUTFI AL-SAYYID, "Athar al-jamal wa-jamal al-athar," *al-Jarida* 1748 (December 12, 1912) in *Taʾammulat fi-l-falsafa*

In 1869, 'Ali Mubarak and his patron, Ismaʿil Pasha, hired the renowned German scholar Heinrich Brugsch to open a school to train Egyptian Egyptologists. According to Donald Malcolm Reid, the school's life was short, and its legacy far from clear. Only a handful of students ever enrolled in the School of Ancient Language (*Madrasat al-Lisan al-Qadim*). Instructions had been given to recruit dark-skinned Egyptian students from the south on the assumption that they were racially closest to the ancient inhabitants of the country.[34] Accounts of the filthy, dilapidated condition of the building in which the school was housed suggest that it was not a high priority for the Ministry of Education, even though Mubarak was a sponsor. In the long run, official neglect would not matter. Following the Franco-Prussian war of 1871, French Egyptologists made it increasingly difficult for German scholars to work in the country: by 1874, Brugsch's school was closed and its pupils dispersed to posts in state bureaucracies. Reid observes that Brugsch's final report placed blame for the failure of the school on Mariette, the director of the Antiquities Service. Brugsch writes, "The Viceroy [Ismaʿil Pasha] was highly satisfied with my work, the minister of education ['Ali Mubarak] was delighted, and the director of government schools almost burst with envy . . . my old friend Mariette worried that it might lead the Viceroy to have it up his sleeve to appoint officials who had studied hieroglyphics to his museum. No matter how much I tried to set his mind at ease, he remained so suspicious that he gave the order to museum officials that no native be allowed to copy hieroglyphic inscriptions."[35] Even if the school was short-lived, two of its students, Ahmad Najib and Ahmad Kamal, later went on to work in the Antiquities Service, where, despite the systematic discrimination they suffered, their careers would have an impact.

Nonetheless, the founding of the school marks a starting point for a new public pedagogy on ancient Egypt, one whose curriculum included studies in history and ancient religion. It is true that the bulk of Egyptian scholars and students (who continued to work in religious institutions such as al-Azhar) were not addressed, let alone affected by the new pedagogy. Yet, in the new elite government schools opened by Mubarak and others, such as the new teachers' college (Dar al-'Ulum, founded in 1871), ancient Egypt entered the curriculum. Moreover, the new pedagogy was not limited to schoolwork: it also began to appear in the press.[36] Even these developments were not enough, for the call continued for more Egyptians to learn about the Pharaonic past since they, unlike Europeans, were organically connected with the material of the past. As one writer put it,

> Not a year goes by without us hearing about an Egyptian discovery that lifts the lid off the past for us. . . . But it is a cause of regret that most of those working to solve the riddles of the past, to uncover what is hidden there, are Westerners. They have written books on the history of the ancient Egyptians, their monuments, their customs, morals, language— everything having to do with them. And they continue to work toward this goal. Still, we see that some of our Egyptian brothers have undertaken the study of these artifacts. . . . In our opinion, they are more capable than Westerners to engage in this study because of their connection to those ancient peoples, and the familiarity of their customs.[37]

Significantly, the new pedagogy included lessons in experience. This was illustrated most vividly in the growing practice among elites to tour the Egyptian countryside and, like European tourists, to make pilgrimages to important Pharaonic antiquities sites. Thus, learning about ancient Egypt was not just about facts, it was also fundamental to an emerging set of national ethics. From the 1880s on, a new attitude—thematized in terms of shame and resurrection—arose among Egyptian intellectuals, especially those who studied at the School of Ancient Language or in Europe. Earlier writers noted the disparity between European and Egyptian learning on the subject, but none had described it in terms of shame. The feeling of shame described by the new generation of intellectuals was not just the sentiment of a few cranks. Rather, it was part of a wider ethical message directed at all modern Egyptians, namely, that the shame of their ignorance of the ancient past should spur them to educate themselves. However, while there was a certain degree of negativity in these accounts, they also offered something positive in compensation. The rewards of learning were considerable because knowing about the Pharaonic past would create the conditions under which modern Egyptians would begin to experience national renaissance.

As for the new history presented in schools and in the press, much of it consisted of translating European sources directly into Arabic: the names of important Pharaonic rulers; the dates of the dynasties; descriptions of periods in which Egypt expanded its empire or was dominated by foreign rulers. At the same time, premodern Muslim sources were relegated to a lower status and less often cited in scholarly and popular essays on ancient Egypt. Not surprisingly, the presentation of historical and cultural information in schoolbooks and guidebooks is dry and pedantic. For instance, a textbook from the 1890s presents the facts of ancient Egypt in a series of questions and answers:

Q. How many historical periods does Egypt have?
A. The history of Egypt is divided into three stages: the pagan (al-Jahiliyya); the Christian; and the Muslim.
Q. How many periods are there in the pagan stage?
A. With regard to Egypt's strength and its decline, there are four phases: the first lasted 1940 years, beginning with the rule of Mena (Misra'im) in 5004 B.C., and ending with the demise of the Tenth Dynasty; the second lasted 1361 years, beginning with the Eleventh Dynasty and ending with the collapse of the Seventeenth Dynasty; the third lasted 1371 years, beginning with the Eighteenth Dynasty and ending with the Thirty-First Dynasty, that is, the triumph of the Persians over Egypt; the fourth phase lasted 713 years, beginning with Alexander the Macedonian and ending with the Roman ruler Theodosius, who issued the order forbidding the

worship of idols, who destroyed temples and shrines, and who ordered the implementation of law according to Jesus (Peace be upon him), in the year 241 before A.H.[38]

The new pedagogy was marked by a new form of address: writers like Tahtawi and Mubarak asserted the relevance of the ancient past by way of explicit argument; now, relevance could be assumed as if it were a point of factual information. Despite the references to the paganism of pre-Christian Egypt, much of the textbook presentation accentuates and even invents similarities between modern, Islamic Egypt and the ancient past. In this regard, Donald Reid notes that as director of the Egyptian school of Egyptology, Brugsch "tried to make the Egyptian pantheon palatable to Muslims. Finding that some epithets of Amon of Thebes, Ptah of Memphis, and other divinities were identical to Islam's ninety-nine 'names' or attributes of God, he emphasized that a single being underlay the surface pluralism of the ancient religion."[39] This did not mean the taint of paganism was forgotten: it was just recontextualized. For instance, an article from the early 1880s discusses the topic of Pharaonic polytheism with great delicacy: "Polytheism [shirk], i.e., the belief in many gods, has been at all times more widespread than monotheism [tawhid]. According to historians who have informed us about the ancient Egyptians, and to what the ancients left behind, their religion was clearly polytheistic, that is, they worshipped many gods. In his *Manners and Customs of the Ancient Egyptians*, the English Egyptologist, Wilkinson, mentions seventy-three gods."[40] Besides historicizing Pharaonic beliefs, the author concludes by stressing the prevalence of monotheism among Egyptians: "Their wise men were monotheists, believing in one God, the Single Creator of all that is in heaven and on earth, the Uncreated One, the One Real God, the Necessary, Who-Exists-Unto-Himself from Eternity."[41] Along these same lines, the textbook cited above states,

The priests of the Egyptians worshipped God the Almighty, praise to Him! And they acknowledged God's oneness. But they hid that from others in order to protect their leadership position. For others, the priests placed statues [tamathil] by whose worship they drew near to God. As time passed, their belief in the oneness of God dissipated, and they began to take the idols [asnam] as gods. Thus, they worshipped Amun, Ptah, Osiris (the Sun), Isis (the Moon), the Sphinx, dogs, crocodiles, cats, scarab beetles, and the greatest of their gods, the calf Ibis. For these deities, they built sanctuaries and temples.[42]

As a story about the development of religion among the ancient Egyptians, this account is fascinating because it places the exceptional moment of Akhenaton's monotheistic heresy at the origin of Pharaonic culture. The point is to assert that the original religion of the Pharaohs was monotheistic and was corrupted only with the passing of time. The language of this passage is also striking in that it reveals a shift in the terminology used to describe this class of artifacts from the pagan past. The less freighted word, *timthal* (likeness, statue), had a long pedigree, appearing in the Qur'an and also in the earliest geographical descriptions of Egypt's wonders. Yet, for the most part, the ancient statuary of Egypt had been most often described as *asnam* (idols, sing. *sanam*) in classical texts. Jabarti, as noted, referred to ancient statuary by this word, with all of its negative cultural connotations. Yet, in the mid-nineteenth century, the word *timthal* began to appear more commonly.[43] In *'Alam al-Din*, Mubarak uses the two words interchangeably, as when he describes the idol worship of the Hindus, Chinese, and pre-Islamic Arab tribes.[44] In one of his first published pieces, the Egyptian Egyptologist Ahmad Kamal also uses both words, as do other authors.[45] Tahtawi was perhaps the first modern to consistently use *timthal* when discussing statuary.[46] The force of the new usage is manifest because it dissociated the objects from the negative connotations of the older, more common word. By the early 1900s, guidebooks, textbooks, and newspaper accounts had completely replaced the term *sanam* with *timthal*.[47] The language used to describe the stuff of ancient Egypt, even those artifacts most implicated in pagan worship, was being stripped of its negative associations: much of the negative pagan imprint ancient Egypt had in the mid-nineteenth century was now gone for some Egyptian intellectuals.

In time, claims about Pharaonic monotheism would become quite common. For instance, the Pharaonic-themed journal *Ra'msis* (Ramses) wrote often on the subject during the 1910s and 1920s, asserting that "like the high priests, Pharaoh believed in the existence of a living god, like our God. This is confirmed in an ancient psalm discovered by Egyptologists and translated by the famous English historian, Wilkinson. It says: 'God is one, the One, with no equal. God is one, He is the One who created

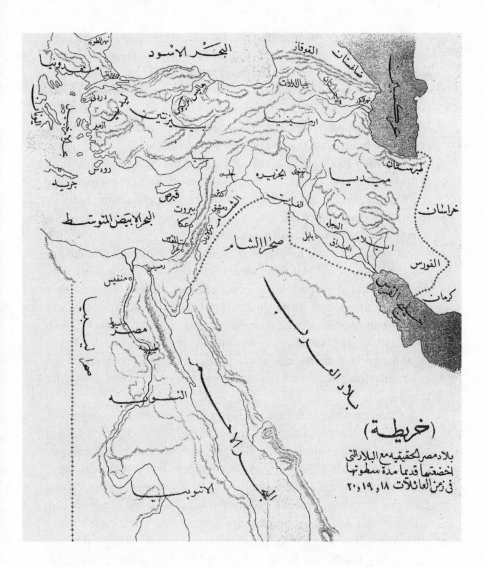

Figure 7. Map from al-Sayyid 'Azmi, *Ithaf abna al-'asr bi-dhikr qudama' muluk Misr* (Bulaq: al-Matba'a al-Amiriyya, 1900). Caption reads: "Map of the actual territories of Egypt, along with its subject countries, from ancient times during the period of its great power, the 18th, 19th, and 20th Dynasties." Note the absence of borders to the south of present-day Egypt.

every thing."[48] Over the next decade, the journal would repeat the same assertion almost verbatim: "The ancient Egyptians believed in a single god. This explains the strength of their faith in the afterlife, the care with which they preserved the bodies of the dead, and erected timeless monuments like the pyramids."[49]

Besides teaching that Pharaonic religion was not quite pagan, the new pedagogy emphasized the imperial power of ancient Egypt. The 1890s textbook cited above presents ancient Egypt as the most powerful nation in the known world. Its detailed list of Pharaonic dynasties pays particular attention to periods of expansion and contraction, explaining that only when Egyptians worked together were they strong and that it was civil wars or treachery that led to Egypt's downfall.

Textbook maps of ancient Egypt show its reach southward through Sudan and Ethiopia and east into Palestine and beyond. Such borders were not just images of the past. It is hard to read such maps of Pharaonic empire during this period—of the joint British-Egyptian imperial venture into Sudan—without considering how they might explain to readers Egypt's nineteenth-century ambitions to dominate its southern neighbor.[50] Echoing the expansionist message of Cairo elites, this same textbook claims that the natural geographic borders of Egypt extended beyond the second cataract.

The imperial Pharaonic past was also a rich source for thinking about Egypt's own ambiguous status as an unofficial British colony following military occupation in 1881. Writing some years later, the influential journalist Ahmad Lutfi al-Sayyid would make this association in unambiguous terms in his influential newspaper *al-Jarida*: "Egypt possessed such greatness in that bygone time that the [Pharaoh] king had approximately twelve princes and others who saw to state protocol. The ambassadors of other kingdoms came to him prostrate, rubbing their noses in the dirt, supplicating before him in hushed voices from fear of the king and his majesty."[51] During a moment when modern Egyptians were attempting to understand their relation to the imperial British crown, such comparisons powerfully implied that the relation could be reversed. Al-Sayyid continues in this vein:

The Egyptians formed an important expansionist nation, proceeding in its empire along the most modern lines of European colonialism today.

When emissaries went forth from Egypt to different regions in Africa they brought with them strong-scented perfume and brightly colored textiles and such, just as Europeans in this era do for the inhabitants of the remote areas of Africa. The object of the art of travel for the ancient Egyptians was not limited to commercial profit. Those travelers won for their country the same benefits that England concealed in the East India Company before it conquered India. Or like Cecil Rhodes. Or what France gained from its missions to the Congo and Sudan. When these emissaries returned to Egypt, they described those countries, and they entrusted the information they had gathered to their government. The Egyptian army would soon follow to conquer those wild countries, conquered easily thanks to the information provided by Egyptian travelers.[52]

In contrast, presumably to the British empire, al-Sayyid describes the Pharaonic empire as one that was tolerant, decentralized, and promoted free trade.

Narratives of history, of course, are never merely about the past. This is especially true of the new Egyptian pedagogy on Pharaonic Egypt at the turn of the century. Authors writing in different media and genres—newspapers, textbooks, guidebooks—would repeatedly and explicitly announce that the point of modern Egyptians' learning about ancient Egypt was that they would learn about themselves. This lesson—that the history of ancient Egypt was the history of the modern Egyptian patriots—was an innovation: relying on European Egyptology, Egyptian intellectuals in different fields transformed that knowledge into something new. The most important aspect of this innovation was that it was not about an object of knowledge that lay outside of Egyptians: in fact, it was more about self-identity than about pieces of information. This chain of reasoning is clearest in the journalism of al-Sayyid during the 1910s. Al-Sayyid is perhaps the first Egyptian intellectual to organize into a single narrative the elements explored in this chapter, bringing the materiality of ancient artifacts and the factual information provided by Egyptological study to bear on the concept of the territorial nation (*watan*) and the feelings, duties, and identity of the patriot (*watani*). He wrote,

Our nation today does not exist independently from the nation of our past. The nation is a single unbroken, unbreakable whole. It is a nation whose social body was created on the day this bounded territorial nation became independent, it possessed a recognizable social order. Then it began to swing from health to sickness, and from sickness to health, until it became what it is today. It is impossible for Egyptians who want to elevate their country to succeed in realizing this wish of theirs if they do not know the reality of their country. Egypt's reality is both its past and its present.[53]

One striking element of the argument linking knowledge of ancient Egypt to the modern, nationalist formulation of Egyptian identity is its rhetoric of shame. That is, it is intended to shame its Egyptian audience by implying that if they have not studied ancient history, they are not authentically Egyptian. He writes, "The patriotism of a person is not complete until he knows his nation, both its ancient past and its present. Whoever is ignorant [*jahala*] of its ancient past is feigning his patriotism, for he who is ignorant of something is treating it with scorn."[54] The innovation of this statement is striking, for only decades earlier Pharaonic civilization had been associated with the ignorance of the pagan era (*al-Jahiliyya*). In al-Sayyid's hands, the terms have been reversed: now any lack of interest in the ancient past has become a sign of ignorance. Thus shame and ignorance became dominant themes in the writing on ancient Egypt by the generation of elite Egyptians who trained in the schools Mubarak and Tahtawi had established. Part of this may have to do with the relationship between the new generation of Egyptian scholars and the Islamic tradition regarding ancient Egypt. Unlike Tahtawi and Mubarak and their contemporaries, who synthesized aspects of older traditions of Pharaonic Egypt with the new science of Egyptology, the new generation ignored or were openly antagonistic toward it.

Although the new discourse relied heavily on the invocation of ignorance and shame, it also offered rewards. In al-Sayyid, to learn about Egypt's glorious past was to set out on the path of national liberation:

Surely, if Egyptians knew these facts recorded in approximately 3500 BC, they would leave behind their depressed self to elevate Egypt, and to show how silly are the opinions of those who suppose that Egypt is naturally incapable of independence and sovereignty. . . . Without a doubt, Egyptians, even educated Egyptians, have so little interest in knowing about ancient Egypt that we are denied the pleasure we once enjoyed. We are denied also the pleasure of persevering in the work of hastening the outcome of our destiny—so that this miserable present might pass, and so that our Egypt might be returned to its ancient past.[55]

The connection between knowledge of the glorious ancient past and a brighter future recurs elsewhere, as when al-Sayyid writes, "The benefit of understanding the ancient Pharaonic and Arab monuments . . . is not limited to the pleasure of seeing the beautiful monuments and achieving a feeling of greatness in the remembrance of Egypt's glorious past. There is an even more powerful benefit, and that is to use knowledge of the past to heal the present, and to replace it with an auspicious future."[56]

Although the Pharaonic past was crucial in Mubarak's formulation of Egyptian modernity, his formulation of knowledge was limited to scholarly learning. For the generation of al-Sayyid, knowledge was something more holistic, involving not just objective facts about the past but their incorporation into personal experience. In this regard, al-Sayyid asserts, "The best model for cultivating taste, to grasp the effects of beauty, is to gaze steadily at the beauty of ruins." In other words, to be real patriots, Egyptians needed to learn to *feel* their ancient history. That is, they needed to visit museums and put themselves in a position to experience their country's ancient monuments. In short, Egyptians were called upon to become tourists in their own country. Earlier writers had made the same plea, arguing that by not touring the countryside of Upper Egypt, Egyptians did not know their own "abode." Ahmad Najib, one of the best-known students from the short-lived School of Ancient Language, was working as antiquities inspector in Upper Egypt by the 1890s. One of the goals of his book *al-Athar al-jalil li-l-qudama' wadi al-Nil* (*The Precious Trace of the Ancients of the Nile Valley*) was to push Egyptians to tour Upper Egypt. Like al-Sayyid and others after him, he connects a number of themes—ignorance of the past, shame of the present, possibility for the future. He writes, "For us [ancient Egypt] is not a distant subject, but one closer than our own jugular. We are the most deserving to study these things, since the owner of the house should best know its condition. It is thus incumbent upon us to be reborn [*nahda*] boldly to ancient Egypt's learning."[57] As we shall see, the language of renaissance (*nahda*) continued to have powerful political and cultural connotations in later decades.

The call for domestic tourism was complicated. The institutions and cultural orientation of tourism in Egypt were largely associated with foreign practices and colonial privileges. Although (or perhaps because) Egyptians had long been exposed to tourists from abroad, the benefits of tourism to Egyptians could not be taken for granted. In the 1890s, authors attempted to explain the merits of antiquities curatorship and foreign tourism. Najib pedantically asserts that there were two benefits to foreign tourism, material and moral:

> As for the material benefits, it is the monuments' fame which has en-larged Egypt's name throughout the world, and attracted so many of the best classes from all over. They are the reason that Egypt has become like a Ka'ba compelling travelers to visit. The travelers spend money as they tour. All types mingle in Egypt's lands, Westerners and Arabs, and foreigners descend on Egypt from the ends of the earth, expending their energy and wealth to see Thebes and Memphis. Commerce spreads through tourism, and the economic situation improves, reinvigorated by the money. Jobs multiply as do opportunities. The face of fate smiles on the poor man. After frowning and distress, his days become seasons of smiles.[58]

Foreign tourism is, in this account, vital to the economic development of the south, a claim that persists to the present. Najib continues, "The people of Upper Egypt liken the season of foreign tourists to the season of the holy pilgrimage in Mecca. What the Antiquities Service receives from tourist expenses visiting museums and monument sites is then spent on the upkeep of the monuments. This sum ends up in the hands of the native Egyptians, since the contractors, agents and laborers are all native Egyptians. It is as if this money no sooner leaves the hand of the foreigner than it goes into the pocket of the native Egyptian."[59] If the benefits of the tourism industry catering to foreigners were largely material, the benefits of Egyptian domestic tourism were deeply moral. Again, Najib writes, "The monuments are Egypt's pride and ornament, and under no circumstance should she be allowed to be stripped of her finery. Moreover, the monuments are like a scroll. . . . You find all that is written on the heart of the stones, as if they were books of the Bible. They are a guide to the sciences of the most ancient of peoples, and reports of a past that had been buried in oblivion. Now, European scientists have nourished us—their writings call out to us."[60]

Egyptian elites did not immediately take up the call to visit museums and tour Pharaonic sites in Upper Egypt, but some, notably the Turko-Circassian royalty, did. Whereas Isma'il Pasha had famously refrained from entering the Antiqakhana when it opened in 1863 (owing, it is said, to his queasy feelings about being in a room with mummies), his successor Tawfiq (r. 1879–92) toured Theban ruins in 1890 and again the following year. By the time of Fu'ad (r. 1923–36) the habit of royal Pharaonic tourism was often reported as news of national importance.

Such tours were sometimes linked to school curricula. In 1891, a group of fifty students from the Teachers' College (Dar al-'Ulum) were taken on a tour of Upper Egypt to study ancient monuments. Their host, John Cook (son of Thomas Cook, founder of the tour company), was "hopeful that 'Abbas II would continue to favor his company,"[61] which had operated steamships on the Nile since 1870 and since 1880 had enjoyed an exclusive concession for steamship travel from Cairo to Aswan and Wadi Halfa. Inviting the Egyptians on board the steamer 'Abbas (named for the new ruler of Egypt), Cook spoke to them: "I met the late Khedive [Tawfiq] and found him very sorry for the Egyptians who thru their good education and knowledge have been appointed in high positions and on account of time the[y] could not voyage in upper-Egypt to visit the monuments and he informed me that very few from the Egyptians [had] voyaged in the country, while we see that tourists come from America and Europe to visit these monuments . . . you must therefore know the history of your ancestors so that you can manage your work after what you have picked up of their good example."[62] As the director of the school, Ibrahim Mustafa, argued, tourism (siyaha) was an important part of education because it exposed students to physical creations of the past and to the sciences, culture, and customs of the people who made them. In other words, it brought students into direct contact with history. For these reasons, Mustafa argues that tourism was an essential component of civilizational progress, "Tourism is the basis of development and civilization ['umran] . . . no country can wear greatness and refinement without it."[63] But, Mustafa notes, Egyptians have a special responsibility to begin their travels in their own country, for becoming a tourist of Upper Egypt was the duty of any serious Egyptian patriot.[64] As a reviewer of the description of the tour would write, its authors "clarified the necessity of traveling first domestically in the traveler's own country."[65] Mustafa writes that the students of Dar al-'Ulum traveled south "to see what the ancient[s] had left for us in the way of monuments, towering structures, fine engravings and skilled frescos, and to see what secrets they had hidden for us in those monuments. It is a fact that Southern Egypt is like the family home as far as all Egyptians are concerned. And a person ought not to be ignorant of his own house, or stay away from it too long, lest the foreigner come to know it better than he."[66] Touring the sites of southern Egypt, Ibrahim's students would have direct experiences of and form attachments to the places, monuments, and artifacts of ancient Egypt. Tourism enabled individuals to connect with and make claims upon the material culture of ancient Egypt—and in so doing, cultivate patriotic sensibilities.

ANCIENT OBJECTS, MODERN SELVES

The new pedagogy involved more than book learning. Its most powerful lessons were intended to help create Egyptian identity itself. And there are good reasons to believe the lessons offered were incorporated by the following generation of Egyptian elites. In memoirs and *Bildungsroman* novels from the 1920s and 1930s, the themes of shame and ignorance, knowledge and resurrection, the ancient Egyptian past and the emerging Egyptian modernity came together to form a new literary culture, commonly referred to by its Arabic name, *al-Fir'awniyya* (Pharaonism).[67] Much of this body of work forms the foundation for the canon of modern Egyptian Arabic literature for the period of the *Nahda* (renaissance). As we shall see, the pedagogy described in the previous pages enabled a coherent and powerful literary narrative of a rebirth that was as personal as it was communal.

The education offered by the tour was crucial to the intellectual formation of Salama Musa (1887–58), whose sponsorship of Pharaonic-themed literature in the 1930s was formidable, as we shall see in the next chapter. As a Copt who became a Fabian as a student in England during the early 1900s and who translated Friedrich Nietzsche, George Bernard Shaw, and others into Arabic, Musa was a central character in Egyptian letters during the 1930s and 1940s.[68] In his autobiography, Musa tells how upon his return to Egypt in 1909, after having spent a year in France, he visited the Thomas Cook travel agency in Alexandria and booked a place on one of their sightseeing tours in Upper Egypt. Because the Thomas Cook Company had, as noted, a monopoly on steamboat travel on the Nile, potential Egyptian tourists had few choices but to visit Upper Egypt on their steamboats. The tour is an important moment in the story of Musa's education, and, in his words, the appreciation of Pharaonic artifacts became more than simply a matter of good taste: it served as the necessary precondition for becoming a modern Egyptian patriot. Musa writes, "I was motivated to take this trip [to Upper Egypt] for rather painful, even shameful reasons. In Europe, whenever I met someone, I was immediately asked questions about the history of the Pharaohs, but I had no answers. We had completely ignored this history, because the English had felt it had better be left unstudied by the twentieth-century descendants of the ancient Egyptians as it might incite in them an undue sense of pride and glory, and even feed our demand for independence."[69] This chain of reasoning expands on that of earlier texts. Musa's account begins with the shameful admission that ancient Egypt has come to belong to Europe, at least morally speaking. This recognition generates a desire to recover that lost tradition. Because this tradition is, in Musa's account, a rightful inheritance, there emerges a powerful sense of self-identification with Pharaonic civilization: learning about the distant Pharaonic past becomes tantamount to learning about himself. This generates a shift from self to community, seen in the pronoun shift from "I" to "we." In other words, Musa's discovery of his Pharaonic self implies that his personal Pharaonic experience is (or should be) typical of his generation, and thus the recovery of the self is tantamount to the recovery of Egyptian community. Finally, this recovery leads inevitably to a sense of patriotism opposed to the English occupation. The most striking element here may be the contexts in which Musa's motivation develops. His interest in ancient Egypt first arises in the context of his colonial encounter with France, where he is asked about ancient Egypt but is unable to answer. Musa claims to be motivated by shame, the result of his ignorance of European knowledge. He even attributes the general ignorance of Egyptians to the scheming of the colonial power. And finally, there is the obvious irony: even as he says it is the English colonial regime that prevented him from learning about ancient Egypt, it is an English tour company which takes him on his tour.

These sentiments are expanded even further in the experiences described by the Egyptian nationalist Ahmad Husayn. Husayn's political party, Misr al-Fatat (Young Egypt), was heavily invested in the idea of resurrecting the glory of the ancient Egyptian dynasties.[70] His memoir describes how as a youth he toured southern Egypt in 1928 and constantly connects the grandeur of the monuments to the power of the Egyptian folk, the peasantry. Learning and teaching this connection becomes especially imperative for Husayn, but he focuses on the fact that for most Egyptians outside the elite the tie between ancient and modern Egypt was neither obvious nor especially relevant. Husayn's tone is emphatic as he admonishes his fellow countrymen: "Egyptians have cut their ties to their ancestors, and they talk about them and look at their accomplishments exactly as tourists and foreigners do. God forbid! Egyptians look upon them with less awe and respect than tourists do!"[71] His condemnation is so strong that it makes of Egyptians who ignore or deny the connection in effect traitors to the nation, obstacles to its progress: "Nothing distinguishes us [as a nation] so much as one thing. This is what keeps us underdeveloped. It keeps us in a wretched condition, tortures us, leads us off the right path. This thing is ignorance, ignorance of our country, ignorance of our history, ignorance of ourselves and our potential."[72]

Husayn's memoir describes his conversion into a Pharaonist, and this censure is key to how he narrates the process. Significantly his personal transformation occurs in relation to Egyptian monuments and artifacts: concrete objects, the frescoes of tombs, temple walls, and columns. This process (according to Husayn) is spontaneous and intuitive but not untutored. It reaches a climax when his group visits the Luxor Temple at night:

Everything that surrounded us filled our souls with enchantment. The moon, the silence and those walls. Even the place itself, in whose shadow tens of thousands of people had once stood to touch the [sacred] pool and ask blessings of God. This place has witnessed the triumphant armies of Egypt departing, filled with strength and spirit, only to return, singing songs of victory. . . . Suddenly, powerful feelings overcame me and I launched into some songs from *The Glory of Ramses*. . . . [73] I began to shout from the depths of my soul, while some of my companions who knew the words joined me: "Carry on in the face of passing time, O Egypt,

O beautiful homeland! Destroy your enemy on Judgment Day! Heed the call and sacrifice yourselves!"[74]

The process of becoming a self for Husayn involves a double possession: he lays claim to the Pharaonic objects around him only insofar as they too lay claim to him. This sense of possession increases as Husayn's tour group enters the temple complex:

> My blood was burning in my veins from the anthems we had been singing. My heart was beating on account of my passing into this solemn monument that I had heard about for so long. I wanted to swallow everything around me. I wanted to carry it with me and hide it in the folds of my soul. . . . I stood while my companions marveled at the extraordinary expertise which had raised these walls and which had righted these cloud-scraping columns. We stood next to these columns, when suddenly the place engulfed us and we almost lost consciousness of our own existence.[75]

After standing dumbfounded by the sublimity of the temple, Husayn goes on to say, he suddenly stood on a rock and, in a scene that prefigures his career as a public speaker, used the example of the antiquities to exhort his companions to (re)build the Egyptian nation: "This greatness which surrounds you should not seem foreign to you. Those who have built it have bequeathed upon you their determination and strength. And Egypt, which at one time carried the banner of humanity, should be resurrected anew and returned to her original path. We need to shake off the dust of indifference and sloth. We need to fill ourselves with faith and determination. We need to gird ourselves with inner strength. We need to labor until Egypt is reborn with her strength, with all her sublimity and greatness."[76] Husayn concludes his account of Luxor Temple by describing it as a personal rebirth that could become the model for a national renaissance: "I was reborn, a new creature. . . . I had been resurrected. And in this way every young man in Egypt ought to be resurrected. I had been created anew, just like every young man in Egypt ought to be created. I [now] saw the columns of Karnak and its monuments, not as ruins, but as if they were a living thing that spoke. . . . I stood there as if I were receiving orders and instructions."[77] This passage further illuminates the theme of double possession. Husayn's account features the relationship between patriot and ancient monument as more than merely that between a living subject and an inanimate object. Insofar as the objects of his description remain as active as his human subjects, Husayn suggests that subjects and objects relate in a fully dynamic and animate fashion. In this memoir, as elsewhere, the material culture of ancient Egypt was not just a backdrop for literature. The objects themselves provided tangible proof of the sorts of civilizational claims Egyptian intellectuals were posing, concrete indicators that the imaginary community of Egypt was not merely a recent fiction.

Experience figured prominently not only in Pharaonist memoirs, but also in novels. Of these, the most emblematic text of the Pharaonist movement is Tawfiq al-Hakim's 'Awdat al-ruh. The novel tells the story of the popular Revolution of 1919 as seen through the eyes of a young boy, Muhsin, whose identity is torn between his loyalty to his Egyptian father, who is of humble peasant origins, and his aristocratic Turkish mother. In one particularly rich segment of the novel, Muhsin returns from studying in the capital to his family's provincial home. Immediately he finds himself alienated from his bickering parents and, acknowledging his attraction to the peasants, takes to wandering among them, all the while wearing the clothes of the effendi class of educated urban elites. In a scene that exemplifies the novel's attempts to imagine a natural alliance between the urban middle class and the peasantry, Muhsin wanders out into the fields and arrives at a primitive hut. Curious, he gazes into the dwelling and sees a cow nursing her calf. Muhsin is astonished to see a tiny child pushing against the calf, struggling to reach the cow's udder. This pastoral image precipitates a transformation within the character of Muhsin himself:

Muhsin marveled at this scene and felt deep, powerful emotions. His mind, however, had nothing to add to that deep feeling. Emotion is the knowledge of the angels, whereas rational logic is human knowledge. If one wanted to translate his feelings into the language of reason and intellect, then it'd be said that he responded in his soul to that union between the two different creatures joined together by purity and innocence. . . . Although Muhsin did not yet know this with his tender intellect . . . he did perceive with his heart and inner eye. . . . But there was one thing Muhsin was able to grasp with his intellect and that was thanks to his study of ancient Egyptian history: this scene reminded him suddenly, for no particularly strong reason, that the ancient Egyptians worshipped animals, or at least portrayed the one God with images of different animals.[78]

Along with his sense of alienation, Muhsin struggles throughout the novel with his ability to understand without feeling and to feel without understanding. It is a tension that remains unresolved until, well into the second half of the novel, the theme of ancient Egypt suddenly intrudes. The ability of the ancient to unite the apparent differences of the modern and to synthesize feeling and understanding is precisely what the Pharaonic signifies in the remainder of the novel: "Didn't the ancient Egyptians know that unity of existence and that union that transcended the different groups of creatures? Aren't all these creatures God's creation? The feeling of being merged with existence—of being merged in God—that was the feeling of that child and calf suckling together. It was the feeling of that ancient, deeply rooted Egyptian people. Wasn't there an angelic, pure-hearted Egypt that survived in Egypt? Egypt had inherited, over the passing generations, a feeling of union, but without knowing it."[79] Soon after this scene, Muhsin passes through a village inhabited by peasants who work for his father. When he overhears that feuding neighbors have poisoned a water buffalo, he draws near. The entire village mourns the loss of the animal as if it were human. Slaughtering the animal, the peasants split up the meat to share among themselves. The scene is important because it prompts Muhsin to begin to think of himself as part of a nation of peasants inextricably rooted in the past. Moreover, this new identification finds its expression as a resurrection after death:

That luminous happiness, the essence of which was unknowable for him, returned to him. It came back to him . . . like life coming from death. What an amazing nation these Egyptian farmers were. Could such a beautiful sense of solidarity and feeling of unity still exist in this world? The next day . . . for the first time, he felt the beauty of life deep within him. For the first time, he perceived that spirit which pervades Creation. . . . An obscure, buried feeling welled up in him: eternity was an extension of just such a moment. And Muhsin's intuition was sound. If he had known more about the history of the [Nile] Valley, he would have understood that its ancient inhabitants had believed that there was no paradise beyond theirs and no other form of eternity, that God had not created any paradise save Egypt.[80]

If he had any doubts about whose child he was, they are dispelled: from this point on he feels descended from the peasantry, descended from the ancient Egyptians, and thus truly Egyptian. With this transformation, the novel's references to the Osiris myth become slightly more overt: the figure of resurrection expresses Muhsin's identification with the peasant nation of Egypt, the recovery of his authentic self, and the nation's uprising against colonial rule.[81]

Here the text changes course, transforming this intuitive identification with the Pharaonic past into a self-conscious one. The patriotic feeling of unity with the Pharaonic past is not complete until it is also explicitly known. At this point in the narrative, Muhsin's parents entertain a British inspector and a French archaeologist while Muhsin is treated to a lesson about the history and relevance of ancient Egypt. The scene begins when, relaxing after lunch, the French expert criticizes the British colonial figure for not giving Egyptian peasants the respect they deserve: "These 'ignorant' people know more than we do! . . . It's a truth that unfortunately Europe doesn't understand. This people, whom you consider ignorant, does know many things. It knows by means of the heart, not Reason. Supreme wisdom is in their blood although they do not [consciously] know it. There is a force within them of which they are not aware."[82] The irony is unequivocal. In a story about how Egyptians become conscious of their true self, conscious of the ancient spirit of Egypt and, in this consciousness, rise up against the oppression of colonial rule, it is a French Egyptologist who connects the dots for the protagonist. The European archaeological expert becomes the central figure in articulating the notion of an unconscious connection to the past, a force which lies buried in the identification with ancient Egypt: "Yes, the Egyptian may not know it, but there are brief moments when that knowledge and experience surface to assist him even without him knowing their source. For us Europeans, this explains those moments of history when we see Egypt leap forward quickly. . . . You don't imagine, Mr. Black, that the thousands of years in Egypt's past have disappeared and left no trace in these descendants?"[83] The statement that "the Egyptian may not know it" lends urgency to the project to make explicit what is now merely latent. Later the French

Egyptologist adds that Egyptians "don't know the treasures they possess."[84] The interpretive authority of European characters in this passage is significant and surfaces throughout the literature of Pharaonism. Despite its apparent affirmation of Europeans' scientific superiority, this literature poses an essential difference between the superficial quality of their knowledge about ancient Egypt and the deeper knowledge of ancient Egypt that only modern Egyptians can directly experience. Hakim's novel presents two colonial figures in discussion of the possibilities if modern Egyptians would only remember their distant past: how they would reinherit their land and modernize and increase its productive capacities. As Muhsin listens and groups of peasants continue to work outside the window, the French Egyptologist tells the British official,

> There is definitely a tie [between modern and ancient Egypt]! Those peasants singing in unison represent individuals who, by faith and feeling, have merged into a single social body. Here today these grandchildren, these peasants, feel the unity which surrounds them. . . . It was such feeling which built the Pyramids. . . . How do you suppose this people was able to build such an edifice unless they transformed themselves into a single human mass enduring pain for a single goal? . . . Don't look down on those poor people today. The force lies buried within them. . . . Don't be surprised if . . . they bring forth another miracle besides the Pyramids.[85]

Muhsin then returns to study in Cairo, where he now not only knows what patriotism is, but feels it, and he joins the revolution when it breaks out. The revolution in the novel is channeled through these assertions about ancient Egypt: the Pharaonic represents the eternal soul of the Egyptian and remains an enduring source of national strength, even under colonial rule.

Admittedly, Hakim's novel does not know what to do about the colonial, mediatory role played by Europeans. Europeans separate modern Egyptians from their ancient past and also rejoin them. Just as much as those of the nineteenth century, twentieth-century Egyptian intellectuals coming to terms with the ancient past would be confronted by European domination of the field of Egyptology. Pharaonist enthusiasts and nationalists alike had no choice but to read texts composed by European authors, conduct tours of their own country via European transportation networks, and study under European Egyptologists. European Egyptologists were as much a sign of colonial rule as they were the key to modern Egyptian self-discovery, renaissance, and revolution. Still, if the lessons of Egyptology could be used by people like Cromer to colonize Egypt, they could also be transformed in the hands of nationalists to contest colonial rule.

From the mid-nineteenth century, Egyptological discourse on Pharaonic antiquity had enabled European archaeologists and curators, administrators and casual tourists to make informed statements about ancient Egypt that were also claims on modern Egypt. Now, as Egyptian elites began to take this discourse to heart, it became a powerful language for articulating a new sense of Egyptian identity, encompassing experiences and aspirations that were profoundly personal and collective. Inescapable are the ironies of the process of cultural translation which allowed the same group of cultural artifacts, narratives, and images to mean such different things to different actors: Pharaonic Egypt was no less a source for contesting colonial hegemony than it had been for legitimating it. In the work of Tahtawi and 'Ali Mubarak, cultural Pharaonism was central to Egyptian responses to growing European power in the Middle East even before direct colonial rule. In the autobiographies and fictions of nationalist intellectuals growing up during the British occupation of Egypt (1882–1956), the significance of ancient Egypt expanded even further: to know and feel ancient Egypt was crucial to national liberation.

The theme of resurrection, inspired in part by the Osiris myth, dominated Pharaonist literary and political culture. Yet this theme recurred throughout *Nahda* culture, and Pharaonism pointed to only one of the classical pasts that could be brought back to life. Indeed, social and cultural modernists of the period attempted to resurrect pasts that were variably Islamic, Coptic, Arab, or Ottoman in orientation. During the early 1900s, there was a wide variety of cultural-political symbolic systems from which Egyptian intellectuals might draw inspiration. There were images of Islamic civilization institutionalized locally in neighborhood mosques and in regionwide religious brotherhoods. The enduring legacy of the Islamic past was broadly deliberated throughout the region, as in the press debates about the *Umma*, or the Caliphate. In this period pan-Arabism had wide circulation in the Levant and to the east, first in order to contest Ottoman rule and, later, French and British domination.

As an ideology, Pharaonism differed from other ideologies in that it was grounded in images of territory and civilization that were simultaneously concrete and abstract, both familiar and distant. In fact, its very distance from the modern period made it quite flexible. The Pharaonic past allowed for an image of Egyptian nationalism that transcended and reconciled existing class, regional, and, especially, sectarian differences. That early proponents of Egyptian territorial nationalism embraced Pharaonism was no accident. The monuments were undeniably present in the Egyptian countryside, and their ubiquitous local visibility lent the Pharaonic past a sense of concreteness and familiarity. Also, contrary to Islamist and pan-Arab concepts of community, Pharaonism was wholly indigenous to the Nile River Valley. This allowed for a distinct territorial nationalism in Egypt—an image of Egyptian community that was rooted in the landscape of Egypt. Moreover, Pharaonism was flexible enough to represent the particularity of local landscapes of Egypt while also general enough to transcend the actual social divisions within these landscapes. It was this local visibility, combined with its strategic distance from the antagonisms of modern society, that made Pharaonism so powerful to this generation of Egyptian intellectuals.

Given the century of distance between them, there is no straight line from Tahtawi's studies in Paris to al-Hakim's novel. But the theme of national rebirth through an informed appreciation of the past, originally championed by Tahtawi and Mubarak and then transformed by a later generation, remained basically the same. However, as the source of what counted as authoritative learning and science changed, what it meant to be informed also changed. For the first Egyptian intellectuals confronting the West during the colonial period, this meant synthesizing Arabo-Islamic scholarship on the ancient past with European knowledge and science. For later generations, it meant increasingly ignoring the former while absorbing more and more of the latter. Along with this shift in knowledge came shifting notions of what it meant to appreciate. By the early 1900s, as authors insisted that Egyptian patriots internalize the kind of knowledge they were learning about the Pharaonic past, the notion of appreciation was also changing, taking on a personal tone that was often linked to feelings of shame. The rhetorical power of shame discourse and pedagogy lay in its ability to challenge and convert negative moral judgments into positive knowledge of the self. Indeed, the theme of resurrection hinged on the understanding that pedagogy would transform Egyptian ignorance into enlightenment, backwardness into development, stagnation into dynamism, weakness into strength, and so on. In this way, learning to appreciate artifacts of the ancient past was tantamount to learning to recognize one's true self and community, and the repossession of the past was also the repossession of the present. For all these reasons, it is tempting to read the rise of Pharaonism in its own terms, that is, as an uncomplicated narrative of gradual enlightenment culminating in national liberation. As we shall see in the next chapters, such a reading is only preliminary, since the terms of Pharaonism were more ambivalent and contested than this initial presentation makes them out to be.

Figure 9. *Abu Naddara Zarqa'* 3:11 (May 30, 1879). French caption reads: "After having sold the harvests of seven fat years as futures, Pharaoh auctions off the Pyramids." Colloquial Egyptian Arabic caption reads: "Pharaoh calls out: Hey tourists! Step on up to an auction! Hey antiquities lovers! The Sphinx. Stones from the Pyramids. The sale's in cash, and pounds are our currency, though not brass ones. A one and a two—let's go! Start your bids, people!"

Two Pharaohs

In countless cartoons, fictional scenes, and dialogues (*muhawarat*), the journalist Ya'qub Sanu', an Egyptian Jew of Italian descent, derided Isma'il for acting the Pharaoh in the pages of his popular colloquial periodical, *Abu Naddara*. The depictions appearing in the late 1870s were unflattering, harsh, and hilarious, poking fun at the tyranny, capriciousness, and illegitimacy of Egypt's Turko-Circassian rulers as well as their supposed lack of religion. How did these images of Pharaoh, which had more to do with age-old Qur'anic narratives than with recent Egyptological discoveries, come into being? The answer to this question goes to the root of colonial rule in Egypt: as public intellectuals like Sanu' grasped the injustices of the emergent colonial order, they found inspiration in those traditions of considering ancient Egypt that modern education had begun to eclipse.

The development projects of Egypt's nineteenth-century rulers were expensive. By 1876, as Khedive Isma'il began to default on his loans, British and French interests had established the Commission of the Public Debt, which oversaw increasingly greater shares of the Egyptian economy. The loss of economic sovereignty was bound to create serious political repercussions, and in 1879 the commission forced Isma'il to abdicate, replacing him with Tawfiq, whose inexperience they correctly guessed would play in their favor during the tempestuous negotiations over Egypt's finances. Rather than resolve Egypt's economic and political crisis, Tawfiq's accession only intensified the resentment felt by Egyptians. Not only did they direct their anger at Europeans for their hegemonic position in Egypt's economy, they also challenged the Turko-Circassian elites whose spending had largely created the debt crisis. It did not help that these same elites appeared all too willing to capitulate Egypt's sovereignty in order to maintain their privileges over Egypt's Arabic-speaking populace. In 1881, questions about undue foreign influence and the legitimacy of Tawfiq's rule became intractable. In the army, ethnic Egyptian junior officers chafed at a new draft law that officially reserved the military's higher ranks for Turko-Circassian elites. Under the leadership of a junior Egyptian officer of peasant descent, Col. Ahmad 'Urabi, Egyptian officers petitioned Tawfiq to consider their protest. Tawfiq replied by ordering their arrest. By the time their regiments rescued 'Urabi and the others from the barracks in which they were being detained, an uprising was under way in the military ranks. As others, including ethnic Egyptian notables, constitutionalists, discontented Ottoman elites, and peasants, joined 'Urabi, the demands widened: first, representation in the government, and then a constitution.

To Egypt's creditors, the situation was alarming. Not surprisingly, both the French and British opposed the new government. Likewise, European powers were frightened by the reformers' demands for an end to the system of extraterritoriality known as the capitulations, which gave European citizens special privileges in Egypt's freewheeling economy. As the power of the nationalists grew, the British and the French turned increasingly anxious. As Tawfiq saw his power waning, he turned more and more to the French and British ambassadors for help. In 1882, when it began to seem only a matter of time before the Assembly would depose Tawfiq, the British and the French began to move more openly to support him. After British warships anchored in Alexandria's harbor in a show of strength, riots between Egyptians and foreign nationals broke out in the city. The British responded by bombarding the city, devastating much of it. Invited by Tawfiq, British troops landed. Within weeks they defeated the Egyptian army and arrested 'Urabi and other members of the nationalist government. Egypt fell under British colonial rule.

By all accounts, Sanu' was the most articulate journalist supporting 'Urabi's government.[1] A publisher, satirist, and fiction writer, Sanu' is credited with coining the nationalist slogan of the era: Egypt for the Egyptians.[2] Throughout this period Sanu' spoke out vehemently against the abuses and structural injustices of the international finance system that had created Egypt's debt crisis: from the usurious practices of European financiers to the foreign political and military cliques who enforced the power of the banks. He complained about corrupt local elites and inept notables, and how peasants were forced to bear the economic and social burdens of the Pashas' bankrupting development schemes. At one point, Isma'il Pasha had been Sanu''s patron. But as the debt crisis intensified, Sanu''s criticism of the ruler became increasingly sharp and daring. Among the many forms his criticism took, Sanu' drew on Pharaonic images in the struggle he waged in the pages of *Abu Naddara*.

When Isma'il closed *Abu Naddara*, Sanu' moved to Paris. There he continued to publish the journal, changing its name and appearance often to fool censors and customs officials. After the end of the 'Urabi revolt, his printing shop became a regular meeting place for other exiles from Egypt, from Muhammad 'Abduh to Jalal al-Din al-Afghani. Though illegal, copies of *Abu Naddara* were smuggled into Egypt, where they were especially popular with Egyptians who had supported the 'Urabi revolt. When Isma'il was deposed and sent into exile in 1879, *Abu Naddara* took special delight in the fall of the tyrant, that is, the modern Pharaoh. In a long fictional dialogue published in the pages of one of the instantiations of his journal, Sanu' resurrects Mehmed 'Ali Pasha, who is appalled by the state of Egypt under Isma'il. He puts the latter on trial. Isma'il's prosecutor, the persona of Abu Naddara, exclaims, "Isma'il! Isma'il! . . . You have ruined Egypt and made its children unhappy. Unbridled liar! Wicked hypocrite! I have not forgotten your words when you mounted the throne of the great Mehmed 'Ali. You said: ' . . . I will open the eyes of my subjects to the lamp of civilization! . . . Under my reign, Egypt will be happier than it ever was under the Pharaohs, more resplendent and glorious than it was under the Ptolemies!' . . . But alas, you misled us. Later you betrayed us. And finally, you murdered us!"[3] Isma'il responds to his accuser, "I dug canals, I imported machines . . . and I followed the French formula: liberté, égalité, fraternité!" The 'ulama' then step forward to make their case against Isma'il: "The infidel Isma'il is mistaken! May God's curse fall on him!" Tawfiq is similarly tried and is told, "Just as Pharaoh and Haman were punished on earth, so too will you and your father be." At this point in the story, "Six large peasants armed with whips seize the two tyrants," who are then beaten, fed slow poison, and drowned in the Nile.[4]

Isma'il and Tawfiq were not the only rulers of modern Egypt to be called Pharaohs. This ancient Egyptian figure of tyranny was famously invoked again a few years later to refer to Evelyn Baring (later Lord Cromer), the former head of the commission who governed Egypt from the outset of the British occupation. Cromer ruled Egypt for a quarter of a century and resigned shortly during the economic collapse of 1907, just months after the Dinshiway incident and trial, in which a number of Egyptians were unjustly tried and executed.[5] For Egyptians (and many others), the incident illustrated the injustice and gross negligence of decades of British rule, and they were glad to see Cromer leave. For his part, Cromer was unapologetic and used his departure as an occasion to boast about the legacy of British rule. Congratulating England for the favors it had done for Egypt, Cromer concluded that Egypt was still not ready for self-government, reiterating the same theme of modern Egyptian stagnation and decline that appears throughout his writing: "Can any sane man believe that a country which has for centuries past been exposed to the worst forms of misgovernment at the hands of its rulers, from Pharaohs to Pashas, and in which, but ten years ago, only 9.5 per cent of the men and 3 per cent of the women could read and write, is capable of suddenly springing into a position which will enable it to exercise full rights of autonomy?"[6] In a farewell address at the Cairo Opera House in May 1907, Cromer singled out for attack the nineteenth-century rulers of Egypt, from Mehmed 'Ali to Isma'il Pasha. The audience, which included many Egyptian notables, sat in silence. The furor created by Cromer's parting shots prompted a number of Egyptians to reply to Cromer's address. Only days after the speech, the Egyptian poet Ahmad Shawqi published these lines, which remain among the greatest of neoclassical Arabic poetry:

> Are these your times, or those of Isma'il? Or are you Pharaoh lording over the Nile?
> Or are you absolute ruler in the land of Egypt, never questioning, never responding?
> O you who enslaves necks with your power, could you not have taken a path to men's hearts?
> When you departed, the country thanked God, as if you were an incurable disease taking leave.[7]

While the gist of Shawqi's attack on Cromer is clear, his citation of Pharaoh is slightly complicated. In the first line of the poem, Shawqi asks about whether Egypt's present moment belongs to Cromer, Isma'il Pasha, or Pharaoh before them. Shawqi appears to be compiling a list of despots, punctuated by the figure of Pharaoh. In this reading, the poem invokes the figure of ancient Pharaoh to criticize Cromer's tyranny in the present: like Pharaoh, he has established himself as the absolute sovereign; like Pharaoh, the colonial viceroy rules by force and violence. Shawqi continues:

> You threatened us with perpetual slavery and continuing humiliation, and a
>   state of being that would never see change,
> Did you think that God was less powerful than you, incapable of effecting
>   change or alteration?
> God rules over kings, and states that vie with him for power do not last.
> Before you Pharaoh was greater in strength, and a mightier backer to have
>   in this world.[8]

Here again, the subject is Cromer's tyranny and injustice. There is nothing ambiguous in his accusation that the British ruler had attempted, like Pharaoh, to place himself on the level of God. Yet Shawqi makes a distinction: while Cromer's tyranny may resemble that of Pharaoh, the scope of his power falls far short. Shawqi's figure is thus not merely a citation of a received figure—"Pharaoh as tyrant"—but a careful poetic reinvention of it. Pharaoh here articulates the despotism of the British viceroy while also insisting upon the superiority of Egypt's ancient past over its colonial present.

Though mainstream literary Pharaonism often imagined the rulers of ancient Egypt as benign, others were there to remind Egyptians of the less savory aspects of ancient Egyptian life. The figure of tyrannical Pharaoh has recurred at key moments in modern Egyptian history, to refer to rulers who abuse the power they wield or who fail to use it for the right and the good. As Shawqi's poem illustrates, the modern reference to Pharaoh is not a mere citation of a very old tradition, but something new. At the same time, the persistence of the negative figurative tradition of Pharaoh indicates an abiding tension within the modern appreciation of the ancient past.

4

The Discovery of Tutankhamen's Tomb: Archaeology, Politics, Literature

The work on which I am engaged has been done not for gain, but in the interest of science. The discovery of the tomb [of Tutankhamen] has produced great benefits for Egypt, and for the Egyptian Antiquities Department in particular. It has also produced rights in the Earl of Carnarvon, the author of those benefits.—HOWARD CARTER, *The Tomb of Tut•Ankh•Amen*

My young king, are they going to transport you to the museum and set you next to the Qasr al-Nil barracks to add insult to injury? So that, my free king, you might look out over your occupied country? So that you might see your enslaved people? So that you might learn that those who robbed your grave now dig another for your nation?—FIKRI ABAZA, "Ila Tutankhamun," *al-Ahram*, February 20, 1924

In the autumn of 1922, the British archaeologist Howard Carter focused his seventh season of excavations near a site where Belzoni had dug a century earlier. Sifting through the area Egyptian workers found the entrance to an unknown tomb that had been buried under the debris accumulated by a century of intense digging and exploration. In his popular account of the discovery, Carter described the dramatic moment he and his team of excavators punched through the wall separating the entrance passage and the antechamber of what they would soon identify as King Tutankhamen's tomb:

> At first I could see nothing, the hot air escaping from the chamber causing the candle flame to flicker, but presently, as my eyes grew accustomed to the light, details of the room within emerged slowly from the mist, strange animals, statues, and gold—everywhere the glint of gold. For the

moment—an eternity it seemed to the others standing by—I was struck dumb with amazement, and when Lord Carnarvon, unable to stand the suspense any longer, inquired anxiously, "Can you see anything?" it was all I could do to get out the words, "Yes, wonderful things."[1]

Wonderful things. Carter's famous understatement is more complicated than it first appears. On the one hand, it captures a sense of marvel, a recognition of the significance of the discovery he had just made. On the other hand, it conveys Carter's inability to comprehend the stuff before his eyes. Positioned at the end of a chapter, this coy description of wonder—important, but as yet uncomprehended—serves to heighten the dramatic tension of Carter's narrative. He admits as much in the subsequent pages.

Of the two words, "wonderful" seems the more significant at first glance because it resonates with the long literary history of the wonders and marvels of ancient Egypt. Like others writing in this tradition, Carter dwells on the sense of immediacy in the scene of discovery. In a set of exhilarating passages on the theme of wondrous discovery, Carter describes how time itself seems to recede in the mind of the excavator:

> I suppose most excavators would confess to a feeling of awe—embarrassment almost—when they break into a chamber closed and sealed by pious hands so many centuries ago. For the moment, time as a factor in human life has lost its meaning. Three thousand, four thousand years maybe, have passed and gone since human feet last trod the floor on which you stand, and yet, as you note the signs of recent life around you . . . you feel it might have been but yesterday. The very air you breathe, unchanged throughout the centuries, you share with those who laid the mummy to its rest. Time is annihilated by little intimate details such as these, and you feel an intruder.[2]

He then turns to describe the wonder of the space in which he finds himself, not purely in terms of a subjective experience, but rather as something arising in relationship with the objects he beholds: "The effect was bewildering, overwhelming. I suppose we had never formulated exactly in our minds just what we had expected or hoped to see, but certainly we had never dreamed of anything like this, a roomful—a whole museumful it seemed—of objects, some familiar, but some the like of which we had never seen, piled one upon another in seemingly endless profusion."[3] In part, it is the "excess," with novelty and variety in abundance, of the material which bewilders Carter in his account and which provokes his sense of awe and wonder. The "endless profusion," this chaotic pile of stuff—or, as Carter called it in his report, "boodle"—is likewise a source of amazement. Carter's unlikely comparison between this chamber of undifferentiated stuff and that of a museum not only conveys a description of the vast quantity of material contained in the space, but also prefigures its eventual destination.

The museum analogy sheds some light on the unlikely complexity of Carter's initial exclamation about "things." Following Heidegger, Bill Brown has recently observed that, a thing is not merely an object.[4] Indeed, it is often used to refer to matter not yet named, not yet specified—a placeholder for stuff not yet properly defined as objects. In other words, "wonderful *things*" might be said to express the moment of first encounter between the archaeologist and the material on which he will work. The things Carter describes as wonderful exist in a moment of indeterminacy. That is to say, "things" describes a moment that comes before the normative relationship that exists between the archaeologist and his proper objects—artifacts. In Carter's account, it is a fleeting moment. Soon the wall to the antechamber is broken open and laid bare to the eyes, electric lamps, and camera lenses of the excavation team. Before long, these "things" become artifacts to be catalogued, antiquities for public exhibition, images and figures for mass audiences.

WONDERFUL THINGS, EGYPTOLOGICAL ARTIFACTS

Carter's account of the Tutankhamen excavation invites one to reexamine the discourse of the artifact one century after its emergence. In some senses the discovery of Tutankhamen in 1922 might be thought of as a repetition of Belzoni's removal of the Memnon head in 1816. Yet, like all repetitions, it is not just the similarities but also the divergences that are significant. As was true of the Memnon head, the transformation of Tutankhamen's things into artifacts involved work that happened to (and in) the matter itself. The physical quality of some of this labor was obvious, such as the excavation of material from tombs, the transportation of material for study and exhibition in the colonial metropole, and the literary description of such objects. Each of these activities took the material as its direct object, shifting its location and contexts, framing and reframing it to foreground and background different meanings.

At the same time, the transformation of things into objects also involved subjective shifts within the agents of archaeological labor. For Carter and his contemporaries, there was no question whether the treasures of King Tutankhamen's tomb were valuable artifacts. It was axiomatic for them to assert the objects' aesthetic and historical value even before their original significance to ancient Egyptians was understood. These values, embedded within the very matter of the artifact, appeared to Carter and others to be facts. At the same time, these objects were critical to the constitution of divergent senses of the self in modern Egypt. As we saw earlier, the transformation of "things-found-in-Egypt" into artifacts and the scientific methods that attended this transformation, were essential for European attitudes about their own identity as Europeans in the metropole. In colonial Egypt, artifacts helped to express an essential difference between Europeans and Egyptians. Likewise, for many modern Egyptians antiquities became material facts attesting to their own history and identity. This was especially so with regard to the artifacts produced from the discovery of King Tutankhamen's tomb, an event that placed the appreciation of ancient Egypt squarely in the center of modern Egyptian political and expressive culture. Thus, while the scientific value of these artifacts appeared to be neutral, there was nothing neutral at all about their broader significances. European Egyptologists made reasonable though increasingly expansive claims that they were in the best position to care for Egyptian antiquities as scientific objects. The precarious state of objects found at excavation sites like those at Tutankhamen's tomb served to make such assertions appear self-evident. In this way, the claims of Egyptologists such as Carter resonated deeply with the long-standing arguments that legitimated the European administration of modern Egypt on the basis of disinterested, rational governance. For their part, Egyptians made claims on the same objects, asserting that they were the descendents of the civilization that produced them and that they were uniquely positioned to be the moral caretakers of King Tutankhamen's tomb. Arguments in favor of Egyptian management of the Tutankhamen excavation site were explicit analogues to arguments for Egyptian self-rule.

Noting the social processes by which things became artifacts allows one to inquire into both kinds of histories—those that focus on human subjects and those that focus on material objects—and to see them as imbricated in one another. Moreover, it allows one to see them both as largely constructed, the result of deliberate (and indeliberate) products of thought and labor. It is crucial, if obvious, to note that there was nothing natural or inevitable about the kind of archaeological activity in which Carter and other Europeans were involved in colonial Egypt. This is not to deny that there were good reasons for allowing highly skilled archaeologists to search for Tutankhamen's tomb and to put its artifacts on display in a national showcase, the Egyptian Museum in Cairo. Rather, it is to begin to ask about the innovation and ambiguities of the institutions of exhibition and appreciation—from the archaeological dig to the Antiquities Service to the collection of the Egyptian Museum—that not only transformed Carter's "wonderful things" into something else entirely, but also transformed the self-perception of museum visitors, Egyptian and European alike. The peculiarity of these institutions becomes all the more significant when one considers how Carter's assumptions about the stuff he encountered diverged from those of earlier generations of European travelers (then archaeologists), and even more radically from those of the subaltern Egyptians who provided the bulk of the local knowledge and labor necessary for the excavation. To interrogate the disparities in attitudes toward the objects is to ask about the institutions and habits that framed how Europeans and Egyptians viewed and experienced the objects in shared and diverging ways. For instance, the institutions supporting Carter's excavation (such as the Metropolitan Museum of Art) and those Egyptian governmental agencies regulating his activity (the Antiquities Service and the Department of Public Works) were very much in a state of development. Within months of the discovery, whatever mutually beneficial arrangements they once enjoyed fell apart as the various actors began to fiercely struggle with one another in court and in the press. Such institutions—such conflicts—were part of what it meant to turn "wonderful things" into artifacts.

Showing how "wonderful things" started to become artifacts in 1922 requires a mapping out of the various institutions, traditions, practices, and habits which produced the effect of artifaction so effectively enacted in Carter's narrative. Yet this process was neither single-minded nor centralized. Instead, the transformation of things into artifacts was incremental and subject to reversals. As we saw in the example of the Memnon head, an object's value might change drastically depending on how it moved in and out of antiquities markets, from the control of one institution to another, or how its image appeared in one medium of representation rather than another. Similarly, the networked quality of artifacts with one another—the fact that an individual article's significance existed in constellation with other objects, institutions, and people—meant that its value would inevitably change with the discovery of other artifacts. At the same time, the entangled quality of artifacts meant that efforts to recontextualize and reframe them were bound to remain incomplete, that traces of their earlier contexts would trail them.

Even taking into account these ambiguities of discovery, it is impossible to overestimate the degree to which the discovery of King Tutankhamen's tomb changed everything about how Egyptian national elites looked at their past. If there was a single event that pushed the largely scholarly interest in the Pharaonic past and its artifacts into the forefront of the mainstream political and expressive cultures of modern Egypt, it was this. King Tutankhamen's tomb yielded tangible objects and indelible images of what an Egyptian sovereign might look like. Moreover, the Pharaonist vision of the past converged in many places with the central ideas and slogans of the national liberation movement, led by Sa'd Zaghloul's Wafd Party, which was territorialist and nonsectarian, as opposed to Ottoman, Arabist, or Islamist in character. While Pharaonist iconography had been relatively marginal to the ideology of Egypt's Revolution of 1919, it soon became quite significant to many of the era's nationalist leaders. That sovereignty was something ancient to Egypt; that Egypt possessed an eternal national spirit that deserved the right to be reborn and the right to express itself; that Egyptian national identity predated and transcended the religious, class, and regional differences of modern Egyptians: these ideas coincided with the central aspirations and demands of Egyptian nationalists throughout the 1920s.

Thus the significance of the discovery of Tutankhamen—Tut—goes well beyond the science of Egyptology to reach the entire range of political and expressive cultures in Egypt, from architecture to literature, from nationalist politics in the new Parliament to how Egyptian elites negoti-ated issues of sovereignty under British occupation. In Europe and North America, Tut's discovery fueled a similarly popular taste for Pharaonic themes and styles, from design and art to cinema and literature.[5] For all these reasons, one cannot tell the story of Pharaonism in Egypt without exploring the multiple meanings that the discovery—as archaeological find, as national treasure, as symbol of national sovereignty, and as mate-rial index of the kind of cultural resurrection the *Nahda* represented—produced in the Egypt of the 1920s.

Yet the ambiguities are crucial to understanding how this single event provided so much fuel for the expression of conflict, and how the study of material objects gave rise to the production of so much creative political and literary culture. The conflicts and cultural fecundity of the moment derived from the connections and gaps between the various discourses informing how King Tutankhamen's discovery was absorbed by Egyp-tians. Many of these ambiguities can be brought to light by examining how Carter's discovery has been remembered. The official history of Egyptology, as we saw, distinguished a "before" and "after" located around the moment when the Memnon head was collected, when the profession-alism of Egyptology is said to have triumphed over the amateurism of antiquarianism. This separation implied a number of other triumphs as well: empirical method over received tradition, public transparency over private modes of knowledge, disinterested research over bias and specu-lation, order and enlightenment over chaos and commercialism. Hereaf-ter it was understood that historical inquiry would inform issues of taste concerning Egyptian art rather than taste informing the writing of his-tory. In terms of writing, this meant that the literary and impressionistic character of earlier accounts of excavation gave way to more scientific styles—that is, less voiced, less anecdotal styles—of description.

In the narrative of enlightened Egyptology, the discovery of Tutankha-men's tomb plays front and center. In this regard, it is useful to note that Carter had worked under William Matthews Flinders Petrie, conven-tionally remembered as the father of scientific Egyptology for the meth-odological and technical innovations he introduced to the field. Key to Petrie's scientism was the understanding that the study of artifacts would be separate from earlier concerns with taste or the confirmation of Biblical narrative. Excavation, in this model, did not seek to confirm preexisting notions about the Pharaonic past, nor to provide evidence about the development of beauty within a universal history of art. Rather, it used material culture to explore the context in which objects were made in order to ascertain the particularities of the moment in which they were made. Following this, the artifact quality of objects was no longer tied to their value as individual works, but rather how they existed in a web of material culture the embeddedness of which within a site was crucial to its meaning. Following Petrie, the Egyptological artifact was no longer regarded as a single creation but rather as a taxonomical piece that revealed the historical period of its origin in addition to the social categories and connections congealed in its matter. As we shall see, the scientism did not prevent audiences—or Egyptologists—from speaking about artifacts in the language of wonder and beauty. The event of Tutankhamen's discovery is hailed as a hallmark of modern Egyptology's professionalism, an affirmation of the scientific methods introduced by Petrie. Yet how does one square the scientism of Carter's discovery with the literary pretensions of his best-selling account? How does one make sense of the fact that the account he prepared for publication draws heavily from styles of literary expression associated with pre-Egyptological forms of excavation? The question is by no means minor to understanding the cultural significances of the event of Tutankhamen's discovery. On the contrary, in the official history of Egyptology, there is a long-standing delight in the tension between the pure scientism of archaeological research and the fact that Egyptological discoveries have always aroused widespread curiosity and intense aesthetic interest whose tone and motivation diverge sharply from the interests of dispassionate study. In this history, the tension between these two kinds of interest—the first scholarly, the second popular—is resolved by way of sequencing them in a narrative of cause and effect. According to this story, the modern archaeological excavation is an institution of pure scientific research, while the cultural dissemination of images and themes from archaeology appear as secondary, derivative, and nonessential to Egyptology's claims. Whether or not one believes it, the point of this narrative is, of course, to "purify" Egyptology's science from the popularizing influences of culture and politics.[6] That is, to make sure that the unreason of Egyptomania does not contaminate the rationality of Egyptology.

As noted throughout this book, it is true that archaeology made possible new aesthetic and political material cultures. But at the same time, expressive and political cultures directly impacted the research agenda of Egyptological science. Indeed, following the discovery, Carter reluctantly became a public celebrity determined to get his version of the Tutankhamen story out to the widest possible audience. He had competition, for within months of the discovery no less than four other sensational book-length narratives of the event—some quite critical of Carter—appeared in print, alongside countless retellings in the press. With the help of his colleague, A. C. Mace (and photographs by Harry Burton), Carter quickly published his popular account, *The Tomb of Tut•Ankh•Amen*. During the autumn of 1923, Carter embarked on a tour of Britain, delivering a talk accompanied by 145 slides to audiences that numbered in the thousands. In the spring of 1924, as Carter went on a lecture tour in North America, the British Empire Exhibition opened a replica of Tutankhamen's tomb, excavated from the sand at Wembley. The example of Tutankhamen's discovery illustrates how it is that literature, entertainment, and the arts were not merely derivative of archaeological research. Rather, the relation between the Egyptomanic "literature" on archaeological artifacts and the "science" of Egyptology was dynamic and two-way. Furthermore, as Carter's discovery was disseminated through the press in Egypt and abroad, these media representations began to impact the conduct of the excavation itself. For these reasons, the story of the discovery of King Tutankhamen's tomb never really began with inchoate original things that were turned into artifacts of a pure science and subsequently transmogrified, by cultural processes, into derivative so-called representations. Even the empirical claim of pristine discovery was itself derived from a long literary tradition.

This chapter begins by exploring the persistence of literary tropes in the account Carter composed for popular audiences, then examines the tensions between the science and the spectacle of Carter's archaeology. The point is not to tar the scientific methods Carter employed by showing that they have an illicit association with literature and leisure entertainment, but rather to suggest that Carter's account (and the science he employed) was quite implicated in the forms of popular leisure culture that Carter openly despised. The issue of how science and culture might exist in a hybrid form explains how the pure Egyptology of Carter's period repeats, though with difference, many of the themes and tropes associated with the pre-Egyptological writings of Belzoni and his contemporaries.

Next, I explore the legal and political contexts surrounding the discovery of Tutankhamen's tomb. In each case, while something very methodical and precise was happening in Carter's excavation, it is impossible to separate the scientific elements of the event from issues of political culture. Finally, I survey the poetry and prose inspired by the archaeological event. Indeed, the emergence of this culture was a precondition for the later Pharaonist culture treated in the last chapter. Here, it is difficult to think of expressive culture as merely secondary to the event of Egyptology because the Pharaonist literature composed around Tutankhamen's discovery contributed greatly to the creation of political iconography and sentiment in Egypt and thus bore directly upon how the science of archaeology was conducted on site.

THE AESTHETICS OF DISCOVERY: FEELING

Carter's exclamation of wonder upon encountering ancient Egyptian antiquities was both spontaneous and derivative of a long tradition in colonial travel writing. Likewise, his aesthetic descriptions of the artifacts drew upon this same discourse. Upon entering the small chamber holding Tutankhamen's sarcophagus, Carter writes, "Facing the doorway, on the farther side, stood the most beautiful monument that I have ever seen— so lovely that it made one gasp with wonder and admiration. . . . There is a grandeur about this monument that made an irresistible appeal to the imagination, and I am not ashamed to confess that it brought a lump to my throat."[7] Carter's description of beauty and wonder is both immediate and interior, one of the most personal moments of his narrative—and is part of the same unfolding aesthetic discourse in which Tawfiq al-Hakim and Ahmad Husayn wrote. Carter's description of beauty is not about objects, but rather about the feelings aroused by seeing them. What is significant is not the novelty of Carter's description of aesthetic experience, but rather the way in which it replicates, with little or no innovation, the very habits of aesthetic description that had colored European travel writing in Egypt since the late eighteenth century.[8] Thus the most subjective descriptions of aesthetic feeling in Carter's text—the personal, embodied moments when the narrator describes feeling—were both unique and routine, original and derivative. Indeed, when viewed in the context of nineteenth-century travel writing, they appear as clichés of colonial travel writing in Egypt. Carter's description of the general speechlessness of his party as it entered the small chamber of Tutankhamen's tomb is exemplary: "Each had a dazed, bewildered look in his eyes, and each in turn, as he came out, threw up his hands before him, an unconscious gesture of impotence to describe in words the wonders that he had seen. They were indeed indescribable, and the emotions they had aroused in our minds were of too intimate a nature to communicate, even though we had the words at our command."[9] Like the assertion of wonder, that of speechlessness—figured here as the (mute) signal of a subjective, aesthetic experience too powerful to express in language—was, by Carter's time, a common feature of European travel writing in Egypt and, by the twentieth century, a regular feature of accounts written by modern Egyptians. Certainly no Europeans had ever seen what Carter's companions saw in the tomb chamber, but they had often described their experience in the very same way—as indescribable.

Most pertinent for illuminating the relations between subjects and objects, Carter's description replicates the most common feature of aesthetic travel writing in Egypt, namely, a reversal of agency, in which the objects discovered seem to discover the onlookers.[10] Immediately upon entering the tomb, Carter begins to distinguish various objects in the gloom. This moment of differentiation is the first moment in the transformation of "wonderful things" into the objects they become. Significantly, at this moment it is the objects that seem to come alive and transfix the beholders:

> Gradually the scene grew clearer, and we could pick out individual objects. First, right opposite to us . . . were three great gilt couches, their sides carved in the form of monstrous animals, curiously attenuated in body, as they had to be to serve their purpose, but the heads of startling realism. Uncanny beasts enough to look upon at any time: seen as we saw them, their brilliant gilded surfaces picked out of the darkness by our electric torch, as though by limelight, their heads throwing grotesque distorted shadows on the wall behind them, they were almost terrifying. Next, on the right, two statues caught and held our attention; two life-sized figures of a king in black, facing each other like sentinels, gold kilted, gold sandalled, armed with mace and staff, the protective sacred cobra upon their foreheads.[11]

Wonder, indescribability, and a reversal of agency are three distinguishing rhetorical features of Carter's aesthetic description of his discovery. These figures depict Carter's subjective experience in terms of passivity; they present the objects of discovery as animate agents that act upon human consciousness.

THE SCIENCE OF DISCOVERY: KNOWING

In contrast, the scientific code of Carter's narrative of discovery puts objects in their proper place, as material viewed, copied, moved, and catalogued by a group of professionals. Part of the authority of Carter's account is thus tied to how it describes a well-organized team of experts working in specialized fields. With him, Carter had a crack team of academic scholars, including James Henry Breasted of the University of Chicago's Oriental Institute, whose focus was on the historical aspects of the site; Alan Gardiner, tasked with the textual aspects of the tomb; and Arthur C. Mace, an Egyptologist from New York's Metropolitan Museum of Art, who, like Carter, had trained under Petrie. On loan from the Egyptian government was a chemist, Alfred Lucas, whose expertise was critical to the successful preservation of the Tutankhamen find. Finally, there was Harry Burton, a photographer also from the Metropolitan Museum, whose camera was key to providing a visual record of the site and objects in their found states. Pinned to the verbal description, the Burton photographs offer more than just crisp images of remarkable objects—they also figure as clear signs of the methodical thoroughness of the excavation itself. Indeed, the first experience of "wonderful things" is presented as if through the lens of a camera: the archaeologist perceived the image through the small aperture made in the entrance wall. The figure is not insignificant: Carter invites his readers to "imagine how [the wonders of the tomb] appeared to us as we looked down upon them from our spyhole in the blocked doorway, casting the beam of light from our torch . . . from one group of objects to another, in a vain attempt to interpret the treasure that lay before us."[12] If the narrative's aesthetic code portrays the event of discovery in terms of a richly textured interior of feeling, the trope of the camera turns the account of the experience outward, toward the objects themselves. In Carter's account, the figure of the camera thus marks a shift from one code to another, from describing the event in terms which foreground subjective experience to describing the event in terms which bracket such experience in favor of a presentation of the objects as matter to be recorded. The objectification of the "wonderful things" appears in Carter's account by way of a number of acts of such recording representations, from photography to copious note taking and catalog description. In the description of the objects within the entrance chamber Carter details the following,

> exquisitely painted and inlaid caskets; alabaster vases, some beautifully carved in openwork designs; strange black shrines, from the open door of one a great gilt snake peeping out; bouquets of flowers or leaves; beds; chairs beautifully carved; a golden inlaid throne; a heap of curious white oviform boxes; staves of all shapes and designs; beneath our eyes, on the very threshold of the chamber, a beautiful lotiform cup of translucent alabaster; on the left a confused pile of overturned chariots, glistening with gold and inlay; and peeping from behind them another portrait of a king.[13]

Such descriptions, which mimic the technical prose of Carter's excavation diary and the handlists of the excavation, interrupt the dramatic flow of the narrative and effectively shift the aesthetic scene of discovery (the dramatic description of subjective experience) toward a listing of objects. They also serve to transform the chaotic profusion of undifferentiated material into individual items ready for detailed study. Writing about the objects in their initial state of discovery was important because such information was crucial for "working over" the objects later. Carter writes, "Detailed and copious notes should be taken at every stage of this preliminary work. It is difficult to take too many, for, though a thing may be perfectly clear to you at the moment, it by no means follows that it will be when the time comes for you to work over your material. In tomb-work as many notes as possible should be made while everything is still in position. Then, when you begin clearing, card and pencil should be kept handy, and every fresh item of evidence should be noted immediately [when] you run across it."[14] The point of such notes, according to Carter, was "to ensure the complete scientific record . . . which it was our duty to make."[15]

Alongside notes, photography plays a central role in the treatment of found objects, since it records their initial "found state" for posterity:

Figure 10. Example of Harry Burton's photographic cross-record for the excavation catalog. The texts in the accompanying "boodle report" and handlist categorize and describe objects in greater detail. Photograph by Harry Burton. © Copyright Griffith Institute, University of Oxford.

"Obviously, our first and greatest need was photography. Before anything else was done, or anything moved, we must have a series of preliminary views, taken in panorama, to show the general appearance of the chamber. For lighting, we had two movable electric standards, giving 3,000 candle-power, and it was with these that all the photographic work in the tomb was done."[16]

The objects were mapped after they were photographed, and their relations to one another plotted:

> Our next step . . . was to devise an efficient method of registering the contents of the chamber, for it would be absolutely essential, later on, that we should have a ready means of ascertaining the exact part of the tomb from which any particular object might have come. Naturally, each object or closely allied group of objects, would be given its own catalogue number, and would have that number securely attached to it when it was moved away from the chamber, but that was not enough, for the number might not indicate position. So, far as possible, the numbers were to follow a definite order, beginning at the entrance doorway and working systematically round the chamber.[17]

Then, the objects were moved to the "laboratory" (located in an adjacent tomb), where they were cleaned, rephotographed, catalogued, and cross-indexed. In other words, within days and weeks, the objects were transformed from material whose existence was not known into artifacts ready for museum study:

> As the objects were brought in they were deposited . . . and covered up until they should be wanted. Each in turn was brought up to the working bay for examination. There, after the surface dust had been cleared off, measurements, complete archaeological notes, and copies of inscriptions were entered on the filing cards. The necessary mending and preservative treatment followed, after which it was taken just outside the entrance for scale photographs to be made. . . . As each object arrived its registration number was noted in an entry book, and in the same book a record was kept of the successive stages of its treatment. . . . Not infrequently it happened that the component parts of a single object, scattered in the tomb, were entered under two or more numbers, and in this case cross-references in the notes were necessary. Note-cards, as completed, were

filed away in cabinets, and in these filing cabinets we had, by the end of the season, a complete history of every object from the tomb.[18]

Even though Carter's account was written for popular audiences, much of the narrative plot following discovery resembles the static form of a catalogue. Indeed, the following chapters of Carter's account, some of which contain limited descriptions of subsequent openings and excavations, are in the main devoted to lists of specific articles, whose location and features are described, numbered, and ordered. In other words, Carter's things become, before long, objects to be catalogued, artifacts for museums, antiquities for display. The narrative arc of Carter's account shifts from the dramatic first-person story of discovering active objects, to a still-life taxonomy of inert objects fixed in their place by scientific method.

THE ARTIFACTION OF DISCOVERY: PRESERVATION

Described from the point of view of the Egyptologist and his objects, these processes of organization and representation are not in the least remarkable: such are the activities of a professional archaeologist, and such are the objects of archaeological work.[19] But if the process is viewed as one of material worked upon—things transformed into artifacts—then the constitutive character of the transformation which made found things into meaningful artifacts embedded within an elaborate array of institutions and grids of cross-referenced texts becomes salient.

It is not merely a figure of speech to talk about this transformation as a process of construction. This is especially clear in the example of preservation, which stands at the core of the process of artifaction. As Carter points out, the discovery and excavation of Tutankhamen's tomb threatened the material integrity of the objects by exposing them to the elements of nature for the first time in thousands of years. This was a recurring problem, particularly with wooden objects, arising "not from the condition in which [they are found], but from subsequent shrinkage owing to change of atmosphere."[20] Some of the most fascinating passages in Carter's account describe how Alfred Lucas chemically reconstituted wooden objects as they broke or disintegrated. Describing how Lucas reworked a casket that initially seemed in good condition, Carter writes,

It seemed as though but little treatment was necessary. The surface dust was removed, the discoloration of the painted surfaces was reduced with benzine, and the whole exterior of the casket was sprayed with a solution of celluloid in amylacetate to fix the gesso to the wood, particular attention being paid to tender places at the cracks. . . . Three or four weeks later we noticed that the joint cracks were getting wider, and that the gesso in other places was showing a tendency to buckle. It was clear enough what was happening. Owing to the change of temperature from the close, humid atmosphere of the tomb to the dry airiness of the laboratory, the wood had begun to shrink once more, and the gesso, not being able to follow it, was coming away from the wood altogether. The position was serious, for we were in danger of losing large parts of the painted surface.[21]

The near-deterioration of the casket led Lucas to try another preservation technique, which involved heating the wood as much as possible, then infusing it with paraffin wax. When the preservation of an object entails such a radical alteration in its chemical composition, it involves a process that constitutes as much as it conserves.[22]

Preservation techniques were aimed not only at deterring threats posed by time and the elements, especially since humans are the most immediate threat mentioned in Carter's account. In fact, before the tasks of photographing, writing, mapping, and chemically preserving the objects can be carried out, Carter writes, "the first thing to be done was to render the tomb safe against robbery."[23] In this sense, preservation of the objects entailed enclosing them, restricting access to them, in short, securing them:

Danger of theft . . . was an ever-present anxiety. The whole countryside was agog with excitement about the tomb; extravagant tales were current about the gold and jewels it contained; and, as past experience had shown, it was only too possible that there might be a serious attempt to raid the tomb by night. This possibility of robbery on a large scale was negatived, so far as humanly possible, by a complicated system of guarding, there being present in The Valley, day and night, three independent groups of watchmen, each answerable to a different authority—the Government Antiquities Guards, a squad of soldiers supplied by the Mudir of Kena, and a selected group of the most trustworthy of our own staff. In addition, we had a heavy wooden grille at the entrance of the passage, and a massive steel gate at the inner doorway, each secured by four padlocked chains; and that there might never be any mistake about these latter, the keys were in the permanent charge of one particular member of the European staff.[24]

As these last words make clear, the issue of security was coded within a particular colonial antagonism and entailed a familiar colonial fantasy: white Europeans saving Egyptian antiquities from Egyptian peasants.[25] Similarly, Carter's reference to "extravagant tales" refers not to European beliefs, but to those of local Egyptians. Additionally, although the wording in this passage may not be explicit, the policing measures Carter describes effectively restricted only local Egyptians from the sites. While Carter complains about the interruptions caused by visiting European tourists and Cairene politicians demanding tours, his text simply does not consider the possibility of visits by local Egyptians. Admittedly, security is not the explicit focus of Carter's writing on preservation. Rather he emphasizes his studied expertise and a code of professional ethics:

> It was slow work, painfully slow, and nerve-wracking at that, for one felt all the time a heavy weight of responsibility. Every excavator must, if he have any archaeological conscience at all. The things he finds are not his own property, to treat as he pleases, or neglect as he chooses. They are a direct legacy from the past to the present age, he but the privileged intermediary through whose hands they come; and if, by carelessness, slackness, or ignorance, he lessens the sum of knowledge that might have been obtained from them, he knows himself to be guilty of an archaeological crime of the first magnitude. Destruction of evidence is so painfully easy, and yet so hopelessly irreparable.[26]

The dispassionate tone in this section of Carter's account is not unusual, nor is there much novelty in his talk of ethics. Yet, as this last passage makes clear, the scientific code of Carter's narrative articulates a careful descriptive theory to the relationship between the Egyptologist and his objects: he photographs, studies, describes, preserves, and restricts access to them. These activities are part of the responsibility the Egyptologist has to his artifacts; they are how he practices an ethical relationship to his objects. In some ways, this relationship might be called one of property, except that, as Carter acknowledges, the artifacts do not belong to him. But neither do they belong to just anyone, especially not to the local Egyptian peasants and workmen, who, he fears, would steal and sell them. (Significantly, not long afterward the thorny issue of control and property rights is what caused the Egyptian government to suspend Carter's work on Tutankhamen's tomb.) Carter makes the assertion that the authority for his control over the objects stems from the fact that they belong to "the present age," for which he is merely a trained caretaker. The Egyptologist may have a unique privilege to work upon the objects, but he is merely a steward whose work will be judged by the strictest standards of disinterested scientific objectivity. If the aesthetic code of Carter's narrative emphasized the agency of things upon the feeling subject, this code reverses that relationship, predicating artifacts as objects worked upon by the archaeologist. If the aesthetic code described the way in which Carter's interest and feeling were piqued by the objects, this code insists that he treat the objects in a detached manner, not as his property, but as a legacy of civilization which belongs to the whole of humanity. If the aesthetic code described the objects as they presented themselves immediately to the excavator, this code describes how the archaeologist catalogues and preserves them so as to present them as objects of study and display.

PUBLIC ACCESS

Nothing better exemplifies the overlap of and tension between aesthetic and scientific codes in Carter's account than the issue of public access. The discovery of the tomb generated wide interest, especially among Europeans living and touring in the country. As an antiquities inspector noted, "Day after day the crowd which assembled to watch the removal of different objects increased in size. Now it was a glistening chariot that was taken to the workshop; now a gilded chest or casket; and now a tray bearing bouquets of flowers or a collection of odds and ends. As each of these loads was carried along the valley, soldiers armed with rifles marched behind it, and pressmen and visitors ran by the side, clicking their cameras and scribbling their notes."[27] Like other monuments on the tourism circuit in southern Egypt, many tombs in the Valley of the Kings were open to European visitors, and now they began to press Carter to open his. By January 1923, the *London Times* reported, "All roads lead to 'Tutankhamun' these days, and whenever one rides out along the picturesque canal bank, past the native cemetery leading to the Valley of the Kings, there is a never-ending string of people on donkeys, or in sandcarts along the road or over the hill, all moving in the direction of, or from, the newly discovered tomb. Urchins at every turn offer you effigies in plaster of Tutankhamun."[28] Given the extraordinary richness of the discovery, many in the press argued that Carter had a scientific duty to open up his findings to the touring and reading public. As pressure mounted to allow access to Tutankhamen's tomb, Carter resisted, pointing out the real dangers such access would pose to the preservation of artifacts within the tomb:

[The] presence of a number of visitors creates serious danger to the objects themselves, danger that we, who are responsible for them, have no right to let them undergo. . . . The tomb is small and crowded and sooner or later—it actually happened more than once last year—a false step or hasty movement on the part of a visitor will do some piece of absolutely irreparable damage. . . . The unfortunate part of it is that the more interested and the more enthusiastic the visitor is, the more likely he is to be the cause of damage; he gets excited, and in his enthusiasm over one object he is very liable to step back into or knock against another. Even if no actual damage is caused, the passage of large parties of visitors through the tomb stirs up dust, and that in itself is bad for the objects.[29]

As if that were not enough, Carter points out that the humidity caused by the breathing of tomb visitors would threaten the objects as well. More than this, though, visits would be a nuisance in an active excavation site:

The second [danger], due to the loss of actual working time that visitors cause, is not so immediately apparent, but is in some ways even more serious. This will seem a terribly exaggerated view to the individual visitor, who will wonder what difference the half-hour that he or she consumed could make to the whole season's work. Perfectly true, so far as that particular half-hour is concerned, but what of the other nine visitors, or groups of visitors, who come on the same day? . . . The danger of constant interruption is obvious. . . . What would a chemist think if you asked him to break off a delicate experiment to show you round his laboratory? What would be the feelings of a surgeon if you interrupted him in the middle of an operation?[30]

Carter was not against opening up the tomb to the public eye. He was well aware that his efforts would eventually result in public access to the tomb and museum display of the artifacts it contained. Rather, he was reluctant to grant demands for full public access to his project while the work of excavation, organization, and preservation continued. The disruptiveness of tours and correspondence was considerable and well noted in his excavation diaries. Many of the entries for February 1923 consist of no more than "Given up to visitors," "Press to tomb of Tutankhamen," and "Visitors to Tomb of Tutankhamen."[31] In this light, Carter's resistance seems more than reasonable.

But Carter's resistance went deeper than this. It is not just that visitors disrupted his work and threatened the material integrity of the artifacts he was unearthing. At times he was simply hostile to public scrutiny of any kind, which may not have been unreasonable either, considering how negative the press coverage of him was. Much of this was brought on by the exclusive deal that Carter's patron, Lord Carnarvon, had made with the *Times*. Grieved at having to purchase day-old reports of the excavation from the *Times*, other British papers ran a constant stream of critical articles on the arrangement, many of which focused on Carter's attitude toward publicity. The Egyptian press was so amplified in its criticism that even Carter noticed their reporting. More than once he resentfully refers to "the local press" in his diaries. Significantly in this regard, when Ahmad Kamal and Salim Hasan, Egypt's most recognized Egyptologists, first weighed in on the issue of Tutankhamen's tomb, they both focused on the norm of publicizing one's scientific discoveries in a timely fashion. Both strongly implied that that norm was being broken by Carter.[32] As the excavation came under increasing scrutiny, such accusations were no longer merely implied. Carter's reluctance to open up the site publicly became tied to open complaints about the Antiquities Service's failure to enforce Egyptian rights over the Carnarvon concession, a failure tantamount to an infringement on the country's sovereignty itself. As we shall see, the tensions around Carter's perceived failure to grant public access to the excavation had resonances in both archaeological and political registers.

This hostility gives rise to a tension throughout his account. On the one hand, the scientific code of Carter's account is closely associated with the issue of publication, and the book itself is a response to the criticisms against him. In some passages, Carter critiques the work of earlier generations of excavator antiquarians who had not done enough to preserve their objects of discovery and who worked far from public scrutiny. Crucial to his distinction between the amateur practices of earlier times and the modern profession of Egyptology was the primary role that publication played in the latter. Indeed, Carter emphasizes, he was motivated to publish his account by "public interest."[33] On the other hand, Carter is bewildered by and resents the popular attention his efforts gained:

Archaeology under the limelight is a new and rather bewildering experience for most of us. In the past we have gone about our business happily enough, intensely interested in it ourselves, but not expecting other folk to be more than tepidly polite about it, and now all of a sudden we find the world takes an interest in us, an interest so intense and so avid for details that special correspondents at large salaries have to be sent to interview us, report our every movement, and hide round corners to surprise a secret out of us. It is, as I said, a little bewildering for us, not to say embarrassing, and we wonder sometimes just exactly how and why it has all come about. We may wonder, but I think it would puzzle anyone to give an exact answer to the question. One must suppose that at the time the discovery was made the general public was in a state of profound boredom with news of reparations, conferences and mandates, and craved for some new topic of conversation. The idea of buried treasure, too, is one that appeals to most of us. Whatever the reason, or combination of reasons, it is quite certain that, once the initial *Times* dispatch had been published, no power on earth could shelter us from the light of publicity that beat down upon us.[34]

The tension here is thus between two overlapping but divergent notions of the public in Carter's account: the enlightened public composed of scientific peers and the entertainment-seeking public of the colonial tourist

Figure 11. Howard Carter (behind and to the right of the bearded Pierre Lacau) surrounded by guests in front of the entrance to the tomb of Sethos II, known as the "laboratory," possibly taken February 16, 1923. Front row, from left to right: Abdel Hamid Soliman, Undersecretary of Public Works; Lacau, Director of the Antiquities Service; Lady Evelyn Carnarvon; 'Ali Shamsi, soon to be appointed Minister of Finance. On the far left of the second row is Murqus Hanna, soon to be appointed Minister of Public Works. Photograph by Harry Burton. © Copyright Griffith Institute, University of Oxford.

mob. The possibility of a third public—an intellectual Egyptian public—never seems to have occurred to the author.

A series of staged official openings expresses most clearly the conflicts that existed between the exigencies of public archaeological work and the public demand for exhibition. As Carter's work proceeded, the Egyptian Antiquities Service forced him to open up the tomb to visits. Some of these visits, for example, the first official opening of the antechamber on November 29, 1922, were elaborately staged. Among those invited were Lord Allenby, the high commissioner for Egypt, and his wife, 'Abd al-Aziz Yahya, the Egyptian governor of Qena, and Muhammad Fahmy, the *ma'mur* of the district, along with other Egyptian officials. In a snub to both the Antiquities Service and to the Ministry of Public Works, neither Pierre Lacau, director of the service, nor Paul Tottenham, cultural and archaeological advisor to the ministry, was invited. During the early spring of 1923, thousands of European travelers descended upon Luxor to be on hand to visit the tomb following a second official opening, the breaking of the sealed wall separating the antechamber from the rest of the tomb. That event was set to take place partly in honor of the visit of Queen Elisabeth of Belgium and her son Prince Leopold. On February 16, Lord Carnarvon and Carter staged an opening of the burial chamber. Although they had hoped to limit the guest list to under twenty-five, by one account over forty-five were present as Carter broke the seal. The guest list reads like a who's who of Egyptian elite politics and Egyptology. King Fu'ad had been invited, but declined (though he later visited the excavation). A number of princes, including Hussein Kamal al-Din, 'Umar Tusun, and Yusuf Kamal, were listed in attendence, along with present and former ministers, including 'Adli Yakan, Tawfiq Nasim, 'Abd al-Khaliq Tharwat, Isma'il Sidqi, and Isma'il Sirri. So too were the ambassadors of France, Belgium, and the United States; Lord Carnarvon and Lady Evelyn Herbert; the former British commanding officer in Egypt, Sir John Maxwell; the French director of the Antiquities Service, Pierre Lacau; and other luminaries.[35]

As A. C. Mace described the event:

The tomb looked as though set for a stage scene. We had . . . made a small stage to enable us to attack the upper part of the sealing thinking it was safest to work from the top downwards. A little way back was a barrier, and behind that chairs for the visitors as it was likely to be a long job. Inside the barrier were, Carter, Callender and myself. Carter made a little speech first and then Carnarvon said a few words and then the exciting moment arrived and Carter mounted the stage, stripped to trousers and vest and struck the first blow with hammer and chisel. He first located the wooden lintel over the door and then very carefully cleared below it; fortunately the stones at the top were small. After about a quarter of an hour he had made a hole big enough to put an electric torch in, and we could all see a huge wooden erection covered with gold leaf, evidently the tabernacle which covered the sarcophagus. At this point he asked me to come up and help him, and the rest of the clearing we did together. It was an odd sensation standing on the stage and gradually widening the hole, you could feel the spectators behind the barrier just tingling with excitement.[36]

The theatricality of the event was not lost on the participants who spoke in terms of the same aesthetic code—wonder, awe, and indescribability—that characterized moments in Carter's account. For instance, immediately upon leaving the opening, Lord Carnarvon told the *London Times*, "I find it difficult to describe what I felt when I entered that inner chamber, for of a surety, I never dreamt I should gaze upon the amazing sight which met my eyes. . . . With the greatest of care I followed Mr. Carter in and whatever emotion and excitement I may have felt when I entered the first chamber were as nothing when I was going into what undoubtedly was the practically untouched tomb of an Egyptian king."[37] Throughout the week, other European dignitaries visited the tomb with elaborate ceremony and considerable publicity. As the *Times* reported,

[Tutankhamen] is paid tribute from everywhere. His name is all over the town. It is shouted in the streets, whispered in the hotels. While in the local shops Tutankhamun advertises everything: art, hats, curios, photographs, and tomorrow probably "genuine" antiquities. Every hotel in Luxor had something on the menu à la Tut. The Queen of the Belgians, though a prominent figure—and she will view the tomb tomorrow—is merely the modern queen of a nation. But to be the thing today in Thebes one has got to show some, any, connection with the ancient King. Slight acquaintances buttonhole one another and tell of dreams they had yesterday of Tutankhamun. There is a Tutankhamun dance tonight at which the first piece is to be a Tutankhamun RAG.[38]

Reports like these only fueled popular demand for opening the tomb up more generally to tours and touched off even more conflicts between Carter and the state agencies overseeing the administration of antiquities. Carter's response to the publicity and growing demand for tours was couched in a register of scientific disdain:

> The claims of archaeology for consideration are just as great as those of any other form of scientific research. . . . Why, because we carry on our work in unfrequented regions instead of in a crowded city, are we to be considered churlish for objecting to constant interruptions? I suppose the reason really is that in popular opinion archaeology is not work at all. Excavation is a sort of super-tourist amusement, carried out with the excavator's own money if he is rich enough, or with other people's money if he can persuade them to subscribe it, and all he has to do is enjoy life in a beautiful winter climate and pay a gang of natives to find things for him.[39]

Carter's complaint points to an opposition within the institutions of archaeological exhibition between scientific study on the one hand and commodified entertainment on the other. As Tony Bennett and others have suggested, the spectacular nature of scientific exhibition—whether in on-site archaeology or in museum display—shared much with popular entertainment industries, especially those associated with tourism and leisure activities.[40] Such a resemblance did not bother the institutions of tourism. On the contrary, the supposedly useful knowledge collected during leisure travel was an important selling point for touring packages to destinations such as the Valley of the Kings.[41] The institutions of Egyptology, however, found the resemblance between scientific demonstration and commercial spectacle a source of real anxiety. For Carter and others who legitimated their work through a language of professional disinterest, it was anathema to associate the work of Egyptology with the leisure of the tourist.[42] But, more than that, it was a structural antagonism because without the public interest and commerce generated by tourism and museum patronage, archaeological projects would not have been publicly and privately funded to the degree they were in Carter's time.

In Carter's account does *exhibition* signify leisure and distraction or work and scientific study? The answer is equivocal. Carter writes,

We have an opportunity in this tomb such as no archaeologists ever had before, but if we are to take full advantage of it . . . [then] it is absolutely essential that we be left to carry on the work without interruption. It is not as if all our visitors were all keen on archaeology, or even mildly interested in it. Too many of them are attracted by mere curiosity, or even worse, by a desire to visit the tomb because it is the thing to do. They want to be able to talk at large about it to their friends at home, or crow over less fortunate tourists who have not managed to secure an introduction themselves.[43]

Here, it seems as if what Carter objects to is the indifferent tourist, the one who not only lacks the knowledge required to appreciate the sight of the tomb, but who is also uncurious. For this kind of visitor the archaeological site is something of an exhibit fetish, sought not out of a sincere desire for knowledge, but rather to emulate the experiences of others. At the same time Carter acknowledges there are tourists whose interest is proper and sincere:

Six cases of objects from the tomb are already on exhibition in the Cairo Museum, and we would earnestly beg visitors to Egypt to content them- selves with these, and with what they can see from the outside of the tomb, and not to set their hearts on getting into the tomb itself. Those who are genuinely interested in archaeology for its own sake will be the first to realize that the request is a reasonable one. The others, the idly curious, who look on the tomb as a side-show, and Tut•ankh•Amen as a mere topic of conversation, have no rights in the matter, and need no consideration.[44]

The place of exhibition in Carter's account is wholly ambiguous for what it says about the difference between the science of archaeology and the pleasures of commercial culture: the objects of exhibit lend themselves to both serious, scientific consideration and to leisurely entertainment; the exhibit is an event that might provoke subjective experiences as easily as object-oriented understanding. In sum, the exhibit is where the aesthetic, entertainment, and scientific codes of Carter's account mingle uneasily with one another.

THE LAW OF DISCOVERY: ARTIFACTS AS
PROPERTY AND THE AFTERMATH OF 1919

When looked at from the perspective of modern Egyptian social history, Carter's popular account is startlingly silent about the context in which he worked. While occasionally politics enters the horizon of his account of the discovery, it is only ever as a distraction or nuisance. Reading his published account, one would never understand that his excavations took place during a time of revolutionary upheaval, or that this revolution was directed at the sorts of privileges that granted Europeans such access to Egyptian soil. This silence is no oversight. On the contrary, the lack of discussion of the revolutionary context in which his research took place is part of the excavation's scientific claim, namely, that it stands apart from all such considerations. Despite this, the political context is critical to understanding not just the wider meanings of Tutankhamen's discovery but also how Carter, as a professional archaeologist, was compelled to practice his science.

Although the British had been the de facto rulers of Egypt since 1882, Egypt remained technically part of the Ottoman empire. When World War I erupted, and the British found themselves in direct conflict with the Ottomans, this legal fiction became a source of contradiction. The British thus resolved to make Egypt a protectorate in 1914. Though waged elsewhere, World War I impacted Egypt in many ways, since much of its economy was subordinated to the British war drive. When the war ended, questions were raised about Egypt's political status just as throughout former Ottoman provinces political activists questioned the status of their governments. The Egyptian elites best positioned to raise the question of Egyptian independence were a group associated with Ahmad Lutfi al-Sayyid and the Umma party. Led by a prominent lawyer named Sa'd Zaghloul, a self-appointed delegation (or *wafd*) of members of this group attempted to travel to participate in the diplomatic meetings that followed the war, only to be prevented from traveling by British officials. When the British arrested Zaghloul and exiled him to Malta, mass protests broke out in Cairo and Alexandria. Though initially spontaneous, they gathered force and eloquence in their demands for independence and British evacuation from Egypt. Within weeks workers, students, professionals, bureaucrats, men, women, and children were participating in the largest direct challenge to British rule in the country. Throughout the countryside, rail and telegraph lines were cut, isolating British garrisons who were besieged by guerrillas. Famously, the leaders of Zifta in the Delta boldly declared their town an independent republic. Likewise, the revolution galvanized segments of Egypt's population that had not been previously active in the anticolonial struggle, let alone risked going to the streets to express their convictions. The wide participation of women in the revolution is especially remembered as proof of its popular and modern appeal. The slogans of the revolution and the multisectarian composition of its Christian and Muslim leadership underscored the fact that the nationalist movement was secular, not Islamist, in its orientation.

The British response was a mixture of repression and cooptation. Hundreds of Egyptians died and thousands were arrested as colonial authorities put down the rebellion. Bowing to pressure, the British began to negotiate, in limited ways, with Zaghloul's delegation (al-Wafd), which emerged as the dominant voice of the Egyptian nationalist movement. Though the Revolution of 1919 did not succeed in its chief demand—complete and immediate independence from Great Britain—it did force the British to make concessions. In 1922, the British viceroy issued the Unilateral Declaration, which gave Egypt formal independence. With formal independence, the status of Egypt's Khedival family changed: Sultan Fu'ad became King Fu'ad in 1922. In 1923, the British permitted the drafting of an Egyptian constitution as well as a law that allowed for parliamentary elections.

These developments are critical to understanding the political pressures put on the legality of Carter's excavations. For instance, when Carter wrote in 1923, "The things [the archaeologist] finds are not his own property," he was expressing a commitment to scientific disinterest. But the statement was true in other ways as well. In February 1924, following the election of Egypt's first Parliament, which was dominated by Zaghloul and his Wafd Party, the Antiquities Service abruptly canceled the concession under which Carter conducted his excavations. Details of the concession agreement appeared during this time in the Egyptian press, where they became the subject of sustained public critique of their legality, along with wry commentary about how they resembled the infamous "concessions" (imtiyazat) of the Ottoman era.[45] The question of property rights had come to overshadow other aspects of the discovery. This development under-scores the fact that the various institutions of the Egyptological artifact (the aesthetic, the scientific, the exhibitionary) obtained to the extent they did only within legal frameworks that governed the colonial administra-tion of antiquities in Egypt, frameworks that clearly understood "things to be discovered" in Egypt as already the patrimony of the Egyptian nation and property of the state.

Carter began his operations in the Valley of the Kings in 1915, when Lord Carnarvon won the right to excavate there with the expiration of the concession belonging to Theodore Davis, an American millionaire who, after twelve years of digging, declared the valley to be empty of other finds. Though the pace of exploration was hobbled by World War I, the Carnarvon concession was renewed annually with no amendments. Many of the concession's articles later proved to be crucial in the legal fights over access and property rights and, finally, state sovereignty. In part they read as follows:

1. The work of excavation shall be carried out at the expense, risk and peril of the Earl of Carnarvon by Mr. Howard Carter; the latter should be constantly present during excavation.

2. Work shall be executed under the control of the Antiquities Ser-vice, who shall have the right not only to supervise the work, but also to alter the manner of the execution if they so deem proper for the success of the undertaking.

3. If a tomb, or any other monument, happens to be discovered, the Permittee or his representative is bound to give notice at once to the Chief Inspector of Upper Egypt, at Luxor.

4. To the Permittee himself shall be reserved the privilege of open-ing the tomb or monument discovered, and of being the first to enter therein.

5. At the moment of the opening the Chief Inspector of the Antiqui-ties Service shall, if he considers necessary, place on the spot the number of guardians he shall deem to be required.

6. The Permittee, or his representative, after examining the said tomb or monument, and having taken such notes as he may judge neces-sary, shall, if so desired, hand it over to the Inspector of the Antiquities Service or to any other agent to be appointed by the said Service.

7. The Permittee, or his representative, is bound to draw up forth-
with a "Procès-verbal" showing the particularities observed at the moment of the opening and the place occupied by each object, sub-joining
thereto as many photographs and drawings as possible.[46]

As the balance of duties and risks versus rights and benefits in articles 1–3
and 5–7 would suggest, the Antiquities Service insisted on maintaining a
privileged position with regard to claims on "things-to-be-discovered."[47]
These articles not only stipulate that activities would be conducted under
the supervision of the Antiquities Service, but also that it is the duty of the
concessionaire to submit—verbally, in writing, and through inspections—
all findings to the service. Other articles insisted upon timely publication
of field notes and itemized lists in the annals of the Egyptian Museum.
Hence, many of the recording techniques referred to in Carter's published
best-seller were not just scientific standard practices, but also require-
ments of the concession. As if it were not clear enough, the final article
insures that the service has the right to intervene in, and not just observe,
the excavation of the concessionaire:

Any infraction, on the part of the Permittee or his agents, of the conditions above stated shall entail the cancellation of the present authorization, without any notice being given or any formality being taken. In such
case the Antiquities Service, acting departmentally, shall at once stop
all work and shall take such steps as it may deem necessary in its own
interests and for the safeguarding of the monuments or objects already
discovered at the moment of the stoppage of the excavations, and this
without the Permittee, or any agent of his, having the right to claim any
indemnity or compensation whatsoever or for any reason.[48]

As we have seen, though Egyptian antiquity laws sought to determine
the treatment of artifacts, the actual application of such laws in the field
often deviated substantially from their language. Much of the history of
colonial antiquities law in Egypt is filled with exceptions rather than rules,
with concessionaires successfully maximizing their claims at the expense
of the Antiquities Service. But, for a number of reasons, including the new
formal independence of the Egyptian state, this old arrangement did not
survive the discovery of Tutankhamen's tomb. One of the most remarkable facts of the event was that the Antiquities Service was able to sustain

its claims against Carter and the Carnarvon concession better than it ever had in the past. Among the many points of dispute between Carter and the Antiquities Service, three stand out: public access, state domain, and public property.

The first serious disputes between the Carnarvon concessionaires and the Antiquities Service arose around the issue of press access. When Lord Carnarvon realized the importance of the Tutankhamen discovery, he negotiated, as noted above, an exclusive reporting contract with the *London Times*. Besides the obvious convenience, he had ample financial incentives for doing so, given the substantial amount of capital he had spent in over fifteen years of excavations in Egypt. As part of this business contract, a *Times* reporter, Thomas Merton, accompanied Carter's team at the excavation site, and other news agencies were barred entry. Despite the outcry this arrangement caused in the local and foreign press, the exclusivity contract was maintained for months after the discovery. The Antiquities Service sought to change the arrangement when it came time to renegotiate the Carnarvon concession for the 1923–24 season, which, following Lord Carnarvon's death in April 1923, had been ceded to his wife. Meeting with Carter in Cairo in early October 1923, James Edward Quibell, secretary-general of the Antiquities Service, proposed greater public and press access to Tutankhamen's tomb so as to alleviate the quarrel which was now in the public's eye. Carter responded by shifting the terms of the discussion. Merton's privileged position at the excavation site, Carter asserted, was due to the fact that he had been taken on as a member of the archaeological team. Seeking to split the complaints of the local press from those of the foreign press, Carter proposed that daily press bulletins be made available to both, though on different terms. As Quibell notes, "The *Times* news would be cabled out in the evening, to be printed in the next day's paper. The same news would be given to the Egyptian Press early in the morning, in ample time to be printed in the papers of the day. Thus the news would reach the public in London and in Cairo practically at the same time. The Cairo newspapers will get for nothing what all Europeans and American papers will have to pay for."[49] This proposed arrangement failed. European news agencies charged that having to pay the *Times* for day-old news amounted to extortion. Similarly, Egyptian agencies complained vociferously about the arrangement, charging that the Egyptian public deserved unfettered access to an archaeological find that should, by all rights, be under the jurisdiction of its proper Egyptian state agency. In a rare moment of national unity, Egypt's biggest news outlets—*al-Ahram*, *al-Balagh*, *al-Jumhur*, *al-Akhbar*, and others—jointly petitioned the government on the issue. One can see two points within the complaint: first, that the *Times* arrangement amounted to a monopoly (*ihtikar*) over information that was vital to the Egyptian public; and second, that it was unconscionable, following independence, that a foreign news agency would exclude Egyptians from reporting events in their own country.[50] Quibell, under pressure from British newsmen, had suggested that a communiqué be issued to the general press on the same evening that Merton wired his reports to London, ending the privileges of the *Times* and effectively annulling its exclusivity contract. Carter's response to the Department of Public Works was indignant: "There is no necessity and no justification whatever either in the interest of science or of the public for establishing an additional news service. The information now given is official—that is to say, it is supplied by the excavator himself—and every paper can, and most papers do, obtain and publish the information at one and the same time by arrangement with the *Times*."[51] The Department of Public Works insisted: the Press Bureau would issue reports daily, representatives of the press would be given more regular access to the site, and finally, the Antiquities Service would post an inspector and three Egyptian officials to oversee all operations at the tomb.[52]

The Antiquities Service began to assail the *Times* agreement by questioning Carter's decision to add Merton, who was no archaeologist, to his official staff.[53] After taking the unusual step of asking Carter to submit a list of his official staff, Antiquities Director Lacau wrote to clarify his motivation: "His Excellency the Minister for Public Works . . . would like to have a list of all your collaborators, and reserves the right to approve or to refuse the presence of any one of the collaborators. This right of acceptance of collaborators stems logically from the Government's unquestionable right of material and scientific control over the whole excavation."[54] At the same time, the Antiquities Service stepped up pressure to allow public visits, proposing a system of tickets issued by the Department of Public Works to allow small groups of the press and Egyptian officials to visit the tomb. Even while Carter resisted this demand, on the grounds that such visits interfered with his work, he was granting informal visits to the tomb to colleagues and acquaintances from his and Carnarvon's circles. Director Lacau responded by asking that Carter's guests apply to an Antiquities Service officer when visiting the tomb.[55]

The crisis over access came to a head during the tomb's third official opening, when Carter would open Tutankhamen's sarcophagus. In the run-up to the opening, scheduled to take place on February 12, 1924, Carter received many requests for invitations. According to Carter, members of his staff were adamant about inviting their wives. In its coverage of the crisis, *al-Ahram* reported, "Carter asked Muhammad Zaghloul, Undersecretary of State in the Ministry of Public Works, whether twenty-two ladies—all relatives of his assistants—might be allowed to visit the tomb after the press has departed. Zaghloul replied in jest, 'Are any of your assistants Muslims?' Carter responded, 'What do you mean by that?' Zaghloul replied, 'I wouldn't begrudge you the visits of twenty-two ladies over and above your sixteen men if there was at least one among them who was Muslim!'"[56] As it turned out, the Ministry of Public Works refused to allow family members to enter without prior authorization, and Lacau ordered Egyptian guards to prevent the wives of Carter's European collaborators from entering the tomb.[57] In response, Carter abruptly locked the tomb. Posting a complaint at a nearby luxury hotel in Luxor, Carter announced, "Owing to the impossible restrictions and discourtesies on the part of the Public Works Department and its Antiquities Service, all my collaborators in protest have refused to work any further upon the scientific investigations of the discovery of the tomb of Tut•ankh•amen."[58]

Perhaps Carter did not realize how tenuous his position had become with the death of Lord Carnarvon. By all accounts, Carter had long been rude to the Europeans in the Antiquities Service and openly contemptuous of its Egyptian bureaucrats and officers.[59] Since 1922, their complaints had found ample hearing in the Egyptian press, which charged that Carter's assertion of independence was chauvinistic and that his handling of Egyptian public property—as all antiquities were—was inappropriate.

Acting as he did in February 1924, Carter's sense of timing could not have been worse. The previous autumn, Zaghloul's Wafd Party had overwhelmingly won Egypt's first parliamentary elections. In the weeks prior to the scheduled sarcophagus opening, Zaghloul was in the process of forming his government and had just appointed new ministers to oversee reform in many government agencies, including the Department of Public Works.[60] In light of pressure to show that the Antiquities Service was effective in its efforts to protect the national patrimony, Lacau's response to Carter's self-proclaimed "archaeological strike" was swift: the Carnarvon concession was canceled on the grounds that Carter had abrogated its conditions. The locks were changed and antiquities officers ordered to prevent Carter from reentering the tomb. Addressing an assembly of Egyptian lawyers at the Semiramis Hotel, Prime Minister Zaghloul articulated the issue in terms that linked the struggle for national self-determination with correct scientific method: "Howard Carter does not have the right to lock tombs that are not his. In fact, the interest of science forbids this kind of behavior. Howard Carter is welcome to raise whatever petitions he likes, but the government, who looks to the public interest, will do all it can to protect its rights and dignity, and it will protect science itself. The government is firm in following this path because it is the right one and it is the one that will lead to the preservation of its dignity, its commitments and the caretaking of the public conscience."[61] According to another report of the event, the audience enthusiastically responded with shouts of "Long live Minister Tutankhamen!" and "Let's set our artillery on the Valley of the Kings!"[62]

As King Tutankhamen became an icon of national independence, Egyptian politicians, especially Wafdist statesmen like Murqus Hanna and Saʻd Zaghloul, began to associate themselves with it, making highly publicized tours of the tomb. Such visits did not just confirm that ancient Egypt had become a mainstream fascination, but also a way to assert a newfound Egyptian sense of sovereignty over the modern excavation sites in the country and, by extension, over the ancient past they helped to reconstruct. Over the next decade, such pilgrimages were de rigueur for politicians—what was arguably first a Wafdist ritual was soon taken up by the Liberal Constitutionalists and others.

Carter raised a suit in the Mixed Courts against the Antiquities Service. As many have pointed out, Carter's ill grasp of politics only exacerbated the siituation: he hired the same lawyer, F. M. Maxwell, who had, as British prosecutor, once argued for the death penalty in a case of treason raised against Murqus Hanna, Zaghloul's new minister of public works. In court, Maxwell claimed that the government had behaved "like a bandit," a phrase that became explosive when translated as *haramiyya* (thieves).

Figure 12. Howard Carter (left) with prominent members of the Liberal Constitutionalist Party in front of the entrance to the "laboratory." Immediately behind Carter to his left is Muhammad Tawfiq Nasim; 'Adli Yakan is in the center with a cane. Muhammad Mahmud stands between him and Carter. These three Egyptians all served as prime ministers during the 1920s. Photograph by Harry Burton. © Copyright Griffith Institute, University of Oxford.

Zaghloul's government took offense at the insult and supported the Antiquities Service's case against Carter, arguing the court had no authority to adjudicate in procedural issues within the Antiquities Service.[63]

The issue of access was only one part of Carter's disputes with the Antiquities Service. From the start, there were ugly rumors that Carter and Carnarvon had stolen the mummy of Tutankhamen from the tomb and transported it to England. More real, Carter faced a legal battle with the Egyptian Museum over artifacts from the tomb that had been put on display in, but not (yet) officially added to, the collection of the museum. When the Egyptian Museum published information on the items in its catalogue, Carter claimed it was tantamount to a premature annexation of the objects. In his defense, Carter pointed to articles 8–10 in the text of the concession. These dealt with the property rights around discoveries:

> 8. Mummies of the Kings, of Princes, and of High Priests, together with their coffins and sarcophagi, shall remain the property of the Antiquuities Service.
>
> 9. Tombs which are discovered intact, together with all objects they may contain, shall be handed over to the Museum whole and without division.
>
> 10. In the case of tombs which have already been searched, the Antiquities Service shall, over and above the mummies and sarcophagi intended in Article 8, reserve for themselves all objects of capital importance from the point of view of history and archaeology, and shall share the remainder with the Permittee. As it is probable that the majority of such tombs as may be discovered will fall within the category of the present article, it is agreed that the Permittee's share will sufficiently recompense him for the pains and labour of the undertaking.[64]

As this last article makes explicit, the expectation was that, aside from the mummies of notables, most "found objects" would be divided between the concessionaire and the Antiquities Service. The disagreement over the possession of those items advertised by the Egyptian Museum in Cairo arose out of a dispute over how Article 9 applied to the case of Tutankhamen's tomb. During the initial official opening in 1922, Carter presented the tomb as intact, going so far as to cover up evidence that the antechamber had been broken into during antiquity. What was at stake was the fact that, if it had been discovered intact, the tomb and its contents would have become the property of the museum, a point on which Lacau was clear.[65] Carter shot back:

> The tomb of Tut•ankh•amen has been searched. It was not found intact. The conclusions to be drawn from these documents appear to me to be sufficiently obvious. Until the Antiquities Department has selected the articles which it proposes to reserve, and fixed their value, until the executors of the Earl of Carnarvon have put their value on these objects, until the Antiquities Department has exercised the option of taking or leaving these objects at the last-named valuation, until the remaining articles have been divided, and until finally the executors have chosen their share, the articles found do not form part of the Public Domain, the rights of the Administration are not exclusive, and the reservation of the rights of the executors is not irrelevant. . . . The articles described do not yet—and perhaps some of them never will—form part of the collection of the Museum.[66]

These claims became moot after Carter lost control of the tomb. But his dispute with the Antiquities Service over property (and propriety) was not yet over: in early April, workmen discovered an uncatalogued wooden statue of Tutankhamen in Carter's workshop. Carter had found the piece while clearing out the debris of the entrance passage. Because he had failed to catalogue the rare piece and had hidden it in a tea crate, there were discussions about Carter's professionalism. At the least, he had broken professional norms and Antiquities Service regulations by treating the object this way. More skeptical minds accused Carter of trying to smuggle the statue out of the excavation site.

As these disputes over access and property rights developed, the Department of Public Works increasingly expressed its position in terms of state power and public domain. For instance, in a letter of November 1923, Lacau asserts, "[The] Egyptian Government, whilst ready and willing . . . to advise you beforehand of the measures which it proposes to adopt, cannot admit any limitation on its own exclusive right to regulate matters of a purely administrative character, such as carrying into effect of a concession over the Public Domain, or matters of public policy and of general interest, such as access of the public to a part of the State's Domain, and reports to the public of operations conducted under the control of the Antiquities Service."[67] In the popular Egyptian press, these issues were commonly linked to state sovereignty. This in itself was something of an innovation. Had Carter's discovery come even months before or perhaps even some months after, the terms of the Carnarvon concession might not have been interpreted in such a fashion. Indeed, never had the control of foreign excavation in Egypt—and the restriction of the press—been so politicized. Likewise, rarely before had the existing antiquities laws been so strictly interpreted and so vigilantly applied by these two state agencies. True, decrees concerning the excavation, transportation, and treatment of antiquities had been issued since the 1830s and had developed as a body of law from the 1880s onward. More often than not, however, the laws were inconsistently applied. Never had they been associated so closely with the ideas of national self-determination or state sovereignty. When Carter and his supporters showed indignation at the strictness with which the Antiquities Service began to interpret the terms of the Carnarvon concession, it was in no small part owing to their expectation that the state agencies would cater to the interests of the concessionaires, rather than vice versa. Given the previous decades' history of the interpretation and enforcement of laws guiding European excavation in Egypt, these expectations were not unrealistic. However, in this case they proved to be sorely mistaken.

Two factors in the Tutankhamen case contributed to this change and to the strengthening of the antiquities laws governing the Carnarvon concession. First, there was the fact that this tomb was certainly more intact than previous finds. The sheer splendor and value of the objects meant that far more was at stake in this site that in any previous discovery. Thus, part of what contributed to the way Carter's dispute transformed the interpretation of antiquities law is rooted in the quality of the antiquities in question. Second, one cannot emphasize enough the coincidence between the discovery and the emergence of parliamentary politics in Egypt. The proceedings which ended in Carter's expulsion from the tomb site—the strengthened interpretation of the terms of the Carnarvon concession, the Antiquities Service's decision to bring the site under its direct control, and the very public state ceremonies around the various openings at the time—owed as much to developments in the political sphere as they did to events taking place in the Valley of the Kings.

It is not possible to appreciate how these developments in the political sphere took place and how they were so easily attached to Egyptological discoveries without situating them within Egypt's print culture. Here, Pharaonist icons and themes had been appearing for decades. From the late nineteenth century, the discoveries of Egyptology had not only been the subject of regular reporting in omnibus journals such as *al-Muqtataf*, but had inspired a distinctive iconographic style in various public arenas, from official state images (such as postage stamps and currency) to urban spaces (such as architecture). In the print culture of the late nineteenth century, Pharaonic imagery remained relatively marginal, though there were notable exceptions. For instance, the image of the Pyramids served as the masthead of Egypt's first serial, *al-Waqa'i' al-Misriyya*, founded by Tahtawi in 1829. Again, in the 1870s, the Pyramids became the banner icon of another newspaper, *al-Ahram* (The Pyramids), founded by the pro-French Syrian-Christian journalist Bishara Taqla. But it was not until the 1910s that the Arabic-language press in Egypt began to incorporate Pharaonic iconography more widely. Copt publishers played a large role in this development, starting small, often short-lived journals like *Ra'masis* (Ramses), *Fir'awn* (Pharaoh), *Abu Hawl* (The Sphinx), and *'Ayn al-Shams* (Heliopolis) that offered a political and cultural point of view that was either explicitly Coptic or secular in orientation. More than any other public figure before the 1920s, it was Ahmad Lutfi al-Sayyid, whom I discussed in chapter 3, who linked the interpretation of ancient Egypt to an anticolonial political program. Following the discovery of King Tutankhamen's tomb in 1922, however, Pharaonic themes exploded across the mainstream culture of Egypt's press iconography.

Some of these journals, like *Kliyubatra* (Cleopatra) and *Wadi al-Muluk* (Valley of the Kings) (which boasted that ten thousand copies of each edition were printed and distributed throughout Egypt and the Sudan), soon disappeared. Other journals from the 1920s such as *al-Siyasa al-Usbu'iyya* (The Weekly Political), the mouthpiece of the Liberal Constitutionalist Party, were to have a much wider impact and survive much longer. The Pharaonist visual style that appeared in the journals was often ornamental, since many treated Pharaonic topics only seldom in their print articles, and not all related the ancient past so directly to the political

Figure 13. *Kliyupatra* 1:2 (August 1924): "The Head of State and Exalted President, Sa'd Zaghloul Pasha."

present. Yet their style was significant to the creation of wider Pharaonist messages. In this regard, consider the iconography of *Kliyubatra*, which is not atypical of the style of visual Pharaonism found in the press during the 1920s. The first issue featured an image of King Fu'ad, the second, of Sa'd Zaghloul. The magazine's hieroglyphic and architectural allusions are superficial, meant to suggest ancient Egypt as a mood. Yet even as mere ornament, the journal's iconography conveys more than an empty gesture toward history in that it links the past and present by way of the theme of royalty and state power. The same is true throughout much of the Pharaonist visual style of the press during the period: it is an iconography that depicts the Pharaonic past as a time when Egypt was ruled by royal sovereigns and powerful governments. It is not surprising that such an association would be made at the same time Tutankhamen's tomb was discovered: only in 1922 was the title of the sultan of Egypt transformed into the title king of Egypt, the first since ancient times. Just as the interest in King Tutankhamen proved to be useful for thinking about the new institution of royalty in modern Egypt, so were the press images of the royal Pharaonic past engaged in this same conversation.

At the same time, there were calls for ancient Egypt to be the source of an authentically Egyptian corpus of modern art and literature. Chief among the proponents of this idea was Muhammad Husayn Haykal, who had studied law in France and began his career as a public intellectual in the pages of al-Sayyid's influential journal of the 1910s, *al-Jarida*. Haykal, one of the literary luminaries of the period, was the author of novels, biographies, and criticism. Moreover, Haykal was a major political figure of the post-1919 period. As the leader of the Liberal Constitutionalist Party, he edited *al-Siyasa al-Usbu'iyya* and eventually came to serve as minister of education on more than one occasion in the 1930s and 1940s. From the mid-1920s, Haykal was a strident champion of Pharaonism in literature and in politics, and in his journalism the literary and political strands are tied together most seamlessly. In its early years, *al-Siyasa al-Usbu'iyya*'s visual image was unabashedly Pharaonist and depicted Thoth, the god of writing and knowledge. Its Pharaonic themes were by no means decoration since they also figured prominently in its coverage and analysis of Egyptian culture. Throughout the 1920s and into the first part of the next decade, *al-Siyasa al-Usbu'iyya* served as the premiere platform for literary Pharaonism. In one of his most influential essays on Egyptian culture,

Haykal spoke of historical unities between the present and the past which, when properly understood, would transcend contemporary social and political differences. In a permutation of the old moralist theme, Haykal chides readers:

> Between modern and ancient Egypt is an abiding spiritual tie. Many forget this, thinking that the developments Egypt has experienced since the age of the Pharaohs in political systems, religious creeds, and language . . . have definitively cut the ties between the present nation and the ancient Egyptian nation. We consider the Arabs or Romans closer relatives to us than those who built the civilization of the Nile Valley thousands of years before Christianity. The majority of Egyptians are Muslim, a minority Christian; their beliefs are based on the Holy Books, which are themselves joined by a strong tie. How could anyone think that they share any beliefs with the worshippers of Amon, Ra and the many other gods they worshipped? How could anyone see any tie linking their beliefs with those ancient beliefs?[68]

Relying on contemporary ethnographic accounts of the rural south, Haykal goes on to assert that the bond between the past and present is based not merely on archaeological research and patriotic feeling, but crucially on the persistence of ancient manners and customs among modern Egyptian peasants:

> The blood that ran through their veins runs through yours. Those instincts which drove them on in their life are what drive you on in yours. . . . You cannot deny that abiding spiritual tie that joins the history of Egypt from its beginning to the age of the present to the end of the future eras that history might know. The motivations of life may change. Railroads, steamships and airplanes may bring the corners of the world into close contact with one another. International borders may crumble and national sentiment wither away. But this abiding spiritual tie will remain forever, this tie that makes Egypt an eternal whole. The Nile remains, the skies of Egypt remain, the essential environment of this valley remains, and people continue to inhabit the place. Grandfathers bequeath to their grandsons what their environment generously bestows upon them.[69]

The timelessness of the Egyptian peasant, a feature of Cromer's colonial rhetoric, becomes here an organic component of nationalist discourse. If Haykal was clear about the European origins of Egyptology, it was only to sharpen the moral obligation of modern Egyptians:

> [We should] search for contact points between ancient and modern Egypt in the fields of literature and books, beliefs and religious rituals. Westerners have opened the door for us in this area. Since Champollion uncovered the secret of the Hieroglyphs by deciphering the Rosetta Stone, there's been an unbroken string of missions from Europe and America coming to explore and excavate Egyptian antiquities and to bring to life what the silent stones speak and the papyri conceal. This has been a gift from them which we should acknowledge. But it puts a great burden upon us, the burden of neglecting to absorb this glorious tradition which joins bright civilizations that might be to us today a lantern for creating a civilization whose brightness and glory will not be less than those.[70]

For Haykal, Egyptians would best absorb the lessons of Pharaonism by way of art. In numerous articles in *al-Siyasa al-Usbu'iyya* during the late 1920s, Haykal called upon Egyptian artists and writers to create an indigenous style that would serve as the aesthetic counterpart to nationalist politics. The list of early- to mid-twentieth-century poets, playwrights, and novelists who heeded the Pharaonist call is long. It includes most of the major poets of the day, including Ahmad Shawqi, Khalil Mutran, Hafiz Ibrahim, Ahmad Zaki Abu Shadi,[71] and 'Abbas Mahmoud al-'Aqqad, all of whom, following the discovery of King Tutankhamen, abandoned neoclassical themes to experiment with Pharaonist motifs. The list also includes playwrights Tawfiq al-Hakim,[72] Ahmad Shawqi,[73] Ahmad Zaki Abu Shadi,[74] and 'Ali Ahmad Bakathir,[75] who joined Mahmud Murad[76] in composing dramas set in ancient Egypt. Murad's musicals featured music composed by Egypt's most famous musician and composer of the period, Sayyid Darwish. It includes novelists like Tawfiq al-Hakim, 'Adil Kamil,[77] and Naguib Mahfouz, all of whom wrote novels which were either set in the ancient past or spoke to the enduring presence of the Pharaonic spirit in the present.[78] In this way, the discovery of Tutankhamen's tomb coincided with an existing public culture, giving it new fuel and helping to create a noteworthy body of Arabic literature in the process.[79]

THE LITERATURE OF DISCOVERY:
ANIMATE ARTIFACTS

Some of this literature was not just inspired by the ancient past, but focused on and recapitulated contemporary archaeological discoveries in a nationalist narrative. These literary texts represented the objects of discovery in two ways: on the one hand, as the still-life patrimony of their nation; on the other, as animated agents within an anticolonial struggle. That is to say, the literary reproduction of the discovery and its objects depicts them both as property belonging to the Egyptian nation and as vanguard subjects of Egyptian nationalist action. Crucial to these representations of national subjects and objects is the depiction of time.

Nowhere are these themes more developed than in the work of the poet Ahmad Shawqi, who dedicated a number of poems to the subject of Tutankhamen.[80] In one poem, Shawqi echoes newspaper reports of visits (and also draws upon the classical figure of the companions), while urging Egyptians to pay their respects to Tutankhamen's tomb:

> O, my two companions, go down to the valley, head toward the chambers
>   of the setting suns,
> Pass through their stony places, pass humbly by their funereal couches,
>   Salute the remains of glory of our Tutankhamen,
> And a tomb that, by its beauty and goodness, almost made the stones shine
>   and the clay smell sweet.
> And which appeared by the splendor of history, as if its sublime stones had
>   been fashioned from those of [Moses'] Mt. Sinai.
> Its guest had been called a king, and its treasure priceless.
> Along with a multitude cheering for that king, as those of old had champi-
>   oned him.
> There is a greatness fixed [in that place] which has stood for forty cen-
>   turies.[81]

Here, the objects of the discovery lie silent before the gaze of visitors, and time comes to a halt. But this still-life representation is the exception in Shawqi's depictions of Tutankhamen. In a contrasting passage from another poem, Shawqi describes at length the objects found in the interior of the tomb—from the embalmed mummy to the statues and the painted reliefs on the walls. Describing the wrappings of the body, he writes,

> Shrouds of embroidery, separated by fine bright gold leaf.
> A somber, careful embalmer gave them the wrapping of bandages.
> As if they were the perianth, and you were the rosebud enclosed.
> In every corner graven images, in every nook a book.
> You see statues, and imagine them scattered about the edges of the gallery.
> Images that show you movement, though their origin is stillness.
> The clarity of their silence passes over the senses, like clear speech.
> Their paint accompanied time, from ancient age to ancient age.
> The paint remains fresh, despite the lengthy trials [of time], and alive, despite the long duration of death.
> The paint tricks the eyes and still challenges those who touch it.
> The young men of your palace taking to riding and hunting.
> The trumpets blaring, the arrows singing, and the bows moaning tenderly.
> Your hunting dogs panting, your horse driven mad.
> The wild beasts stampeding across the plains, leaping across rough ground.
> Wounded birds, strung together, cries still in their beaks.
> As if the forefathers of the earth were brought into the cities.
> As if the Dynasty of the Pharaohs were all around, to your left and your right.[82]

Here, the objects of discovery are not lifeless. Rather, the passage here moves from a description of the mummy being embalmed by the hands of an ancient priest to books and statues that speak eloquently despite their silence. By the time the poem's eye has turned to the bas-reliefs of the tomb walls, these objects are not behaving like objects at all. Instead they become (quite literally) the subjects of the poem's verbs. Moreover, they do more than depict ancient scenes of hunting and royal power: they also enact them and in so doing resurrect them in the present.

The prosopopoeia of Shawqi's poetry plays on the theme of reawakening and rebirth dominant within the literature explored in chapter 3. However, whereas in that literature the theme of resurrection takes place on the level of human protagonists, for Shawqi it occurs in the material of archaeology. Representing the objects in animate terms also speaks to the presentation of time in this kind of literature. For instance, in the above passage, Shawqi's description of the "reliefs-come-alive" projects the ancient past into the colonial present. The meeting of these two eras is not an easy one: the resurrection of the past is a challenge to the present. In this fashion, Tutankhamen's discovery—a sort of resurrection from death—becomes a comment on colonial Egypt's need to be reborn. While the poem recites the passage of different historical eras, each marked by foreign rule (with the example of the Arab era noticeably absent from the list), it also presents Egypt's time as eternal, timeless.

Shawqi's treatment of the confrontation between the colonial present and the ancient past draws upon the classical literary figure of the ruins (*atlal*), which explicitly depicts the event in terms of subject-object relations. In lines that evoke the panegyric rhetoric of classical poetry, Shawqi links praise for his talents as poet to the power of Tutankhamen:

> King of Kings, I salute you with the loyalty of a trustworthy protector.
> I know this sacred saint's tomb, and have outstripped the narrators in praising it.
> I've stood by your remnants [*athar*], adorning and clarifying their sublimity.
> With twenty of its stones, I built my strong poetry.
> The sources of my poems poured forth, and the spring water gushed from stone.
> I made one generation sit for passion and another stand up for it.[83]

As we saw in the classical tradition, the concrete figure of the ruins—the abandoned encampment, the beloved's abodes, etc.—sets into motion a melancholic reflection on the passing of time and on the inability of humans to change this fact. The ruins figure somewhere between presence and absence, signification imagined as full or as empty. The traces (*athar*, also, in the modern period, "antiquities") point to a structure that once existed but is now almost entirely obliterated. Not even the poem can compensate for the loss marked by the figure-object of the ruins: it too becomes yet another trace marked, then erased, by the passing of time.[84] In Shawqi's hands, however, the ruins do not figure in this way at all. Rather, they become the concrete, permanent markers of the past. This recurs elsewhere in another poem on Tutankhamen when Shawqi writes,

> God Almighty, there was enchantment in them, for do not [their] stones speak reasonably [to us]?
> They departed, building what remains, and left immortal things behind the eternities!
> When they embarked on an accomplishment, they prepared for it certainty and solid creation.
> For immortality is not a status [usually] received from the lips of pre-Islamic pagans.[85]

Shawqi's reference to ruins thus turns the classical tradition on its head: Tutankhamen's ruins point not to an ongoing loss of meaning, but to its recuperation; they suggest not the indeterminacy of poetic meaning-making but rather its clear proof. Shawqi depicts Tutankhamen's ruins so as to collapse time, or at least to traverse it. Later in the same poem, Shawqi describes Tutankhamen's victorious reemergence into the modern era as the source of confusion. The poet wonders whether what he is witnessing is an event from Egypt's past or from its present (or even future):

> If your departure yesterday was a journey, or a plain victory [*fath mubin*: also, a clear archaeological discovery],
> If your resurrection was from the slow movement of spirits, or the beating of a heart,
> And if you came out of the Valley of the Kings wearing a garland of victors,
> With bowing horses dressed in gold,
> With two rings of spears and armor in your sword belt.
> And with a train of soldiers driving on shackled kings,
> I would have taken you for another generation of unbowed giants.
> I would have mistaken you for a subjected people who'd exhausted themselves, and then returned as rulers.[86]

The lines of the poem are wonderfully ambiguous: "departure yesterday," suggests both Tutankhamen's death in ancient times and the modern removal of his mummy in modern ones; likewise, *fath mubin* suggests both the modern discovery of Tutankhamen's tomb and a victory on the part of the ancient king. The poet cannot determine whether this military procession from the site of excavation is an ancient one or a modern one. Yet for all its deliberate confusion about time, what is not confused is its relationship to the concept of the nation. The recovery of the nation's timelessness—its eternal identity—is a necessary stage in a political process, the return of Egyptians as rulers of their own country.

The association between the discovery of Tutankhamen's tomb and Egyptian self-rule is one made throughout Shawqi's poetry. Critics have argued that Shawqi's poetics follow from his nationalist politics, but this misses the crucial point that his poetics enable his politics. In other words, it is impossible to imagine Shawqi's nationalist images without reading them in light of the poetic figures which motivate them, key among them the ruins. In one poem, he describes Tutankhamen's emergence in terms of a return home to Egypt, which he finds under English rule:

> He traveled forty centuries, considering them until he came home, and
> found there . . .
> England, and its army, and its lord, brandishing its Indian sword, protecting
> its India.[87]

At the end of his longest poem on Tutankhamen, Shawqi situates Tutankhamen's discovery within a historical moment of decolonization:

> Pharaoh, the time of self-rule is in effect, and the dynasty of arrogant lords
> has passed.
> Now the foreign tyrants in every land must relinquish their rule over their
> subjects![88]

The foreign tyrants (in the Arabic, *al-ru'a*, "the Shepherds") are a reference to a moment in Pharaonic history when the "Shepherd Kings" (the Hittites) ruled over Egypt until they were expelled.[89] Thus ancient history becomes a source not just for analogizing modern colonial history, but also for cultivating a sense of confidence that the outcome, Egyptian self-rule, will be the same. The recollection of King Tutankhamen becomes a rich source for thinking about the return of Egyptian sovereignty. In another poem, Shawqi associates Egypt's formal independence (in 1924) with Tutankhamen's discovery: both are indications of Egypt's recovery of self. The official visits of state politicians become, in this poem, a return of Egyptian sons to mother Egypt:

> Young Egypt has reached her majority, and the pure blood has confirmed her righteousness.
> She balanced on the rope herself, testing slackness and tautness alike.
> She sent her shrewdest and toughest, and they fought for her cause in the West,
> She dispatched her soldiers to Parliament and gathered together her crowds for the festival,
> She urged her old and young to it and showed off her buxom young girls and maidens.
> She spread out her roses along the road, and received her heart [King Fu'ad] and her Wafd delegation . . .
> Tutankhamen has established Egypt's representative body, fortified its convocation, and he conferred the promise [of self-government] to this happy generation.
> Tutankhamen has returned his authority to our sons![90]

Shawqi's poetry not only links and celebrates the coincidence of Tutankhamen's discovery and the emergence of Parliament. It also describes, in clear detail, the conflict that emerged between Carter and the Antiquities Service. Throughout these poems, Carter figures as a representative of colonial dispossession, cutting off modern Egyptians from their history. In one section, he writes of Egyptians attempting to visit Tutankhamen's tomb but being prevented from doing so by Carter:

> We sought out those doors of yours, but Carter shut them in the face of all delegations.
> He would have continued to prevent us from approaching you if we had not made the efforts we did not want to make![91]

More serious, Shawqi reproduces the accusation that Carter was stealing from the excavation site:

Our forefathers, and their greatest [Tutankhamen], are an inheritance that
we should be careful not to let pass into the hands of others.

We refuse to allow our patrimony to be mistreated, or for thieves to steal
it away.

While you were silent, every suspicion swirled around you. Had you spoken
up, the suspicions would not have arisen.

People spoke in secret and in public, and you have no ruse against the gos-
sip mongers.

Aren't those who kidnapped the living Caliph [Wahid al-Din] capable of
stealing off with dead kings?[92]

Elsewhere, the poetry asks for retribution for Carter's arrogance, that he
suffer the same mosquito bite which killed his patron, Carnarvon: "I said
to you, 'Strike his hand and cut it off! And send his way the nuisance of
mosquitoes!'"[93]

Admittedly, Shawqi's poetic representations belong to an elite literary
tradition, but the morbid reference to Pharaonic retribution contained in
the last line connects it with a more popular tradition of Egyptian literature on Tutankhamen. In this popular literature, mummies appear prominently, usually as figures of vengeance striking against those who disturbed
their tombs. Part of this literature was rooted in historical events: Carnarvon died of an infected mosquito bite not long after the discovery in
late 1922, and soon after, other prominent Europeans associated with the
opening of Tutankhamen's tomb also died in unexplained circumstances.
In the press, Arthur Conan Doyle referred to it as the "Pharaoh's curse,"
and (unfounded) reports began to appear telling of the Pharaoh's curse
written in hieroglyphs in Tutankhamen's tomb.[94] In this way the mummy
became something of a national hero in Egyptian literature, vanquishing
the colonizers from beyond the grave. This was a real innovation in the
representation of mummies in the Egyptian press.[95] In one humorous literary vignette from the period, the Sphinx and Tutankhamen debate their
respective nationalist credentials:

The Sphinx: Hey Amun! Amun!
Tutankhamun: Who's that calling my name?
Sphinx: It's me!
Tut: Is that you, Sphinx? [then in English:] How are you, old fellow?

Sphinx: What's this, my son, you're speaking English now?

Tut: Yes, but that's because in my tomb I hear nothing but English.

Sphinx: Aren't you ashamed to let yourself be colored English? Where has your true patriotism gone?

Tut: Leave me in peace! You're not one to talk, letting the English photograph your backside!

Sphinx: That's because they're tourists.

Tut: Is that any excuse? Are they not also English?

Sphinx: I didn't call you to argue about this. I'm angry with you about some things you've done. . . . Aren't you ashamed of how you got rid of those noble men?

Tut: . . . Who are you calling noble? If those people were noble, they wouldn't set foot into other people's tombs. [Normally] when someone yanks something from the hand of a dead person, it's called stealing. But when they snatch it after a thousand years have passed, they call it a great archaeological discovery and all honor goes to the one who committed the crime. . . . I have to defend myself as best I can.

Sphinx: Still, whoever comes near you is in danger! And now that silly judge who had the misfortune to be assigned to preside over the current dispute with Howard Carter has had his foot severed in a tram accident. What do you have to say about that?

Tut: That one was the conductor's fault, [not mine]![96]

Most mummy fictions from this period narrate a far more earnest story of colonial penetration and nationalist retribution. One short story, "Yaqzat Fir'awn" (A Pharaoh Awakes),[97] tells the story of King Tutankhamen on the eve of discovery: Tutankhamen is awakened by an Egyptian deity who advises him to flee before the shovels of the Westerners who are coming to desecrate his tomb. Strangely, the mummy-king tells the messenger that he will surrender: the reign of the Pharaohs is over, they have no more power in the new Egypt. As he prepares for the opening of the tomb, the mummy puts on his finest clothing and jewelry in order to shine before his discoverers. In another story, "al-Yadd al-Muhannata" (The Embalmed Hand),[98] a rebellious princess, punished for eternity by having her hand separated from her body, pursues Lord Hamon, who had come to purchase her hand in Egypt. Back home in Ireland, the lord notices that the hand comes back to life with the full moon—he has the phenomenon verified by scientific experts. One night, as he and his wife chant verses from the Egyptian *Book of the Dead*, the princess arrives, takes her hand, and vanishes peacefully into the night.

These stories, moreover, resonate with a broad range of stories which play with the idea of the revivification of Tutankhamen's mummy as an act of awakening. In February and March of 1923, for instance, there appeared a series of "mummy awakes" stories in the pages of *al-Ahram*—with titles like "Tutankhamen Speaks," "Tutankhamen Addresses Egypt's Interests" and "Tutankhamen Holds the Ministry Accountable"—that playfully tie the enlightenment themes of the Nahda to issues of governance. The figure of the mummy in these short Egyptian fictions is not that of the mummy in European literature or cinema: rather than being objects of desire or horror, the Egyptian mummies are relatively benign. They incite neither desire nor fear and do not disrupt social order. But the most telling characteristic of these figures of the mummy is how they appear as benevolent ancestors and patriarchs who seek restitution for Egypt. These mummy fictions transform the objects of discovery one more way—turning Tutankhamen's mummy into something more human than artifact. The objects as figured in these texts belong not to institutions of (Western) scientific description or (colonial) public exhibition, but rather to the mystical origins of an eternal national identity.

The process of Tutankhamen's artifaction—at the archaeological site and in law, literature, and the press—was contentious, and its consequences were sometimes ambiguous. By highlighting the contingency of this history one can denaturalize the commonsensical understanding of such objects and their discovery. The objects discovered by Carter *matter* to our understanding of colonial archaeology in Egypt in every sense of the word: they were important not just for what they said about the past, but also for how they signified in modern Egypt as material upon which identities and sovereignties could be expressed. Without a doubt, the antiquities discovered in the Valley of the Kings in November 1922 were privileged objects serving as the material grounds for grand colonial and nationalist narratives about time and civilization. The ambiguities of value and meaning also suggest that these material objects could be a source for confounding such narratives or for producing better ones. A more complete reckoning of the processes enacted by Tutankhamen's discovery and the subsequent struggles over property rights and public exhibition would have to explore more than the brief period of months considered here. As the eighty plus years since their discovery have shown, the significance of the objects from Tutankhamen's tomb has only continued to expand.[99] While the event of the discovery of Tutankhamen's tomb belongs to Egyptology's mature and professional period, its science was never separable either from colorful literary sensibilities and impassioned aesthetic judgments or from the pleasures associated with the commercial leisure activities of the European touring classes. Likewise, the practice of archaeological science at Tutankhamen's tomb could never be purely disinterested because it depended upon a legal system that apportioned rights and obligations according to a volatile colonial balance of powers. Finally, the relation between Egyptology and the expressive—especially literary and political—cultures surrounding it cannot be described in terms of (archaeological) cause and (cultural) effect. It is impossible to extricate the science of the Egyptological moment of Tutankhamen's discovery from the literary and political cultures in which it occurred and to which it then gave rise. Indeed, Carter's discovery stemmed directly from his reading of Belzoni's travel narrative, itself a response to Hamilton's *Aegyptiaca*, which had depended upon Vivant Denon's best-selling *Voyages*, which in turn responded to an eighteenth-century tradition of aesthetic travel writing, which in turn cited medieval Arabic sources, which referred to ancient Greek and Latin ones, and so on. Moreover, the amount of Arabic literature produced in the wake of Tutankhamen's discovery helped to fuel the political interpretation of the event that nationalists were developing, which in turn bore directly upon the execution of scientific practices at the archaeological site.

When Carter described his initial encounter with the stuff of Tutankhamen's tomb in terms of wonder, he meant it in the sense that for him these objects existed beyond and outside any regular cognitive framework. More wondrous perhaps is how such an intelligent person ever thought that such objects could ever be estranged from the histories, traditions, and institutions—which is to say, the *conflicts*—in which the work of colonial Egyptology proceeded. Separating itself from and then forgetting the networks and contexts in which it works may be how Egyptology has often secured its unique intellectual authority. Yet, if we were to accept that version of the event, we would, of course, think that Egyptologists worked in Egypt as if it were a sterilized laboratory, as if their discoveries belonged exclusively to the world of academic science, and as if the rest—the colonial context, the literary productions, the political conflicts—were mere externalities in the production of knowledge about the ancient past. To do so, however, is to accept an intentionally fractured view of the world. In this sense, among the wonderful things revealed by the analysis of Tutankhamen's discovery is that one might recombine those contexts and claims—the scientific, the literary, the political—differently in order to see the event of Egyptology otherwise.

Nahdat Misr

Let the curtain be raised on your sublime statue. O *Nahda*, you embody the hopes of generations!—AHMAD ZAKI ABU SHADI,
from "Timthal al-Nahda"

—Did your alarm clock wake you up in time to see the unveiling of the statue, "Egypt's Awakening" [*Nahdat Misr*]"?
   —I had a headache. The only "getting up" [*nahda*] I saw was commotion and bickering.—Cartoon from *al-Kashkul*

The career of the sculptor Mahmoud Mukhtar (1891–1934) illustrates the close identification between the Wafd-led nationalists and Pharaonist aesthetic style. Mukhtar was the first student to enroll in the Egyptian School of Fine Art when it opened in 1908. The school's patron, Prince Yusuf Kamal, sent Mukhtar to Paris in 1911. Before leaving Egypt, the artist had worked on busts of national heroes, sculptures of heroes from Islamic history, and rustic themes from the Egyptian countryside.[1] In Paris, Mukhtar turned toward ancient Egyptian themes, producing a statue of Aïda in 1912, the first sculpture by an Arab artist to exhibit internationally. Indeed, Pharaonism was literally thrust upon him almost as soon as he arrived in Paris: "I had to go through the experience of being a new student at the Beaux Arts. I was stripped stark naked and tied to a chair. I was crowned with a pharaoh's crown made of paper and given the title of Rameses II. I was then carried all around the streets of Paris until we reached the Café Bonaparte while the passers-by just looked at us and smiled. They deposited me on a sofa, still naked as ever, and called for food and drink."[2] After producing wax models of the heroes of World War I and the Peace Conference, Mukhtar turned to commemorate the Revolution of 1919, eventually sculpting a work entitled *Nahdat Misr: Le Réveil de L'Égypte* (Egypt's Renaissance), which instantly became an icon not just of Pharaonist aesthetic style, but of the Egyptian national liberation movement and *Nahda*-era culture more generally. *Nahdat Misr* won the annual exhibition in the Grand Palais, another first for an Arab artist. It also attracted the attention of Egyptian elites visiting Paris in 1920. Wisa Wasif, a prominent Copt leader in the Wafdist movement, was one of those who saw it: "[*Nahdat Misr*] is an Egyptian woman. A peasant woman standing, her head raised, the marks of pride and hope clear on her face. At her feet, the Sphinx. This peasant woman stands with her right hand on the Sphinx's head, calling him to arise from his prostration. He has heard her beckon and raises his head toward her, bringing his chest off the sand, his ears toward the call of the one who awakens him."[3] Wasif's report was part of a larger campaign to raise funds for erecting a larger version of *Nahdat Misr* in a public square in the Egyptian capital. Within months, the committee overseeing the project had raised sixty-five hundred Egyptian pounds. In 1921, the Egyptian Cabinet granted permission for the statue to be erected in the square directly facing Cairo's rail station. The place chosen by the committee was highly symbolic and designed to be the first thing a passenger getting off the train would see. Though one intended audience of the statue was the Egyptian public, supporters of the plan admitted it was above all meant for foreign consumption, since it would "convince the world that Egypt still cared about the fine arts and that it was attempting to bring back its ancient glory in this field," and "advertise the Egyptian cause in a way that would attract the most attention."[4]

In granting permission for the statue to be placed in a public square, Prime Minister 'Adli Yakan noted that the project was privately funded, though that was to change. Because of the cost of building special lines to connect the railways to the Aswan granite quarry, the project's costs began to expand precipitously. By 1924, over twelve thousand Egyptian pounds of public funds were tied up in *Nahdat Misr*, and the project had become part of the Department of Public Works. At this point, the history of the statue became bound up in ministerial politics, and its fate decided in no small part at the level of struggles between competing parties and factions within the new Egyptian parliamentary government. Work was stopped and plans put under bureaucratic scrutiny that was partisan. At one point, Salah 'Anan, public works commissioner, suggested that

Figure 14. *Ruz al-Yusuf*, 1928: "*The Renaissance of Egypt* as it should be." Caption below image reads: "Egyptian Peasant Woman: Stop the fuss and headaches! We've been standing on our feet for seven years—where were you? My feet hurt from standing so long! As long as Mr. Mukhtar is sitting, you should sit down too, Sphinx. Egypt won't be getting up [*nahida*] until we see the light of day!"

the sculpture would be better placed in front of the zoo. He also recommended the "formation of a committee composed of people with aesthetic taste to look into the statue's appropriateness."[5] In 1926, Mukhtar's salary was stopped while he was traveling abroad.

When the statue was completed in 1928, its unveiling became a state occasion of the highest order. Most of the major political players were present, including King Fu'ad, the British high commissioner, Prime Minister Mustafa al-Nahhas, the Wafd Party leadership, and many members of Parliament. Shawqi recited a poem he had composed for the occasion, while others—Khalil Mutran and Ahmad Zaki Abu Shadi most notably—also panegyrized the statue. What is remarkable in the press accounts of the event is the shared perception of the statue as an object that brought together abstract concepts and expansive historical perspective. Moreover, *Nahdat Misr* did not just join these themes, it made them into something concrete and tangible. This allegorical reading is one that has remained virtually unchallenged to this day. Speaking of the statue as an object linking past, present, and future, Prime Minister al-Nahhas asserted, "It represents the glory of the past, the earnestness of the present, and the hope of the future. It represents a picture of young Egypt preoccupied with the Sphinx so that it may revive through her and she through it, directing its glance towards its old power and copying the glorious precedent of its reawakening. . . . If there is a single nation whose ancient past vindicates its current rebirth, that nation is Egypt."[6]

As a public event, the unveiling of *Nahdat Misr* in 1928 was without precedent. While poetry had long had a prominent place in state functions, the plastic arts, particularly sculpture, did not; there were a handful of other statues in modern Cairo's public squares, but they all depicted specific royal figures and national heroes, not symbolic themes or abstract concepts. Reports of the unveiling suggest that the crowd's response was overwhelming and spontaneous:

Last Sunday at 6:30 PM, thousands upon thousands gathered in Cairo Station Square. Thousands had been invited by the Department of Public Works. Thousands of others came from all over Egypt to witness collectively the unveiling of the sculpture *Nahdat Misr*. The hour arrived and the order to unveil the statue was given. The soldier began to lift it off slowly for the spectators. No sooner did the head of the Egyptian woman appear . . . when a shiver went through the souls and bodies of those present. Instantly, thousands of hands clapped and a cry split the heavens, "Long live *Egypt's Renaissance!*" No Egyptian who was gathered there in the square could help himself from being overwhelmed by this powerful, wondrous feeling . . . joining thousands of years of a past long gone to a future composed of thousands of years still to be revealed. Individuals were not individuals at that spot. They were spirits joined together in one spirit, the timeless, eternal spirit of Egypt. These thousands of hearts became one heart, the heart of Egypt beating with pride in the glory of its past, and with faith in the greatness of its future.[7]

In the pages of the Wafdist press, the significance of the event, like the significance of the statue itself, was presented as unambiguous and universal. Many leading public intellectuals were effusive in their praise of the statue. Yet, on closer inspection, traces of controversy and conflict can be seen. Of course, there was the issue of public financing: once the project of the statue had fallen under the control of the Department of Public Works, bureaucrats had used the issue of public funds to delay the project or redesign its content. It may be tempting to dismiss these maneuvers as personal or bureaucratic politics, but there is reason to think there was some degree of principle at stake. In this vein, the opening paragraphs of Mahmud 'Abbas al-'Aqqad's essay on *Nahdat Misr* are telling in that they give indications of some dispute about whether the government was in a position to afford paying so much for the completion of Mukhtar's statue. Al-'Aqqad dismisses "those who do not want to see a single statue or hear a single [national] anthem in Egypt until it is has sewer systems, hospitals, factories and quarries."[8] While al-'Aqqad insists that art is no less necessary than economic and social development, he is defensive and forced into conceding the point that if public funds are used for the construction of public art there could be no escape from public debate. Yet, as the history of the project's funding suggests, after the initial public appeal to donors in 1920, there was insufficient public debate on the statue. Proponents of Pharaonism assumed the naturalness of the undertaking (even though it was the first of its kind in Egypt). Furthermore, they assumed that the statue's appeal would be unquestionably universal.

While the press was uniformly enthusiastic about the work of art, the mouthpiece of the Liberal Constitutionalist Party, *al-Siyasa al-Usbu'iyya*, chose to downplay the Wafdist elements of the unveiling even as it praised the work's Pharaonist style.[9] One prominent critic, Ibrahim 'Abd al-Qadir al-Mazini, dared to critique the statue. Mazini's critique is significant not because it represents a majority opinion, but because as a minority critique it exposes some of the assumptions underlying Pharaonism. What is wrong with Mukhtar's statue, in Mazini's reading, is not its content. Mazini's is a formalist critique of the statue as a composition, a topic for the most part ignored by other critics, poets, politicians, and journalists who weighed in on the subject.

Mazini's attack on *Nahdat Misr* is composed of two parts, the first satirical and presented as a fictional dialogue between himself and a street urchin. In the conversation, Mazini plays dumb and lets the boy explain Mukhtar's art in his own words:

al-Mazini: Do you know this lady? . . . Is this the first time she's been standing around here?

Boy: That's not a lady. She's stone. A statue. Understand?

M: Yes, I get it. But how long is she going to stand here like this? Won't she get tired?

B: Look, didn't I tell you that the name of the sculpture is *Egypt's Renaissance*? This is the Sphinx getting up. Do you understand now?

M: I wish I did. . . . But where's "Egypt" here?

B: It's the Sphinx.

M: Then what about this lady standing next to him?

B: That's Egypt.

M: You mean there are two Egypts? . . . No offence, but you told me that the Sphinx was Egypt and then that the lady was Egypt. And so I understood that to mean that one plus one equals two.

B: No, no! This isn't math. This one is Egypt waking up the Sphinx.

M: You mean, an Egypt wakes up an Egypt?

B: Yes, that's the meaning.

M: Sorry, but I still don't understand. . . . Where are the pyramids? Did Mukhtar move them?

B: Move them how? Why bring the Pyramids into this?

M: It's just that I read in books the Pyramids are located next to the Sphinx. Looks like someone must have moved them.[10]

Mukhtar's fans could not have failed to hear their own words in the mouth of the young boy. The critique that Mazini levels in this deceptively simple dialogue strikes at the core of the work's allegorical impulse. The street boy becomes, in al-Mazini's hands, the voice of the commonsensical nationalist interpretation of the work. The dialogue thus serves to deconstruct the allegorical interpretation that was entertained by Egypt's most prominent cultural critics.

The second half of Mazini's critique recapitulates these same ideas in a more earnest tone. Mazini's chief critique here is directed at the sculpture's lack of realism. He points out that when animals rise from their crouch, they lift their back legs first. He observes that since the woman's hand is not resting for support on the head of the Sphinx, her gesture is rigid and ambiguous. Finally, he asks whether Mukhtar should have represented Egypt in two separate figures, and he concludes that *Nahdat Misr* would have been clearer had Mukhtar not included the mythical animal. Together, Mazini's satirical dialogue and his more conventional critique show that one could dispute the nationalist interpretation on which there was a general consensus in the Egyptian press. Mazini shows that when one reads the figures closely and with an eye to their literal denotations, the statue's allegorical connotations become muddled. Underneath Mazini makes another point, namely, that the medium of the work, sculpture, was quite novel if not wholly foreign to Egyptian public spaces and that it was unrealistic to think the public would know how to read *Nahdat Misr* as an allegory. The fact that the sculpture and its creator were lampooned as boring and pretentious in the popular press suggests that Mazini's skepticism was shared to some extent. Taken together, the critical and satirical commentaries on *Nahdat Misr* should give one pause about making larger claims about the public reception of Pharaonist art. If this, the most visible, iconic example of the Pharaonist allegorical style, could be so easily disputed within the circumscribed culture of elite arts and letters, what resonance did such allegories have for the wider Egyptian public?

5

Pharaonism after Pharaonism:
Mahfouz and Qutb

I did not write a historical story in the precise sense of the term. In other words, I was not interested in transporting the reader to a past life. Rather, I was constantly depicting the present.—NAGUIB MAHFOUZ, *Atahaddith ilaykum*

Islam is not a historical event that once happened and then was left behind as history moved on. . . . The *Jahiliyya* is a condition, not a temporal, historical period. The *Jahiliyya* has driven its stakes into every corner of the world, in the diversity of beliefs, doctrines, political regimes and circumstances.
—SAYYID QUTB, *Fi-zilal al-Qur'an*

More than a decade after the major literary and political figures of the 1920s had turned their back on Pharaonism, the ancient past still remained vibrant in the minds of a younger generation of intellectuals. Before he became known as a novelist, Naguib Mahfouz (1912–2006) spent much of the 1930s writing articles on Pharaonic history and its influence on modern culture. His first book-length work, which he published while still a teenager, was a translation of a children's book on ancient Egypt, and his first novelistic experiments were historical romances set in Pharaonic times. While his first novel, *'Abath al-aqdar* (Play of Fates), was not widely discussed in the press, his second novel, *Radubis* (Rhodopis), garnered favorable reviews. His third novel, *Kifah Tiba* (The Struggle of Thebes), began to turn the heads of readers. One critic, Sayyid Qutb (1906–66), a protégé of 'Abbas Mahmoud al-'Aqqad, wrote, "If I had a say in the matter, I would put this novel in the hands of every boy and girl. I would publish it and distribute it free of charge to every household."[1] For Qutb, Mahfouz's novel made ancient Egypt come alive and represented a unique success in Pharaonist literature. It not only taught about ancient history, it renewed the spirit of Egypt in the hearts of its readers:

> I have listened to those hollow [Pharaonic] anthems which provoke in us only a superficial zeal because they do not emanate from a genuine connection between [ancient] Egypt and us. What are they but deafening clichés, whose content is hidden in a noisy clamor! Only once have I encountered a book that brought ancient Egypt to life in our souls, and gave it form in our minds: 'Abd al-Qadir Hamza's *'Ala hamish al-tarikh al-Misri al-qadim* (On the Margins of Ancient Egyptian History). I rejoice today in the novel *Kifah Tiba* like I did in that book. I call upon the Ministry of Education to take the dead books from the hands of students and replace them with this book![2]

In the late 1920s, Muhammad Husayn Haykal had called for an Egyptian national literature based on just this idea, a pedagogy that was as spiritual as it was scientific. In this rendition, literary Pharaonism differed from other modes of discourse about the Pharaonic past in that it claimed to be not about the ancient past but of it. In other words, Haykal's call for a literary Pharaonism did not treat ancient Egypt as an object of study, but rather conceived of it as a vital source for self-expression. Whether Qutb was explicitly citing the debates of the 1920s, his discussion of Mahfouz revived the call for a national literature rooted in the appreciation of Pharaonic civilization, its history, aesthetic styles, and modern relevance. In a tone of blame that could have been Haykal's from fifteen years earlier, Qutb linked forgetfulness of the ancient past with cultural and political decline:

> I can see the national and human character clearly in the literatures of every country, especially in poetry and the novel. But the Egyptian character appears pallid and faint in our artistic works despite their high level of accomplishment, and the fact that some of them rank among the finest of world literature. I attribute the pallor of the Egyptian national complexion to the fact that ancient Egypt lives neither in our souls nor in our imaginations. I blame the faded quality of our national hue on the fact that we are cut off from this great past and know nothing of this history but hollow phrases. We neither take this past as an example for us,

nor do we share any vibrant association with it. Our art, spirit, emotions and instincts lack no less than 5000 years of our glorious history! Our national character has faded because there is a profound gap in time and language, neglect and forgetfulness, that lies between us and [ancient] Egyptian monuments, [ancient] Egyptian arts, [ancient] Egyptian life, and [ancient] Egyptian innovations.[3]

Kifah Tiba reminded Qutb of his desire to translate the entire corpus of the Pharaonic past and to make ancient Egypt the central lesson of a national curriculum:

I propose that every literary fragment discovered from Ancient Egypt be translated into Arabic, that the images of [ancient] Egyptian life, in all of their shades, be drawn in the Arabic language, that a strong bond be forged between [ancient] Egyptian monuments and youths at every stage of their development, that life be breathed into those monuments and statues and histories by the creation of stories, myths, epics and information around them. I call for the lives of Ahmose, Tutmose, Ramses, Nefertiti and others like them to be within the grasp of every school child and advanced student and for [ancient Egyptian] myths to come alive in nurseries.[4]

Kifah Tiba accomplishes more than just making history come alive, however. In Qutb's eyes, Mahfouz's novel, a story of ancient Egyptians throwing off the yoke of foreign rule, is powerful because it is not only convincingly real, but because it tells a story of national liberation whose relevance was paramount for modern Egyptians:

I read the novel, and stopped every so often to say: Yes! These are the [real] Egyptians. I know them well as they appear in the novel. They may fall victim to political pressure and economic pillage, but they explode when someone assails their family or religion. They may appear subdued to the point you think they have died, then they rise up and their rebellion knows no limits, and they produce miracles that you never before thought them capable of. . . . They are people whose souls flood with a love of the land and people, and they don't leave these things behind unless for a great purpose. And when they return, they return passionately. They are people who wait endlessly for a leader, and when one appears, they gladly march behind him to the death. These are the eternal Egyptians, confident and sure.[5]

Mahfouz's stature in Egyptian letters needs little introduction. Decades before he won the Nobel Prize for literature in 1988, Mahfouz was recognized throughout the Arab world as the writer who had transformed the Arabic novel from an uncertain experiment into a solid tradition. His novels have sold more than all others. Published in multiple editions and adapted in countless films, his work has permeated Egyptian culture far beyond what might be suggested by the country's low reading rates.

If contemporary readers in the West are aware of Qutb, it is through his connection to the late twentieth-century Islamist movements which have taken inspiration in his Qur'anic commentary. During the 1990s, while Egyptian Islamists fought the corrupt and brutal Mubarak regime and began to attack his patron, the United States, Americans began to seek out information on Egypt's Islamists. As the mainstream press turned to look at the history of Islamist political movements in Egypt (and across the Arab and Muslim world), the name of Qutb began to appear. As this conflict morphed after 9/11 into an open-ended "war on terror," Qutb began to loom large in the Western understanding of political Islam, though never as a man of letters.

As poet and critic during the 1930s and 1940s, Qutb occupied a pivotal position in the literary culture of Cairo. Though educated largely in secular schools, as a *hafiz* (one who has memorized the Qur'an) Qutb had a grasp of the primary text of Islam unlike many of his literary colleagues. His most original writings of the 1940s were applications of modern philosophy and literary theory to the reading of the Qur'an. By this time, Qutb was already exploring Islamic traditions that many of Egypt's literary elites largely ignored. By 1948, when he completed *al-'Adala al-ijtima'iyya fi-l-Islam* (Social Justice in Islam), Qutb's interest in Islam went beyond questions of literary appreciation to a systematic critique of secular forms of governance. Though sympathetic to the Muslim Brotherhood, it was arguably while he was living in the United States as an exchange student in 1948–50 that Qutb began to break decisively with the secular elements of the *Nahda* version of Egyptian modernity.[6] Shocked by the moral emptiness of American consumer society and angered by the extrajudicial execution of the Brotherhood's spiritual guide, Hasan al-Banna (1906–49), Qutb decided to join the movement. Within months, he was one of the organization's leading spokesmen and remained so through the 1950s and 1960s. Though close to Gamal Abdel Nasser's junta during the first months following the Revolution of 1952, Qutb and other Brothers soon realized that the Free Officers were headed down a path that was not their own. When the junta and the Brotherhood came into direct conflict in 1954, Qutb was arrested along with thousands of others. He spent most of the rest of his years in prison until he was executed in 1966. *Fi-zilal al-Qur'an* (In the Shade of the Qur'an), the exegesis of the Qur'an that Qutb wrote while in prison, remains one of the most original and powerful modern readings in Islam and should be appreciated as one of the major works of modern literary criticism in any language. As for the issue of ancient Egypt in Qutb's post-1951 phase of thought, it was inseparable from a general state of apostasy and ignorance, *al-Jahiliyya*, an accusation he hurled against Egyptian and European modernity alike.

The irony of the critical encounter between Mahfouz and Qutb during the mid-1940s is too rich to pass by, especially since the subsequent careers of the two authors represent the most compelling intellectual trends of the second half of the twentieth century in Egypt. On the one hand, Mahfouz exemplifies the continuation of the core, liberal assumptions of *Nahda* modernity, working at the center of its literary culture, though increasingly skeptical—if not critical—of the Egyptian state's many failures. On the other hand, Qutb represents the emergence of a powerful countertradition of dissident Islamist thought, modernist in outlook, though opposed to the Western and secular character of the elite's expressive culture and opposed to the corrupt and violent character of the modern state's political culture. If the translation of their respective oeuvres is any indication, Qutb and Mahfouz are the two most influential Arabic literary figures of the twentieth century.

It was not accidental that Mahfouz and Qutb would meet on the terrain of Pharaonism, or that it was the Pharaonic subject matter of Mahfouz's novels that caught Qutb's attention. Both were steeped in the lessons of Pharaonist pedagogy in school and in the literary culture of the 1920s, the period of their formation as young authors. For these reasons, the early careers of Qutb and Mahfouz are fertile ground for the study of the life of

Pharaonist literary culture following the deflation of Pharaonist political culture.

It is tempting to read Pharaonist literature from the 1940s, including works like Mahfouz's novels, under the sign of anachronism. However, even while Pharaonist public monuments were no longer so popular, Pharaonic themes were still being taught in classrooms and discussed in literary journals, even as they are today. In other words, while Pharaonism was eclipsed on one level by the 1940s, it survived because it had been successfully institutionalized during the 1920s and 1930s. Just because the literary and political elites of the *Nahda* generation had distanced themselves from Pharaonism does not mean that a younger generation of Egyptian intellectuals stopped drawing upon an ancient Egyptian past as a source for thinking about the colonial present.

Rather than thinking of belated Pharaonism in terms of anachronism, one might conceive of it through the metaphor of a minor refrain. "The Pharaonic" had been a major theme of 1920s Egyptian national culture until the parliamentary struggles broke apart the political consensus to which it was attached. After the mid-1930s, "the Pharaonic" no longer figured prominently in mainstream Egyptian political culture, though ruling elites continued to rely on the image of the ancient past when marketing Egypt to the West. Within Egypt's secular national culture, "the Pharaonic" often recurred as a refrain among the larger motifs of pan-Arabism, Third-Worldism, Islamism, and so on. Likewise, though with very different connotations, "the Pharaonic" has also featured as a refrain within Egypt's Islamist culture. In this discourse, ancient Egypt is associated with what is wrong with modern secular culture, with the moral foundations of the nation-state, and with the tyranny of Egypt's rulers whether of the ancient past or modern present.

This chapter explores Naguib Mahfouz's early career and in particular his first three "Pharaonic novels," works that are rarely discussed in contemporary criticism. My point is not to present an aesthetic appreciation of these works or their place within the author's wider oeuvre but to situate them within the context of their emergence. Though set in ancient Egypt, these novels raise concerns whose modern applicability would have been obvious to Mahfouz's first readers. *'Abath al-aqdar* deals with issues of royal succession and political authority, *Radubis* with the loss of royal authority, and *Kifah Tiba* with colonial condominium and national liberation. Thus, each novel treats major political issues of the period: the complicated accession of Faruq following King Fu'ad's death in 1936; King Faruq's loss of authority in the face of personal scandals in the late 1930s; and the reconfiguration of Egyptian national sovereignty and the national liberation movement following the 1936 Treaty, which both granted a greater share of autonomy to Egypt's politicians and also brought Egypt more firmly into the British sphere of power. As the initial contexts of these allegories have faded, the significance of the novels has suffered. In fact, there is reason to think that their significance was always fairly limited: they are Pharaonist texts that emerged after Pharaonism had been largely eclipsed as a source of political image-making. While the allegorical messages may have resonated with their immediate cultural and political contexts, their fictional grounding, ancient Egypt, no longer did. As allegories whose readings could not be taken for granted, Mahfouz's first three novels expose some of the limits of literary Pharaonism. They also pose a problem for allegorical reading more generally, a point to which I will return in the conclusion.

Alongside Mahfouz's fictions, I will explore the image of ancient Egypt in the writings of Hasan al-Banna and those of Sayyid Qutb after his turn toward Islamism. For these authors, the Pharaonism of literary and political elites was naïve and derivative of European colonial discourse. When Pharaonist intellectuals claimed that Egyptian modernity ought to be grounded in an appreciation of and identification with the ancient past, Islamists like Qutb in the 1950s might have agreed, though for very different reasons. Like the Pharaonists, Qutb saw the ancient past as more than a mere historical period. The pre-Islamic past was a timeless spirit. That this past might be resurrected as a source of Egyptian modernity, as the Pharaonists claimed, was, for Qutb, cause for concern rather than celebration. Unless modern Egypt returned to the rule of religion, it would resemble the heedless culture of the *Jahiliyya*. Though critical of colonial modernity and its expression in the Pharaonism of the *Nahda*, Banna and Qutb's critique does not mark a return to the Islamic textual tradition discussed in chapter 2. Ancient Egypt is not, in their reckoning, a source of wonder or an object for contemplation. Rather, their understanding of the past is largely derived from that of Pharaonism, though the terms are reversed. If for Pharaonists the ancient past had a positive value, for Banna, Qutb, and others, it did not. If Mahfouz's works suggest how Pharaonist allegory depended heavily on a wider political culture that had receded, Qutb's and Banna's work represents a counterdiscourse for thinking about secularism, nationalism, and the state.

NAGUIB MAHFOUZ, PHARAONISM, AND HISTORICAL ROMANCE IN CONTEXT

In reality, there are two kinds of historical novels. In the first kind, the novel returns you to history, with all its details, its rituals, as if it grasped life in that historical past, or reanimates movement in its lifeless limbs. The other kind evokes the historical ambiance only, then gives itself relatively free power within its outlines. My writing is closer to the second kind.
—NAGUIB MAHFOUZ, *Atahaddith ilaykum*

As a child, Naguib Mahfouz's mother, who, according to her son, "loved antiquities," took him on trips from their neighborhood in Gamaliyya to modern Cairo or across the river to Giza: "We used to go to the *Antiqakhana* often, or to the Pyramids nearby the Sphinx. To this day, I still don't know what was behind this pastime of my mother's. We would go off by ourselves, sometimes with my father, she would drag me by her hand, and go to the museum, especially the mummy room. We went to the mummy room often."[7] Mummies were to remain on the author's mind. In one interview, Mahfouz acknowledged it was his experience of viewing one particular mummy, that of Seqenenre', whose body shows indications of a violent death, that led him to write *Radubis* the way he did. Another vengeful mummy is the focus of an early short story. But Mahfouz was not only seeing mummy exhibits in the museum; he was also reading about them in schoolbooks on Egyptology and in the stories of H. Rider Haggard. But the point is not simply that Mahfouz was inspired by objects from ancient Egypt. Rather, it is that Mahfouz was in a position to be inspired largely because during his youth the antiquities were displayed in museums and extensively discussed in the press.

At Fu'ad I University Mahfouz majored in philosophy but read widely, especially in literature and ancient Egyptian history. His boundless interest in ancient Egypt led him to audit courses in Egyptology. Speaking on the subject, Mahfouz has said, "I had studied the Pharaonic history of Egypt completely, almost to the point of specialization. . . . I religiously attended lectures in the Antiquities Department. I studied everything connected with the Pharaonic period, the everyday life, methods of war, religion."[8] As a student in the philosophy department, where courses were conducted in English and French, Mahfouz was pressed to improve his foreign language skills. In order to practice his English, Mahfouz sought out translation.[9] In light of his abiding interest in ancient Egypt, the book Mahfouz decided to translate was a popular children's book entitled *Misr al-qadima* (Ancient Egypt). Mahfouz's first book-length publication was thus a highly derivative, now unremembered import from the English series *Peeps at Many Lands*.

Mahfouz seems to have been well aware that the evangelical, racist, and imperial agenda of the original text's author, the Reverend James Baikie, would be jarring and offensive to mainstream Egyptian audiences, Copts and Muslims alike. Throughout his translation Mahfouz attempts to take the edge off some of the sharpest differences. For instance, the original text of *Ancient Egypt* closes with these words about the beliefs of ancient Egyptians:

> Remember that these men of old [Egypt], wonderfully wise and strong as they were in many ways, were still young; like children, forming many false and even ridiculous ideas about things they could not understand; like children, too, reaching out their groping hands through the darkness to a father whose love they felt, though they could not explain His ways. We need not wonder if at times they made mistakes and went far astray. We may wonder far more at the way in which He taught them so many true and noble things and thoughts, never leaving Himself without a witness even in those days of long ago.[10]

In his translation, Mahfouz rewrites the specifically Christian phrases (such as the anthropomorphic representation of God) in terms which neutralize and even Islamicize them. And so, whereas Baikie's children reach out to a fatherly God, in Mahfouz's translation, the children simply reach out to a human father. Instead of being unable to "explain His ways," in Mahfouz's translation these children are "ignorant" in terms which suggest the *Jahili* past superceded by Islam. Even as Mahfouz works to transform the specifically Christian tone of Baikie, he is unable to undo the condescension of *Ancient Egypt*. These attitudes, here and elsewhere in Baikie's text, ought to have made it an unlikely candidate for inclusion in Salama Musa's Egyptocentric journal *al-Majalla al-jadida*, which was unwavering not just in its secularism, but also in its support for the idea that ancient Egypt was a civilization of knowledge, not ignorance. The Christian original, published for British teens, must have appeared childish to the sophisticated, secular elites who subscribed to Musa's journal. His embarrassment at this youthful publication may explain Mahfouz's longtime reluctance, maintained until the late 1980s, to allow the publication of new editions of *Misr al-qadima*.[11] Despite the strangeness of *Misr al-qadima* and its obscurity within critical considerations of Mahfouz's career, this translated text contained a number of elements which recur importantly in Mahfouz's Pharaonist fictions, and thus I will return to it later.

Al-Majalla al-jadida was the same venue in which Mahfouz had been regularly publishing essays on philosophy and literature, many of which were school lessons repackaged for a wider public.[12] From 1930 to 1939, Mahfouz published roughly twenty articles in Musa's journal on subjects that ranged from the existence of God to Henrik Ibsen's drama and Henri Bergson's vitalist philosophy.[13]

An affinity for Fabian socialism was only part of what brought Mahfouz and Musa together. Musa was impressed not just by the essays, but also the stories that Mahfouz wrote for *al-Majalla al-jadida* from 1930 to 1936. As Musa began to cool toward Mahfouz's essays, he began to lend support and mentorship to Mahfouz's fiction. With Musa's encouragement, Mahfouz wrote a historical romance set in ancient Egypt, *Hikmat Khufu* (Cheops' Wisdom). Musa's intervention in this text was notable: he both gave the novel a new title (*'Abath al-aqdar*) and published it in September 1939, again as a special book issue of *al-Majalla al-jadida*. Though Mahfouz had been writing novels since he was a teenager, this was the first to see publication.

Mahfouz's association with Musa during the first years of his life as an emerging public intellectual and literary artist is crucial, since it places Mahfouz directly at the center of one of the most prominent institutions of cultural and political Pharaonism. Moreover, Pharaonism is never disconnected from the nationalist ideology in Mahfouz's early work. Indeed, there is the assumption that literary Pharaonism was the aesthetic style most appropriate for articulating his views of Egyptianist (as opposed to Arabist or Islamist) nationalism. As he put it, "Egyptian nationalism was burning brightly at that time. And there was a real surge in Pharaonism, and there were objective reasons for this. The Pharaonic age was the one bright age that stood in the face of the humiliation and decline we were living at the time. The humiliation of British imperialism along with the domination of the Turkish [aristocracy]."[14] For Mahfouz what was useful about the image of community that Pharaonist nationalism had to offer was that it sharply opposed itself both to the colonial rule of the British and the creolized Turkish classes who dominated elite Egyptian politics. As we shall see, the anti-Turkish aspect of the movement was hardly submerged in Mahfouz's fiction. However, though Mahfouz's Pharaonism was no less ethnocentric than Ahmad Husayn's brand, he not only distanced himself from the latter, but also repeatedly attached himself to the liberal Wafdist vision, especially as it was embodied in the figure of Sa'd Zaghloul.[15]

In political terms, Pharaonism articulated a form of territorial nationalism in Egypt that was distinct from the images of community offered by pan-Arab and pan-Islamic movements. The other political movements also had literary correlates, especially in the realm of historical romance. Girgy Zaydan, the scholar, journalist, and best-known novelist of the generation at the turn of the century, wrote twenty-one historical romances before his death in 1915. These novels form a series extending from the time of the Prophet to the end of the Ottoman empire.[16] Popular throughout the Arab world, the stories tell a long narrative of Christian and Muslim Arabs unified by a single history. While Egypt appears in many of these novels, their center of gravity lies east of Suez. Zaydan's project was on the mind of Mahfouz and his mentors when he began to dedicate himself to writing fiction.[17]

Mahfouz downplayed the notion that his proposed but never completed series of thirty-five to forty historical novels on Egypt was a response to Zaydan, a Syrian Christian who had resided in Egypt since the 1880s. Elsewhere he mentions Zaydan's novels as a direct model. Moreover, Mahfouz was aware of similar works by his contemporaries, writers like Muhammad Farid Abu Hadid, 'Ali al-Garim, Muhammad Sa'id al-'Aryan, and 'Ali Ahmad Bakathir, all of whom worked in Egypt but whose fictions treated Arab and Muslim history, rather than that of the Egyptians. Mahfouz knew these authors and their works well: he competed with them in the literary contests of the 1940s. It is useful to associate Mahfouz's early career with Zaydan's formula, just as it is to associate him with some of Zaydan's later imitators. These were the models from which and against which Mahfouz began to write. The project of writing a series that was twice as long as Zaydan's and that focused exclusively on Egyptian history was nothing less than an attempt to nationalize a literary genre which had, until then, been dominated by non-Egyptian themes and by authors who, even if they resided in the country, were often non-Egyptian. As part of a preexisting, mainstream literary movement inspired by ancient Egypt and as part of this popular genre of historical romance, Mahfouz's Pharaonist novels were poised to rewrite the image of contemporary and ancient Egypt in undeniably indigenist terms.

HASAN AL-BANNA:
PATRIOTISM AND PAGANISM

The Muslim Brothers do not . . . advocate Pharaonism, Arabism, Phoenicianism, or Syrianism.
—HASAN AL-BANNA, from "Da'watuna fi-tawr jadid"

The *Nahda* literary project was only one part of the Egyptian response to colonial rule and modernity. A very different form of response is embodied in the career of Hasan al-Banna. The group Banna founded in 1928, the Muslim Brotherhood, represented more than just the popular political movement that endures to this day in Egypt. It also proposed a comprehensive counterproject of modernity, an intellectual, spiritual, and political alternative to the *Nahda* vision of Cairo *littérateurs*. Banna was born in the Delta and was involved in Muslim charity groups and Sufi brotherhoods from a very young age. After studying at the Teachers' College in Cairo (Dar al-'Ulum), Banna was assigned to teach in a government school in the town of Isma'iliyya. The location proved to be decisive because it was a center of conflict between Egyptian nationalists and the British occupation. In Isma'iliyya, Banna taught Arabic in school. After hours, he preached to Egyptian canal workers and bureaucrats in mosques and cafes, and helped to found the Young Men's Muslim Association as a response to the youth-oriented activities of Christian missionaries in the city. In 1928, the Society of Muslim Brothers (*Jama'iyyat al-Ikhwan al-Muslimin*) was born when Banna was approached by a group of Egyptians who worked in British military camps nearby. The following report of the conversation of that meeting is revealing for what it says about the Brotherhood's reliance upon Banna's charisma as a leader:

> We are weary of this life of humiliation and restriction. . . . We see that the Arabs and the Muslims have no status and no dignity. They are not more than mere hirelings belonging to the foreigners. We possess nothing but this blood . . . and these souls . . . and these few coins. . . . We are unable to perceive the road to action as you perceive it, or to know the path to the service of the patria [*watan*], the religion, and the nation [*umma*] as you know it. All that we desire now is to present you with all that we possess, to be acquitted by God of the responsibility, and for you to be responsible before Him for us and for what we must do. If a group contracts with God sincerely that it live for His religion and die in His service, seeking only His satisfaction, then its worthiness will assure its success however small its numbers or weak its means.[18]

The Society grew quickly in the Canal Zone and beyond. When Banna was transferred to Cairo in 1932, the headquarters of the Muslim Brotherhood moved with him. Throughout the 1930s, they established a nationwide network of branches, formed youth groups, and regularly convened national conferences. Throughout the revolt in 1936–39 in British Mandate Palestine, the Muslim Brothers stood at the vanguard of Egyptian solidarity with Palestinians, demonstrating against British repression and Zionist settlement while organizing relief aid campaigns. At the outset of World War II, the Brothers, like other groups, opposed aiding the British war effort. For these activities, Banna and others were exiled from Cairo, but this only helped the organization strengthen its ties throughout the countryside. By the end of the war, the society had grown to the point where its members were successfully challenging Wafd supremacy on university campuses and in unions. When armed struggle broke out in Palestine again in 1947, the Brotherhood sent arms, military trainers, and soldiers to fight. At this same time, they were among the loudest in demanding an immediate end to the British occupation of Egypt and participated actively in the military strikes against the British from 1945 to 1956. Though the Brotherhood made ill-advised alliances with the king and the Sa'dists against the Wafd and the Communists, on the whole they enjoyed a respect few parties had. Throughout this period, the fate of the Brothers was closely tied to that of its leader. In 1948, Muslim Brothers assassinated an Egyptian judge who had sentenced another Brother to prison for attacking British soldiers in a nightclub. Banna was unable to distance himself from the assassination and also unable to maintain complete control of militant cadres. In retaliation, state agents assassinated Banna, changing the history of the Muslim Brothers drastically.

It is impossible to write the history of Egyptian resistance to colonial rule without placing the Muslim Brothers in a leading role. Though Banna was not a prolific author, his letters and sermons provided much content to the society's ideology. During the Brotherhood's conferences of the 1930s, Banna and others formulated positions on a wide range of subjects: family, sexual, and gender relations; colonialism; capitalism and socialism; secular culture and secular states. In one of the clearest expositions of nationalist thought ever offered in Egypt, Banna surveyed the major political strands of the 1930s and 1940s in a series of letters. Banna's focus throughout these essays is the relationship between Islam as a religious faith and Islam as a source of politics. Of particular concern to Banna was the topic of nationalism, or rather the various competing forms of nationalist thought—such as Egyptianism, Arabism, Easternism—some of which posed a challenge to Muslim conceptions of community. His discussion of patriotism (*wataniyya*) and nationalism (*qawmiyya*) is nuanced and provocative. Most forms of patriotism and nationalism are, Banna finds, compatible with Islam, either because they resonate with the value of community or because they strengthen tradition and attachment to the lands of Islam. But, the author points out, they are not substitutes to the kind of community offered by Islam. There are, however, nationalisms which cannot be assimilated into Muslim culture. He singles out factionalism along with ethnic nationalism for excoriation. The topic of Egyptianism is slightly more problematic in Banna's treatment. He writes,

Egyptianism [*Misriyya*] . . . has its place in our mission, and its status and right in the struggle. We are Egyptians, living in the great valley of the

Earth where we were born and raised. Egypt is a country of faith that has generously embraced Islam. How could we not strive for Egypt and for Egypt's welfare? How could we not strive to defend Egypt to our utmost? We are proud that we are true to this beloved country [*watan*], that we work on its behalf and strive for its welfare. We will persist . . . believing that Egypt is the first link in the chain of our sought-for *Nahda*, and that Egypt is part of the wider Arab world, and that when we work on Egypt's behalf, we work on behalf of Arabism, the East and Islam.[19]

The cause of tension in this passage rests not in Egyptianism per se, but in the way in which Egyptianism had been so closely associated with Pharaonism. In other words, what makes Banna halt in his discussion of the territorialist versions of Egyptian nationalism is his unease with its image of ancient Egypt: "There is nothing in any of this preventing us from being interested in the ancient history of Egypt, and all that the ancient Egyptians possessed in the way of knowledge and science. We welcome ancient Egypt as a history containing glory, science and learning. But we resist with all our strength . . . the program that seeks to re-create [ancient] Egypt after God gave Egypt the teachings of Islam . . . and provided her with honor and glory beyond that of [the ancient past], and rescued her from the filth of paganism, the rubbish of polytheism, and the habits of the *Jahiliyya*."[20] In another essay on nationalism in Egypt, Banna writes,

If what is meant by nationalism is: the revival of the customs of a pagan age [*jahiliyya*] that have been swept away; or the reconstitution of extinct mores that have disappeared; or the erasure of a benevolent civilization that has been established; or the dissolution of the bonds of Islam under the banner of nationalism and racial pride (as some regimes have done, going so far as to destroy the traits of Islam and Arabism in names, script and expressions), so as to resurrect long-forgotten pagan customs; if this is the kind of nationalism that is meant, then it is despicable and harmful in its effects. It will lead the East to enormous ruin, cause the East to forfeit its tradition. It will cause a decline in its prestige, and cause it to lose its most special characteristics along with its most sacred traits of honor and nobility. Yet, this harms not God's religion: "If you turn your backs

on Him, He will replace you with another people who will be unlike you"
[Qur'an 47:38].[21]

Pharaonists might have reasonably replied that Banna was misinterpret-
ing their claims. After all, throughout the 1920s, they had been publicly
asserting that they were not so much trying to return to ancient Egypt as
to resurrect its timeless spirit. Yet Banna is keenly attuned to the lacunae
in the Pharaonist message. That discourse had attracted secular modernists precisely because it provided a source for inventing a modern tradition evacuated of most religious content. Likewise, territorial nationalists
had found Pharaonist discourse useful for thinking of a polity unmarked
by religious specficity. At the same time, it has to be admitted that Pharaonism allowed secularists to speak without having to engage directly in
discussions of laicism and allowed modernists to speak without having to
engage fully with the force of Muslim tradition. This, then, is part of what
Banna's discussions of nationalism illuminate about Pharaonism, and
about *Nahda* modernity more widely. While ancient Egypt may appear
marginal in Banna's thought, its function is crucial since it sheds light on
the agnostic (if not antireligious) foundations of Pharaonism and *Nahda*
culture more widely.

'ABATH AL-AQDAR: PETRIFIED TABLEAUX AND POLITICAL SUCCESSION

Naguib Mahfouz's first novel, *'Abath al-aqdar* (Play of Fates), does not
seem to offer much at first glance. The story is set in the Fourth Dynasty
(2700 BCE) and is based on an ancient story that appears in Baikie's *Ancient Egypt*. The novel tells two intertwined stories: the tale of the crisis
of political succession brought on by the retirement of Pharaoh Khufu
(Cheops) and the tale of the education of the young protagonist, Dadaf,
and his subsequent rise within the ranks of the army. The two narratives
are joined by the fact that it was Dadaf, not Khufu's son, who is proph-
esied to succeed Pharaoh, and again when Dadaf and Khufu's daughter
fall in love. When Dadaf leads Pharaoh's army against the Sinai Bedouins,
he discovers the prophecy but returns humbly to serve under the prince.

Only when the prince moves to usurp his father's throne by force does Dadaf reveal himself. The novel ends with Khufu anointing Dadaf as his political heir, thus fulfilling the unavoidable prophecy while also maintaining a legitimate succession of Pharaonic power.

The subject material, plots, and characters of 'Abath al-aqdar owe quite a bit to *Ancient Egypt*. Only by reading them beside each other can one appreciate how 'Abath al-aqdar, following that children's book, is not as interested in developing plot or character as in presenting scenes of everyday life in ancient Egypt. Many of the novel's scenes appear as tableaux copied directly from Baikie's book, itself copied from accounts of the walls of ancient Egyptian monuments. Indeed, much of 'Abath al-aqdar is composed of tableaux of processions, rendered in the derivative image of monumental bas-reliefs, as in this decription of Dadaf's victorious return from Sinai:

> In front marched groups of prisoners, arms bound, beards shaven. Behind them followed great carts carrying the captive women and children and spoils of war. Then appeared a squadron of chariots, led by the young captain, surrounded by the great men of the realm who had come out to greet him. Behind him followed lines of huge chariots, all moving in awe-inspiring precision. Behind them came the brigades of archers and lightly-armed soldiers. They advanced in lines, each marching to the rhythm of their music. They left empty spaces for those who had fallen in the victory, a salute to their memory and the memory of their noble martyrdom in the service of nation and Pharaoh.[22]

Scenes like this read like an ekphrasis of a great temple wall, and within this aesthetic it is statues (*tamathil*) embedded within tableaux that serve as the novel's most privileged figure for representing ancient Egypt.[23] Representing ancient Egypt in this way—through tableaux and figures of the statuesque—creates a petrified mood at odds with dynamic narrative structure.

Nonetheless, the monumental style is arguably well suited to the novel's two great allegorical themes: Egyptian nationalism and the political authority of the Pharaoh. These two strands form the strongest ideological thread running through the novel. First, from the outset there is a strong identification between love of country (*watan*) and love of Pharaoh. To worship the king is, in the words of Pharaoh's vizier, "a divine patriotism" (*wataniyya samiyya*).[24] At the same time, the kind of nationalism articulated in *'Abath al-aqdar* is rooted in an ethnic understanding of who rightly belongs to the Egyptian nation. The contours of this identity are most clearly defined in the story of the war against the Sinai Bedouins, where it becomes clear what is meant by terms like "Egypt" (*Misr*) and "the patria" (*al-watan*). On first introduction, the Bedouin tribes of Sinai are typed by their "attacks on villages, their kidnapping of lost and misguided souls, and their brigandage against caravans."[25] Later, during the Sinai campaign the difference—and threat—posed by the Bedouins is further spelled out: they speak a different language, they worship strange gods, they live outside of the Nile Valley, they are not an agricultural society. In short, the Bedouin Arabs are anything but Egyptian. In such a context *'Abath al-aqdar* tells an allegory of racial purity and territorial nationalism, a thinly veiled response to the Arab-centered images offered by Arabist nationalists.

If the novel is allegorical, its sharpest focus is on political authority and the problems of political succession. On the literal level, *'Abath al-aqdar* tells the tale of the realization of the prophecy about Pharaoh's legacy; allegorically, it relates a crisis of succession and political legitimacy. There is no doubt Mahfouz's first generation of readers would have recognized this aspect. Throughout much of the 1930s, the issue of legitimate succession was a pressing concern in the two dominant political institutions of elite Egyptian society, the Wafd Party and the royal family. Much of the popularity of the Wafd Party rested on the image of Sa'd Zaghloul and on the notion that after his death it alone bore the mantle of his authority. This strategy succeeded (and failed) to varying degrees throughout the 1920s and 1930s but it rarely wavered: the party always presented itself as the heir to the leader who had once galvanized the nation. More immediate to readers in 1939 would have been the crisis brought on by the death of King Fu'ad in 1936. Fu'ad's heir, the sixteen-year-old Faruq, was initially installed as king, but within two weeks' time his powers had been transferred to a Regency Council. Only after Faruq reached his majority in July 1937 was he invested with full power. Even as the problem of succession was resolved, the problem of legitimacy was not. As we shall see in the discussion of *Radubis* below, many doubted whether the young king was ready to inherit the throne.

In the novel, the issue of political authority develops as a relationship between Pharaoh and nation. Pharaoh argues that his legitimacy as ruler does not emanate from himself, but rather from his relationship to the Egyptian nation, both present and future:

> Khufu is Pharaoh of Egypt. What is Egypt but a great labor undertaken by builders sacrificing individuals? What is the value of an individual's life? It does not equal a dry tear in the eye of one who looks toward the distant future and sublime creation. For this reason, I am cruel without hesitation. I strike with a hand of iron, I drive hundreds of thousands of souls to misery, not because of a stupid disposition or arbitrary selfishness. It's as if my eyes pierce the horizon's veil and look down upon the glory of this awaiting nation. Once, the Queen accused me of cruelty and ruthlessness. No. Pharaoh is but a wise man with far-reaching vision.[26]

These comments come during a conversation about the slaves who are building Khufu's pyramid and thus offer a theory of the relationship between Pharaoh and his subjects. In a scene which alludes to Tawfiq al-Hakim's 'Awdat al-ruh, the novel denies that the relationship between Pharaoh and his subjects is one of slavery since "their hearts believe that the hard labor they give their lives to is a sublime religious obligation, a humbled undertaking for the lord they worship, a willing obedience to the emblem of their glory who sits on the throne. Their calling is to worship, their hardship is a pleasure, their mighty sacrifices an eternal duty to the will of the sublime person. You see them . . . in the withering heat of the afternoon, under the burning fires of the sun, breaking rocks with forearms like lightning, with resolve like the fates, all the while singing songs and reciting hymns."[27] Whereas the labor needed for Pharaoh's tomb is simple misery for non-Egyptians, for Egyptians it is a sacred medium for expressing their love of Pharaoh and country. This, then, is the vision 'Abath al-aqdar offers of Egyptian society: subjects willing to work under the strong rule of the leader because they have faith in him. The faith of Egyptians is confirmed by the gods, who, when they choose Pharaohs to rule, give them "knowledge and wisdom" to "do well for the country and make the worshippers happy."[28] In this way, the power of Pharaoh is subjected to a process of legitimization and confirmation: he rules because he knows what is best for the nation; his subjects are willing to carry out his projects because of their faith in him; the gods confirm this in granting Pharaoh wisdom and strength.

Mahfouz's second novel, *Radubis* (Rhodopis), is set in a very different period in Pharaonic history, roughly 2150 BCE. Whereas the plot of *'Abath al-aqdar* explores ancient Egyptian civilization at its first high point, *Radubis* looks at a later moment of decline, the Sixth Dynasty, the last years of the Old Kingdom, after the capital had moved from Memphis to Thebes. In telling its story, *Radubis* weaves together two separate narratives from the ancient world. The first, taken from Herodotus and Sappho, embellishes the story of the fabled courtesan Rhodopis, whose sexual "gifts were so great she gained a fortune."[29] While the sources of the Rhodopis narrative are Greek, in Mahfouz's hands the story becomes essentially Egyptian. The second narrative tells of the decline and collapse of the historical Pharaoh Merenre, about whom little is known except that he ruled for only one year and died a violent death. Mahfouz's novel develops the account of this short, unsuccessful rule into an epic romance, and the story of an epic struggle between pleasure and duty, royal desire, and the welfare of the country.

The bulk of the narrative treats Radubis's seduction of the Pharaoh and the problems their subsequent love affair causes for the Pharaoh's family and his kingdom. At the same time, *Radubis* tells of the Pharaoh's disastrous policy of confiscating priestly resources and privileges, ostensibly one of the major causes of the collapse of the actual Old Kingdom. In the novel, as in historical records, this policy pits the two traditional bases of political power against each other, the royal court and the priestly caste. As their illicit, though public, affair grows, Merenre neglects his sister-wife Queen Nikrotis while squandering the kingdom's wealth upon his mistress. The priests, already angered by the fact that Merenre had confiscated temple wealth for the throne, are enraged to find that Pharaoh has been spending the bulk of it decorating Radubis's palace. With Egypt in a state of neglect, the people of the land begin to signal their dissatisfaction with Merenre and with the courtesan who overshadows the queen. In this climate of popular unrest, Merenre begins to realize that a direct confrontation with the priests would be disastrous. And so, on the false pretense of a foreign threat, he devises a plan to raise a standing army that he might turn against the popular priestly class. When the plot is exposed, the people rise against Pharaoh, who repents and attempts to engage peacefully with the army of priests and peasants standing outside the gates. Before he can do so, however, he is struck down by an arrow. Saddened by his death, Radubis takes her own life with poison.

Mahfouz's novel is remarkable in that it features a female character whose sexuality is explicit and not immediately condemned. Indeed, even though the very adjective to describe her (*fatina*) conjures up images of the disorder and strife (*fitna*) caused by feminine sexuality, much of the novel takes delight in elaborating on her gifts and charms in thick description. The novel's erotic qualities sharply distinguish it from other Egyptian novels of this (and later) periods: *Radubis* breaks an implicit rule that, while sexual desire might be alluded to in novels, it was not to be explicitly described. But the novel's overt eroticism is remarkable not just because it presents erotic themes in terms of content, but also because it is an important component of the book's narrative arc and ultimately of its political ideology.

The ancient historical setting undoubtedly allowed Mahfouz to present such eroticism without apology. However, foregrounding the sexual desire of his protagonists also allowed Mahfouz to experiment with the sentimental genre in ways that no other author had. There were, after all, good narrative reasons for avoiding the kind of eroticism that colors *Radubis* in the sentimental novel. In that genre, the most dominant strain of the Egyptian novel at that time, explicit erotic description might reasonably be said to undermine the tensions driving the narrative. Part of this is due to the peculiar sort of sentimental narratives of Egypt during this era. Whether set in the present or in the historical past, few of these romances end in sexual consummation. If there is a constancy throughout these novels it is one of unconsummated desire, of maintaining desire by leaving it unfulfilled. Thus in starting with a courtesan and in describing with great relish her erotic qualities, *Radubis* effectively inverts many of the most important conventions of the canonical Egyptian sentimental narrative. Rather than appearing as a socially proper object of desire, Radubis appears as a prostitute; rather than creating narrative tension by placing the possibility of sexual consummation at the end of the narrative, this novel presents it up front; rather than withholding this consummation, this novel makes it readily attainable; rather than alluding to feminine eroticism by way of euphemism, *Radubis* describes it explicitly;

rather than explaining the feelings of desire within the protagonist, only *Radubis* attempts to incite them in the reader as well.

After beginning in this vein, however, *Radubis* does evolve into a traditional sentimental novel as Rhadubis purifies herself in the temple and sets out to leave her life as a courtesan behind for the innocent and pure form of love she shares with Merenre. After her conversion, the romance narrative becomes exceptional only in its lack of tension. But this is precisely the moment at which the novel becomes interesting, since their relationship sets in motion a number of deeper social conflicts. These conflicts extend beyond the relationship between Merenre and his family to the priestly class and the kingdom more widely. In this sense, the novel speaks far more about political matters in the kingdom of Egypt than it does about affairs of the heart. As the conflict worsens, the Pharaoh's character flaws intensify: he overturns the traditional power arrangement between king and priests, rejects all counsel, and proves steadfast in his stubbornness. The conflict eventually results in his death, and even that appears more or less legitimate, the consequence of his own faults.

There is no doubt that this story of justifiable regicide was read as a comment upon Faruq's contemporary legitimacy problems when it first appeared. If *'Abath al-aqdar* addressed the problems of the court by indirect references to succession, *Radubis* attacked the issue head-on. From the outset of the second novel, the people wonder whether the young king is fit to rule. His rivalry with the prime minister and his conflicts with the powerful priestly class expose his lack of experience and wisdom as a sovereign, while his frivolous spending of public wealth raises opposition from all sides. These were problems Faruq faced even from before his coronation.[30] Like the Pharaoh Merenre, Faruq came from a once-illustrious ruling dynasty founded by a charismatic patriarch but now widely regarded to have fallen in decline. Like Merenre, Faruq acted more like a playboy than a husband and was criticized for his indiscreet relationships with nightclub performers.[31] By the climax of the novel, the populace is up in arms about the behavior of their king, calling out, "Our King is a playboy," "We need a king who's for real" and "The Worthless King" (*al-malik al-'abith*).[32] These last words echoed a popular slogan about Egypt's modern king, even though it claimed to be speaking about a figure from the past. According to Mahfouz's publisher, the court was angered by these allusions to Faruq and by the suggestion that the Egyptian people could get rid of the king by killing him.[33]

KIFAH TIBA: NATIONAL LIBERATION

Set around 1600–1525 BCE, Mahfouz's third novel, *Kifah Tiba* (The Struggle for Thebes), describes the struggle of Egyptians to overthrow the tyrannical foreign rule of the Hyksos and the founding of the New Kingdom. Historically, the Hyksos were a nomadic people from central Asia who conquered Egypt and ruled there for over two hundred years before being driven out. Drawing on contemporary interest in this period, Mahfouz's novel rewrites history in crucial ways.[34] For instance, in *Kifah Tiba*, the Hyksos only rule for one hundred years before their expulsion. Historically the Hyksos introduced the chariot into ancient Egypt, and this invention was to a large part responsible for their conquest. In Mahfouz's hands, however, the Hyksos, in collaboration with Egyptian artisans, steal the invention from the Pharaohs. Such changes were read by critics as historical mistakes; for Mahfouz, they were attempts to assert the nationalist spirit of Egyptians of all eras.

The story of *Kifah Tiba* takes place over three generations. The first book of the novel begins by describing the humiliating power condominium by which the Hyksos rulers of lower Egypt allowed the Egyptian throne to rule over Upper Egypt from the royal city of Thebes. This arrangement ends when the Hyksos provocatively redraft the terms of their suzerainty and then treacherously invade. The king is killed defending Thebes while the rest of the royal family flees. The second book of the novel describes the exile of the royal family in Nubia, and the royal Prince Ahmose's covert reconnaissance missions to Egypt. During these trips, Prince Ahmose meets "common Egyptians" and also inadvertently falls in love with a Hyksos princess. The prince eventually sublimates his desires into building an army of national liberation. The final book of the novel describes the long campaign to liberate Egypt, city by city, from south to north. With the death of his father, Ahmose is crowned Pharaoh, and he eventually expels the Hyksos from Egypt. The Pharaonic family and throne are restored, while Egypt returns to native rule.

Mahfouz's first two novels were concerned with the legitimacy of political power and focused particularly on the legitimacy of royal power. *Kifah Tiba* addresses these concerns, but, more important, it frames them within a narrative of national liberation. Whereas *'Abath al-aqdar* is concerned with a problem of dynastic succession and *Radubis* with an acute crisis in royal legitimacy, *Kifah Tiba* places these issues of political succession and legitimacy within a rubric of anticolonial struggle: the legitimacy of the royal family is never in doubt (as it is in the first two novels) because they are clearly identified as native Egyptians against foreign oppressors. And with undoubted legitimacy, kingly succession is accomplished without hesitation or question: when Seqenre and Kamose die, each is succeeded by a son as able and respected as the last. The three generations of Pharaohs in *Kifah Tiba* are not whimsical despots, but beloved leaders who inspire and defend the honor of the Egyptian people.

There is little doubt that critical elements of the novel's nationalist allegory were readily visible to early readers. The semi-independent nature of the Thebes government clearly resembled the power arrangements of domestic Egyptian governance under British suzerainty in effect since 1924 and revised in 1936. Likewise, the novel hints at elements of the history of two recent armed struggles against foreign occupation—1882 and 1919—in which national leaders were struck down and Egyptian hopes for independence were dashed. In this way, the novel suggests that a third generation might launch a successful rebellion against foreign rule. Finally, the slogan of the Theban nationalists, "Struggle, Egypt, Amun" (*al-Kifah, Misr, Amun*), recalls a popular nationalist slogan of the 1930s, "God, King, Country" (*Allah, al-Malik, al-Watan*).[35] Crucially, however, Mahfouz substituted "Struggle" for "King," a meaningful, perhaps even risky, change.

The theme of slavery plays a central role in *Kifah Tiba* and is closely tied to the nationalist allegory. The Hyksos regularly refer to common Egyptians as slaves. In a reprise of early twentieth-century colonial discourse in Egypt, one of the Hyksos characters proclaims in the first pages of the novel, "There is no better medium for communicating with Egyptians than the whip."[36] The Hyksos king announces after vanquishing Seqenre', "We are white, you are brown. We are the masters, you are the peasants. The throne, the government, the obedience belong to us. . . . Whoever works on our lands is a slave who earns his wage. . . . And I will shed the blood of an entire village if anyone lifts a hand to harm any of my men."[37] Like other novels, *Kifah Tiba* argues that the servility of Egyptians is not an essential character trait, but rather the result of foreign rule. It is not that Egyptians are slaves but rather that they become slaves under the Hyksos. For Egyptians to end the foreign occupation is thus to return themselves to their free nature. Still, Pharaoh does more than merely liberate the Egyptian people from slavery under the Hyksos. He also frees Egyptian lands from foreign usurpation. In scenes which anticipate Nasser's land reforms of the 1960s, the victorious Ahmose transfers all lands over to the masses of Egyptian peasants. By the end, national liberation is one not just of native Egyptians from foreign masters, but also a liberation of Egyptian peasants from foreign landlords.

In the novel, the conflict between native Egyptians and their foreign rulers is also a racial one, underscored by the central (and problematic) signification of skin color and physiognomy throughout the national liberation narrative. Almost without exception, the national conflict between the native Egyptians and the foreign Hyksos is described in racial terms: brown-skinned, lean, clean-shaven Egyptians and white-skinned, squat, bearded Hyksos. One imagines, yet again, a bas-relief origin to this sharply contrasting depiction of national differences. The first Hyksos character to appear in the narrative is introduced via a description of his body: he is a "short, stocky, white-skinned man with a round face and long beard."[38] In fact, whenever Hyksos characters enter the narrative, it is the whiteness of their skin that is first described. Besides being a marker of physical sickness, the Hyksos' physiognomy signals moral failings. In another scene, the Hyksos are referred to as "stupid, proud white men with filthy beards."[39] They act as "excessively proud and swaggering men. They are overly strong, but lazy, which leads them to exploit others to do their work."[40] If that were not enough, the novel puns with the names of central Hyksos characters, which might be read as "Sanmut" ("we will die"), "Khanzir" ("pig"), and "Khiyan" ("treachery"), thus underscoring their immoral and ill-fated essence.

Readers quickly recognized that *Kifah Tiba*'s talk about foreign occupation in ancient Egypt was also a way to speak about modern Egypt under British occupation. But, importantly, the white-skinned Hyksos in *Kifah*

Tiba were not merely allegorical ciphers for the British. The novel's ruling Hyksos class also hinted at the ethnic Turkish-Egyptian aristocracy, whose power was largely based on their extensive landholdings. Moreover, like the novel's villainous Hyksos, modern Egypt's Turkish elite was white-skinned and had ties to the ancient nomadic peoples of Central Asia.

The contrast with the native Egyptians could not be more pronounced, and it too is underscored by physiognomy. The brown skin color of the royal family attests not just to their difference from the Hyksos, but also to their likeness to the Egyptian people. Again, the allegorical implications are striking: unlike modern Egypt's royal family, in the novel the Pharaoh's skin color and facial features resemble those of Egyptian peasants in the fields and Egyptian artisans in the cities. The consanguinity of the brown-skinned Egyptians becomes the visible sign of what joins the victorious Pharaoh to the people he has come to liberate. Indeed, Pharaoh Ahmose describes the conflict between the Egyptian and Turkic races as follows:

Who are the slaves and who are the masters? You know nothing, you deceived young woman, because you were born in the embrace of this valley which inspires glory and greatness. If your birth were a century ago, you would have been born in the furthest cold reaches of the Northern deserts. You would not have heard anyone call you a princess or your father a king. From these deserts your people came and usurped the masters of our valley and brought the highest down lowest. Mistaken and ignorant, they said that they were princes and that we were peasant slaves. They said that they were white and we were brown. But today, justice has taken its due course and returned to the master his power. The slave has overthrown his enslavement. And whiteness becomes the mark of those who wander in the cold deserts, while brownness is the slogan of the masters of Egypt, those who have been purified by the light of the sun![41]

Using racial discourse in the service of a nationalist ideology leads *Kifah Tiba* into some uncomfortable and unsustainable realms, particularly because it expresses national liberation in terms of racial purification. National liberation becomes, in this novel, a process of re-Egyptianizing Egypt (*i'adat misriyyatiha*).[42] To expel the foreign oppressors is to cleanse the land of its blemishes and to purify "the land of Egypt from its enemy."[43] What does purity mean in this context? As Ahmose explains to his commanders, "After today, nobody but Egyptians will rule Egypt. Nobody but

Egyptians will own land. The land is Pharaoh's land, and the peasants take care of it for him. They will keep what they need and what will provide for them a full life. And they will give to Pharaoh the surplus to spend for the public good. Egyptians will be equals before the law. Nobody will be raised above another, except if he should wish it. There are no slaves in this land, except the Hyksos!"[44] The story of national liberation in *Kifah Tiba* is, in fact, one of racial purification and emancipation from slavery.

SAYYID QUTB: ALLEGORY
OF PHARAONIC TYRANNY

The foundation of the institutions of life suggests that the entire world to-day is living in a state of ignorance (*jahiliyya*). It is a *jahiliyya* which remains unameliorated by any of the extraordinary material conveniences of modern material inventions. This *jahiliyya* is founded upon a rebellion against the rule of God on the Earth, and against the most particular of God's attributes: sovereignty.—SAYYID QUTB, *Ma'alim fi-l-tariq*

Sayyid Qutb, the first literary critic to champion Mahfouz's talents as a novelist, was an avid proponent of Pharaonism through the mid-1940s. However, his enthusiasm for Pharaonist style was by that time already separated from any particular political program, since he had already somewhat distanced himself from the politics of Egypt's main parties.[45] In fact, the period in which he discovered Mahfouz was a transitional one for Qutb: in his critical work, he was already bringing the lessons of Western philosophy to bear upon the sacred text which had comprised much of his education as a youth; in his poetry and fiction, he had turned to more existential topics. Qutb's thought at this time still remained very much within the mainstream of *Nahda* literary culture. By all accounts, the years Qutb spent studying in the United States were decisive in bringing him out of this mold. It was at places like Stanford University that Qutb first confronted the depth of the West's misunderstanding of Islam, its racism toward Arabs, and its different moral attitudes toward gender and sexuality. Only then did Qutb begin to understand the extent to which the *Nahda* model of modernity was based on Western norms, on models that were not just foreign to Egypt's autochthonous culture, but that effectively repudiated the values of Muslim civilization.[46]

Qutb was greeted upon his return by young Muslim Brothers. Within months, he joined the Brotherhood. Later, he described the experience as one of rebirth.[47] The loss of Banna had deeply affected the Brothers, and they quickly moved to promote Qutb through the ranks to fill the gap. In 1952, he was elected to the Brotherhood's leadership council, made head of the organization's public outreach mission, and appointed editor in chief of the society's newspaper, *al-Ikhwan al-Muslimun*.[48] That year, when a Brother attempted to assassinate Nasser in Alexandria, the state pounced on the organization: the paper was closed, and Qutb, along with hundreds of others, was arrested, tortured, and sentenced to a lengthy prison term. He would not emerge from Nasser's prisons until 1964, during which time he had written five books, including his monumental exegesis of the Qur'an, *Fi-zilal al-Qur'an* (In the Shade of the Qur'an), and another, more polemical book, largely excerpted from that work, *Ma'alim fi-tariq* (Signposts Along the Road).

Even on his return to Egypt in 1951, Qutb was already building a comprehensive analysis of Muslim culture and a systematic critique of Western modernity. When it began to appear in the 1950s, Qutb's exegetical work was offered, and received, as a repudiation of the secular culture of *Nahda* modernity. By the time he joined the Brotherhood, Pharaonism's sun had already set, and there are few moments in his work when he explicitly addresses the Pharaonist culture he had advocated only a few years earlier. Yet reading Qutb alongside Mahfouz's allegories illuminates some of the problems of Pharaonist literary discourse. More immediately, it exposes affinities between Pharaonism and Qutb's Islamist writing. In this regard, Qutb's method of reading the ancient past stands out. For Qutb, no less than Mahfouz, Egypt's ancient past was not only alive in the present moment but was arguably its most relevant truth.

Critics have noted the eclectic citations of Qutb's writing. His is a library that stretches from Karl Marx and Friedrich Nietzsche to Ibn Taymiyya and Abu al-'Ala' al-Mawdudi. In his exegesis of the Qur'an, Qutb goes beyond elucidating holy text to offer compelling critiques of colonialism and capitalism. He writes with equal insight on the blindnesses of Western scientific methodology, not to mention the failures of socialism and nationalism. Moreover, Qutb's work speaks in a range of registers, from political theory to theological apologia to sociological analysis. Yet throughout, the method of his major piece of writing, *Fi zilal al-Qur'an*, was primarily literary. As a work of literary analysis, it is of a particular kind: Qutb reads the text of the Qur'an as a comment on his own social-historical context and relies on his own context to elucidate his reading of the text. In other words, Qutb's exegesis is profoundly allegorical, in that his reading of the Qur'anic text is through reference to the present. At the same time, his reading of the present is grounded in the Qur'anic text. Thus emerges in Qutb's method a dialectic in which Qur'anic text elucidates the world outside it and in which the world brings into focus the kernel truths of the Qur'an. *Fi zilal al-Qur'an* implies that one cannot read the text without an eye on the world in which one lives; nor can one hope to live in this world without using the Qur'an as a guide.

Before turning to Qutb's monumental work, I will glance at his most popular tract, *Ma'alim fi-l-tariq*, itself mostly taken from his commentary on Sura 7 ("Surat al-A'raf," or "The Heights"). In *Ma'alim*, Qutb describes two spheres of problems in modern Muslim society: one, a sphere of culture, in which morality, belief, behavior, and thought fall short of the cultural norms established in the Qur'an; and another, a sphere of politics, in which state power is wielded in illegitimate and tyrannical ways. In Qutb's account, the two spheres are interlocking: problems of the political order are rooted in problems of modern Muslim culture; problems of culture have their origins in the political order. Similarly, the problems individual Muslims face are analogous to those facing the collective, and vice versa. Qutb's analysis of these interlocking spheres has two main foci, the conditions of legitimate power and the conditions of tyranny: on the one hand, problems that have to do with the origins of power; and on the other, problems that have to do with the justness of power. Again, these issues—origins and justice—are inseparable in that each is both the cause and effect of the other.

Power in modern states, Qutb notes, derives from human laws. It is not just that humans make the law, but that they emphasize the human character and origin of those laws. In the best cases, the highest values of European humanism are prominently embedded in the laws of the modern state, while in the worst cases they are forgotten. But in either case, the law of modern states is made by humans and made according to human standards which are eminently fallible and often arbitrary. By Qutb's reasoning, human legal regimes have nothing in common with those Muslim states that have been rightly governed. In such states, Qutb avers, Muslims have enforced laws whose origins were divine, rather than earthly. When Muslim states have not implemented the laws as revealed in holy text, they have not been rightly governed.

At this point Qutb asserts that obedience to law is a form of worship (*'ibada*). In making this claim, Qutb raises the stakes considerably. The legitimacy of government is thus attached to the issue of practiced faith. If to live by law is a form of worship, Qutb alleges, then to abide by human-made law is to worship something human. In contrast, to abide by laws whose origin is divine is to worship their Maker. Here, then, are the outlines of Qutb's political theory of Islam: on the one hand, to abide by Islamic law is to worship its Maker, to submit to the only power worthy of the trait of sovereignty and to be free of those illegitimate forms of power; on the other hand, to follow human law is tantamount to worshiping something other than God. In short, it is a form of idolatry (*shirk*). To explain the difference between legitimate and illegitimate power, Qutb relies upon a reading of the narrative of Moses' confrontation with Pharaoh as it appears in "Surat al-A'raf."

Since Qutb's contextualization of the Qur'anic text is crucial to his commentary, I will trace its elaboration. Qutb's approach to the text of "Surat al-A'raf" might be called narratological in the sense that what concerns him foremost is its development of a story, the confrontation of Pharaoh and Moses. Here, Qutb immediately acknowledges a thorny issue, namely, that even the most plotted segments of the Qur'an often cannot be read as discrete narratives. This is due partly to the fact that many of the narratives of the Qur'an are told in pieces scattered throughout the text and partly to the fact that many of the narratives of the Qur'an are recounted more than once in different parts of the Qur'an. The second is the case of "Surat al-A'raf": there is a coherent narrative that takes the forgetfulness and ingratitude of humans toward God as its central theme, but this narrative, and especially the portion devoted to the Moses-Pharaoh story, is one that is developed at length in six other books of the text and appears many, many other times in fragments or by way of citation. This fact of repetition is crucial for Qutb's reading because it acknowledges some of the fundamentals of Qur'anic interpretation, namely, that the arrangement of the Qur'an text is not linear and that any particular narrative episode ought to be read in conjunction with the other versions of that narrative which appear elsewhere.[49] Qutb's political theory and theological propositions thus hinge upon a close reading of the Pharaonic past as depicted in the Qur'an. Qutb lived with the Qur'an most of his life, but his training was in Egypt's secular schools and under the tutelage of critics like 'Abbas Mahmud al-'Aqqad. His exegesis of the Qur'an thus belongs to the history of modern literary criticism and differs significantly from the kinds of commentaries studied and produced in religious institutions like al-Azhar. Most important, Qutb's commentary was addressed to a non-specialist audience, which is part of its lasting popularity.

Qutb's reading of Moses' challenge to Pharaoh as narrated in "Surat al-A'raf" is thus determinative. Qutb notes that the Sura as a whole tells a long history of human frailty and arrogance: from the time of Adam, God has revealed himself to humans; each time they take his mercy for granted and forget his commandments, and each time they are punished. The story of Moses' challenge to Pharaoh is but one part of this longer narrative. Qutb, like other exegetes, notes that only part of the significance of Pharaoh's story lies on the level of the ancient past of the Egyptians and the Israelites. One must read it as part of an address to an audience that occurs in a specific context and also in multiple contexts. Thus part of the significance of the story relates to the context in which God directly addressed this story to the lives of Muhammad and the first Muslims. The significance of the text when comprehended in this context opens up the narrative of Pharaoh in rich ways. First, it can speak to the kind of persecution early Muslims experienced at the hands of Mecca's pagan rulers. Second, in Medina, where early Muslims resented Jewish opposition to their growing power, it can speak to the special kind of failure marked by example of the Israelites' forgetfulness. But where Qutb is most inventive is in his opening of this horizon further to encompass the present. Here it might resonate with any number of contemporary struggles and conflicts. It is in this play between ancient, Islamic, and modern contexts that Qutb's reading begins to transform into something more than literary.

Paraphrasing verse 137 of the Sura, Qutb writes, "Thus falls the curtain on the scene of destruction on one side, and on the scene of a new civilizing order on the other. Drowned are Pharaoh, the tyrants' tyrant, along with his people. The life they created, the foundations they built, the vineyards and orchards they cultivated: all of this was destroyed in the flash of an eye and in the space of a few words."[50] In the following sentence, Qutb opens the frame of interpretation onto the context of its revelation in Arabia: "This was an example given by God to a small group of believers in Mecca who suffered at the hands of idolaters." He then opens the aperture again: "These are wide views offered to every Muslim group who encounters the likes of Pharaoh and his idolatry, that they might learn what befell the weak of the world: when they were patient, God gave them the reaches of the Earth." In Qutb's reading, the past is a lesson to the present, much like the example of the pre-Islamic heathens who were a lesson to early Muslims. Similarly, the present is what illuminates this past: the fact that the condition of the modern world resembles the moment of Muhammad's mission is what enables him to read the text cogently.

Qutb's close reading of Pharaoh is illuminating in this regard, for it allows him to define the kernel of tyranny and godlessness. What was so objectionable about Pharaoh as he appears in the narrative of the Israelites is that he not only makes himself lord, but does not recognize any other. While this might be reasonably interpreted as an act of apotheosis, Qutb offers a more nuanced interpretation:

> Pharaoh did not claim divinity in the sense that he was Creator and Ruler of the world, or that he had power over the forces of nature. He claimed divine status over his downtrodden people, in the sense that he ruled over this people by way of his law and that by his will and order things were done and matters completed. This is what a sovereign [*hakim*] who rules by law does. This is what lordship means, both in its linguistic and practical senses. Likewise, the people in Egypt did not worship Pharaoh in the sense that they performed religious rituals toward him. They had their gods, and Pharaoh had his gods that he worshipped. This is clear in the speech of Pharaoh's advisors when [he was confronted by Moses] and they counseled him "[Will you allow Moses to] forsake you and your gods . . . ?" [al-Qur'an 7:127] This is likewise confirmed by what is known of the history of ancient Egypt. They "served/worshipped" Pharaoh in the sense that they submitted to his will, did not disobey him, and did not violate his law. This is the linguistic, practical and technical sense of the word "worship." Whenever people accept and accede to human legislation they are worshipping/submitting to humans.[51]

Qutb's reading of the passage is motivated by an ambiguity in the verb *'abada*, which means both to serve as a slave and to worship. As Qutb goes on to make clear, the difference between worshiping (*al-'ibada*) and submitting as a slave (*al-'ubudiyya*) should be critical to Muslims. In fact, he asserts, Islam's political meaning lies in the fact that it came to free people from their enslavement to humans. Submitting to God in worship is proper because God truly is sovereign and stands over humans in power and knowledge.

Slavery, the illegitimate rule of humans over humans, is thus the core meaning of the pre-Islamic period (*al-Jahiliyya*) for Qutb. In his reading, Islamic law rejects this proposition, just as Islamic faith would reject the notion of worshiping anything but God as idolatry and apostasy. Here, then, Qutb's commentary begins to build out from the text. This reading is based in his insistence on interpreting the Qur'an in a figurative manner. This is especially clear in his use of the terms *Islam* and *Jahiliyya*, which take on a significance that goes beyond their historical relation. Relying on the interpretative work of al-Mawdudi in this regard, Qutb glosses the words as metaphors, transforming them into figures of a transhistorical binarism and abiding human struggle:

> Islam is not a historical event that once happened and then was left behind as history moved on. Today, Islam is called to play the role it once played. The circumstances, social customs, conditions, political regimes, beliefs, faiths, values, and traditions [of today] resemble those Islam confronted when it first appeared. The *Jahiliyya* is a condition, not a temporal, historical period. The *Jahiliyya* has driven its stakes into every corner of the world, in the diversity of beliefs, doctrines, political regimes and circumstances. It founds itself on the basis of the sovereignty (*hakimiyya*) of servants over servants, and rejects the absolute sovereignty of God over men. [This *Jahiliyya*] makes any kind of human passion its foundation and ruling deity while preventing the law of God from being the ruling code.[52]

In Qutb's writing, a state of *jahiliyya* exists in the hearts and minds of individuals, and it exists across societies and time. Moreover, it is not just non-Muslim individuals or non-Muslim societies whose character might be *jahili*. Following al-Mawdudi's radical innovation, Qutb denounces modern Muslim societies living under human laws as having forfeited their Muslim character, as having reverted to a state of *jahiliyya*. Here, Qutb employs the neologism *al-Islami* (the Islamist) to differentiate those modern Muslims who insist on living in obedience with revealed law from those Muslims still living *jahili* lives. Beginning with his reading of Pharaoh and Moses, Qutb extends the violence of the Pharaonic tyranny into a contemporary reading of secular legal regimes in Muslim society.

Around this scenario develops a line of thought about the political and moral duties and rights of *Islami* Muslims living under the rule of *jahili* government. Qutb urges Muslims to purify themselves of the *jahiliyya* in their hearts and minds and to confront and repudiate *jahiliyya* wherever they find it in their modern societies:

> In this time of ours, we see different styles and shades of paganism, even among those who claim to be monotheists and who claim to submit to God. . . . We fool ourselves if we limit paganism to crudely formed idols and ancient gods, and to the rituals people performed in their worship, seeking the aid of such idols before God. Only the shape of the idols and idolatry has changed. The rituals have become more complex and taken on new titles, yet the nature and underlying truth of paganism remain the same behind the changing shapes and rituals. . . . These are examples of what occurs today in the world. Humans who are lost are well acquainted with them. They are examples which reveal the paganism that dominates today, and the truth of idols that are worshipped in place of the old candid paganism, and the idols which were once seen as idols. The changing shapes of paganism and idolatry should not deceive us about their constant truth.[53]

Of course, the most prominent sites where Muslims would find the *jahiliyya* of modern societies would be in those governments that do not implement divine law, a list which included, in Qutb's reckoning, all modern Muslim and Arab states. The coherence of Qutb's thought and the power of its continuing relevance to so many people lie in the fact that he took a philosophy of individual faith, derived partly from older strands of Islamic theology, and synthesized it within a far-reaching critique of modernity and an astute concept of political authority. Much of the power derives from his reading of *jahiliyya*, a reading which allowed him to unmoor the word from its traditional narrow denotation of a moment located in a receding historical past. Resemanticizing the word, turning it into a figure that connoted far more than ever before, Qutb opened the text onto a discussion of the contradictions of the modern liberal society under colonial rule and to the failures and violence of the nation-state emerging with formal independence. Qutb encourages his readers to look at modern Egypt, whose state of corruption and heedlessness they could see reflected in the text of the Qur'an.

Paradoxically, this move to free the ancient past from its literal, historical meaning had a precursor in Egypt: the Pharaonist project in which Qutb had invested so heavily earlier in his career. Arguably, then, one might trace Qutb's effort to resurrect the past in the present, his insistence that the pre-Islamic past was alive today in the lives of modern Egyptians, to the likes of Salama Musa, Tawfiq al-Hakim, and Muhammad Husayn Haykal. Of course, the differences between the two projects are salient: the Pharaonist *Nahda* appeared in the minds of its creators as an ideal dream, while for Qutb the persistence of the *jahili* past was a nightmare; for the former, the Pharaonic past was the ground for imagining national sovereignty; for the latter, it was the image of political tyranny. Nonetheless, the cultural mechanism of the two projects is the same, in that both rested on a largely allegorical conception of ancient history in which Pharaonism played a leading role.

CONCLUSION

History died. What was there to resurrect, what was the cause of its death? . . . I studied everything connected with the Pharaonic period, the everyday life, methods of war, religion. How did I ditch the massive effort [of historical fiction] after *Kifah Tiba*? . . . Maybe history became incapable of allowing me to say what I wanted to say.—*NAGUIB MAHFUZ YATADHAKKIR*

Today, people erect gods, calling one "the nation," another "the homeland," "the people," and so on. These amount to nothing more than shapeless idols [*asnam*], like the crude idols that pagans created in the past.
—SAYYID QUTB, *Fi-zilal al-Qur'an*

Fredric Jameson's essay "Third World Literature in the Era of Multinational Capitalism" (1986) proposed a method of reading literature in developing and formerly colonized countries.[54] Novels especially, he asserted, might be read as "national allegories." Those familiar with Jameson's essay will recognize that I have already misrepresented his argument. He did not propose *a* method of reading, nor did he *suggest* that novels *might* be read allegorically. Rather, he roundly asserted that "all third-world novels are necessarily . . . national allegories." Critics rightly pounced on the essentialisms in Jameson's essay: his problematic definition of "Third World," his blanket generalizations about life in the Third World, his comments about the mature form of the modernist novel and the anachronistic feel of literature from the formerly colonized world, his Fourth International assumptions about the innately progressive revolutionary character of anticolonial national liberation movements.[55] In the ensuing storm, many missed Jameson's most intriguing and productive observations about the enduring relevance of allegory to modern fiction.[56]

A more defensible rephrasing of his proposition might read as follows: quite often one finds novels in which the psychological narratives of individual characters have a clear relation to wider political narratives; in such novels, the two narrative arcs are quite often mediated through the image of the nation. Jameson elaborates on this idea by way of reading two novels. His reading, in my opinion, remains compelling despite the other problems of the essay. In each novel, Jameson finds the two narrative arcs—one psychological and libidinal, the other sociological and collective—exist in a dynamic relation to one another. Through close reading, Jameson shows us that the two novels do not pose a realm of collective experience that is merely reflective of personal experience. Rather, each of the novels he considers stages a dialectic in which the personal informs and drives the political and in which changes in the wider political plots transform the feelings and desires of the individual characters. The hinge between the two levels of narrative is nationalist discourse, hence the term *national allegory.*

In Jameson's hands, national allegory remains intratextual. That is, those levels of the text that might be called the grounding and allegory relate to elements that are within the narrative plots. It is on this point that Jameson's concept of allegory becomes not so traditional. In his readings, he proposes that the narrative of individual psychology might function as the ground on which the collective narrative is expressed. Thus, the personal might be said to represent the literal level of the narrative while the political represents something more figurative. But this is only half of Jameson's model, for he also insists that the narrative of the collective might also function as the literal level on which the more figurative narrative of individual psychology is expressed. In this way, the political becomes the ground, while the personal now appears as figure. His reading of national allegory thus attempts to describe a dynamic mode of narrative in which the terms *ground* and *figure* shift, reverse, and drive each other onward.

Throughout this chapter, I have attempted to put to use Jameson's model of national allegory, looking for moments when the narratives of internal lives and the narratives of polities speak to and argue with one another. At the same time, I have been considering allegory in another way, considering the political or historical world outside Mahfouz's novels as ground and his texts as figures. This is admittedly a conventional method of reading allegory, and one with faults, since it often implies a reflective theory of cultural production.

Here is where Jameson's dialectical model of allegory seems useful. The same kind of dynamism he finds within individual texts also exists between different texts, of course, and also between those texts and their sociohistorical contexts. In other words, one might imagine texts in contexts which compel readers to see what they take as ground shift into figure, or the two—ground and figure—exchanging places and transforming each other. Arguably, this kind of dynamism is where allegorical fiction is at its most powerful, where the inner lives of readers are transformed by reading narratives, and where collective narratives out in the world bear the traces of narratives that may have first appeared on tongues or pages. For this dynamic mode of allegory to work, however, readers must see a piece of fiction as much more than a reference to the world in which they live; they have to recognize that a particular fiction could also serve as the grounding for the world in which they live, or one in which they would rather live. This utopian element is crucial for Jameson's reading of allegory, for it is the desire to imagine in an otherly fashion that drives this dynamic. Put differently, allegory arguably thrives only in contexts in which readers feel invited to reimagine the relationship between the text they are reading and the context in which they are living. Only in that position might the power of figures usurp the ground of historical contexts only to reverse again, the positions now forever shifted by the process. Conversely, one might also argue that where there is not a widely held consensus about this need and potential for play between sociohistorical ground and textual figure, allegory's life will be short and flat.

Such dynamism is not at work in the kind of national allegories offered in Mahfouz's novel. The novels appear less like allegories, more like romans à clef. It is easy to see how these novels comment upon their political and social contexts, but difficult to see how readers might have recognized this fictional commentary as vital and relevant. To address this point, I want to turn to the question of reception. It is true that some critics praised the debut of *Kifah Tiba*, though none to the extent that Qutb did. But if reception is any gauge, these novels were minor from the moment they appeared in print. In fact, given the attention that critics paid at first to issues of historical accuracy in the novels, it is clear that readers looked at the novels primarily as history texts and only secondarily as fictions that spoke to the present. This fact frustrated Mahfouz, who felt he had been misread.[57] Though the novels have been reprinted over the decades, Mahfouz's critics still do not know how to approach them. After completing *Kifah Tiba*, Mahfouz abandoned the writing of Pharaonist literature for four decades and also the massive project of writing the complete history of Egypt in a series of novels.

Usually, Mahfouz's first novels are dismissed as the works of an immature author, an opinion that Mahfouz himself has voiced on a number of occasions. I would like to propose instead that Mahfouz's Pharaonist novels fail not because of the supposed immaturity of the novelist at the time (though that may also be true) but because the post-Pharaonist context in which they emerged could not support anything but the flattest kind of reading. They were offered to the public as the resurrected spirit of the past brought to bear upon the present but were received as still-life portraits of antiquity. They are novels whose potential force comes from the assertion that the past lives in the present, yet they were published at a time when the literary world had decided that the past, at least the Pharaonic past, was the distant past. Mahfouz's novels illustrate how, in the secular culture of the *Nahda*, the Pharaonic past had ceased to function as an enduring spirit and returned to being simply the past. The Pharaonic had returned to being a topic better suited to historical research than literary experimentation.

This last point highlights the uncanny parallelism in the kind of Islamist thinking exemplified by Banna and Qutb. In the classical Islamic tradition, the objects and narratives of ancient Egypt were topics that inspired the contemplation of the passing of historical time. In contrast, for Qutb (as for Mahfouz), the Pharaonic was not merely a historic period, nor did it prompt reflection on the passing of time. As a sign of the un-Islamic rather than merely pre-Islamic, the Pharaonic was very much about a timeless present. I would suggest that the innovation in Qutb's thinking has everything to do with the issue of allegory as Jameson describes it, at least insofar as his reading of the *Jahiliyya* loosened it from its literal grounding and offered it as a figure living in the present, and living beyond the narrow confines of Cairo's elite print culture. Qutb's reading of the past has managed to exist in vibrant relation to modern-day readers in ways that those of Pharaonist writers never did. In that way, and despite the fact that the concept of the nation was antithetical to his project, Qutb's writings on the *Jahiliyya* might be thought of as a particularly dynamic form of national allegory. If Mahfouz's novels mark the end of a period, the dying out of an allegorical relationship to the Pharaonic past among secular *Nahda* intellectuals, Qutb's equally allegorical reading of the Pharaonic past was uncommonly dynamic and vibrant and helped to radically shift the Muslim Brothers' conception of themselves and their world. And in so doing, it helped the Brotherhood and its inheritors challenge the world in ways Pharaonists never dreamed of.

Conclusion

Humanity begins with things.—MICHEL SERRES

The invention of the artifact—embedded as it was within a broad network of institutions—enabled European archaeologists and curators, administrators and casual tourists to make informed statements about ancient Egypt. Critically, these were also claims on modern Egypt. Likewise, as Egyptian elites began to take the lessons of Egyptology to heart, they developed a powerful language for articulating a new sense of Egyptian identity encompassing experiences and aspirations that were profoundly personal and also collective. We cannot miss the ironies of the process of cultural translation and adaptation which allowed the same group of cultural artifacts, narratives, and images to mean such different things to different actors: Pharaonic Egypt was no less a source for contesting colonial hegemony than it had been for legitimating it. As we saw in the work of Tahtawi and 'Ali Mubarak, cultural Pharaonism was central to Egyptian responses to growing European power in the Middle East even before direct colonial rule. In the autobiographies and fictions of nationalist intellectuals growing up during the British occupation of Egypt (1882–1956), the significance of ancient Egypt expanded even further: to know ancient Egypt and, more important, to *feel* it were crucial within a developing nationalist sensibility. With the discovery of Tutankhamen's tomb, these sensibilities became more than assertions, they began to appear as forms of common sense.

Even as one recognizes the forces weaving aesthetic, historical, and political claims on ancient Egypt into one another, one needs to question the assumption that this process was natural and necessary, or that different modes of Pharaonist discourse were identical or even always compatible. This is yet another ambiguity I have attempted to indicate by returning to the conflicted aspects of the various moments and texts I have surveyed. A brief exploration of the term *Pharaonism* (*Fir'awniyya*) will reveal just how many conflicts it contains. Beginning in the 1920s, elite Egyptian intellectuals used the word *Fir'awniyya* to describe the aesthetic and political assertion that ancient Egypt was the wellspring of Egypt's modern identity. In the press, it referred to a wide range of things: a Pharaonic style of expressive culture (in literature, art, and architecture); an emphasis on the Pharaonic period in historical discussions of Egypt; a register of political discourse that linked the national liberation movement under British rule to images and narratives drawn from ancient Egypt. Pharaonism entailed a combination of any and all of the above. Together, these articulations created powerful narratives and images of Egyptian national identity, one in which individual and communal identity were interchangeable: an identity that was historical and also transcendent; an essence that had its own natural style of artistic expression; a springboard for political action that was based in the present moment of Egypt's colonial subjection and in a past moment of Egyptian colonial might. Pharaonism addressed Egyptians as individual citizens of a modern nation and also as members of a collective that was timeless. It appealed to hearts no less than minds.

The flexibility of these claims made Pharaonism a potentially powerful discourse. But its elasticity begs the following question: What did Pharaonism mean if it was: (a) an aesthetic style; (b) a style of historiography; (c) a political idiom for speaking about colonial power; (d) a political discourse for creating a new sense of national community; and (e) a register for translating back and forth claims about communal and individual feeling, experience, and identity? How does one grasp this as a coherent cultural phenomenon while remaining attuned to the specificity and heterogeneity of the texts and activities composing it? The beginning of the answer to these questions lies in the observation that Pharaonism was not a unified symbolic system, even during its clearest and most powerful moments. The differences between various forms and registers of Pharaonist discourse were, as I have shown, spaces for heightened ambiguities and significant contestations.

While there is good reason to consider the wide range of aesthetic and political texts together under the rubric of a single cultural phenomenon called Pharaonism, registers of artistic expression are clearly different from those of political expression in ways that beg further exploration. Moreover, while the different registers of Pharaonism often invoked each other, they did not always work in easy harmony together. Pharaonist gestures, whether political, aesthetic, or both, contained significant divergences and ironies. This goes beyond differences of genre or, for instance, the distinction between a parliamentary speech, poetry recitation, or the unveiling of statues. It also consists of real conflicts in the Pharaonist claims launched by competing parties of secular nationalists in Egypt's fledgling Parliament of the 1920s. This was evinced in the conflicts between the Wafd and the Liberal Constitutionalists, the two major parties of the period, both of which invested heavily in Pharaonist iconography. As they jockeyed for position through the late 1920s, however, and as they accentuated their differences by reference to the ancient past, they each developed a slightly variant form of Pharaonism. While Wafd and Liberal Constitutionalist claims about the Pharaonic past drew upon the same source, their competition over its interpretation had, in time, the effect of reshaping Pharaonist discourse. Thus Pharaonism in 1936 was not what it had been in 1924. Taken together, the pluralism, tensions, and developments within Pharaonism suggest that it was neither a monolithic nor static discourse.

If this was true for those who participated in it, it was even more so for those—such as the first generation of Islamists—who spoke of the ancient past in radically divergent ways. This raises the most fundamental controversy of Pharaonist discourse: its place at the center of an emerging elite secular culture at times imposed on, but mostly isolated from, the popular classes of Egyptian society, who remained aloof from and indifferent toward the culture of Pharaonism. In reading closely the secular claims of Pharaonism, one cannot help seeing the points where they clashed with the claims of religious traditions and nonsecular social movements that maintained a connection with older, more complex understandings of the relation between the pre-Islamic past and the present.

That my book stops in the 1940s is not to imply that modern Egyptians suddenly stopped talking about the ancient past. They did, however, back off from earlier Pharaonist cultural and political investments. Still, ancient Egyptian history has remained a central part of the national curriculum at all levels, and the results of this pedagogy ensure that many of the fundamental tenets and slogans of an earlier nationalism remain alive in the public culture. In the popular press and media today, it is not uncommon to hear pundits talk about Egypt's "five thousand years of civilization" as if there were no ruptures or discontinuities over those eons and as if the ancient past were an open book to the present. Such clichéd phrases and familiar images of monuments and artifacts are common currency within state media. During the Nasserist era, Pharaonic motifs occasionally surfaced in state monumental architecture (the Cairo Tower, for example), while elsewhere they remained a constant feature on postage stamps, currency, and tourist advertising. The relation of modern to ancient Egypt became especially pointed again during the final stages of the building of the Aswan Dam during the 1960s and the subsequent inundation of antiquities sites (and all of historical Nubia) under Lake Nasser. A few years later Anwar Sadat quite consciously employed Pharaonic images—the most iconic artifacts from the Cairo Museum's Tutankhamen collection—as he courted the United States during the 1970s. More recently, the Mubarak regime has often drawn on Pharaonic themes in its conflict with militant Islamists: as symbols of secularism, many new state buildings, including the Constitutional Supreme Court, are designed in a neo-Pharaonist style, even though it clashes with republican ideals. With the ascendency of political Islamism in the country during the 1990s, secular intellectuals, in alliance with the Ministry of Culture, once again resurrected discourse on ancient Egypt to promote the image of a unified, eternal, nonsectarian nation. This posture found echoes in literature and film as ancient Egyptian themes have staged a small comeback, most notably in the work of the novelists Naguib Mahfouz (*Akhenaton*) and Gamal al-Ghitani (*Mutun al-ahram*) and the film director Yusuf Chahine (*al-Muhajir*). It is difficult to compare this relatively circumscribed wave of cultural production to earlier ones. Times had changed—and the relation that many more Egyptians now have to ancient Egypt is colored by increasing desperation. Since the late 1970s, when the International Monetary Fund initiated policies to deindustrialize Egypt and rechannel its agricultural output, an increasing share of the local economy has been forced to rely on a single, fragile source of income—foreign tourism. Thus there has been a return to an age, perhaps not seen since 1881, when much of the economy of the Egyptian south depends on the leisure of people from elsewhere. Now, as then, tourism in Egypt almost exclusively means pilgrimages to Pharaonic monuments and antiquities sites. In the 1920s Egyptian elites became temporary tourists in Upper Egypt in order to acquaint themselves with what they saw as their national patrimony. Now, lacking other career opportunities, many college-educated Egyptians serve as professional tour guides showing off national treasures for the entertainment of tourists, as Egyptian archaeologists feel compelled to play host to New Age Pyramid worshipers from abroad.[1] While such scenes—the present-day legacy of secular Pharaonism—are thoroughly ambiguous, they are only one potential endpoint to this story. Other scenes seem less ambiguous, as when in October 1981, Khalid Islambuli, Sadat's assassin, took credit for the deed by announcing, "I have killed Pharaoh." Indeed, to this day, the figure of Pharaoh retains its semantic power for Islamist critics of the modern Egyptian state: Egypt's autocratic presidents continue to be called Pharaohs. And it is likely Qutb, rather than the celebrated secular authors and poets of the *Nahda*, who is now most widely read both in Egypt and abroad. Perhaps it will be this Islamist understanding of the past, and not the Pharaonist one, that will have the most profound impact on the world. Despite the ironies, this too is a legacy of the specific form of colonial modernity that emerged when Europeans and Egyptians contended with one another over the control of Egypt's Pharaonic artifacts and, with that, the power to interpret its ancient past.

Notes

INTRODUCTION

1. In Greek literature, Memnon was the king of Ethiopia who fought in the Trojan war on the side of Troy. He was killed by Achilles. In classical and pre-Egyptological modern traditions of travel writing this statue was linked to Memnon and others, such as Sesostris and Ozymandias. Growing acceptance of Champollion's theories about the ancient hieroglyphics in the 1830s led to the statue's being relabeled as belonging to Ramses II.

2. Heidegger, "The Age of the World Picture," in *Off the Beaten Path*, 67.

3. Ibid., 66.

4. Ibid., 69–70.

5. Ibid., 67–8.

6. Mitchell, *Colonising Egypt*.

7. Horkheimer and Adorno, *Dialectic of Enlightenment*, 9.

8. On the early history of the British Museum, see Miller, *That Noble Cabinet*, and Ian Jenkins, *Archaeologists and Aesthetes*. In the House of Commons, sharp debates over public funding for the museum would continue through the 1860s.

9. British Museum trustees consistently relied upon nationalist appeals to increase state support for acquisitions. In one proposal from this period they argue, "It has often been noticed with surprize that the British government should not have availed themselves of the means they possess, through their diplomatic and other agents in different parts of the globe, towards enriching, and as far as possible completing their public collections of rare and valuable productions and thereby essentially contributing to the advancement of science and the useful arts. The Trustees of the British Museum, who preside over the only national scientific repository in the United Kingdom, aware of the justness of this observation, think it becomes them to make a representation to His Majesty's government, requesting them to establish a correspondence with such of their representatives and agents abroad, as may have any

opportunity of contributing toward so patriotic an object." British Museum: Central Archives: Trustees' Manuscripts: Original Letters and Papers, 3:1450 [c. 1818]).

10. Duncan, *Civilizing Rituals*.

11. Fisher, *Making and Effacing Art*, 18.

12. McClellan, *Inventing the Louvre*.

13. Bal, "Telling Objects."

14. Duncan, *Civilizing Rituals*, 21–47.

15. What Andrew McClellan says about the Louvre in the 1790s is also true of the British Museum in the nineteenth century: "In the late 1790s French commitment to conservation was stretched to justify the appropriation of art confiscated as the booty of war in conquered lands. Portraying itself as a politically and culturally superior nation, France claimed to be uniquely qualified to safeguard the world's treasures for the benefit of mankind." *Inventing the Louvre*, 7. On museum ethics more widely, see *Embedding Ethics*, eds. Meskell and Pels, and Karen J. Warren, "A Philosophical Perspective on the Ethics and Resolution of Cultural Properties Issues."

16. Trigger, *History of Archaeological Thought*, 78.

17. Moser, *Wondrous Curiosities*, 43.

18. Richardson, *Travels Along the Mediterranean and Parts Adjacent*, 1:523.

19. A partial list of popular and scholarly histories in this vein would include: James Baikie, *A Century of Excavation in the Land of the Pharaohs*; Fred Gladstone Bratton, *A History of Egyptian Archaeology*; C. W. Ceram, *Gods, Graves and Scholars*; Warren Dawson, *Who Was Who in Egyptology*; Stanley Mayes, *The Great Belzoni*; Barbara Mertz, *Temples, Tombs and Hieroglyphs*; John A. Wilson, *Signs and Wonders Upon Pharaoh*; and John David Wortham, *The Genesis of British Egyptology*.

20. For critical accounts of this term and its deployment in institutions of excavation, collection, and display in the wake of the French Revolution, see Dario Gamboni, *The Destruction of Art*; and Andrew McClellan, *Inventing the Louvre*.

21. For recent versions of this argument, see Deborah Manley and Peta Rée, *Henry Salt*; Ronald Ridley, *Napoleon's Proconsul in Egypt*; Claudine Le Tourneur d'Ison, *Mariette Pacha*; and Maya Jasanoff, *Edge of Empire*.

22. Brian M. Fagan, *The Rape of the Nile*; and Peter France, *The Rape of Egypt*.

23. Martin Bernal, *Black Athena*; and Cheikh Anta Diop, *The African Origin of Civilization*.

24. See Cohn, "The Transformation of Objects into Artifacts, Antiquities and Art in Nineteenth-Century India," in *Colonialism and Its Forms of Knowledge*, 76–105.

25. The debate on *Black Athena*'s positive claims persists. See Mary Lefkowitz, *Not Out of Africa*; *Black Athena Revisited*, ed. M. Lefkowitz and G. Rogers; Jacques Berlinerblau, *Heresy in the University*; and *Black Athena Writes Back*, ed. David Chioni Moore.

26. See James Stevens Curl, *Egyptomania*; Rosalie David, *The Experience of Ancient Egypt*; and Jean-Marcel Humbert, *Egyptomania*.

27. A vivid example of this can be found in Philip Kuberski's essay "Dreaming of Egypt." At one point Kuberski notes (ostensibly as critique) that, "[The] curiosity of the imperialist is accompanied by an identification, not with colonial peoples who were thought to be unconcerned with their archaeological treasures, but with the ancient dead. . . . It is impossible . . . to appreciate what ancient Egypt is without recognizing that it has always been an artifact of Western desires." In one sense, Kuberski is correct in noting the central imaginary role Egypt (as image) plays in European philosophy and literature. Yet Kuberski's essay is not merely analytical. It performatively *reinscribes* the very problem it claims to describe in critical terms. See Kuberski, *The Persistence of Memory*, 23–24.

28. Donald Reid, *Whose Pharaohs?*; "Indigenous Egyptology"; and "Nationalizing the Pharaonic Past," in *Rethinking Nationalism in the Arab Middle East*, eds. J. Jankowski and I. Gershoni. More popularly, the writings of the celebrity Egyptologist Zahi Hawass fall in this vein. See, for example, Hawass's memoir *Secrets from the Sand*. For examples of school textbook accounts of ancient Egyptian history, see al-Sayyid 'Azmi, *Ithaf abna al-'asr*; Ibrahim Mustafa, *al-Qawl al-mufid*; Ahmad Najib, *Kitab al-athr al-jalil*; and, especially, Jamal Hamdan, *Shakhsiyyat Misr*.

29. A particularly striking example of this can be found in Okasha El-Daly's recent claim that medieval Egyptians never lost their tie to Pharaonic civilization and that Muslim scholars, working within an unbroken scholarly tradition, were the world's first Egyptologists. See Okasha El-Daly, *Egyptology: The Missing Millennium*.

30. For example, Hawass describes modern Egyptian peasants with a paternalism reminiscent of colonial-era travel literature. Complaining about the difficulty of separating poor Egyptians from antiquities sites, he writes, "Thousands of illegal houses and farms have been built on Antiquities land. The present law is very weak and does not provide for the removal of squatters. The people who live in these villages smuggle artifacts and sell them on the black market; many have been caught stealing antiquities. In addition to the theft of artifacts, the villages pose more general dangers to the tombs by producing acid pollution, water pollution, and fire and smoke from cooking" (247).

31. Jacques Tagher, "Fouilleurs et antiquaires en Égypte au XIXe siècle."

32. Antoine Khater, *Le Régime juridique*.

33. See Neil Asher Silberman, *Between Past and Present*.

34. Gershoni and Jankowski, eds., *Egypt, Islam, and the Arabs*, 164–190.

35. See Jan Assmann, *Moses the Egyptian*.

36. See Steven Shapin, *Leviathan and the Air-Pump*; Bruno Latour, *The Pasteurization of France*.

37. Meskell, "Introduction: Archaeology Matters," in *Archaeology Under Fire*, 1–12; "An Archaeology of Social Relations in an Egyptian Village"; "Deir el Medina in Hyperreality"; and below.

38. On how archaeology intervenes in the making of its objects, see Nadia Abu El-Haj, *Facts on the Ground*.

39. See Mitchell, "Heritage and Violence," in *Rule of Experts*, 179–205.

40. The work of Bruno Latour is especially germane to this subject. See *Pandora's Hope*; and, with Steve Woolgar, *Laboratory Life*.

41. See Meskell, "Sites of Violence," in *Embedding Ethics*, 123–146; Timothy Mitchell, "Heritage and Violence"; and Kees van der Spek, "Dead Mountain Versus Living Community."

42. See Ann Laura Stoler and Frederick Cooper, "Between Metropole and Colony: Rethinking a Research Agenda," in *Tensions of Empire*; and Timothy Mitchell, *Rule of Experts*.

43. See Nicholas Thomas, *Entangled Objects*.

44. The concept that agency might be dispersed across networks or shared between human actors and prosthetic objects is not new. See Michel Callon, *The Laws of the Market*; Gilles Deleuze and Félix Guattari, *The Anti-Oedipus*; and Donna Haraway, *Primate Visions*.

45. In particular see the work of Bruno Latour, Michel Serres, Michel Callon, and John Law. Bruno Latour, *The Politics of Nature*; *We Have Never Been Modern*; Michel Serres, *The Natural Contract*. Michel Callon, "Four Models for the Dynamics of Science"; with John Law, "Agency and the Hybrid *Collectif*"; John Law, *Organizing Modernity*.

46. On the concept of the *actant*, see Latour, *Reassembling the Social*, 54–55.

1. THE ARTIFACTION OF THE MEMNON HEAD

1. Taylor Combe, Report of January 9, 1819. British Museum: Central Archives: Officers Reports, 5:1168.

2. Belzoni, *Narrative of the Operations and Recent Discoveries*, 50.

3. The Egyptian chronicler 'Abd al-Rahman al-Jabarti notes this event, though he places it on another date. See al-Jabarti, *Tarikh 'aja'ib al-athar fi-1-tarajim wa-1-akhbar*, 572.

4. Belzoni, *Narrative of the Operations*, 133, 134–35.

5. British Museum, Trustees' Manuscripts, Original Letters, and Papers, 4:1394.

6. British Museum, Department of Ancient Egypt and the Sudan, Salt and Sloane Collections, MS Catalogue of Egyptian Antiquities and Various BM Correspondence, "Letter from H. Salt to Lord Castlereagh, October 12, 1817." See also Henry Salt, *The Life and Correspondence of Henry Salt, Esq.*, 2:296.

7. "Letter from Rear Admiral Charles Penrose, December 9, 1817," British Museum Trustees' Manuscripts, Original Letters, and Papers, 4:1432.

8. British Museum, Standing Committees, Antiquities Department, 2691; and British Museum, Trustees' Manuscripts, Original Letters, and Papers, 4:1431.

9. "Letter of April 10, 1818," British Museum, Trustees' Manuscripts, Original Letters, and Papers, 4:1443.

10. "Letter of April 17, 1818," British Museum, Trustees' Manuscripts, Original Letters, and Papers, 4:1447.

11. "Observations Relating to Some of the Antiquities of Egypt, from the Papers of the Late Mr. Davison," *Quarterly Review* 10 (1817), 391–424; "Belzoni's Discoveries in Egypt and Nubia," *Quarterly Review* 17 (1818), 230–62; "Light's Travels in Egypt," *Quarterly Review* 19 (1819), 178–204; "Notice of Memnon Head Delivery," *Quarterly Review* 18 (1818), 368; Edmé Jomard, "Notice sur les nouvelles découvertes faites en Égypte" [Extrait de *La Revue Encyclopédique* (Mai 1819)] (Paris: Imprimerie de Baudoin Frères, 1819).

12. Under the pseudonym Glirastes, Shelley published his "Ozymandias" in *The Examiner*, January 11, 1817. Smith's "Ozymandias" was published in the same venue on February 1, 1818.

13. Among others of the period, George Gliddon noted this distinction: "The firmans for antiquities, although the exportation was to the individual forbidden, were not refused to the consuls-general of powerful nations." Gliddon, *An Appeal to the Antiquaries of Europe*, 127.

14. Echoing the reports of eighteenth- and nineteenth-century travelers to Gurna, the local acquisitions agent for French consul Drovetti remarked at the time, "The traveler who visits Thebes (and especially Gourna) in order to explore, should expect to find there a great deal of difficulty from the inhabitants. These people seem to think that they have inherited a monopoly right over ancient objects. Likewise, they never fail to look jealously at those Europeans who come to excavate the soil looking for antiquities. The Arabs of Gourna live in the tombs and it is in the nooks of their innermost chambers where their collections of antiquities are hidden. These collections are shown piece by piece to purchasing agents from Europe" (Rifaud, *Voyages en Égypte 1805–1827*, 221).

15. Henry Salt, Letter of June 28, 1816. British Museum, Department of Ancient Egypt and the Sudan, Salt and Sloane Collections, MS Catalogue of Egyptian Antiquities and Various BM Correspondence.

16. Salt claimed to have been principally inspired by Hamilton's account of the piece in *Aegyptiaca*. See his letter of October 1817 to Lord Castlereagh. British Museum, Department of Ancient Egypt and the Sudan, Salt and Sloane Collections, MS Catalogue of Egyptian Antiquities and Various BM Correspondence.

17. On Salt's life, see Bryn Davies, "Henry Salt"; Rashad Rushdy, "English Travellers in Egypt During the Reign of Mohamed Ali"; and Deborah Manley and Peta Rée, *Henry Salt*.

18. *Diodorus of Sicily*, 169.

19. Strabo, *The Geography*, 123.

20. Pococke, *A Description of the East*, 101–07. On Pococke, see Anita Damiani, "Richard Pococke."

21. Norden, *Travels in Egypt and Nubia*, 61–84.

22. Bruce, *Travels to Discover the Source of the Nile*, 1:120–38.

23. Denon, *Travels in Upper and Lower Egypt*, 2:224.

24. *Description de l'Égypte*, Antiquités vol. 2, planche 25.

25. Hamilton, *Remarks on Several Parts of Turkey: Part 1, Aegyptiaca*, 177. Hamilton's role in British Museum acquisitions during this period is central. In 1801, as a British officer overseeing the French evacuation from Egypt, Hamilton seized the Rosetta stone, hidden by Bonaparte's savants, and ensured its transportation to the British Museum. Later, he served as Lord Elgin's secretary and supervised the conveyance of the Acropolis friezes—the Elgin marbles—to London.

26. John Lewis Burckhardt, *Travels in Nubia*.

27. Capt. Henry Light, *Travels in Egypt*.

28. Manley and Rée, *Henry Salt*, 87.

29. Mayes, *The Great Belzoni*, 115.

30. The 1810s was a decade of intense research into the nature of the hieroglyphic language. See Erik Iversen, *The Myth of Egypt*, 123–44; and discussion of Champollion in chapter 2. For a colorful example of hieroglyphic speculation applied to the Memnon head, see J. F. Lake Williams, *Letter I. of a series, on a fragment of the Plmyooymyyz [sic]*.

31. As quoted in Mayes, *The Great Belzoni*, 114.

32. Ronald T. Ridley, *Napoleon's Proconsul in Egypt*.

33. Salt, *The Life and Correspondence of Henry Salt, Esq.*, 1:485, 472.

34. On Belzoni's life see Maurice Willson Disher, *Pharaoh's Fool*; and Mayes, *The Great Belzoni*.

35. See Mayes, *The Great Belzoni*, 17–45; and Richard Altick, *The Shows of London*.

36. The contract is quoted in full in Belzoni, *Narrative of the Operations*, 26–27. See also British Museum, Department of Ancient Egypt and the Sudan, Salt and Sloane Collections, MS Catalogue of Egyptian Antiquities and Various BM Correspondence, "Instruction, Boulak June 28, 1816."

37. A copy of the Ottoman firman acknowledging Salt's rights and privileges as a consul in Egypt is in the British Museum archives. Strangely, although the document describes the scope of Salt's authority (including his unique authority over the English merchant community in Egypt and his exemption from taxation), it says nothing about antiquities collection. In this sense, there is nothing in the document that speaks to the legality of the antiquities he collected for himself or for the museum. See British Museum Department of Ancient Egypt and the Sudan, Firman of Salt (EA 74092).

38. D'Athanasi, also known as Yanni, later relocated to Luxor as Salt's full-time agent. At the end of his career, he published his own account of travel and acquisition work in Upper Egypt: *A Brief Account of the Researches and Discoveries in Upper Egypt*.

39. Belzoni, *Narrative of the Operations*, 30.

40. European physicians in the employment of Ottoman officials also seem to have played a leading role in the antiquities trade. Count Forbin ironically described the physician of the Bey at Assyut in the following terms: "Subsequently, I saw Italians who claimed to be doctors in Upper Egypt. They bury Agas, and disinter statues, and make out very well by the exchange." Louis Nicolas de Forbin, *Voyage dans le Levant*, 327–28.

41. Belzoni, *Narrative of the Operations*, 30.

42. Ibid., 37.

43. See Jean-Marie Carré, *Voyageurs et écrivains français en Égypte*; and Elliott Colla, "Hooked on Pharaonics."

44. The literature on this topic is extensive. See M. H. Abrams, "From Addison to Kant: Modern Aesthetics and the Exemplary Art"; Rudolph Arnheim, "A Review of Proportion"; Erwin Panofsky, "The History of the Theory of Human Proportions"; John Summerson, *The Classical Language of Architecture*; Rudolf Wittkower, *Architectural Principles in the Age of Humanism*.

45. On these debates, see Curl, *Egyptomania*; and Humbert, *Egyptomania*.

46. Michael Podro, *The Manifold in Perception*.

47. Elizabeth A. Bohls, *Women Travel Writers and the Language of Aesthetics*.

48. Belzoni, *Narrative of the Operations*, 37–38.

49. Alois Riegl, "The Modern Cult of Monuments."

50. Malcolm Andrews, *The Search for the Picturesque*; Ann Bermingham, *Landscape and Ideology*.

51. Johannes Fabian, *Time and the Other*. See chapter 2 below for discussion of the classical Arabic literary tradition of ruins (*atlal*), including ancient Egyptian monuments.

52. Belzoni, *Narrative of the Operations*, 40–41.

53. Ibid., 43–44.

54. Ibid., 50–51.

55. Belzoni would venture into Nubia more than once. These journeys were documented by others as well: see Charles Leonard Irby and James Mangles, *Travels in Egypt and Nubia*; Robert Richardson, *Travels Along the Mediterranean and Parts Adjacent*; and the interesting account of Belzoni's dragoman in Nubia, Giovanni Finati: *Narrative of the Life and Adventures of Giovanni Finati*.

56. The systematic, state-sponsored expulsion of peasants from temple complexes in southern Egypt would not begin until later, although decrees permitting such removals were in place by the 1860s. John Gardner Wilkinson describes Mehmed 'Ali's expulsion of peasants from Esna in 1842: see Wilkinson, *Modern Egypt and Thebes*, 2:267. For similar expulsions under Isma'il Pasha in the 1860s and 1870s, see Auguste Mariette, *Voyage dan la Haute-Égypte* (1878).

57. Belzoni, *Narrative of the Operations*, 56–57.

58. Ibid., 82.

59. Ibid., 119.

60. Ibid., 93.

61. Ibid., 93.

62. Ibid., 94–95.

63. Ibid., 99.

64. Ibid., 131.

65. Ibid.

66. Ibid., 131–32.

67. Taylor Combe, Report of January 9, 1819. British Museum, Central Archives, Officers' Reports, 5:1168.

68. Combe, Report of February 13, 1819. British Museum, Central Archives, Officers' Reports, 5:1180.

69. Ibid.

70. See "Letter of Objects Presented to the Trustees of 1819," British Museum, Central Archives, Ellis Scrapbook, 94.

71. Joseph Banks to Henry Salt, February 14, 1819, in Salt, *The Life and Correspondence of Henry Salt, Esq.*, 2:303.

72. In contrast, the Louvre's directors celebrated Egyptian antiquities wholeheartedly at the time. The French abandonment of conservative attitudes to-

ward Egyptian art may have been tied to anticlerical attitudes. Whereas the art of Greece and Rome had been coopted by the Catholic church, Egypt was free from any such association. Even before the Revolution, Egypt had (among Masons and Rosicrucians, for example) come to symbolize a pre- and non-Christian source of enlightenment. This was quickly institutionalized in the early years of the Revolution. See Curl, *Egyptomania, the Egyptian Revival*; and Humbert, *Egyptomania*.

73. Salt, *The Life and Correspondence of Henry Salt, Esq.*, 2:304.

74. Belzoni, *Narrative of the Operations*, 104.

75. When Belzoni mounted his commercial exhibit (actually, simulated re-creation) of the tomb of Seti I, this confusion/tension around Belzoni's acquisitions would only increase. See Susan M. Pearce, "Giovanni Battista Belzoni's Exhibition of the Reconstruction of Pharaoh Seti I in 1821." See also Moser, *Wondrous Curiosities*, 96–123.

76. William Hamilton to Henry Salt, February 16, 1819, in Salt, *The Life and Correspondence of Henry Salt, Esq.*, 2:305.

77. Jenkins, *Archaeologists and Aesthetes*, 18.

78. The Department of Antiquities was redivided in 1860, into Oriental Antiquities, Greek and Roman Antiquities, and Coins and Medals; soon after that, they were subdivided again. The Department of Egyptian Antiquities was not formed until 1955. See Miller, *That Noble Cabinet*, 364–68.

79. This innovation was part of the broader shift from the *Kunstkammer* of earlier times to the universal survey organization that was critical to the pedagogical design of nineteenth-century national public museums. See Carol Duncan, *Civilizing Rituals*, and Tony Bennett, *The Birth of the Museum*.

80. Long, *The British Museum*, 2:1.

81. Winckelmann, as quoted in Jenkins, *Archaeologists and Aesthetes*, 59.

82. Such ideas are most clearly expressed in Hegel's *Introductory Lectures on Aesthetics*.

83. See Jenkins's discussion of Winckelmann, Caylus, and Westmacott, *Archaeologists and Aesthetes*, 56–61.

84. Long, *The British Museum*, 1:4–5.

85. Miller, *That Noble Cabinet*, 114–16.

86. Joseph Planta, "Report on Contents of the Basement Story and the First Two Rooms of the Upper Story, February 18, 1808," British Museum, Trustees' Manuscripts, Original Letters, and Papers, 2:888.

87. "A Report Concerning the More Valuable Parts of the Collections Deposited in the Basement Story of the British Museum," February 27, 1809, British Museum, Trustees' Manuscripts, Original Letters, and Papers, 2:907.

88. Taylor Combe, "Report of June 8, 1811," British Museum, Central Archives, Officers' Reports, vols. 1, 2.

89. Combe, "Report of February 8, 1812," British Museum, Central Archives, Officers' Reports, vols. 1, 2.

90. "Extracted by William Hamilton of the Foreign Office for the British Museum," March 23, 1817, British Museum, Trustees' Manuscripts, Original Letters, and Papers, 4:1394.

91. The word *artifact* means "anything made by human art and workmanship; an artificial product," with the special sense in archaeology of being "applied to the rude products of aboriginal workmanship as distinguished from natural remains." According to the *Oxford English Dictionary*, the first English usages appear following an 1821 essay by Samuel T. Coleridge. Arguably, the substantive noun "artifact," from the Latin words "ars" (art) and "facere" (to make), derived from the adjective "artificial," meaning "man-made." The transformation of what had previously been conceptualized as an attribute of objects (artificiality) now became a thing in itself.

92. *Synopsis of the Contents of the British Museum* (1821), 105–06.

93. It reads: "[Article] No. 11. The head and upper part of the body of a colossal statue, brought from the ruins of the Memnonium, a building dedicated to Memnon, at Thebes. This fragment is composed of one piece of granite of two colours, and the face, which is in remarkably fine preservation, is executed in a very admirable manner. Presented by Henry Salt, Esq. and the late Louis Burckhardt, Esq." (*Synopsis of the Contents of the British Museum*, 107).

94. Translated excerpts from Noeden's essay, "Über das sogenannte Memnons-Bild im Brittischen Museum in London" (1822), appear in Long, *The British Museum* (1832), 1:247–54.

95. Long, *The British Museum* (1832), 1:5.

96. Ibid., 2:9–11.

97. See *The Penny Magazine* (May 26, 1832). British Museum, Department of Prints and Drawings, Folder "Views of the British Museum and Plans of the Museum," Wrapper 9, "Egyptian Galleries and Antiquities."

98. Bonomi and Arundale, *Gallery of Antiquities*, 1.

99. Ibid.

100. Vaux, *Handbook to the Antiquities in the British Museum*, 289. This is the first museum guidebook to present an extensive chart of Egyptian history into which the objects of the collection could be placed, 335–44.

101. Westmacott, as quoted in Jenkins, *Archaeologists and Aesthetes*, 113.

102. Quoted ibid., 42.

103. See Miller, *That Noble Cabinet*, 102–08; Jenkins, *Archaeologists and Aesthetes*, 18–32.

104. Miller, *That Noble Cabinet*, 106.

105. 56 George, Sect. 99: "Act to Vest the Elgin Collection of Ancient Marbles and Sculpture in the Trustees of the British Museum for the Use of the

Public" (July 1, 1816), British Museum, Trustees' Manuscripts, Original Letters, and Papers, 4:1310.

106. Miller, *That Noble Cabinet*, 44.

107. Ibid., 43.

108. The exclusion of the wider public was accomplished through a number of policies from the earliest days. First, the museum was open only during weekdays, during business hours. It was closed on Sundays as well as on national and religious holidays. Second, the process of applying for tickets gave ample discretion to officials wishing to facilitate the visits of certain patrons and discourage others. Third, later rules concerning "decent and orderly . . . appearance and behaviour" effectively barred those not recognized to be part of polite society. For early rules, see "Directions to Such as Apply for Tickets to See the British Museum" [January 14, 1803], British Museum, Central Archives, Trustees' Manuscripts' Original Letters and Papers, 2:760. Such rules were repeatedly confirmed through the 1810s, and only incrementally changed after the 1820s.

109. Miller, *That Noble Cabinet*, 136. See British Museum, Central Archives, British Museum Cuttings and Extracts, to c. 1862 (Ellis Scrapbook), 276.

110. British Museum, Central Archives, British Museum Cuttings and Extracts, to c. 1862 (Ellis Scrapbook), 288.

111. "House of Commons, Committee of Supply: Address by Mr. Croker," as reported in *The Times* (June 21, 1823). British Museum, Central Archives, British Museum Cuttings and Extracts, to c. 1862 (Ellis Scrapbook), 106.

112. On sacralization, see Dean MacCannell, *The Tourist*.

113. On the ambiguities of the market and non-market value of objects, see Igor Kopytoff, "The Cultural Biography of Things."

114. See Latour's discussion of the "factish" (fact/fetish) in *Pandora's Hope*, 272–76.

115. See Nicholas Thomas, *Entangled Objects*.

116. See Lynn Meskell, "Object Orientations."

117. See Lynn Meskell and Peter Pals, "Embedding Ethics."

118. Thompson, *Sir Gardner Wilkinson and His Circle*, 25–27.

119. See Timothy Mitchell, *Rule of Experts*.

120. See, for instance, Edward de Montulé, *Travels in Egypt*; Wolfradine Von Minutoli, *Recollections of Egypt*; Richard Robert Madden, *Travels in Turkey, Egypt, Nubia and Palestine*.

121. The intermittent, modest complaints of Egyptian officials are no exception. Consider in this regard Zahi Hawass. Though a government official, Hawass speaks longingly of his wish that the head of Nefertiti (in Berlin), the Rosetta stone (in London), and the Dendara zodiac (in Paris) be repatriated. Yet he admits that this is just fanciful thinking. See Hawass, *Secrets from the Sand*, 251.

122. Dalia N. Osman, "Occupiers' Title to Cultural Property."

123. Consular reports from the early 1800s give some sense of the amount of this traffic. In terms of value, antiquities were consistently among the leading luxury exports tracked by the French consulate in Alexandria. For the year 1812, the value of mummy exports (to be used in pharmaceuticals) was equal to that of lentils shipped. Among the luxury exports recorded in the same year, the value of mummy was comparable to that of goods like gum arabic and coffee. The same is true for 1824: both the volume of antiquities and their value increased, the latter ahead of many raw and finished agricultural products such as natron, lentils, though far behind cotton and grains. See, for instance, Ministère des Affaires Étrangères (Quai d'Orsay), Correspondance Consulaire et Commerciale, Alexandrie, 18:431 (1805–12); and Ministère des Affaires Étrangères (Quai d'Orsay), Correspondance Consulaire et Commerciale, Alexandrie, 22:10 (1825–27).

124. Thanks to Fred Cooper for this observation. See his *Colonialism in Question*, 158.

OZYMANDIAS

1. Bequette, "Shelley and Smith," 29–31.

2. This point is made by Anne Janowitz in "Shelley's Monument to Ozymandias."

3. See James Brown, "Ozymandias."

4. See, for example: H. M. Richmond, "Ozymandias and the Travelers."

5. This concept, derived from A. J. Greimas's work on literature, has been expanded in Actor-Network-Theory to apply not just to the semiotic relations between elements of a text, but also to those of social organizations and natural fields. See Robert Scholes, *Structuralism in Literature*, 103–07; and Latour, *Reassembling the Social*, 54–55.

6. Law, "On the Subject of the Object," 2.

2. CONFLICTED ANTIQUITIES

1. Al-Jabarti, *Tarikh 'aja'ib al-athar fi-l-tarajim wa-l-akhbar*, 571. Translation is, with some modifications, from *'Abd al-Rahman al-Jabarti's History of Egypt*, trans. and eds. T. Philipp and M. Perlman, 398–99.

2. See Bosworth, "Al-Jabarti and the Frankish Archaeologists," 233.

3. Jabarti, *Tarikh 'aja'ib al-athar fi-l-tarajim wa-l-akhbar*, 572; *al-Jabarti's History of Egypt*, 399. Bosworth points out that the historian is likely conflating two events: the arrival of the Memnon head, which, being too heavy to be unloaded from the boat, was seen by visitors to the quay in

Bulaq in late 1816; and the findings of subsequent excavations undertaken by Caviglia and Belzoni at Giza, which were displayed in Salt's residence in late 1817.

4. See Hawting, *The Idea of Idolatry and the Emergence of Islam*, 55–66. In this regard, it is curious to note that, in addition to the term *sanam*, which carried heavy implications about paganistic worship, classical Muslim authors also sometimes employed the more neutral term *timthal* (statue, likeness) when speaking of monuments encountered in Egypt. In one lively passage the early geographer Ibn Khurradadhbih recounts breaking into a subterranean vault during the reign of Ibn Tulun. The author describes finding 360 ancient Egyptian statues (*timthal*) in a vault with frescoed walls that depicted, among others, the Prophets Moses, Jesus, and Muhammad! See, Ibn Khurradadhbih, *Masalik wa-l-mamalik*, 159–60.

5. See Okasha El-Daly, *Egyptology: The Missing Millennium*.

6. All translations here, with occasional modifications, are from *al-Qur'an: A Contemporary Translation*, trans. Ahmed Ali. The story is told at length in a number of places in the Qur'an, most notably Sura 7: 103–57; 10: 75–92; 20: 9–135; 28: 1–50; 40: 23–37. See also *Encyclopædia of Islam*, s.v. "Musa."

7. See Mahmoud Ayoub, *The Qur'an and Its Interpreters*; Mustansir Mir, "The Qur'an as Literature"; *Literary Structures of Religious Meaning in the Qur'an*, ed. Issa Boullata; and Michael Sells, *Approaching the Qur'an*. There is more than one Pharaoh alluded to in the Qur'an and Prophetic traditions (*hadith*): there is the Pharaoh confonted by Moses (the same Moses discussed in chapters 1–14 of the book of Exodus), while other Pharaohs, from periods before and after Moses, are associated with the Amalekites. See A. J. Wensinck and G. Vajda, "Fir'awn."

8. Respectively, Qur'an, 23: 46 and 29:39; 10: 83; 44: 31; 28: 4; 20: 24, 43; and 10: 83 and 44: 31. For a semantic analysis of these terms, see Toshihiko Izutsu, *Ethico-Religious Concepts in the Qur'an*; and also Muhammad 'Abd al-Rahman al-Sayyid 'Awad, *al-Fir'awniyya kama sawwarha al-Qur'an al-karim*. Among Sufis, Pharaoh is understood in more figurative terms. The confrontation between Moses and Pharaoh in this reading represents a struggle, within the human spirit, between higher and lower levels of the soul. For his part, the Sufi philosopher Ibn 'Arabi (1165–1240 CE) asserts that Pharaoh understood the truth of Moses' words and that he was an initiate (*'arif*) of divine revelation. See Denis Gril, "Le Personnage Coranique de Pharaon d'après l'interprétation d'ibn 'Arabi." Likewise, there is the interpretative debate surrounding verses 10: 90–92, in which Pharaoh, on the point of drowning in the Red Sea, attests to the truth of Moses' God. See Paret, "Le Corps de Pharaon," 235–37; and also, Ayoub, *The Qur'an and its Interpreters*, 95–96.

9. Qur'an, 28: 38

10. This point is made powerfully in Sayyid Qutb's reading of Sura 7. See Sayyid Qutb, *Fi-Zilal al-Qur'an*, vol. 6 (Cairo: Dar al-Shuruq, 1996).

11. As Tarif Khalidi puts it, "The most prominent enemies of the Prophets are the kings, who typify human pride as its peak. At their head stands Fir'awn (Pharaoh), a major Qur'anic figure. His struggle against Moses prefigures the entire history of the relationship between prophets and kings, a theme of recurring importance in Islamic historical thought and writing. Fir'awn is tyrannical, blasphemes before the 'signs of God,' fights divine truth with magic, and sows discord among the people. . . . Fir'awn is the Anti-Prophet" (*Arabic Historical Thought in the Classical Period*, 10–11). See also Haarman, "Regional Sentiment in Medieval Islamic Egypt," 56.

12. Qur'an, 69: 2–6, 9–10, 12.

13. See *Encyclopedia of Islam*, s.v. "Fir'awn."

14. As Khalidi notes, Islam intervened in Arabian culture by offering an understanding of history as events with "moral significance," rather than merely as unfathomable sequences of occurrences. Not only are humans able to "read" history for its signs (*ayyat*) and lessons (*'ibar*), they have a moral duty to do so. Khalidi, *Arabic Historical Thought in the Classical Period*, 9.

15. Qur'an, 28: 51–53. *Tadhkir*, (reminding or warning) is, by any standard, one of the major themes of the Quranic message. As al-Zarkashi puts it, "The Quranic sciences are, at their source, divided into three parts: *tawhid* [the principle of God's oneness], *tadhkir* [reminding, warning], and *ahkam* [judgments]. *Tawhid* comprises a knowledge of creations and their Creator, in all His names, attributes, and deeds. *Tadhkir* includes promises and threats, Heaven and Hell, and separating appearances from essences. *Ahkam* consists of all the kinds of behavior, and clarifying beneficial acts from harmful ones, virtuous acts from prohibited and lamentable ones" (*al-Burhan fi-'ulum al-Qur'an*, I: 17).

16. This tenet is expressed many times in the Qur'an, as in 4: 137: "Those who believe, then reject faith, then believe again, and again reject faith and go on increasing in Unbelief,—God will not forgive them nor guide them on the Way."

17. See A. A. Vasiliev, "The Iconoclastic Edict of the Caliph Yazid II"; Marshall G. S. Hodgson, "Islam and Image"; Oleg Grabar, "Islam and Iconoclasm." Much of this scholarship has noted that official policies encouraging iconoclasm were the exception, not the rule, of Muslim governments. More recent scholarship stresses that, even if there were official sanctions of iconoclasm, this never meant an end to the creation of art in the Muslim world. See Finbarr Barry Flood, "Between Cult and Culture." Finally, with regard to Muslim sanctions against pre-Islamic art in Egypt, the bulk was directed at Coptic, not Pharaonic, institutions and symbols. See G. R. D. King, "Islam, Iconoclasm, and the Declaration of Doctrine."

18. Compare this to Jewish and Christian attitudes toward pagan images and objects. See Moshe Halbertal, "Coexisting with the Enemy," and Guy Stroumsa, "Tertullian on Idolatry and the Limits of Tolerance."

19. On the *fada'il* literature about Egypt, see Michael Cook, "Pharaonic History in Medieval Egypt"; and Haarman "Regional Sentiment," 55–56.

20. As in Ahmad ibn 'Ali al-Maqrizi's history of Egypt, *Kitab al-muwa'iz wa-l-i'tibar bi-dhikr al-khitat wa-l-athar*, al-Baghdadi's *Kitab al-ifada wa-l-i'tibar*, and Ibn Khaldun's proposed "History of the World," *Kitab al-'ibar*, of which *al-Muqaddima* was to serve as introduction.

21. Other works in this vein would include sections of 'Abd al-Rahman ibn 'Abdallah ibn 'Abd al-Hakam (d. 871 CE), *Futuh Misr*; Abu al-Hasan 'Ali ibn al-Husayn al-Mas'udi (d. 956 CE), *Muruj al-dhahab*; and Ahmad ibn 'Ali 'Abd al-Qadir al-Maqrizi (d. 1442 CE), *Kitab al-muwa'iz wa-l-i'tibar bi-dhikr al-khitat wa-l-athar*. See also the extensive bibliography in El-Daly.

22. Idrisi, *Kitab Anwar*, 1.

23. Quran, 6: 11.

24. Idrisi, *Kitab Anwar*, 14–15.

25. This point is made by Haarman, "In Quest of the Spectacular," 58.

26. *Sharh al-mu'allaqat al-'ashira*, 74–5, translation mine.

27. See Jaroslav Stetkevych, *The Zephyrs of Najd*; Mohammed A. Bamyeh, *The Social Origins of Islam*, 7–11.

28. Walter Ong, *Orality and Literacy*.

29. See James Monroe, "Oral Composition in Pre-Islamic Poetry."

30. As quoted in Suyuti, "The Treatise on the Egyptian Pyramids," 38; see also, Idrisi, *Kitab anwar*, 18.

31. This point has been made by Michael Sells: "Traces of an abandoned campsite mark the beginning of the pre-Islamic Arabian ode. They announce the loss of the beloved, the spring rains, and the flowering meadows of an idealized past. Yet they also recall what is lost—both inciting its remembrance and calling it back." *Desert Tracings*, 3.

32. Idrisi, *Kitab Anwar*, 8. The Quranic verse is 44: 25. Other resonances of the word *athar* should be noted. In addition to referring to the monuments of antiquity, it is also used to refer to relics of the Islamic period and signs of the divine, as in verse 30:50 of the Qur'an: "Look, then, at the signs (*athar*) of God's mercy, and how he resurrects the earth after its death. . . ." It is also used synonymously to refer to the traditions and narrations of the sayings and deeds of the prophet Muhammad and his companions.

33. See *Encyclopedia of Islam*, s.v. "Adja'ib." Syrinx von Hees notes that there is no single genre of writing called "*aja'ib* literature," but rather that the writing on the exotic and the marvelous appears across a wide range of texts—from geographical treatises and writings known as "ways and kingdoms" (*masalik*

wa-mamalik), to travel writing and even fiction. See von Hees, "The Astonishing." It is associated especially with cosmographical writing and the work of al-Qazwini. See Tawfiq Fahd, "Le Merveilleux dans la faune, la flore et les minéraux." For a recent, provocative consideration of the philosophical, literary, and theological implications of the concept of wonder in Arabic and Persian literature, see Zadeh, "Translation, Language, and Identity."

34. As one dictionary puts it, "Among the various meanings is to marvel (*ta'ajjub*) at something whose cause is hidden. Wonder (*'ajab*) is to look at something unfamiliar and unusual—it is a state in which a human is presented with his ignorance about the cause of a thing. . . . Such a thing is a wonder (*'ajib*, *'ajiba*, and *'ujuba*)," (*Mu'jam alfaz al-Qur'an al-karim*, 410). Likewise, there is also a deep connection between wonder and the marvelous status of the Quranic *ayya* (sign, verse). As al-Zarkashi defines their relation in his classic work: "The *ayya* is a marvel (*'ajab*). . . . It is as if each verse were a marvel, on account of its composition and the meanings contained within it" (al-Zarkashi, *al-Burhan fi-'ulum al-Qur'an*, 1:266). Later, al-Zarkashi elaborates on the concept of *ta'ajjub*, which appears more than once in the Quranic text, "The word *al-ta'ajjub* suggests the way in which God wishes for an action to be performed, as in the saying, 'Your Lord marvels at the youth who is not driven by childish passions,' and the saying, 'Your Lord delights in the man who rises straight from his bed to pray.' Likewise, the word may also suggest God's wish for an action to be avoided, as in this verse: 'If you marvel, then marvelous are the words of those . . . ' [13:5] and this: 'While you are filled with wonder, they scoff . . . ' [37:12]" (al-Zarkashi, 2:14). Greenblatt writes that there is an "ease with which the very words *marvel* and *wonder* shift between the designation of a material object and the designation of a response to the object" (*Marvelous Possessions*, 22).

35. Idrisi, *Kitab Anwar*, 19.

36. Baghdadi is referring to accounts of the Caliph al-Ma'mun's destructive expeditions in the Giza plateau. Baghdadi, *The Eastern Key: Kitab al-ifadah wa-l-i'tibar*, 137. See also "Extract from the Relation Respecting Egypt of Abd Allatif," in *Voyages and Travels in All Parts of the World*, ed. Pinkerton, 15:810.

37. As quoted in Suyuti, "The Treatise on the Egyptian Pyramids," 39.

38. Al-Baghdadi, *The Eastern Key*, 147.

39. As quoted in Idrisi, *Kitab Anwar*, 17.

40. Idrisi, *Kitab Anwar*, 21–23; Suyuti, "The Treatise on the Egyptian Pyramids," 32–38. See also the discussion in El-Daly. Ibn Hawqal returned to classical claims that they were granaries. See Ibn Hawqal, *Surat al-ard*, paragraph 19.

41. This subject is treated at length in Cook and also in M. Plessner, "Hermes Trismegistus and Arab Science"; Alexander Fodor, "The Metamorphosis of Imhotep"; and D. P. Walker, *The Ancient Theology*. See also M. Plessner, "Haram."

42. In this respect, they have much in common with European travel accounts, from the Greeks until the eighteenth century. See Elliott Colla, "The Measure of Egypt."

43. Idrisi, *Kitab Anwar*, 27–28.

44. See Grabar, "Islam and Iconoclasm," and G. R. D. King, "Islam, Iconoclasm, and the Declaration of Doctrine." Yet there is also the extraordinary account of the Sufi sheikh who defaced the Sphinx. The story is quoted in 'Ali Mubarak: "[According to Ibn al-Mutawwaj] there was a man Sa'im al-Dahr ["the one who fasts a lifetime"] . . . who, around 1378 CE, rose up to rectify abominable things. He went to the pyramids and mutilated the face of the Sphinx and ruined it." 'Ali Mubarak, *al-Khitat al-Tawfiqiyya*, 16:44–45. See also C. H. Becker, *Encyclopaedia of Islam*, s.v. "Abu-l-Hawl."

45. Baghdadi, *The Eastern Key*, 141–43.

46. Ibid., 155–57.

47. Ibid., 119–21.

48. Idrisi, *Kitab Anwar*, 39.

49. Ibid., 45–46.

50. Ibid., 46–77.

51. Baghdadi, *The Eastern Key*, 159.

52. See Eric Iversen, *The Myth of Egypt*.

53. Richardson, *Travels Along the Mediterranean and Parts Adjacent*, 216.

54. A thorough account of this history is given in Robert Solé and Dominique Valbelle, *The Rosetta Stone*.

55. The discovery was first announced in the French journal *Courrier de l'Égypte* 37 (29, Fructidor, Year VII [1799]), 3–4. A report of the discussion of the object at the institute appeared in *La Décade égyptienne* 3 (Year VIII [1800]), 293–94.

56. The "account of pieces of ancient sculptures taken by the British forces in Egypt from the French army" and its subsequent cataloguing and display can be found in British Museum Central Archives, Original Letters and Papers, 3:752, 759, 768–70; and Trustees' General Meetings, 1:970.

57. As quoted in Solé and Valbelle, *The Rosetta Stone*, 95.

58. Ibid., 99.

59. Champollion, *Egyptian Diaries*, 184.

60. Mariette-Bey, *Itinéraire de la Haute-Égypte*, 7–8, 75–76.

61. Champollion, *Egyptian Diaries*, 215.

62. Long, *The British Museum*, 4–5.

63. See Champollion, *Egyptian Diaries*, 253.

64. Jean-François Champollion, *Lettres et journaux écrits pendant le voyage d'Égypte*, 427, translation mine.

65. Ibid., 433.

66. Ibid., 433–34.

67. Ibid., 444–45, 447–48.

68. See Peter France, *The Rape of Egypt*.

69. As quoted in Said, *Orientalism*, 32.

70. As quoted in Khater, *Le Régime juridique*, 37–38.

71. Consider, for instance, the comments of Auguste Mariette writing nearly forty years later on the lax enforcement of such antiquities laws: "Despite all the prohibitions, clandestine excavations are still practiced, particularly in Thebes, where papyri are to be found, as they are among many other monuments. Travelers only have to study up and make inquiries, not only at Thebes, but also wherever their boat stops. In this way, Mr. Harris of Alexandria formed his beautiful collection, and Madame d'Orbiney purchased piecemeal the papyrus which is now in the British Museum and which has given her name such celebrity" (*Itinéraire de la Haute-Égypte*, 79).

72. See Elliott Colla, "The Stuff of Egypt."

73. See Carole Duncan, *Civilizing Rituals*; and Andrew McClellan, *Inventing the Louvre*.

74. See Elliott Colla, "Hooked on Pharaonics."

75. Bowring, *Report on Egypt and Candia*, 3.

76. Ibid., 29. The complaint is echoed in many travel accounts from this period.

77. Ibid., 61.

78. Ibid., 153.

79. George R. Gliddon, *An Appeal to the Antiquaries of Europe*, 1.

80. Ibid., 2.

81. Such claims were repeated in the press. See *Foreign Quarterly Review* 28 (c. 1841), 286.

82. Gliddon, *An Appeal to the Antiquaries of Europe*, 4.

83. Ibid., 4.

84. Ibid., 93.

85. Ibid., 135.

86. Ibid., 138.

87. Ibid., 145.

88. Lord Cromer, *Modern Egypt*, 1:343.

89. Ibid., 2:457–58.

90. Ibid., 2:458–60.

91. Ibid., 2:464–65.

THE ANTIQAKHANA (1835–55)

1. As quoted in Khater, *Le Régime juridique*, 37–38.

2. Reid, *Whose Pharaohs?*, 53.

3. Gliddon, *An Appeal to the Antiquaries of Europe*, 127–28.

4. On the work and life of Wilkinson, see Jason Thompson, *Sir Gardner Wilkinson and His Circle*.

5. Wilkinson, *Modern Egypt and Thebes*, 1:264. Champollion and others also describe Ibrahim's collection in similarly unflattering ways.

6. Ibid., 264; quoted also in Reid, *Whose Pharaohs?*, 58.

7. Reid, *Whose Pharaohs?*, 58.

3. PHARAONIC SELVES

1. On Tahtawi, the mission, and its influence on Egyptian intellectual history, see Daniel L. Newman's introduction in *An Imam in Paris*, 15–92; Edmé-François Jomard, "École égyptienne de Paris," *Journal Asiatique* 2 (1828), 96–116; and Cheikh Réfaa [al-Tahtawi], "Relation d'un voyage en France," *Journal Asiatique* 11 (1833), 222–51.

2. Tahtawi, *Takhlis al-ibriz fi-talkhis Bariz*, 200–01.

3. Ibid., 300–301.

4. See Fodor, "The Origins of the Arabic Legends of the Pyramids," 343.

5. Tahtawi, *Takhlis al-ibriz*, 301. The lines (mis)quoted in Tahtawi are likely taken from Suyuti, "The Treatise on the Egyptian Pyramids," 39.

6. Ibid., 302.

7. See Albert Hourani, *Arabic Thought in the Liberal Age*.

8. Reid, *Whose Pharaohs?*, 100.

9. Some guidebooks remain. See Auguste Mariette, *Description du Parc Égyptien*; and Gaston Maspero, *Guide du Visiteur au Musée de Boulaq*.

10. Auguste Mariette, *Notice des principaux monuments exposés dans les galeries provisoires du Musée d'Antiquités Égyptiennes*, 10.

11. Mariette-Bey, *Furjat al-mutafarraj*, as published in *Wadi al-Nil* (June 25, 1869), 293.

12. *Furjat al-mutafarraj*, 329.

13. See Muhsin Mahdi, *Ibn Khaldun's Philosophy of History*.

14. Tahtawi, *Takhlis al-ibriz*, 18–19.

15. *Anwar Tawfiq al-Jalil*, 20.

16. Ibid., 18.

17. Ibid.

18. Hourani, *Arabic Thought in the Liberal Age*, 80.

19. Tahtawi, *Manahij al-albab*, 2.

20. See the expositions, "al-Umma" and "al-Watan," by Mubarak's contemporary Husayn al-Marsafi (1815–90), in *Risalat al-kalim al-thaman*, 41–61, 62–83. As Charles D. Smith points out, in the Arab context different words for national community and territory (*umma, qawm, milla, watan*) have had

significantly different shades of meaning. See Charles Smith, "Imagined Identities, Imagined Nationalisms." On the evolution of vocabulary on community and territory in the nineteenth century, see Ezzat Orany, "'Nation,' 'patrie,' 'citoyen' chez Rifa'a al-Tahtawi et Khayr al-Din al-Tounsi."

21. As quoted in Hourani, *Arabic Thought in the Liberal Age*, 79.

22. Hourani, *Arabic Thought in the Liberal Age*, 79.

23. Tahtawi, *Anwar Tawfiq al-jalil*, 66.

24. Mitchell, *Colonising Egypt*, 127.

25. Ibid., 65.

26. 'Ali Mubarak, *al-Kitat al-Tawfiqiyya*, 16:11.

27. Dykstra, "Pyramids, Prophets, and Progress," 61–62.

28. See Widad al-Qadi, "East and West in 'Ali Mubarak's 'Alamuddin,'" 24–25. See also B. F. Musallam, "The Modern Vision of 'Ali Mubarak."

29. 'Ali Mubarak, *'Alam al-Din*, 1:6–7.

30. Ibid., 3:914–15.

31. Ibid., 3:988.

32. Ibid., 3:990.

33. Ibid., 3:991.

34. Reid, *Whose Pharaohs?*, 116–18.

35. Brugsch, as quoted ibid., 118.

36. Reid notes that while only two to three books appeared per decade on the subject of ancient Egypt during the 1870s and 1880s, the number grew to ten in the 1890s and twenty-four for the period between 1900 and 1914. Reid, *Whose Pharaohs?*, 210.

37. *Al-Hilal* 2:16 (April 15, 1894), 482.

38. Sayyid 'Azmi, *Athaf abna' al-'asr*, 5.

39. Reid, *Whose Pharaohs?*, 117.

40. "Adyan al-awa'il: diyanat al-misriyyin al-qudama'," *al-Muqtataf* 7:9 (1883), 602.

41. Ibid., 605.

42. 'Azmi, *Athaf abna' al-'asr*, 8.

43. Jabarti also uses the word when discussing the strange use of lamps and figures during public spectacles under the French occupation. See Shmuel Moreh's note on *tamathil* in *Al-Jabarti's Chronicle of Napoleon in Egypt*, 61, 128.

44. *'Alam al-Din*, 948, 950–51.

45. Kamal, "Abu Hawl," *al-Muqtataf* 10:12 (September 1886), 720–23. See also "Adyan al-awa'il."

46. See, for example, *Anwar Tawfiq al-jalil*, 65.

47. See, for example, the first published guidebook for the Giza Museum, opened in 1892, *al-Khalasa al-wajiza fi-bayan ahamm al-athar al-ma'ruda bi-Mathaf al-Giza*; see also "Izhar al-madfun min timthal fir'awn," *al-Manar* 4:7 (May 19, 1901), 225–28.

48. *Ra'masis* 1:1 (February, 1912), 11.

49. *Ra'masis* 12:2 (1923), 162.

50. See Eve M. Troutt Powell, *A Different Shade of Colonialism*.

51. Al-Sayyid, "al-Athar al-qadima," 13.

52. Ibid., 13–14.

53. Ibid., 17.

54. Al-Sayyid, "Athar al-jamal wa-jamal al-athar," 24.

55. Al-Sayyid, "al-Athar al-qadima," 14.

56. Ibid., 17.

57. Ahmad Najib, *al-Athar al-jalil*, 7.

58. Ibid., 99–100.

59. Ibid., 100.

60. Ibid., 101.

61. Reid, *Whose Pharaohs?*, 206.

62. Cook, as quoted ibid.

63. Ibrahim Mustafa, *al-Qawl al-mufid fi-athar al-Sa'id*, 10.

64. Ibid., 12–13. Arguments about the patriotic duty to tour Egypt before touring Europe would recur often in the Egyptian press during subsequent decades. See "Fi-l-Uqsur," *al-Balagh al-Usbu'i* 1:9 (January 21, 1927); and "al-Misri yaktashif biladahu," *al-Risala* 2:60 (August 27, 1934). Other arguments included the benefits of subsidizing Egyptian domestic tourism, as in Ahmad Lutfi al-Sayyid, "Min al-Qahira ila Asna: al-hukuma wa-l-sahafiyun, al-jinab al-'ali fi-l-Uqsur, Maslahat al-athar," *al-Jarida* 584 (February 10, 1909). Much later, there were also arguments in favor of nationalizing the tourist industry, from hotels to transportation, see "Tashji' al-siyaha li-Misr: ma yajib 'ala al-hukuma an ta'milahu," *al-Siyasa al-Usbu'iyya* 2:89 (November 19, 1927); "Fi-mudun al-athar al-Misriyya: mashahadat al-mawsam al-hali," *al-Balagh al-Usbu'i*, April 15, 1927; "Mawsam al-siyaha," *al-Risala* 2:68 (October 22, 1934); and "al-Siyaha fi-Misr: wa-mata taghdu mawradan qawmiyyan?" *al-Risala* 4:135 (February 3, 1936).

65. *Al-Adab* 4:19 (30 Shawwal, 1310 [1893]), 451–52.

66. Mustafa, *al-Qawl al-mufid fi-athar al-Sa'id*, 6.

67. The most authoritative accounts of the culture of Pharaonism are Gershoni and Jankowski, "The Egyptianist Image of Egypt: III. Pharaonicism," in *Egypt, Islam and the Arabs*, 164–90; and Charles Smith, *Islam and the Search for Social Order in Modern Egypt*.

68. See Vernon Eggers, *A Fabian in Egypt*.

69. Citations here refer to the translation of his autobiography, *The Education of Salamah Musa*, 57.

70. On *Misr al-Fatat*, see James P. Jankowski, *Egypt's Young Rebels*.

71. Husayn, "Imani," from *Mu'allafat Ahmad Husayn*, 19.

72. Ibid., 20.

73. *Majd Ra'masis*, a popular play by Mahmud Murad, was first produced in 1923.

74. Husayn, "Imani," 20–21.

75. Ibid., 21–22.

76. Ibid., 22–23.

77. Ibid., 23.

78. Tawfiq al-Hakim, *'Awdat al-ruh*, 35–36.

79. Ibid., 37–38.

80. Ibid., 40.

81. In the Pharaonic myth, Osiris, God of the underworld and illegitimate son of Nut, wife of the sun god Ra, is killed by Set. Isis, his wife, searches for his body, finds his coffin embedded in a tamarisk tree, and takes it home. Isis brings Osiris back to life momentarily and has a child by him, Horus. Set comes across Osiris's coffin, takes out the body, and chops it into pieces, dispersing them throughout the Nile Valley. Isis then travels the length of the valley and, burying all the pieces she can find, raises a number of temples in his honor. His penis, thrown into the Nile, is never found. Horus avenges his father's death by fighting Set a number of times. The first time he captures Set, but Isis lets him go free. Horus eventually kills his father's murderer. Hakim's novel seems to have little to do with the myth on the level of plot. On the level of thematics, the connection is deliberate, even clumsy. The psychological and political transformations that occur throughout the novel are described as rebirths, resurrections, and a recollection of scattered parts.

82. Hakim, *'Awdat al-ruh*, 40–41.

83. Ibid., 58.

84. Ibid., 60.

85. Ibid., 65–67.

TWO PHARAOHS

1. On Sanu'a's impact on Egyptian letters, see Badawi, *Early Arabic Drama*, 31–42; Irene L. Gendzier, *The Practical Visions of Ya'qub Sanu'*; Najwa Ghanus, ed., *al-Lu'bat al-tiyatiriyya*; Jacob M. Landau, "Abu Naddara, an Egyptian-Jewish Nationalist"; Jacob M. Landau, *Studies in the Arab Theater and Cinema*; and Muhammad Yusuf Najm, *al-Masrah al-'arabi: dirasat wa-nusus*, vol. 3.

2. An earlier generation of Egyptian scholarship freely acknowledged Sanu''s central place in the era's political and cultural arena, calling him the father of Arab theater. See Anwar Luqa, "Masrah Ya'qub Sanu'," *al-Majalla* (March 15, 1961). In recent years, with the intensification of the Palestinian-Israeli conflict, the author's Jewishness has been the source of discomfort.

During the 1990s, Egyptian Christians and Muslims seeking to express secular solidarity with one another resurrected the 'Urabist slogan "Misr li-l-misriyyin" (Egypt belongs to the Egyptians). Prominent in these displays were the crescent and cross: no indications were given that the author of the phrase was Jewish. A recent study notes a lack of sources corroborating Sanu''s view of himself as "the Egyptian Molière": Sayyid 'Ali Isma'il, *Mahakamat masrah Ya'qub Sanu'*. Despite the blatant anti-Semitism of the attack, the author presents a real philological problem: to date there exist no eyewitness accounts of Sanu''s plays performed on stage. Though the motivation of the critic is objectionable—to purify early Egyptian theater of possible Jewish origin—he presents a compelling possibility: that Sanu''s dialogues (*muhawarat*) were more experimentations in print fiction than in stage production.

3. Baignières, ed. and trans., *L'Égypte satirique: Album d'Abou Naddara*, 95–96, translation mine.

4. Ibid., 103–04.

5. See Berque, *Egypt: Imperialism and Revolution*, 236–38.

6. Cromer, as quoted in Khouri, *Poetry and the Making of Modern Egypt*, 66.

7. Khouri, *Poetry and the Making of Modern Egypt*, 66–67, translation mine.

8. Ibid., 67, translation mine.

4. THE DISCOVERY OF TUTANKHAMEN'S TOMB

1. Carter and Mace, *The Discovery of the Tomb of Tutankhamen*, 95–96.

2. Ibid., 97.

3. Ibid., 98.

4. Brown, T*he Sense of Things*; Heidegger, "The Thing."

5. See Curl, *Egyptomania*, 211–23; Kuberski, *The Persistence of Memory*, 20–41; and Antonia Lant, "The Curse of the Pharaoh, or How Cinema Contracted Egyptomania."

6. The logic of purification (and its importance to the constitution of modern fields of autonomous knowledge) is described in Bruno Latour, *We Have Never Been Modern*.

7. Carter, *The Discovery of the Tomb of Tutankhamen*, 184.

8. See Colla, "Hooked on Pharaonics."

9. Carter, *The Discovery of the Tomb of Tutankhamen*, 186.

10. Mary Louise Pratt describes this as "the narrative of anti-conquest." See *Imperial Eyes*, 38–68.

11. Carter, *The Discovery of the Tomb of Tutankhamen*, 98–99.

12. Ibid., 98.

13. Ibid., 99.

14. Ibid., 162.

15. Ibid., 102.

16. Ibid., 127.

17. Ibid., 127–28.

18. Ibid., 162–64.

19. See Bruce G. Trigger, *A History of Archaeological Thought*.

20. Carter, *The Discovery of the Tomb of Tutankhamen*, 158.

21. Ibid., 165.

22. This point, made in Riegl and elsewhere, has most recently been elaborated by Nadia Abu El-Haj, *Facts on the Ground*.

23. Carter, *The Discovery of the Tomb of Tutankhamen*, 105.

24. Ibid., 125–26.

25. The phrase is borrowed from Gayatri Chakravorty Spivak's "White Men Are Saving Brown Women from Brown Men," in Spivak, *A Critique of Postcolonial Reason*, 284.

26. Carter, *The Discovery of the Tomb of Tutankhamen*, 124.

27. Arthur Weigall, as quoted in France, *The Rape of Egypt*, 211.

28. As quoted ibid., 211–12.

29. Carter, *The Discovery of the Tomb of Tutankhamen*, 146–47.

30. Ibid., 147–48.

31. See "Tutankhamun: Anatomy of an Excavation. Howard Carter's Diaries. The First Excavation Season in the Tomb of Tutankhamun, Part 2: January 1 to May, 1923." Http://griffith.ashmus.ox.ac.uk/gri/4sea1no2.html (accessed: April 2007).

32. Ahmad Kamal, "al-Athar al-Misriyya," *al-Ahram* (December 29, 1922); Salim Hasan, "Kinz al-Uqsur al-jadid, aw qibr Tut Ankh Amun," *al-Ahram* (January 31, 1923).

33. Carter, *The Discovery of the Tomb of Tutankhamen*, xxix.

34. Ibid., 141.

35. Hoving, *Tutankhamun*, 191–93.

36. "A. C. Mace's Account of the Opening of the Burial Chamber of Tutankhamun on February 16, 1923." Http://griffith.ashmus.ox.ac.uk/gri/4maceope .html.

37. As quoted in Hoving, *Tutankhamun*, 197.

38. Ibid., 200.

39. Carter, *The Discovery of the Tomb of Tutankhamen*, 148–49.

40. Tony Bennett, *The Birth of the Museum*.

41. See, for example, Piers Brendon, *Thomas Cook*.

42. Dean MacCannell, *The Tourist*; and *Touring Culture*, eds. Chris Rojek and John Urry.

43. Carter, *The Discovery of the Tomb of Tutankhamen*, 149.

44. Ibid., 150.

45. See "al-Khilaf bayn Kartir wa-l-hukuma; Kartir yutalib bi-nisf al-athar al-mustakshafa; qarar lajnat qadaya al-hukuma: ilgha' 'aqd al-imtiyaz," *al-Ahram* (February 21, 1924).

46. Text of Concession, signed April 18, 1915, by George Daressy, acting director of the Antiquities Service, 1914–15. Renewed through 1923 by Daressy and Pierre Lacau. From Howard Carter, *The Tomb of Tut•Ankh•Amen: Statement, with Documents, as to the Events Which Occurred in Egypt in the Winter of 1923–24, Leading to the Ultimate Break with the Egyptian Government* (London: Cassell and Company, n.d.) as reprinted in *Tut•Ankh•Amen: The Politics of Discovery*, 4–5.

47. The terms of the concession were far from unusual, see Law 14 of 1912 concerning antiquities in Khater, 286–91.

48. *The Tomb of Tut•Ankh•Amen: Statement, with Documents*, 6.

49. Quibell, "Note on Conversation with Mr. Howard Carter, October 11, 1923," as reprinted ibid., 13.

50. "Fi-wadi al-muluk: ihtijaj al-sahafa al-misriyya," *al-Ahram* (November 21, 1923).

51. *The Tomb of Tut•Ankh•Amen: Statement, with Documents*, 32.

52. Ibid., 34.

53. Ibid., 19–20.

54. Ibid., 47.

55. Quibell, "Note on Conversation with Mr. Howard Carter, October 11, 1923," as reprinted ibid., 49–59.

56. See "al-Khilaf bayn Kartir wa-Wizarat al-Ashghal fi-wadi al-Muluk; Shakayat Maslahat al-Athar al-mutawaliyya min suluk Kartir," *al-Ahram* (February 15, 1924).

57. Letter to Carter from M. A. Zaghl[o]ul (Under-Secretary of State, Ministry of Public Works), February 12, 1924, reproduced in *The Tomb of Tut•Ankh•Amen: Statement, with Documents*, 99.

58. Ibid., 103.

59. There were also lingering feelings of resentment between the parties. Carter worked as inspector in the Antiquities Department from 1899 to 1903 but was unfairly dismissed following an altercation at Saqqara with drunken French tourists. The account appears in James, Howard Carter, 97–120.

60. Berque, *Egypt*, 363–402.

61. "Khutba siyasiyya kubra li-ra'is al-hukuma al-jalil," *al-Ahram* (February 16, 1924).

62. "Al-Khilaf bayn Kartir wa-l-hukuma fi-wadi al-muluk; musa'i Kartir fi-suhuf Lundun," *al-Ahram* (February 16, 1924).

63. Hoving, *Tutankhamun*, 306.

64. *The Tomb of Tut•Ankh•Amen: Statement, with Documents*, 5.

65. Ibid., 71.

66. Carter to Lacau, February 3, 1924. As reproduced in *The Tomb of Tut•Ankh•Amen: Statement, with Documents*, 75, 79.

67. *The Tomb of Tut•Ankh•Amen: Statement, with Documents*, 39.

68. Muhammad Husayn Haykal, "Misr al-haditha wa-Misr al-qadima: khulud hayat al-umam," *al-Siyasa al-Usbu'iyya*, (November 27, 1926), 10.

69. Ibid., 10.

70. Ibid., 11.

71. See his collection: *Watan al-Fira'ina* (1926).

72. See his play *Izis*.

73. See his play *Masra' Kliyupatra* (1917). Shawqi is unique in that his interest predates the Tutankhamen discovery.

74. See his play *Akhnatun, fir'awn Misr* (1927).

75. See his plays *Ikhnatun wa-Nifartiti* (1940) and *al-Fir'awn al-maw'ud* (1945).

76. References to *Majd Ra'msis* (1923) and *Tutankhamun* (1924) appear in Jacob M. Landau, *Studies in the Arab Theater and Cinema* (Philadelphia: University of Pennsylvania Press, 1958).

77. See his novel *Malik min shu'a'* (1945).

78. To this list must be added earlier works in a more popular vein: Mikha'il Bishara Dawud, *Bani al-fira'ina* (1915); and *Ghadat al-ahram* (1905).

79. No less important was the inspiration to Egyptian cinema. One of the first feature-length films produced in Egypt, *Wadi al-Muluk* (1924), was set in the Valley of the Kings.

80. Others did as well. See, for example, Al-Tunsi, "Tut Ankh Amun," *Diwan Bayram al-Tunsi*, 406–07.

81. "Tut Ankh Amun," *al-Shawqiyyat*, 1:271–72.

82. Shawqi, "Tut Ankh Amun wa-hadarat 'asrih," *al-Shawqiyyat*, 2:97–98.

83. Ibid., 2:98–99.

84. See Jaroslav Stetkevytch, *The Zephyrs of Najd*; and Suzanne Pinckney Stetkevych, *The Mute Immortals Speak*.

85. "Tut Ankh Amun," *al-Shawqiyyat*, 1:267–68.

86. "Tut Ankh Amun wa-hadarat 'asrih," *al-Shawqiyyat*, 2:99–100.

87. "Tut Ankh Amun wa-l-barliman," *al-Shawqiyyat*, 2:159.

88. "Tut Ankh Amun," *al-Shawqiyyat*, 1:274.

89. The reference appears elsewhere in literature from the period, most notably in Naguib Mahfouz's novel *Kifah Tiba* (1944). See discussion in chapter 5.

90. "Tut Ankh Amun wa-l-barliman," *al-Shawqiyyat*, 2:159–160.

91. Ibid., 2:159.

92. "Tut Ankh Amun," *al-Shawqiyyat*, 1:270–1. The last line is a reference to the covert British evacuation/abduction of the Ottoman "Caliph" in 1921.

93. *Al-Shawqiyyat*, 2:159.

94. Hoving, *Tutankhamun*, 227. On the history of the representation of mummies in British and Egyptian popular culture, see Nicholas Daly, "That Obscure Object of Desire: Victorian Commodity Culture and Fictions of the Mummy"; Antonia Lant, "The Curse of the Pharaoh"; and Elliott Colla, "Shadi 'Abd al-Salam's *al-Mumiya.*'"

95. For example, compare the sensationalist, supernatural tone of "Tut Ankh Amun wa-l-Lurd Karnarfun: intiqam al-arwah" with the positivist rhetoric of an earlier piece, "al-Ajsad al-Misriyya al-muhannata tataharrak wa-tantahad."

96. "Abu Hawl wa-Tut Ankh Amun," *Ra'msis* 10:3 (1926), 165–67.

97. "Yaqzat Fir'awn," *Ra'msis* 12:9–10 (1923), 696–97.

98. "Al-Yadd al-muhannat," *Ra'msis* (1924), 47–48.

99. See, for example, Melani McAlister's account of Anwar Sadat's use of the King Tutankhamen exhibit to transform Egypt's image in the United States during the 1970s: "King Tut, Commodity Nationalism, and the Politics of Oil, 1973–1979," in *Epic Encounters*, 125–54.

NAHDAT MISR

1. For a comprehensive catalogue of Mukhtar's work, see Abu Ghazi, *Mukhtar*, 157–61. On Mukhtar's life, see Ostle, "Modern Egyptian Renaissance Man"; and the definitive study by Israel Gershoni and James Jankowski, in their *Commemorating the Nation*, 27–140.

2. Mukhtar, as quoted in al-Sharouni, "Mahmoud Mukhtar: A Traditional and Contemporary Artist," 27–28.

3. Wisa Wasif, "Mahmud Mukhtar wa-l-nahda al-fanniyya fi-Misr," *al-Akhbar* (May 2, 1920), as reproduced in Abu Ghazi, *al-Maththal Mukhtar*, 96.

4. Amin al-Rafi'i, *al-Akhbar* (April 30, 1920), as reproduced in Abu Ghazi, *al-Maththal Mukhtar*, 93.

5. Abu Ghazi, *al-Maththal Mukhtar*, 79.

6. Al-Nahhas, as quoted in Gershoni and Jankowski, *Commemorating the Nation*, 187.

7. "Timthal Nahdat Misr qad rufi' al-sitar 'anhu," *al-Siyasa al-Usbu'iyya* (May 26, 1928), as reproduced in Abu Ghazi, *al-Maththal Mukhtar*, 105.

8. 'Abbas Mahmoud al-'Aqqad, "Timthal al-Nahda," *al-Balagh al-Usbu'i* (May 25, 1928), 13.

9. This point is made by Gershoni and Jankowski, *Commemorating the Nation*, 187.

10. 'Abd al-Qadir al-Mazini, "Abu Hawl wa-timthal Mukhtar," *al-Siyasa al-Usbu'iyya* (June 9, 1928), as reproduced in Abu Ghazi, *al-Maththal Mukhtar*, 114–15.

5. PHARAONISM AFTER PHARAONISM

1. Qutb, "Kifah Tiba," [*al-Risala*, October 2, 1944, 89–92], as reproduced in 'Ali Shalash, *Najib Mahfuz: al-tariq wa-l-sada*, 208.

2. Ibid., 197–98.

3. Ibid., 198.

4. Ibid., 198–99.

5. Ibid., 207–08.

6. See Musallam, *From Secularism to Jihad*, 111–36; and John Calvert, "The World Is an Undutiful Boy! Sayyid Qutb's American Experience."

7. As quoted in *Najib Mahfuz yatadhakkir*, 13.

8. As quoted ibid., 44.

9. Mahfouz began to translate the book while in high school: ibid., 39.

10. Baikie, *Peeps at Many Lands: Ancient Egypt*, 89.

11. See El-Enany, *Naguib Mahfouz: The Pursuit of Meaning*, 35.

12. As quoted in *Najib Mahfuz yatadhakkir*, 39.

13. For a complete bibliography of Mahfouz's early publications in magazines, see Badr, *Najib Mahfuz: al-ru'ya wa-1-adat*, 489–501.

14. Mahfuz, *Atahaddith ilaykum*, 89.

15. Ibid., 77, 79. On Misr al-Fatat, see ibid., 79.

16. See Brugman, *Introduction to the History of Modern Arabic Literature in Egypt*, 218–24.

17. *Najib Mahfuz yatadhakkir*, 43.

18. As quoted in Mitchell, *The Society of the Muslim Brothers*, 8.

19. From "Da'watuna," in *Majmu'at Risa'il al-Imam al-Shahid Hasan al-Banna*, 229–30.

20. Ibid., 230.

21. Ibid., 23. See also "Our Mission," in Wendell, *Five Tracts of Hasan al-Banna*, 40–68.

22. Mahfouz, *'Abath al-aqdar*, 167–68.

23. Ibid., 21, 23, 32, 95, 131, 205.

24. Ibid., 10.

25. Ibid., 42.

26. Ibid., 11.

27. Ibid., 9.

28. Ibid., 33.

29. Herodotus, *The History*, 189–90. Herodotus names Charaxus, Sappho's brother, as the man who paid the great fee to liberate Rhodopis from slavery on her arrival in Egypt. For her part, Sappho refers to Rhodopis as Doricha (rosy-cheeked). Elsewhere, Rhodopis is connected with the sandal dropped by an eagle into the lap of King Psammetichus. See Peled, *Religion, My Own*, 42.

30. See Hugh McLeave, *The Last Pharaoh*.

31. McBride, *Farouk of Egypt*, 100–01.

32. Mahfouz, *Radubis*, 171.

33. Sa'id Jawda al-Sahhar, postface to *Kifah Tiba*, A-B.

34. See Princess Kadria Hussein, "La reine Teti-Sheri et la restauration nationale."

35. On the slogan and its ties to Fatat Misr, see Jankowski, *Egypt's Young Rebels*, 13.

36. Mahfouz, *Kifah Tiba*, 6.

37. Ibid., 68–69.

38. Ibid., 5.

39. Ibid., 78.

40. Ibid., 77.

41. Ibid., 203.

42. Ibid., 178

43. Ibid., 193, 194.

44. Ibid., 161.

45. On Qutb's early career, see Adnan A. Musallam: "Prelude to Islamic Commitment: Sayyid Qutb's Literary and Spiritual Orientation"; and *Sayyid Qutb: The Emergence of the Islamicist 1939–1950*. See also Olivier Carré, *Mysticism and Politics*; and William Shepard, *Sayyid Qutb and Islamic Activism*.

46. On this, see Euben, *Enemy in the Mirror*, 58.

47. As quoted in Kepel, *Muslim Extremism in Egypt*, 41.

48. Kepel, *Muslim Extremism in Egypt*, 41.

49. The sciences of reading the Qur'an developed historically to explain just these intratextual relations. The tasks of this tradition are formidable: to establish the historical order of the revelations that were compiled into the Qur'an; to study the specific contexts in which portions of the Qur'an were revealed; to inquire into how specific revelations addressed—admonished, reminded, encouraged—the early Muslim community as it formed itself and encountered its specific trials. The understanding of the Quranic text that emerges from this tradition is one of an address that is often immediate and direct: God speaks to his believers, answers their questions, gives advice. What this

means for reading, however, is all-important: the meaning of any particular narrative is not contained within its plot but is also tied to the other versions of the same narrative. See Nasr Hamid Abu Zayd, *Mahfum al-nass*.

50. Qutb, *Fi-zilal al-Qur'an*, 3:1361.

51. Ibid., 1353.

52. Ibid., 1256.

53. Ibid., 1413.

54. Jameson, "Third World Literature in the Era of Multinational Capitalism," *Social Text* 15 (Fall 1986).

55. Most famously, Aijaz Ahmad, "Jameson's Rhetoric of Otherness and the 'National Allegory,'" in *In Theory*.

56. One critic who did not miss this aspect, and who developed Jameson's observations considerably is Doris Sommer in *Foundational Fictions*.

57. Mahfouz makes this point in an incident he related often in interviews: "I remember the first literary contest I entered was the Qut al-Qulub al-Damirdashiyya contest. I entered the novel *Radubis*. Apparently the committee liked the novel. But they found some historical mistakes in it. I was surprised when . . . Ahmad Amin phoned me. He asked if I would come to meet him at the committee for authorship, translation, and publication, in 'Abdin. I went to him. He began to talk to me generally about Pharaonic civilization, while directing many questions to me about it. My answers surprised him, and he finally said to me: 'Frankly, I asked you to come here thinking that you knew nothing about Pharaonic civilization. But I find you know as well as an Egyptologist. I read your novel, *Radubis*, as a member of the refereeing committee, and I was surprised to find—since the novel is about the sixth dynasty—a horse-drawn chariot in the procession. You know very well that these vehicles did not come into Egypt until the Hyksos. Why did you make this historical mistake?' At the time, I gave him an aesthetic explanation. I told him that the procession, without horse-drawn chariots, would not be as beautiful and spectacular. And that the novelistic situation necessitated this embellishment. I transgressed this simple historical fact in order to realize a kind of artistic plausibility" (Naguib Mahfouz, *Atahaddith ilaykum*, 90–91).

CONCLUSION

1. Again, the career of Zahi Hawass is telling in this regard, since, in him, the science of Egyptology is thoroughly entangled with the popular culture of Egyptomania. As director general of the Giza Pyramids, Saqqara, Heliopolis, and the Bahariyya Oasis, Hawass has the unpleasant task of fending off requests for excavation permits by nonscholars (so-called Pyramidiots) who believe that the Pyramids are of Atlantean origin. At the same time, he has raised

eyebrows for renting access to the Pyramids for visiting groups of New Age tourists, not to mention journalists like Geraldo Rivera. See Alexander Stille, "Perils of the Sphinx," *The New Yorker* (February 10, 1997), 54–66; Douglas Jehl, "Sphinx, Repaired, Is Poker-Faced, But Could It Be Sitting on a Secret?" *The New York Times* (May 24, 1997), 4; Zahi Hawass and Mark Lehner, "The Sphinx: Who Built It, and Why?" *Archaelogy* (September-October 1994), 30–41.

Bibliography

ARCHIVES

British Museum: Central Archives.
British Museum: Department of Ancient Egypt and the Sudan.
British Museum: Department of Prints and Drawings.
Ministère des Affaires Étrangères. Quai d'Orsay. Consular Records: Alexandria.

NEWSPAPERS AND PERIODICALS

Abu Hawl
Abu Naddara
al-Adab
al-Ahram
al-Balagh al-Usbu'i
Fir'awn
al-Hilal
al-Jarida
al-Kashkul
Kliyubatra
al-Manar
al-Muqtataf
Ra'masis
al-Risala
Siyasa al-Usbu'iyya
Wadi al-Muluk

WORKS IN ARABIC

Abu Ghazi, Badr al-Din. *al-Maththal Mukhtar.* Cairo: al-Dar al-Qawmiyya li-1-tiba'a wa-1-Nashr, 1964.
———. *Mukhtar.* Cairo: al-Hay'a al-'Amma li-1-Kitab, 1988.

Abu Shadi, Ahmad Zaki. *Watan al-Fira'ina: muthul min al-shi'r al-qawmi.* Cairo: al-Matba'a al-Salafiyya, 1926.

———. *Akhnatun, fir'awn Misr: Ubira tarikhiyya dhat thalathat fusul.* Cairo: Dar al-'Usur, 1927.

Abu 'Ubayd al-Bakri, Abd Allah. *al-Masalik wa-l-mamalik,* ed. Jamal Talba. Beirut: Dar al-Kutub al-'Ilmiyya, 2003.

Abu Zayd, Nasr Hamid. *Mahfum al-nass: dirasa fi-'ulum al-Qur'an.* Beirut: Markaz al-Thaqafi al-'Arabi, 1994.

'Awad, Muhammad 'Abd al-Rahman al-Sayyid. *al-Fir'awniyya kama sawwarha al-Qur'an al-karim.* Cairo: Maktabat al-Salam al-'Alimiyya, 1981.

'Azmi, al-Sayyid. *Ithaf abna al-'asr bi-dhikr qudama' muluk Misr.* Bulaq: al-Matba'a al-Amiriyya, 1900.

Badr, 'Abd al-Muhsin Taha. *Najib Mahfuz: al-ru'ya wa-l-adat.* Cairo: Dar al-Thaqafa li-l-Tiba'a wa-l-Nashr, 1978.

al-Baghdadi, 'Abd al-Latif. *The Eastern Key: Kitab al-ifadah wa-l-i'tibar.* Trans. and ed. Kamal Hafuth Zand, John A. Videan, and Ivy E. Videan. London: George Allen and Unwin Ltd., 1964.

Bakathir, 'Ali Ahmad. *Ikhnatun wa-Nifartiti.* Cairo: Maktabat al-Khanji, 1940.

———. *al-Fir'awn al-maw'ud: masrahiyya usturiyya fi-sittat manazir.* Cairo: Dar Misr li-l-Tiba'a, 1945.

al-Banna, Hasan. *Majmu'at Risa'il al-Imam al-Shahid Hasan al-Banna.* N.p.: Dar al-Hadara al-Islamiyya, 1981.

Dawud, Mikha'il Bishara. *Bani al-fira'ina: Khu-In-Atun, Amun-Hotib al-Rabi'.* Matba'at al-Muhit, 1915.

Ghadat al-ahram. n.a. Cairo: Musamarat al-Sha'b, 1905.

al-Gharnati, Abu Hamid al-Andalusi. *Tuhfat al-albab,* ed. Gabriel Ferrand. Paris: Imprimerie Nationale, 1925.

al-Ghitani, Jamal. *Najib Mahfuz yatadhakkir,* ed. Gamal al-Ghitani. Beirut: Dar al-Masira, 1980.

al-Hakim, Tawfiq. *'Awdat al-ruh.* Beirut: Dar al-Kitab al-Lubnani, 1984.

———. *Izis.* Cairo: al-Matba'a al-Namudhijiyya, n.d.

Hamdan, Jamal. *Shakhsiyyat Misr: dirasa fi-'abqariyyat al-makan.* Al-Qahira: Maktabat al-Nahda al-Misriyya, 1970.

Husayn, Ahmad. *Mu'allafat Ahmad Husayn.* Cairo: Dar al-Shuruq, 1981.

ibn 'Abd al-Hakam, 'Abd al-Rahman ibn 'Abdallah. *Futuh Misr,* ed. Charles C. Torrey. New Haven: Yale Oriental Series, 1922.

ibn Fadl Allah al-'Umari, Shihab al-Din Ahmad. *Masalik al-absar fi-mamalik al-amsar,* ed. Ayman Fu'ad Sayyid. Cairo: IFAO, 1985.

ibn Hawqal, Abu al-Qasim ibn 'Ali al-Nasibi. *Surat al-Ard.* Beirut: Manshurat Dar Maktabat al-Hayat, 1979.

ibn Khurradadhbih, Abu al-Qasim 'Ubaydallah. *Kitab al-masalik wa-l-mamalik*, ed. and trans. M. J. Goeje. Leiden: E. J. Brill, 1967.

al-Idrisi, Abu Ja'far Muhammad ibn al-'Aziz al-Husayni. *Kitab anwar 'uluw al-ajram fi-l-kashf 'an asrar al-ahram*, ed. Ulrich Haarman. Beirut: Franz Steiner, 1991.

———. *Light on the Voluminous Bodies to Reveal the Secrets of the Pyramids: Kitab anwar 'uluw al-ajram fi 'l-kashf 'an asrar al-ahram*, ed. Ursula Sezgin. Frankfurt: Institute for the History of Arabic-Islamic Science, 1988.

Isma'il, Sayyid 'Ali. *Mahakamat masrah Ya'qub Sanu'*. Cairo: al-Hay'a al-'Amma li-l-Kitab, 2001.

al-Jabarti, 'Abd al-Rahman. *Tarikh 'aja'ib al-athar fi-l-tarajim wa-l-akhbar*. Beirut: Dar al-Jil, 1983.

Kamil, 'Adil. *Malik min shu'a'*. Cairo: Maktabat Misr, 1945.

al-Khalasa al-wajiza fi-bayan ahamm al-athar al-ma'ruda bi-Mathaf al-Giza. n.a.). Bulaq: al-Matba'a al-Kubra al-Amiriyya, 1893.

Mahfouz, Naguib. *'Abath al-aqdar*. Cairo: Maktabat Misr, n.d. [1939].

———. *Radubis*. Cairo: Maktabat Misr, n.d. [1943].

———. *Kifah Tiba*. Cairo: Maktabat Misr, n.d. [1944].

———. *Atahaddath ilaykum*. Beirut: Dar al-'Awda, 1977.

al-Maqrizi, Ahmad ibn 'Ali 'Abd al-Qadir. *Kitab al-muwa'iz wa-l-i'tibar bi-dhikr al-khitat wa-l-athar*. Bulaq: al-Matba'a al-Kubra al-Amiriyya, 1853.

Mariette, Auguste. *Furjat al-mutafarrij 'ala al-antiqakhana al-khidiwiyya al-ka'ina bi-Bulaq Misr al-mahmiyya*, trans. 'Abdallah Abu Su'ud, *Wadi al-Nil*. June 25, 1869.

al-Marsafi, Husayn. *Risalat al-kalim al-thaman*. Beirut: Dar al-Tali'a, 1982 [1881].

al-Mas'udi, Abu al-Hasan 'Ali ibn al-Husayn. *Muruj al-dhahab*. Bulaq: al-Matba'a al-Kubra al-Amiriyya, 1885.

Mubarak, 'Ali. *al-Kitat al-Tawfiqiyya al-jadida li-Misr al-Qahira wa-muduniha wa-biladiha al-qadima wa-l-shahira*. Bulaq: al-Matba'a al-Kubra al-Amiriyya, 1889.

———. *'Alam al-Din*. Alexandria: Matba'at Jarida al-Mahrusa, 1882.

Mu'jam alfaz al-Qur'an al-karim, ed. Ibrahim Madkur. Cairo: Dar al-Shuruq, 1981.

Mustafa, Ibrahim. *al-Qawl al-mufid fi-athar al-Sa'id*. Bulaq: al-Matba'a al-Kubra al-Amiriyya bi-Bulaq, 1893.

Najib, Ahmad. *Kitab al-athr al-jalil li-qudama' wadi al-nil*. Bulaq: al-Matba'a al-amiriyya, 1895.

Najm, Muhammad Yusuf. *al-Masrah al-'arabi: dirasat wa-nusus*. Beirut: Dar al-Thaqafa, 1963.

Qutb, Sayyid. *Fi-zilal al-Qur'an*. Cairo: Dar al-Shuruq, 1996.

———. *Ma'alim fi-l-tariq*. Cairo: Dar al-Shuruq, 1982.

Sanu', Ya'qub. *al-Lu'bat al-tiyatiriyya*, ed. Najwa Ghanus. Cairo: al-Hay'a al-'Amma li-l-Kitab, 1987.

al-Sayyid, Ahmad Lutfi. *Ta'ammulat fi-l-falsafa wa-l-adab wa-l-siyasa wa-l-ijtima'*. Cairo: Dar al-Ma'arif, n.d.

Shalash, 'Ali. *Najib Mahfuz: al-tariq wa-l-sada*. Cairo: al-Hay'a al-'Amma li-qusur al-thaqafa, 1993.

al-Shanqiti, Ahmad ibn Amin. *Sharh al-mu'allaqat al-'ashira*. Beirut: Dar al-Kitab al-'Arabi, 1984.

Shawqi, Ahmad. *Masra' Kliyupatra*. Cairo: Matba'at Misr, 1917.

———. *al-Shawqiyyat: al-a'mal al-shi'riyya al-kamila*. Beirut: Dar al-'Awda, 2000.

al-Suyuti, Jalal al-Din. *Kitab Hasan al-Muhadara fi-akhbar Misr wa-l-Qahira*. Cairo: Isma'il Hafiz, c. 1881.

al-Tahtawi, Rifa'a Rafi'. *Takhlis al-ibriz fi-talkhis Bariz, aw: al-diwan al-nafis bi-iwan Baris*. Tunis: al-Dar al-'Arabiyya li-l-Kitab, 1991 [1834].

———. *Manahij al-albab al-misriyya fi-mabahij al-adab al-'asriyya*. Bulaq: al-Matba'a al-Kubra al-Amiriyya, 1866.

———. *Anwar tawfiq al-jalil fi-akhbar Misr wa-tawthiq Bani Isma'il*, in *al-A'mal al-kamila li-Rifa'a Rafi' al-Tahtawi*, ed. Muhammad 'Imara. Beirut: al-Mu'assasa al-'Arabiyya li-l-Dirasat wa-l-Nashr, 1974 [1868].

———. *al-Murshid al-Amin li-l-banat wa-l-banin*. Cairo: Matba'at al-Madaris al-Malikiyya, 1872), 94.

al-Tunsi, Bayram. *Diwan Bayram al-Tunsi*. Beirut: Dar al-'Awda, 1996.

al-Zarkashi, Abu 'Abdallah Badr al-Din. *al-Burhan fi-'ulum al-Qur'an*, ed. Muhammad Abu al-Fadl Ibrahim. Cairo: Dar Ihya' al-Kutub al-'Arabiyya, 1957.

WORKS IN ENGLISH AND FRENCH

Abrams, M. H. "From Addison to Kant: Modern Aesthetics and the Exemplary Art." In *Studies in Eighteenth-Century British Art and Aesthetics*. Berkeley: University of California Press, 1985.

Abu El-Haj, Nadia. *Facts on the Ground: Archaeological Practice and Territorial Self-Fashioning in Israeli Society*. Chicago: University of Chicago Press, 2002.

Ahmad, Aijaz. *In Theory*. London: Verso Press, 1992.

Altick, Richard. *The Shows of London*. Cambridge, Mass.: Belknap Press of Harvard University Press, 1978.

Ali, Ahmed, trans. *Al-Qur'an: A Contemporary Translation*. Princeton: Princeton University Press, 1984.

Andrews, Malcolm. *The Search for the Picturesque*. Stanford: Stanford University Press, 1989.

Arkoun, Mohamed. "Peut-on parler de merveilleux dans le Coran?" In *L'Étrange et le merveilleux dans l'Islam médiéval: actes du colloque tenu au Collège de France à Paris, en Mars 1974*, 1–60. Paris: Institut du Monde Arabe, 1978.

Arnheim, Rudolph. "A Review of Proportion." In *Toward a Psychology of Art*, 102–19. Berkeley: University of California Press, 1966.

Assmann, Jan. *Moses the Egyptian: The Memory of Egypt in Western Monotheism*. Cambridge, Mass.: Harvard University Press, 1997.

d'Athanasi, Yanni. *A Brief Account of the Researches and Discoveries in Upper Egypt made under the Direction of Henry Salt, Esq., to which is added a detailed catalogue of Mr. Salt's Collection of Egyptian Antiquities*. London: John Hearne, 1836.

Ayoub, Mahmoud. *The Qur'an and Its Interpreters*. Albany: SUNY Press, 1984.

Badawi, M. M. *Early Arabic Drama*. Cambridge: Cambridge University Press, 1988.

al-Baghdadi, 'Abd al-Latif. "Extract from the Relation Respecting Egypt of Abd Allatif." Translated by Silvestre de Sacy in *Voyages and Travels in All Parts of the World*, ed. John Pinkerton. London: Longman, Hunt, Rees, Orme and Brown, 1811. Vol. 15.

de Baignières, Paul, ed. and trans. *L'Égypte satirique: Album d'Abou Naddara*. Paris: Lefebvre, 1886.

Baikie, James. *Peeps at Many Lands: Ancient Egypt*. London: A. and C. Black, 1912.

———. *A Century of Excavation in the Land of the Pharaohs*. London: Religious Tract Society, 1924.

Bal, Mieke. "Telling Objects: A Narrative Perspective on Collecting." In *The Cultures of Collecting*, eds. J. Elsner and R. Cardinal. Cambridge, Mass.: Harvard University Press, 1994.

Bamyeh, Mohammed A. *The Social Origins of Islam: Mind, Economy, Discourse*. Minneapolis: University of Minnesota Press, 1999.

Baring, Evelyn. Lord Cromer. *Modern Egypt*. New York: Macmillan Company, 1908.

Becker, C. H. "Abu-1-Hawl," *Encyclopaedia of Islam*.

Belzoni, Giovanni. *Narrative of the Operations and Recent Discoveries within the Pyramids, Temples, Tombs, and Excavations in Egypt and Nubia*. London: John Murray, 1820.

Bennett, Tony. *The Birth of the Museum: History, Theory, Politics.* New York: Routledge, 1995.

Bequette, M. K. "Shelley and Smith: Two Sonnets on Ozymandias." *Keats-Shelley Journal* 26 (1977), 29–31.

Berlinerblau, Jacques. *Heresy in the University: The Black Athena Controversy and the Responsibilities of American Intellectuals.* New Brunswick: Rutgers University Press, 1999.

Bermingham, Ann. *Landscape and Ideology: The English Rustic Tradition, 1740–1860.* Berkeley: University of California Press, 1986.

Bernal, Martin. *Black Athena: The Afroasiatic Roots of Classical Civilization.* New Brunswick: Rutgers University Press, 1987.

Berque, Jacques. *Imperialism and Revolution,* trans. Jean Stewart. New York: Praeger, 1972.

Bohls, Elizabeth A. *Women Travel Writers and the Language of Aesthetics: 1716–1818.* Cambridge: Cambridge University Press, 1995.

Bonomi, Joseph, and Francis Arundale. *Gallery of Antiquities Selected from the British Museum.* London: John Weale, 1842–43.

Bosworth, C. E. "Al-Jabarti and the Frankish Archaeologists." *International Journal of Middle East Studies* 8 (1977).

Boullata, Issa. *Literary Structures of Religious Meaning in the Qur'an.* Richmond: Curzon Press, 2000.

Bowring, John. *Report on Egypt and Candia Addressed to the Right Hon. Lord Viscount Palmerston.* London: W. Clowes and Sons, 1840.

Bratton, Fred Gladstone. *A History of Egyptian Archaeology.* New York: Thomas Y. Crowell, 1968.

Brendon, Piers. *Thomas Cook: 150 Years of Popular Tourism.* London: Secker and Warburg, 1991.

Brown, Bill. *The Sense of Things: The Object Matter of American Literature.* Chicago: University of Chicago Press, 2004.

Brown, James. "'Ozymandias': The Riddle of the Sands." *Keats-Shelley Journal* 12 (1998), 51–75.

Bruce, James. *Travels to Discover the Source of the Nile, in the Years 1768, 1769, 1770, 1771,1772, and 1773: in Five Volumes.* Edinburgh: J. Ruthven, 1790.

Brugman, J. *An Introduction to the History of Modern Arabic Literature in Egypt.* Leiden: E. J. Brill, 1984.

Burckhardt, John Lewis. *Travels in Nubia.* London: John Murray, 1819.

Callon, Michel. *The Laws of the Markets.* Oxford: Blackwell Publishers, 1998.

———. "Four Models for the Dynamics of Science." In *Handbook of Science and Technology Studies,* ed. S. Jasanoff et al. Beverly Hills: Sage Publications, 1995.

Callon, Michel, with John Law. "Agency and the Hybrid *Collectif.*" *South Atlantic Quarterly* 94:2 (1995), 481–508.

Calvert, John. "The World Is an Undutiful Boy! Sayyid Qutb's American Experience." *Islam and Christian-Muslim Relations* 11:1 (2000).

Carré, Jean-Marie. *Voyageurs et écrivains français en Égypte, tome I: du début à la fin de la domination Turque.* Cairo: L'Institut Français d'Archéologie Orientale, 1956.

Carré, Olivier. *Mysticism and Politics: A Critical Reading of Fi Zilal al-Qur'an by Sayyid Qutb (1906–1966),* trans. W. Shepard. Leiden: E. J. Brill, 2003.

Carter, Howard, and A. C. Mace. *The Discovery of the Tomb of Tutankhamen.* New York: Dover Publications, 1977 [1923].

———. *Tut•Ankh•Amen: The Politics of Discovery.* London: Libri, 1998.

Ceram, C. W. *Gods, Graves and Scholars.* London: Gollancz, Sidgwick and Jackson, 1952.

Champollion, Jean-François. *Lettres et journaux écrits pendant le voyage d'Égypte.* Edited by H. Hartleben. Paris: Christian Bourgois Éditeur, 1986.

———. *Egyptian Diaries: How One Man Solved the Mysteries of the Nile.* London: Gibson Square Books, 2001.

Cohn, Bernard. *Colonialism and Its Forms of Knowledge: The British in India.* Princeton: Princeton University Press, 1996.

Colla, Elliott. "Hooked on Pharaonics: Literature and the Appropriations of Ancient Egypt." Ph.D. diss., U.C. Berkeley, 2000.

———. "Shadi 'Abd al-Salam's *al-Mumiya*': Ambivalence and the Egyptian Nation-State." In *Beyond Colonialism and Nationalism in North Africa,* ed. Ali Ahmida, 109–46. New York: Palgrave, 2000.

———. "The Stuff of Egypt: The Nation, the State and Their Proper Objects." *new formations* 45 (Winter 2001–02), 72–90.

———. "The Measure of Egypt." *Postcolonial Studies* 7:2 (Winter 2005), 271–93.

Cook, Michael. "Pharaonic History in Medieval Egypt." *Studia Islamica* 57 (1983).

Cooper, Fred. *Colonialism in Question: Theory, Knowledge, History.* Berkeley: University of California Press, 2005.

Curl, James Stevens. *Egyptomania, the Egyptian Revival: A Recurring Theme in the History of Taste.* Manchester: Manchester University Press, 1994.

Daly, Nicholas. "That Obscure Object of Desire: Victorian Commodity Culture and Fictions of the Mummy." *Novel* 28:1 (1994), 24–51.

Damiani, Anita. "Richard Pococke (1704–1765)." In *Enlightened Observers: British Travellers to the Near East, 1715–1850,* 70–104. Beirut: American University of Beirut, 1979.

David, Rosalie. *The Experience of Ancient Egypt*. London: Routledge, 2000.

Davies, Bryn. "Henry Salt." *Bulletin of the Faculty of Arts Fouad I University* 2:1 (1934), 67–81.

Dawson, Warren. *Who Was Who in Egyptology*. London: Egypt Exploration Society, 1952.

Deleuze, Gilles, and Félix Guattari. *The Anti-Oedipus: Capitalism and Schizophrenia*. New York: Viking Press, 1977.

Denon, Vivant. *Travels in Upper and Lower Egypt, During the Campaigns of General Bonaparte*. London: J. Cundee, 1803.

Diop, Cheikh Anta. *The African Origin of Civilization: Myth or Reality*. Chicago: Lawrence Hill Books, 1974.

Disher, Maurice Willson. *Pharaoh's Fool*. London: Heinemann, 1957.

Duncan, Carole. *Civilizing Rituals: Inside Public Art Museums*. London: Routledge, 1995.

Dykstra, Darrell. "Pyramids, Prophets, and Progress: Ancient Egypt in the Writings of 'Ali Mubarak." *Journal of the American Oriental Society* 114:1 (January-March 1994).

Eggers, Vernon. *A Fabian in Egypt: Salamah Musa and the Rise of the Professional Classes in Egypt, 1909–1939*. London: University Press of America, 1986.

El-Daly, Okasha. *Egyptology: The Missing Millennium: Ancient Egypt in Medieval Arabic Writings*. London: UCL Press, 2005.

El-Enany, Rasheed. *Naguib Mahfouz: The Pursuit of Meaning*. New York: Routledge, 1993.

Euben, Roxanne L. *Enemy in the Mirror: Islamic Fundamentalism and the Limits of Modern Rationalism, a Work of Comparative Political Theory*. Princeton: Princeton University Press, 1999.

Fabian, Johannes. *Time and the Other: How Anthropology Makes Its Object*. New York: Columbia University Press, 1983.

Fagan, Brian M. *The Rape of the Nile: Tomb Robbers, Tourists, and Archaeologists in Egypt*. New York: Charles Scribner's Sons, 1975.

Fahd, Tawfiq. "Le Merveilleux dans la faune, la flore et les minéraux." In *L'Étrange et le merveilleux dans l'Islam médiéval: actes du colloque tenu au Collège de France à Paris, en Mars 1974*, 117–165. Paris: Institut du Monde Arabe, 1978.

Finati, Giovanni. *Narrative of the Life and Adventures of Giovanni Finati, Native of Ferrara; Who, Under the Assumed Name of Mahomet, Made the Campaigns Against the Wahabees for the Recovery of Mecca and Medina; and Since Acted as Interpreter to European Travelers in Some of the Parts Least Visited of Asia and Africa*, trans. and ed. W. J. Bankes. London: John Murray, 1830.

Fisher, Philip. *Making and Effacing Art: Modern American Art in a Culture of Museums*. New York: Oxford University Press, 1991.

Flood, Finbarr Barry. "Between Cult and Culture: Bamiyan, Islamic Iconoclasm, and the Museum." *Art Bulletin* 84:4 (December 2002), 641–59.

Fodor, Alexander. "The Origins of the Arabic Legends of the Pyramids." *Acta Orientalia Academiæ Scientiarum Hungaricæ* 23 (1970).

———. "The Metamorphosis of Imhotep: A Study in Islamic Syncretism." *Abhandlungen der Akademie der Wissenschaften in Göttingen* 98 (1976), 155–81.

de Forbin, Louis Nicolas. *Voyage dans le Levant en 1817 et 1818*. Paris: Imprimerie Royale, 1819.

France, Peter. *The Rape of Egypt: How the Europeans Stripped Egypt of Its Heritage*. London: Barrie and Jenkins, 1991.

Gamboni, Dario. *The Destruction of Art: Iconoclasm and Vandalism Since the French Revolution*. London: Reaktion Books, 1997.

Gendzier, Irene L. *The Practical Visions of Ya'qub Sanu'*. Cambridge, Mass.: Harvard University Press, 1966.

Gershoni, Israel, and James Jankowski, eds. *Egypt, Islam, and the Arabs: The Search for Egyptian Nationhood, 1900–1930*. New York: Oxford University Press, 1986.

———. *Commemorating the Nation: Collective Memory, Public Commemoration, and National Identity in Twentieth-Century Egypt*. Chicago: Middle East Documentation Center, 2004.

Gliddon, George. *An Appeal to the Antiquaries of Europe on the Destruction of the Monuments of Egypt*. London: James Madden, 1841.

Grabar, Oleg. "Islam and Iconoclasm." In *Iconoclasm: Papers Given at the Ninth Spring Symposium of Byzantine Studies, University of Birmingham, March 1975*, eds. A. Bryer and J. Herrin. Birmingham: Centre for Byzantine Studies, 1977.

Greenblatt, Stephen. *Marvelous Possessions: The Wonder of the New World*. Chicago: University of Chicago Press, 1991.

Gril, Denis. "Le Personage Coranique de Pharaon d'après l'interprétation d'ibn 'Arabi." *Annales Islamologiques* 14 (1978), 37–57.

Haarman, Ulrich. "Regional Sentiment in Medieval Islamic Egypt." *Bulletin of the School of Oriental and African Studies* 43:1 (1980).

———. "In Quest of the Spectacular: Noble and Learned Visitors to the Pyramids Around 1200 AD." In *Islamic Studies Presented to Charles J. Adams*, eds. Wael Hallaq and Donald P. Little. Leiden: E. J. Brill, 1991.

Halbertal, Moshe. "Coexisting with the Enemy: Jews and Pagans in the Mishnah." In *Tolerance and Intolerance in Early Judaism and Christianity*, eds. Graham Stanton and Guy Stroumsa, 159–72. Cambridge: Cambridge University Press, 1998.

Hamilton, William. *Remarks on Several Parts of Turkey: Part 1, Aegyptiaca or, Some Account of the Antient and Modern State of Egypt, as Obtained in the Years 1801, 1802.* London: T. Payne, 1809.

Haraway, Donna. *Primate Visions: Gender, Race, and Nature in the World of Modern Science.* New York: Routledge, 1989.

Hawass, Zahi. *Secrets from the Sand: My Search for Egypt's Past.* New York: Harry N. Abrams, 2003.

Hawting, G. R. *The Idea of Idolatry and the Emergence of Islam: From Polemic to History.* Cambridge: Cambridge University Press, 1999.

Heidegger, Martin. "The Age of the World Picture." In *Off the Beaten Path*, eds. and trans. J. Young and K. Haynes. Cambridge: Cambridge University Press, 2002.

Heidegger, Martin. "The Thing." In *Poetry, Language, Thought*, trans. Albert Hofstadter, 165–86. New York: Harper Colophon Books, 1971.

Herodotus. *The History.* Translated by David Grene. Chicago: University of Chicago Press, 1987.

Hodgson, Marshall G. S. "Islam and Image." *History of Religions* 3 (1969), 220–60.

Horkheimer, Max, and Theodor Adorno. *Dialectic of Enlightenment.* Translated by John Cumming. New York: Herder and Herder, 1972.

Hourani, Albert. *Arabic Thought in the Liberal Age, 1798–1939.* Cambridge: Cambridge University Press, 1983.

Hoving, Thomas. *Tutankhamun: The Untold Story.* New York: Simon and Schuster, 1978.

Humbert, Jean-Marcel. *Egyptomania: Egypt in Western Art 1730–1930.* Ottawa: National Gallery of Canada, 1994.

Hussein, Kadria. "La reine Teti-Sheri et la restauration nationale." *Le Revue du Caire* 1:3 (1938), 191–210.

Irby, Charles Leonard, and James Mangles. *Travels in Egypt and Nubia, Syria and Asia Minor during the years 1817 & 1818.* London: Privately published, 1823.

d'Ison, Claudine Le Tourneur. *Mariette Pacha, ou le rêve égyptien.* Paris: Plon, 1999.

Iversen, Erik. *The Myth of Egypt and Its Hieroglyphs.* Princeton: Princeton University Press, 1993.

Izutsu, Toshihiko. *Ethico-Religious Concepts in the Qur'an.* Montreal: McGill-Queen's University Press, 2002.

al-Jabarti, 'Abd al-Rahman. *'Abd al-Rahman al-Jabarti's History of Egypt.* Trans. and eds. Thomas Philipp and Moshe Perlman. Stuttgart: Franz Steiner, 1994.

James, T. G. H. *Howard Carter: The Path to Tutankhamun.* London: Kegan Paul International, 1992.

Jameson, Fredric. "Third World Literature in the Era of Multinational Capitalism." *Social Text* 15 (Fall 1986).

Jankowski, James P. *Egypt's Young Rebels, 'Young Egypt': 1933–1952.* Stanford: Hoover Institution Press, 1975.

Janowitz, Anne. "Shelley's Monument to Ozymandias." *Philological Quarterly* 63:4 (Fall 1984), 477–91.

Jasanoff, Maya. *Edge of Empire: Lives, Culture, and Conquest in the East, 1750–1850.* New York: Vintage Books, 2005.

Jenkins, Ian. *Archaeologists and Aesthetes in the Sculpture Galleries of the British Museum 1800–1939.* London: British Museum Press, 1992.

Jomard, Edmé François, et al. *Description de l'Égypte, ou, Recueil des observations et des recherches qui ont été faites en Égypte pendant l'expédition de l'armée française.* Paris: L'Imprimerie Impériale, 1809.

——. *Coup-d'oeil impartial sur l'état présent de l'Égypte, comparé à sa situation antérieure.* Paris: Imprimerie de Béthune et Plon, 1836.

Kepel, Gilles. *Muslim Extremism in Egypt: The Prophet and Pharaoh.* Berkeley: University of California Press, 1986.

Khalidi, Tarif. *Arabic Historical Thought in the Classical Period.* Cambridge: Cambridge University Press, 1994.

Khatab, Sayed. *The Political Thought of Sayyid Qutb: The Theory of* Jahiliyya. New York: Routledge, 2006.

Khater, Antoine. *Le Régime juridique de fouilles et des antiquités en Égypte.* Cairo: Imprimerie de l'Institut Français d'Archéologie Orientale, 1960.

Khouri, Mounah A. *Poetry and the Making of Modern Egypt (1882–1922).* Leiden: E. J. Brill, 1971.

King, G. R. D. "Islam, Iconoclasm, and the Declaration of Doctrine." *Bulletin of the School of Oriental and African Studies* 48:2 (1985), 267–77.

Kopytoff, Igor. "The Cultural Biography of Things: Commoditization as Process." In *The Social Life of Things: Commodities in Cultural Perspective,* ed. Arjun Appadurai, 64–91. Cambridge: Cambridge University Press, 1986.

Kuberski, Philip. *The Persistence of Memory: Organism, Myth, Text.* Berkeley: University of California Press, 1992.

Landau, Jacob M. "Abu Naddara, an Egyptian-Jewish Nationalist." *Journal of Jewish Studies* 3:1 (1952).

——. *Studies in the Arab Theater and Cinema.* Philadelphia: University of Pennsylvania Press, 1958.

Lant, Antonia. "The Curse of the Pharaoh, or How Cinema Contracted Egyptomania." In *Visions of the East: Orientalism in Film,* ed. M. Bernstein and G. Studlar, 69–98. New Brunswick: Rutgers University Press, 1997.

Latour, Bruno. *The Pasteurization of France.* Translated by Alan Sheridan and John Law. Cambridge, Mass.: Harvard University Press, 1993.

Latour, Bruno. *We Have Never Been Modern*. Cambridge, Mass.: Harvard University Press, 1993.

———. *Pandora's Hope: Essays on the Reality of Science*. Cambridge, Mass.: Harvard University Press, 1999.

———. *The Politics of Nature: How to Bring the Sciences into Democracy*. Translated by Catherine Porter. Cambridge, Mass.: Harvard University Press, 2004.

———. *Reassembling the Social: An Introduction to Actor-Network-Theory*. Oxford: Oxford University Press, 2005.

Latour, Bruno, with Steve Woolgar. *Laboratory Life: The Social Construction of Scientific Facts*. Princeton: Princeton University Press, 1986.

Law, John. *Organizing Modernity*. Oxford: Blackwell, 1994.

———. "On the Subject of the Object: Narrative, Technology, and Interpretation." *Configurations* 8:1. (2000).

Lefkowitz, Mary. *Not Out of Africa: How 'Afrocentrism' Became an Excuse to Teach Myth as History*. New York: Basic Books, 1996.

Lefkowitz, Mary, and G. Rogers, eds. *Black Athena Revisited*. Chapel Hill: University of North Carolina Press, 1996.

Light, Henry. *Travels in Egypt, Nubia, Holy Land, Mount Lebanon, and Cyprus, in the Year 1814*. London: printed for Rodwell and Martin, 1818.

Long, George. *The British Museum: Egyptian Antiquities*. London: Charles Knight, 1832.

MacCannell, Dean. *The Tourist: A New Theory of the Leisure Class*. Berkeley: University of California Press, 1999.

Madden, Richard Robert. *Travels in Turkey, Egypt, Nubia and Palestine in 1824, 1825, 1826, and 1827*. London: Henry Colburn, 1829.

Mahdi, Muhsin. *Ibn Khaldun's Philosophy of History*. Chicago: University of Chicago Press, 1957.

Manley, Deborah, and Peta Rée. *Henry Salt: Artist, Traveller, Diplomat, Egyptologist*. London: Libri, 2001.

Mariette, Auguste. *Description du Parc Égyptien*. Paris: Dentu, 1867.

———. *Notice des principaux monuments exposés dans les galeries provisoires du Musée d'Antiquités Égyptiennes de S. A. le Vice-Roi à Boulaq*. Alexandria: Mourès, Rey and Ce., 1868.

———. *Itinéraire de la Haute-Égypte, comprenant une description des monuments antiques des rives du Nil entre le Caire et la Première Cataracte*. Alexandria: Mourès and Cie., 1872.

———. *Voyage dans la Haute-Égypte: Explication de quatre-vingt-trois vues photographiées d'après les monuments antiques, compris entre le Caire et la première cataracte par Auguste Mariette-Bey*. Cairo: A. Mourès, 1878.

Maspero, Gaston. *Guide du Visiteur au Musée de Boulaq*. Boulaq: Musée du Boulaq, 1883.

Mayes, Stanley. *The Great Belzoni: The Circus Strongman Who Discovered Egypt's Ancient Wonders*. London: I. B. Tauris, 2003 [1959].

McAlister, Melani. *Epic Encounters: Culture, Media and US Interests in the Middle East, 1945–2000*. Berkeley: University of California Press, 2001.

McBride, Barrie St. Clair. *Farouk of Egypt, A Biography*. New York: A. S. Barnes, 1967.

McClellan, Andrew. *Inventing the Louvre: Art, Politics, and the Origins of the Modern Museum in Eighteenth-Century Paris*. Berkeley: University of California Press, 1994.

McLeave, Hugh. *The Last Pharaoh: Farouk of Egypt*. New York: McCall, 1970.

Mertz, Barbara. *Temples, Tombs and Hieroglyphs*. London: Gollancz, 1964.

Meskell, Lynn. "Deir el Medina in Hyperreality: Seeking the People of Pharaonic Egypt." *Journal of Mediterranean Archaeology* 7:2 (1994), 193–216.

————, ed. *Archaeology Under Fire: Nationalism, Politics and Heritage in the Eastern Mediterranean and Middle East*. London: Routledge, 1998.

————. "An Archaeology of Social Relations in an Egyptian Village." *Journal of Archaeological Method and Theory* 5:3 (1998), 209–43.

————. "Sites of Violence: Terrorism, Tourism, and Heritage in the Archaeological Present." In *Embedding Ethics*. Oxford: Berg, 2005.

————. "Object Orientations." In *Archaeologies of Materiality*. Oxford: Blackwell, 2005.

Meskell, Lynn, and Peter Pels, eds. *Embedding Ethics*. Oxford: Berg, 2005.

Miller, Edward. *That Noble Cabinet: A History of the British Museum*. London: Andre Deutsch, 1973.

Mir, Mustansir. "The Qur'an as Literature." *Religion and Literature* 20:1 (1988).

Mitchell, Richard P. *The Society of the Muslim Brothers*. Oxford: Oxford University Press, 1969.

Mitchell, Timothy. *Colonising Egypt*. Cambridge: Cambridge University Press, 1988.

————. *Rule of Experts: Egypt, Techno-Politics, Modernity*. Berkeley: University of California Press, 2002.

Monroe, James. "Oral Composition in Pre-Islamic Poetry." *Journal of Arabic Literature* 3 (1972), 1–53.

de Montulé, Edward. *Travels in Egypt during 1818 and 1819*. London: Richard Phillips, 1821.

Moreh, Shmuel, trans. *Al-Jabarti's Chronicle of Napoleon in Egypt*. Princeton: Markus Weiner, 2001.

Moore, David Chioni, ed. *Black Athena Writes Back: Martin Bernal Responds to His Critics*. Durham: Duke University Press, 2001.

Moser, Stephanie. *Wondrous Curiosities: Ancient Egypt at the British Museum*. Chicago: University of Chicago Press, 2006.

Musa, Salamah. *The Education of Salamah Musa*. Leiden: E. J. Brill, 1961.

Musallam, Adnan A. "Prelude to Islamic Commitment: Sayyid Qutb's Literary and Spiritual Orientation, 1932–1938." *Muslim World* 80:3–4 (July–October 1990), 176–89.

———. *Sayyid Qutb: The Emergence of the Islamicist 1939–1950*. East Jerusalem: PASSIA, 1990.

———. *From Secularism to Jihad: Sayyid Qutb and the Foundations of Radical Islamism*. Westport, Conn.: Praeger, 2005.

Musallam, B. F. "The Modern Vision of 'Ali Mubarak." In *The Islamic City*, ed. R. B. Serjeant, 183–99. Paris: UNESCO, 1980.

Newman, Daniel L. *An Imam in Paris: Account of a Stay in France by an Egyptian Cleric (1826–1831)*. London: Saqi, 2004.

Norden, Frederick Lewis. *Travels in Egypt and Nubia*. Edited by Peter Templeton. London: Lockyer Davis and Charles Reymers, 1758.

Ong, Walter. *Orality and Literacy*. London: Methuen Press, 1984.

Orany, Ezzat. "'Nation,' 'patrie,' 'citoyen' chez Rifa'a al-Tahtawi et Khayr al-Din al-Tounsi." *MIDEO* 16 (1983), 169–90.

Osman, Dalia N. "Occupiers' Title to Cultural Property: Nineteenth-Century Removal [of] Egyptian Artifacts." *Columbia Journal of Transnational Law* 37 (1999), 969–1000.

Ostle, Robin. "Modern Egyptian Renaissance Man." *Bulletin of the School of Oriental and African Studies* 57:1 (1994), 184–92.

Panofsky, Erwin. "The History of the Theory of Human Proportions as a Reflection of the History of Styles." In *Meaning in the Visual Arts*. New York: Doubleday Anchor Books, 1955.

Paret, R. "Le Corps de Pharaon signe et avertissement pour la postérité." *Études d'Orientalisme, dédiées à la mémoire de Lévi-Provençal*. Paris: G.-P. Maisonneuve et Larose, 1962.

Pearce, Susan M. "Giovanni Battista Belzoni's Exhibition of the Reconstruction of Pharaoh Seti I in 1821." *Journal of the History of Collections* 12:1 (2000), 109–25.

Peled, Mattityahu. *Religion, My Own: The Literary Works of Najib Mahfuz*. New Brunswick: Transaction Books, 1983.

Pickering, Andrew. *The Mangle of Practice: Time, Agency, and Science*. Chicago: University of Chicago Press, 1995.

Plessner, M. "Hermes Trismegistus and Arab Science." *Studia Islamica* 2 (1954), 45–59.

Pococke, Richard. *A Description of the East, and Some Other Countries*. London: W. Bowyer, 1743.

Podro, Michael. *The Manifold in Perception: Theories of Art from Kant to Hildebrand*. Oxford: Clarendon Press, 1972.

Pratt, Mary Louise. *Imperial Eyes: Travel Writing and Transculturation*. New York: Routledge, 1992.

al-Qadi, Widad. "East and West in 'Ali Mubarak's *'Alamuddin*." In *Intellectual Life in the Arab East, 1890–1939*, ed. Marwan R. Buheiry. Beirut: American University of Beirut, 1981.

Reid, Donald Malcolm. *Whose Pharaohs?: Archaeology, Museums, and Egyptian National Identity from Napoleon to World War I*. Berkeley: University of California Press, 2002.

———. "Indigenous Egyptology: The Decolonization of a Profession." *Journal of the American Oriental Society* 105:2 (1985), 233–46.

———. "Nationalizing the Pharaonic Past: Egyptology, Imperialism, and Egyptian Nationalism, 1922–1952." In *Rethinking Nationalism in the Arab Middle East*, eds. J. Jankowski and I. Gershoni, 127–49. New York: Columbia University Press, 1997.

Reimer, Michael J. "'Ali Mubarak's Description of al-Azhar." *International Journal of Middle East Studies* 29 (1997).

Richardson, Robert. *Travels Along the Mediterranean and Parts Adjacent in Company with the Earl of Belmore, During the Years 1816–17–18*. London: T. Cadwell, 1822.

Richmond, H. M. "Ozymandias and the Travelers." *Keats-Shelley Journal* 11 (1962), 67–71.

Ridley, Ronald. *Napoleon's Proconsul in Egypt: The Life and Times of Bernardino Drovetti*. London: Rubicon Press, n.d.

Riegl, Alois. "The Modern Cult of Monuments: Its Character and Origin." *Oppositions* 25 (Fall 1982), 21–51.

Rifaud, Jean-Jacques. *Voyages en Egypte 1805–1827*. Paris: n.p., 1830.

Rodinson, Maxime. "La Place du merveilleux et de l'étrange dans la conscience du monde musulman médiéval." In *L'Étrange et le merveilleux dans l'Islam médiéval: actes du colloque tenu au Collège de France à Paris, en Mars 1974*, 167–226. Paris: Institut du Monde Arabe, 1978.

Rojek, Chris, and John Urry eds. *Touring Cultures: Transformations of Travel and Theory*. London: Routledge, 1997.

Rushdy, Rashad. "English Travellers in Egypt During the Reign of Mohamed Ali." *Bulletin of the Faculty of Arts, Fouad I University* 14:2 (1952), 1–61.

Said, Edward. *Orientalism*. New York: Pantheon Books, 1978.

Salt, Henry. *The Life and Correspondence of Henry Salt, Esq*. Edited by J. J. Halls. London: Richard Bentley, 1834.

Scholes, Robert. *Structuralism in Literature: An Introduction.* New Haven: Yale University Press, 1974.

Sells, Michael. *Desert Tracings: Six Classic Arabian Odes by 'Alqama, Shanfara, Labid, 'Antara, al-A'sha, and Dhu al-Rumma.* Middletown: Wesleyan University Press, 1989.

———. *Approaching the Qur'an: The Early Revelations.* Ashland: White Cloud Press, 1999.

Serres, Michel. *The Natural Contract.* Ann Arbor: University of Michigan Press, 1995.

Shapin, Steven. *Leviathan and the Air-Pump: Hobbes, Boyle, and the Experimental Life.* Princeton: Princeton University Press, 1985.

al-Sharouni, Subhi. "Mahmoud Mukhtar: A Traditional and Contemporary Artist." *UR* 1 (1984), 27–28.

Shelley, Percy Bysshe. *Shelley's Poetry and Prose.* Eds. D. H. Reiman and S. B. Powers. New York: W. W. Norton, 1977.

Shepard, William. *Sayyid Qutb and Islamic Activism: A Translation and Critical Analysis of Social Justice in Islam.* Leiden: E. J. Brill, 1996.

Silberman, Neil Asher. *Between Past and Present: Archaeology, Ideology, and Nationalism in the Modern Middle East.* New York: Anchor Books, 1989.

Smith, Charles. *Islam and the Search for Social Order in Modern Egypt: A Biography of Muhammad Husayn Haykal.* Albany: SUNY Press, 1983.

———. "Imagined Identities, Imagined Nationalisms: Print Culture and Egyptian Nationalism in Light of Recent Scholarship." *International Journal of Middle East Studies* 29:4 (November 1997), 607–22.

Solé, Robert, and Dominique Valbelle. *The Rosetta Stone: The Story of Decoding the Hieroglyphics.* London: Profile Books, 2001.

Sommer, Doris. *Foundational Fictions: The National Romances of Latin America.* Berkeley: University of California Press, 1991.

Spivak, Gayatri Chakravorty. *A Critique of Postcolonial Reason: Toward a History of the Vanishing Present.* Cambridge, Mass.: Harvard University Press, 1999.

Stetkevych, Jaroslav. *The Zephyrs of Najd: The Poetics of Nostalgia in the Classical Arabic Nasib.* Chicago: University of Chicago Press, 1993.

Stetkevych, Suzanne Pinckney. *The Mute Immortals Speak: Pre-Islamic Poetry and the Poetics of Ritual.* Ithaca: Cornell University Press, 1993.

Stoler, Ann Laura, and Frederick Cooper. *Tensions of Empire: Colonial Cultures in a Bourgeois World.* Berkeley: University of California Press, 1997.

Strabo. *The Geography of Strabo.* Trans. Horace Leonard Jones. Cambridge, Mass.: Harvard University Press, 1967.

Stroumsa, Guy. "Tertullian on Idolatry and the Limits of Tolerance." In *Tolerance and Intolerance in Early Judaism and Christianity*, eds. Graham Stanton and Guy Stroumsa, 173–84. Cambridge: Cambridge University Press, 1998.

Summerson, John. *The Classical Language of Architecture*. Cambridge: MIT Press, 1963.

al-Suyuti, Jalal al-Din. "The Treatise on the Egyptian Pyramids (*Tuhfat al-kiram fi khabar al-ahram*) by Jalal al-Din al-Suyuti." Trans. Leon Nemoy. *Isis* 30 (1939), 2–37.

Synopsis of the Contents of the British Museum. London: Richard and Arthur Taylor, 1821.

Tagher, Jacques. "Fouilleurs et antiquaires en Égypte au XIXe siècle." *Cahiers d'histoire égyptienne* 3:1 (November 1950), 72–86.

Thomas, Nicholas. *Entangled Objects: Exchange, Material Culture and Colonialism in the Pacific*. Cambridge, Mass.: Harvard University Press, 1991.

Thompson, Jason. *Sir Gardner Wilkinson and His Circle*. Austin: University of Texas Press, 1997.

Trigger, Bruce G. *A History of Archaeological Thought*. Cambridge: Cambridge University Press, 1989.

Troutt Powell, Eve M. *A Different Shade of Colonialism: Egypt, Great Britain, and the Mastery of the Sudan*. Berkeley: University of California Press, 2003.

van der Spek, Kees. "Dead Mountain Versus Living Community: The Theban Necropolis as Cultural Landscape." In *Proceedings of the Third International Seminar Forum UNESCO: University and Heritage*, eds. W. S. Logan, C. Long, and J. Martin, 176–82. Melbourne: Deakin University Press, 1998.

Vasiliev, A. A. "The Iconoclastic Edict of the Caliph Yazid II, A.D. 721." *Dumbarton Oaks Papers* 9–10 (1956).

Vaux, W. S. W. *Handbook to the Antiquities in the British Museum: Being a Description of the Remains of Greek, Assyrian, Egyptian, and Etruscan Art Preserved There*. London: John Murray, 1851.

Von Hees, Syrinx. "The Astonishing: a Critique and Re-reading of 'Aga'ib Literature," *Middle East Literatures* 8:2 (July 2005), 101–20.

Von Minutoli, Wolfradine. *Recollections of Egypt*. Philadelphia: Carey, Lea and Carey, 1827.

Walker, D. P. *The Ancient Theology: Studies in Christian Platonism from the Fifteenth to the Eighteenth Century*. Ithaca: Cornell University Press, 1972.

Warren, Karen J. "A Philosophical Perspective on the Ethics and Resolution of Cultural Properties Issues." In *The Ethics of Collecting Cultural Property: Whose Culture? Whose Property?*, ed. P. M. Messenger, 1–25. Albuquerque: University of New Mexico Press, 1989.

Wendell, Charles. *Five Tracts of Hasan al-Banna' (1906–1949)*. Berkeley: University of California Press, 1978.

Wensinck, A. J., and G. Vajda. *The Encyclopaedia of Islam*, s.v. "Fir'awn."

Wilkinson, John Gardner. *Modern Egypt and Thebes: Being a Description of Egypt; Including the Information Required for Travellers in the Country*. London: John Murray, 1843.

Williams, J. F. Lake. *Letter I. of a series, on a fragment of the Plmyooymyyz* [*sic*] . . . *being a Dissertation on the Famous Colossal and Harmonious Statue of Amniphosis, Osmandias or Memnon, at Heliopolis, in the Thebais, Upper-Aegypt; or, an Essay to Account for the Phenomenon of its Music, Upon Philosophical Principles, With a Copious View of the Religion, Customs, Arts, and some popular ceremonies of the Ancient Inhabitants of the Aegyptian Empire. Being the Substance of a Letter or Memorial, Most Respectfully Addressed to the Royal Antiquarian Society of London*. London: E. Wilson, 1815.

Wilson, John A. *Signs and Wonders Upon Pharaoh*. Chicago: University of Chicago Press, 1964.

Wittkower, Rudolf. *Architectural Principles in the Age of Humanism*. London: Alec Turanti, 1952.

Wortham, John David. *The Genesis of British Egyptology, 1549–1906*. Norman: University of Oklahoma Press, 1971.

Zadeh, Travis. "Translation, Language, and Identity: Pre-modern Negotiations along the Frontiers of Islam." Unpublished dissertation, Harvard University, 2006.

Index

Note: page numbers in italics indicate illustrations and captions

Abaza, Fikri, 172

'Abbas I, 120, 124

'Abbas II, 154

'Abduh, Muhammad, 169

Abu al-Salt, 85

Abu al-Su'ud, 'Abdallah, 128–29, 133, 134

Abu Hadid, Muhammad Farid, 244

Abu Shadi, Ahmad Zaki, 215, 227, 230

Abu Simbel, Belzoni's excavations at, 40, 41–43

Abu 'Ubayd al-Bakri, 86

Adorno, Theodor, 3–4

aesthetic experience: Carter's Tutankhamen tomb discovery as, 172–73, 181–83, 190, 225; in European travel narratives, 33–34, 181–82; historical knowledge and interpretation and, 92–93; juxtapositions of ancient and modern and, 40–41; museum going and exhibition viewing as, 5, 198; ruins as, 34–35, 40

aesthetic values: ambivalence of, about Egyptian antiquities, 9, 33–34, 46, 48, 49, 52–55, 57, 286–87 n. 72; museum development and, 47

al-Afghani, Jalal al-Din, 169

Africa Association, 31

Afrocentric Egyptology, 12–13

agency of artifacts and monuments, 4–5, 17–18, 19, 35, 70–71, 158–59, 182–83, 190

Ahmose, 256–57, 258, 259–60

'aja'ib literature, 82–84, 293–94 n. 33

Åkerblad, Johann David, 93

Akhenaton, 146

Akhenukh, 85

alchemy, 21

allegory. See literary allegory

Allenby, Lord, 195

ambiguity and conflict: artifacts as embodiments of, 29, 60; civilization as dialectic and, 130–31; Egyptian adoption of Egyptology and, 116; in Egyptology, 11, 14–16, 18–19, 225–26; within Pharaonism, 14–15, 273–75

Amin, Ahmad, 308 n. 57

'Anan, Salah, 228, 230

ancient-modern opposition, 15, 68–69, 101, 108; European views of, 40–41; in Roberts's lithographs, 104–8

al-Antiqakhana: first, 117, 118–20, 124; second, 126–29, 135, 154

antiquarianism: Egyptology vs., 8–9, 75–76. See also European antiquarianism, Egyptology antiquities acquisitions, collecting, 9–10, 11, 41, 43, 65–66. *See also* antiquities commerce; European antiquarianism, Egyptology

antiquities commerce, 27, 65, 285 n. 40, 290 n. 123; commercialism, 41, 43, 47, 287 n. 75; Gurna in, 15–16, 27, 283 n. 14; Jabarti on, 72–73; repatriation and, 64, 102, 289 n. 121. *See also* antiquities acquisitions, collecting; Egyptian antiquities policy and management; European antiquarianism, Egyptology

antiquities ownership, control. *See* artifact ownership, control

appreciation (of antiquities): in Arabo-Islamic tradition, 86–91; European claims of superiority in, 92, 100–101, 103–4; knowledge and, 7, 48, 53–55, 92–93, 164; among modern Egyptians, 115, 125, 164; shame and, 164. *See also* aesthetic experience; exhibition; museums; tourism in Egypt

al-ʿAqqad, ʿAbbas Mahmoud, 215, 231, 234, 264

Arabo-Islamic literature. *See* literature, Arabo-Islamic

archaeological sites, separation of, from modern context and inhabitants, 15, 41, 68–69. *See also* Pharaonic sites; *and under names of specific sites*

archaeology, 8, 15, 62, 115, 178–79, 187; Egyptian nationalism and, 11, 18. *See also* Tutankhamen tomb discovery, excavations

architecture, modern, 276. *See also under names of specific monuments and sites*

art history, place of Egyptian antiquities in, 48, 53–54

artifaction, 16–17, 19–20, 28–29, 176–77; of the Memnon head, 28–29, 62–63, 70; provenance records and, 26–27; scientific archaeology and, 179; Tutankhamen's tomb artifacts and, 174–77, 187, 189–90. *See also* artifacts

artifact ownership, control, 18, 62–63, 216; Egyptian identity linked with, 123, 125; Egyptian sovereignty linked with, 201, 206, 209–10; interpretation breakthroughs and, 75–76, 96; justifications of, by Europeans, 18, 63, 189, 190; repatriation and, 64, 102, 289 n. 121; of Tutankhamen tomb objects, 200–201, 202, 206, 208–10

artifacts, 60–63, 273; archaeologists' relationship with, 189–90; *artifact* as term, 8, 9, 51, 61, 62, 288 n. 91; as embodiments of conflict, 29, 60; imbuing of, with agency, 4–5, 17–18, 19, 35, 70–71, 158–59, 182–83, 190; literary transformations of, 216, 217–18, 224. *See also* artifaction; artifact ownership, control; exhibition; historical interpretation; Pharaonic antiquities

artificial, as term, 51

al-ʿAryan, Muhammad Saʿid, 244

Assmann, Jan, 15

Aswan Dam, 276

athar (monuments), 79, 82, 128, 135, 293 n. 32; ruins in Arabo-Islamic literature and, 78–86

Austrian consul, 27

Awakening. See *al-Nahda*

al-ʿAziz, 87–88

al-Baghdadi, 'Abd al-Latif, 79, 83–88

Baikie, James, 242; *Ancient Egypt* (*Misr al-qadima*) (tr. Mahfouz), 242–43, 249, 250

Bakathir, 'Ali Ahmad, 215, 244

Balfour, Arthur, Lord, 100–101

Bankes, William John, 30

Banks, Joseph, 31, 46, 47, 59

al-Banna, Hasan, 238, 240, 245–49, 261

Baring, Evelyn, Lord Cromer, 113–15, 169–71

beauty, standards of, 33–34, 52. *See also* aesthetic values

Bedouin tribes, in Mahfouz's '*Abath al-aqdar*, 250, 251

Belzoni, Giovanni, 29, 31–37, 40–45, 66, 68, 172, 225; Abu Simbel excavations of, 40, 41–43; background and reputation of, 31–32; on contemporary Egypt, 40; Memnon head description by, 35, 70; Memnon head removal by, 32–37, 40, 43–45, 46; Seti I tomb exhibit and, 287 n. 75

Bennett, Tony, 197

Bernal, Martin, 12–13, 17

Bonaparte savants, 73, 93, 121, 284 n. 25. See also *Description de l'Égypte*

Bowring, John, 108–9

Breasted, James Henry, 183

British antiquarianism, Egyptology: British-French rivalry and, 11, 13, 37, 59–60, 65–66; public financing concerns and, 57–60; resistance of, to Champollion's findings, 95–96. *See also* British Museum; European antiquarianism, Egyptology; Memnon head; Tutankhamen tomb discovery, excavations

British Empire Exhibition, 180

British Foreign Office, 31

British intervention in Egypt, 93, 115, 148, 166, 168–71, 257; formal Egyptian independence and, 200, 221; legitimacy claims for, 100–101, 113–15; Muslim Brotherhood's resistance to, 246–47; Treaty of 1936 and, 240; World War I and 1919 revolution and, 199–200, 257. *See also* colonialism

British intervention in Palestine, 246–47

British Museum, 1, 279 n. 8; acquisitions funding of, 47, 57–60; acquisitions methods and philosophy of, 31, 46–47, 279–80 n. 9; attitudes of, on Egyptian antiquities, 47, 48–57, 95–96; catalogs and guidebooks of, 48, 51, 52–55; Elgin marbles acquisition by, 46, 55, 57–58, 284 n. 25; growth and development of, 6–7, 47–49, 50, 55, 59; Memnon head acquisition by, 24, 26–27, 29, 65; Memnon head installation in, 25, 45–46; Memnon head reception at, 24, 26, 45–47, 50–51, 58–60; as pedagogical space, 3, 5–6; public access to, 58, 59, 289 n. 108; Rosetta Stone acquisition by, 93, 284 n. 25. *See also* Egyptian Sculpture Gallery, British Museum; Egyptian Sculpture Room, Townley Gallery; Memnon Head; Townley Gallery

Brown, Heidegger, 174

Bruce, James, 30

Brugsch, Heinrich, 142–43, 145

Bulaq Antiqakhana, 126–29, 135, 154

Burckhardt, John Lewis, 30–31, 32

Burton, Harry, 180, 183; photos by, 185, 194, 207

Cairo, redevelopment of, under
Mubarak, 136–38

Carnarvon, Earl of, 172, 173, 195, 196,
201, 208; death of, 203, 205, 222;
Times agreement and, 192, 203–4

Carnarvon, Lady Evelyn, *194*, 203

Carter, Howard, 172, 180, *194*, *207*,
225; conflicts of, with Antiquities
Service, 197, 203–6, 208–10, 303
n. 59; property rights to Tutankhamen tomb artifacts and, 208–10;
public access to Tutankhamen's
tomb and, 191–98, 204–6, 208;
theft accusations against, 208,
221–22. *See also* Tutankhamen
tomb discovery, excavations

Certeau, Michel de, xi

Chahine, Yusuf, 276

Champollion, Jean-François, 7, 53,
92–94, 95–100, 118, 138

Cheops, 122, 138; in Mahfouz's
'Abath al-aqdar, 249–50, 251–52

Chephren, 138

Christianity: Muslim iconoclasm
and views of, 86–87, 292 n. 17;
Pharaonic Egypt and, 21, 22. *See
also* Copts, Coptic tradition

civilization: of Europeans vs. Muslim accomplishments, 131; ibn
Khaldun's view of, 130–31, 141;
legacy of Pharaonic antiquities for,
14, 103, 109, 112–13, 140; tourism
and progress and, 154

collecting. *See* antiquities acquisitions, collecting; European antiquarianism, Egyptology

colonialism, 9–10, 12, 65–66, 76,
100–115, 156; anticolonial allegory
in Mahfouz and, 257–60; antiquities intervention arguments and,
108–12; Egyptian adoption of

Egyptology and, 115, 162–63;
legitimacy claims for European
intervention and, 76, 96, 100–101,
112–15, 175; Muslim Brotherhood's resistance against, 246–47;
Pharaonic imperialism and,
148–49. *See also* British intervention in Egypt; Egyptian nationalism, nationalist themes

Combe, Taylor, 45–46, 49, 50, 51

commercialism: in antiquities collecting, 43, 47, 287 n. 75; commercial
tourism tensions and, 197–98

Communist Party, 247

community, Egyptian identity and,
125, 133–36, 139–40, 164, 244,
297–98 n. 20

conflict. *See* ambiguity and conflict

conservation, preservation: artifaction and, 187, 190; Egyptian calls
for, 117, 135; European recommendations for, 97, 98–100, 108–9; as
justification for European acquisitions, 6, 11–12, 14, 64, 75, 103–4,
280 n. 15; Muslim views on, 87–91;
of Tutankhamen's tomb artifacts,
187, 190, 191. *See also* Egyptian
antiquities policy and management

consular agents, role in antiquities
commerce, 27, 29, 31, 283 n. 13

contemplation (*i'tibar*), 21–22, 79, 80,
82, 83, 85

control. *See* power, control, and
subject-object opposition

Cook, John, 154

Coptic publications, 211

Copts, Coptic tradition, 87, 97,
292 n. 17; Pharaonic antiquities in,
22, 74, 91

Cromer, Evelyn Baring, Lord, 113–15,
169–71

curiosities, 48–49, 50–51, 96

curse and retribution themes, 222

Dar al-'Ulum (Teachers' College),
143, 154–55, 245

Darwish, Sayyid, 215

d'Athanasi, Giovanni, 32

Davis, Theodore, 201

decline, stagnation rhetoric, 112–15,
132, 141, 170

Denon, Vivant, 30, 68, 104, 225

Department of Public Works. *See*
Egyptian Ministry of Public Works

Description de l'Égypte, 5, 30, 93, 104,
110, 121

destruction, defacement of monuments, 87–89, 91; European condemnation of, 98–99, 100, 108–11,
295 n. 44; prohibition against, by
1835 ordinance, 116–17

development: Cairo redevelopment
and, 136–38; development themes in
'Alam al-Din and, 139–41. *See also*
economy, economic development

Dinshiway incident, 170

Diodorus Siculus, 29, 68

disbelief (*kufr*), 78, 292 n. 16

doctors, 285 n. 40; medical interest in
Pharaonic statues and, 86, 87

Doyle, Arthur Conan, 222

Drovetti, Bernardino, 31, 33, 36, 37,
43, 44, 58, 60, 61

Dykstra, Darrell, 138

economy, economic development
(Egypt), 113–15, 152, 157, 166,
168–69

Egypt, ancient. *See* Pharaonic Egypt;
and related entries

Egypt, modern: continuity of, with
Pharaonic past, 14, 101, 124, 133–
36, 149, 161–62, 276; economy and

development in, 113–15, 136–38,
157, 166, 168–69, 276; health of
state correlated with health of
antiquities in, 108–11; Muslim rule
in, viewed as decline, 112–15, 132,
141; recent Pharaonic echoes in,
275–77; reclamation of Pharaonic
past in, 132, 141, 144, 150–51, 157,
158, 164–65. *See also* Egyptians,
modern; Pharaonism

Egyptian antiquities policy and management, 14, 99, 103, 120, 152, 202;
Carter excavations and, 176, 192–
93, 195, 197, 200–210; collection
activity zone division, 100; Department of Public Works, 195, 204, 205,
206, 209–10; 1835 ordinance and
first Antiqakhana, 101–3, 116–20;
foreign recommendations and criticisms of, 99–100, 104, 108–11, 296
n. 71; second Antiqakhana (Bulaq),
126–29, 135, 154; state sovereignty
and, 201, 206, 209–10. *See also*
Egyptian Antiquities Service

Egyptian Antiquities Service, 127,
142, 152, 176; Carter's excavations
and, 192, 195, 200–210

Egyptian history: Champollion's summary of, 97–98; modern Egyptian
views of, 130–36

Egyptian identity: Egyptology's forma-
tive role in, 125–26; Islamic past
and, 163, 164; Pharaonic antiquities
and artifacts and, 12, 13, 14–15, 175,
273, 281 n. 29; Pharaonic literary expression of, 160–61; Pharaonic past
and, 149–50; place and community
and, 125, 133–36, 139–40, 141,
149–50, 164, 244, 297–98 n. 20. *See
also* Egyptian nationalism, nationalist themes; Pharaonism

Egyptianism, 247–48

Egyptian Ministry of Public Works: *Nahdat Misr* and, 228, 230, 231; Tutankhamen tomb excavations and, 195, 204, 205, 206, 209–10

Egyptian Museum, Cairo, 176, 198, 208–9, 241

Egyptian nationalism, nationalist themes, 125, 126, 176, 200; artifact ownership disputes and, 18; Banna's writings on, 247–49; colonial archaeology and, 11, 13–14, 18; Islam and Islamic tradition and, 125, 150, 163, 247; in Mahfouz, 243–44, 250, 251, 257–60; in *Nahdat Misr*, 230, 231–32, 233; in Pharaonic literature, 156, 161, 216, 218, 220–21; Pharaonism and, 14–15, 126, 156, 163–65, 244, 273, 274; in popular literature, 222–24; revolution of 1919 and, 177, 199–200; sovereignty and antiquities control and, 201, 206, 209–10; Tutankhamen tomb discovery and, 177. *See also* Egyptian identity; patriotism

Egyptian peasants, 15, 214–15; expulsions of, from antiquities sites, 15, 286 n. 56; habitation of, at ancient sites, 40–41, 107, 281 n. 30; peasant woman of *Nahdat Misr*, 228, 229, 230–31, 233; political allegory in Mahfouz and, 258; threat to antiquities by, 14, 64, 99–100, 123, 281 n. 30. *See also* Egyptians, modern

Egyptian politics: formal independence and, 200, 221; Muslim Brotherhood and, 238, 246–47, 261; *Nahdat Misr* and, 231–32, 233; political allegory in Mahfouz's work and, 239–40, 250, 251–52,

255–60; political authority and succession issues in, 240, 251; political Pharaonism in, 125, 126, 177, 239, 274–75; revolt of 1882 and, 168, 257; revolution of 1919 and, 177, 199–200; Tutankhamen tomb discovery and, 177, 199–200, 205–6, 209–10. *See also* British intervention in Egypt; Egyptian nationalism and nationalist themes; Islamism

Egyptians, modern: class issues and conflicts of, 14, 18, 281 n. 30; domestic tourism and, 126, 143, 151–56, 299 n. 64; Egyptology adopted and influenced by, 115, 116, 121–24, 135–36, 138–42, 162–63; habitation of Pharaonic sites by, 40–41, 91, 107, 281 n. 30; as ignorant, 113–15; as indifferent to Pharaonic past, 13, 115, 123, 157; in Roberts's lithographs, 104–8, 105, 106; significance and function of Pharaonic past for, 21–22, 34–35, 91, 112, 124, 125, 141–42, 149–50. *See also* Egyptian identity; Egyptian peasants

Egyptian Sculpture Gallery, British Museum, 7, 55, 56, 57

Egyptian Sculpture Room, Townley Gallery, *xii*, 1–3, 5–8, 11, 19, 49; guidebook description of, 51, 288 n. 93; Memnon head installation in, 25, 45–46

Egyptology: adoption of and influenced by Egyptians, 115, 116, 121–24, 135–36, 138–42, 162–63; ambiguity and conflict in, 11, 14–16, 18–19, 225–26; Arabic-language scholarship in, 13, 281 n. 29; colonialism and, 9–10, 12, 76; context and, 16, 17–18; differing narratives of, 11–15; Egyptian training in, 142–43, 145; Egyptomania and, 179; emergence of, 8–9, 10–11, 75, 178; Mahfouz's studies in, 241–42; Orientalist perspective in, 101; role of artifacts in, 17–18, 61–63; science and, 8, 16, 62, 115, 178–79. *See also* archaeology; artifaction; artifact ownership, control; artifacts; European antiquarianism, Egyptology

Egyptomania, 179, 308–9 n. 1

El-Daly, Okasha, 281 n. 29

Elgin marbles, 46, 55, 57–58, 284 n. 25

enlightenment narratives (Egyptology), 11–12, 13–14, 64

eroticism in Mahfouz's *Radubis*, 254–55

European antiquarianism, Egyptology, 9–10, 14, 27–28, 65–66, 100; diplomats' role in, 27, 29, 31, 283 n. 13; legitimacy narratives and, 11–12, 13–14, 64, 65, 75, 96, 103–4, 112–15, 175; Muslim and Egyptian views of, 72–73, 100, 102, 121–22, 135; postcolonial views and criticisms of, 12–13, 61–62, 281 n. 27; as theft, 63, 64–65, 123. *See also* artifaction; artifact ownership, control; artifacts; British antiquarianism, Egyptology; British Museum; Egyptian antiquities policy and management; French antiquarianism, Egyptology

excavation accounts, 178, 179; of Tutankhamen tomb discovery, 173–74, 179, 180, 181–90. *See also* Belzoni, Giovanni

excavation labor: in Belzoni's Abu Simbel excavations, 41, 42–43; Memnon head removal workforce, 35–37, 38–39, 40, 44

exhibition: art and antiquities vs. curiosities, 49–51; development of the public museum, 5, 9, 47, 287 n. 79; historical information and interpretation and, 7–8, 53–55; as pedagogy, 3–4, 5–6, 47, 287 n. 79; science and entertainment opposition in, 180, 197–98; subject-object relations and, 1–4, 19, 137; viewing of, as aesthetic experience, 5, 198. *See also* museums; *and under names of specific locations and artifacts*

exhibitions: Paris 1889, 3; related to Tutankhamen tomb discovery, 180

experience. *See* aesthetic experience; knowledge-experience synthesis

fada'il literature, 79, 133

Fahmy, Muhammad, 195

Faruq, King, 240, 247, 251, 255–56

feelings. *See* aesthetic experience; knowledge-experience synthesis

Fergusson, James, 55

film, 21, 276

Fir'awniyya, 274. *See also* Pharaonism

firmans, 32

Freemasonry, 21

French antiquarianism, Egyptology, 21, 27, 121, 286–87 n. 72; Bonaparte savants' work, 73, 93, 121, 284 n. 25; French-British rivalry and, 11, 13, 37, 59–60, 65–66; Louvre acquisitions, 60, 280 n. 15, 286–87 n. 72; Mariette's position in, 126–29; Memnonium and Memnon head, 30, 52; Tahtawi on, 121–22. *See also* Drovetti, Bernardino; European antiquarianism, Egyptology

French intervention in Egypt, 73, 93, 166, 168

French Revolution, 21, 287 n. 72

Fu'ad, King, 153, 154, 195, 200, 213, 230, 240, 251

Gardiner, Alan, 183
al-Garim, 'Ali, 244
Gershoni, Israel, 14–15
al-Ghitani, Gamal, 276
Gliddon, George, 28 n. 13, 109–13, 118–19
Gourna. *See* Gurna, Gurna natives
"Grand Entrance to the Temple of Luxor" (Roberts), 106, 107–8
Greco-Roman antiquities, 33, 47, 48, 49, 52, 55, 57, 287 n. 72; Elgin marbles, 46, 55, 57–58, 284 n. 25
Greenblatt, Stephen, 294 n. 34
guidebooks: for European travelers, 94–95; for museums, 51, 52–55, 127–29, 288 n. 93
Gurna, Gurna natives, 15–16, 27, 41, 283 n. 14; as Memnon head removal workforce, 35–37, *38–39*, 40

Haggard, H. Rider, 241
al-Hakim, Tawfiq, 215, 268; *Awdat al-ruh* (*Return of the Spirit*), 126, 159–62, 252
Hamilton, William, 30, 31, 47, 225, 284 n. 25
Hamza, 'Abd al-Qadir, 235
Hanna, Murqus, *194*, 206
Hasan, Salim, 192
Haussmann, Georges-Eugène, 136
Hawass, Zahi, 281 n. 30, 289 n. 121, 308–9 n. 1
Haykal, Muhammad Husayn, 213–15, 235, 268
Heidegger, Martin, 1–2, 3, 4
Hermes Trismegistus, 21, 85
Herodotus, 138, 253, 307 n. 29
hieroglyphics, 76, 91–100, 284 n. 30; Champollion's Egyptian travels and, 94, 97–100; collecting and

acquisitions and, 31; decipherment of, 7, 53, 76, 93; Egyptian School of Ancient Language and, 142–43, 144, 145; interpretation of antiquities and, 7, 51, 53, 75–76, 92, 94–96; pre-decipherment European views of, 92; reception of Champollion's work on, 53, 95–96; Rosetta Stone and, 76, 91, 93, 284 n. 25
historical interpretation (of antiquities), 7–8, 48, 53–55, 75–76; hieroglyphic studies and decipherment and, 7, 51, 53, 75–76, 92, 94–96; museum acceptance of Pharaonic objects and, 53–55, 95–97; of Pyramids of Giza, 122–23; Tahtawi's synthesis of European and Arabo-Islamic knowledge, 121–24
historiography: ibn Khaldun, 129–31; Tahtawi, 130–36
homeland (*watan*), 133–34, 135–36, 139–40, 297–98 n. 20
Horkheimer, Max, 3–4
Hourani, Albert, 132, 134
Hunterian Museum, 50
Husayn, Ahmad, 126, 157–59, 244
Hyksos, 256, 257–59

'ibar (lessons), Pharaonic monuments as, 79–80, 81–82, 85, 141
ibn al-Athir, Diya' al-Din, xi
ibn al-Nadim, 122
ibn al-Sa'ati, 'Ali ibn Muhammad, 84
ibn 'Arabi, 291 n. 8
ibn Khaldun, 129–32, 133, 141
ibn Khurradadhbih, Abu al-Qasim, 72
ibn Muhammad, Ahmad, 80
ibn Rabi'a, Labid, 80–81
ibn Taymiyya, 261
ibn Tulun, 87
Ibrahim, Hafiz, 215

Ibrahim Pasha, 32–33, 119
iconoclasm, 79, 86–87, 112, 292
  n. 17, 295 n. 44; Muslim criticisms
  of, 87–88, 89–90
idols (*sanam*), idolatry (*shirk*), 73–74,
  86–87, 131, 144–45, 146, 291 n. 4;
  Qutb on, 263, 265, 267, 268. *See
  also* paganism; Pharaonic religion
Idris, 85
al-Idrisi, Jamal al-Din, 79–80, 82, 83, 85
ignorance (*jahiliyya, al-Jahiliyya*),
  144, 234, 238, 240, 248–49, 260,
  266–67, 272. *See also* knowledge-
  ignorance dialectic
imperialism, European. *See* colonialism
imperialism, modern Egyptian, 148
imperialism, Pharaonic, 98, 148–49
International Monetary Fund, 276
Irby, Charles Leonard, 29
Islam: Pharaonic religion and, 73–74,
  78–79, 124, 128–29, 144–46, 148,
  248–49; Qutb's gloss of, 266. *See
  also* Qur'an, Qur'anic interpretation
Islambuli, Khalid, 277
Islamic iconoclasm, 79, 86–87, 112,
  292 n. 17, 295 n. 44; Muslim criticisms of, 87–88, 89–90
Islamic law, 263, 266–67
Islamic literature. *See* literature,
  Arabo-Islamic; Qur'an, Qur'anic
  interpretation
Islamism, 237, 239, 240–41, 244,
  272, 275; Islamist responses to
  Pharaonism and, 235, 238, 240–41,
  248–49, 275; Muslim Brotherhood
  and, 237, 238, 245–49, 261, 272.
  See also Qutb, Sayyid
Isma'iliyya, 245
Isma'il Pasha, 127, 136, 142, 154, 286
  n. 56; derision of, by Sanu', 166,
  167, 169; removal of, 166

i'tibar (contemplation), 21–22, 79, 80,
  82, 83, 85

al-Jabarti, 'Abd al-Rahman, 72–75, 91,
  115, 146, 298 n. 43
jahiliyya, al-Jahiliyya (ignorance),
  144, 234, 238, 240, 248–49, 260,
  266–68, 272
*Jama'iyyat al-Ikhwan al-Muslimin.
  See* Muslim Brotherhood
Jameson, Fredric, "Third World Lit-
  erature in the Era of Multinational
  Capitalism," 268–71
Jankowski, James, 14–15
Jenkins, Ian, 47
Jewish tradition, Pharaonic Egypt in,
  21, 74
Jomard, Edmé-François, 116, 121

Kamal, Ahmad, 143, 192
Kamil, 'Adil, 215
Kamose, 257
Karnak, Belzoni at, 44
Khalidi, Tarif, 292 n. 11, 292 n. 14
Khater, Antoine, 14, 102
Khufu. *See* Cheops
knowledge-experience synthesis
  (viewing antiquities), 5, 92–93, 96,
  143–44, 160, 198. *See also* aesthetic
  experience; exhibition; historical
  interpretation
knowledge-ignorance dialectic:
  al-Jahiliyya, 144, 234, 238, 240,
  248–49, 260, 266–67, 272; knowledge of past as self-discovery and
  patriotism, 144, 150, 156, 164–65,
  215, 235–36; in Qutb, 235–37; view
  of modern Egyptians as ignorant
  and, 113–15. *See also* Pharaonist
  pedagogy
Kuberski, Philip, 281 n. 27
kufr, 78, 292 n. 16

Lacau, Pierre, *194*, 195, 204, 209
lessons (*'ibar*), Pharaonic monuments
    as, 79–80, 81–82, 85, 141
Liberal Constitutionalist Party, 206,
    207, 211, 213, 231, 275
Light, Henry, 30
literary allegory, 268–72; in Mahfouz,
    239–40, 250, 251–52, 255–60, 271;
    in Qutb, 262, 272
literary Pharaonism, 20, 126, 155–64,
    215–16, 234–36; claims about
    Pharaonic monotheism in, 146,
    148; Hakim and, 126, 159–62, 215;
    Haykal and, 213–15, 235; Husayn
    and, 126, 157–59; Musa and,
    155–56; nationalist themes in, 156,
    161, 164, 216, 218, 220–21; Pha-
    raoh figures in, 171; post-*Nahda* re-
    prise of, 234–39, 240; resurrection
    themes in, 126, 155, 158, 160–61,
    163, 164–65, 214–15, 218; Shawqi's
    Tutankhamen poetry, 216–22;
    theater, 215; visual iconography in
    print, 211–13. *See also* literature,
    Egyptian; al-Tahtawi, Rifa'a Rafi'
literature, Arabo-Islamic, 13, 75,
    76–91, 115; accounts of the Pyra-
    mids in, 78, 79–80, 81, 83, 84–86,
    123, 138; antagonism of nationalist
    thinkers and, 150; antiquities as les-
    sons or reminders in, 78–80; appre-
    ciation ethic in, 86–91; echoes in
    Shawqi's poetry, 218–19; Egyptol-
    ogy scholarship, 13, 281 n. 29; ibn
    Khaldun's *Muqaddima*, 129–32;
    modern Egyptian Egyptology and,
    122–24, 125, 135–36, 138–39,
    140; modern historical romances
    in, 244–45; Pharaoh figure in, 75,
    76–78, 291 n. 7, 291 n. 8, 292 n. 11;
    pre-Islamic poetic tradition and,

80–82, 293 n. 31; ruins and wonder
    in, 21–22, 80–86. *See also* litera-
    ture, Egyptian; Qur'an, Qur'anic
    interpretation; *and under names of
    specific authors and titles*
literature, Egyptian, 155; eroticism in,
    254; inspiration of Tutankhamen
    tomb discovery on, 181, 215–24;
    Mubarak and, 125, 136–42, 151,
    164, 275, 295 n. 44; mummy fic-
    tions in, 19, 222–24; 1930s–1940s,
    234–39; Qutb and, 237–38,
    240–41, 260–68, 272, 275; Sanu'
    and, 22, 166, 167, 168–69, 300–301
    n. 2; sentimental and historical ro-
    mances in, 244–45, 254–55; theater
    and, 215, 300 n. 2. *See also* literary
    Pharaonism; literature, Arabo-
    Islamic; Mahfouz, Naguib
literature, European: Memnon head
    and Shelley's "Ozymandias," 26, 29,
    67–71. *See also* travel narratives
Louvre Museum, 60, 280 n. 15,
    286–87 n. 72
Lucas, Alfred, 183, 187–88
Luxor: Belzoni in, 33, 44; Husayn's
    memoir of, 157–59; Roberts's Grand
    Temple lithograph and, *106*, 107–8

al-Ma'arri, 89
Mace, Arthur C., 180, 183, 195–96
Mahfouz, Naguib, 20, 215, 237, 238,
    239–40, 241–45; *'Abath al-aqdar*
    (Play of Fates), 234, 239, 243, 249–52;
    Akhenaton, 276; background to
    and earliest work of, 241–45; on his
    own work, 234, 241, 268, 271, 308
    n. 57; *Kifah Tiba* (The Struggle for
    Thebes), 234–35, 236–37, 239–40,
    256–60, 271; *Misr al-qadima* (An-
    cient Egypt) translation, 242–43,

249, 250; Musa and, 243–44; political allegory in, 239–40, 250, 251–52, 255–60; *Radubis* (Rhodopis), 234, 239, 253–56, 308 n. 57; reception of early works of, 234–35, 271, 308 n. 57

Mahmud, Muhammad, *207*

al-Ma'mun, 87

Mangles, James, 29

maps, of Pharaonic Egypt, *147*, 148

Mariette, Auguste, 94–95, 126–28, 138, 142, 296 n. 71

marvels. *See* wonder themes, rhetoric

Marx, Karl, 261

al-Mas'udi, 88

al-Mawdudi, Abu al-'Ala', 261, 266

Maxwell, F. M., 206

al-Mazini, Ibrahim 'Abd al-Qadir, 232–33

McClellan, Andrew, 280 n. 15

measurement of Pharaonic antiquities, 52, 85, 138

media. *See* press

Mehmed 'Ali, 124, 127, 286 n. 56; antiquities policies and, 27, 110–11, 118, 119, 135; Champollion and, 97–100; development projects and, 137, 141; Memnon head and, 30–31, 32; in Sanu''s satire, 169

Memnon, 29, 279 n. 1

Memnon head, *xii*, 1, 7, 24–71, 279 n. 1; arrival and reception of, in England, 24, 26, 45–47, 50–51, 58–60; artifaction of, 26–27, 62–63, 70; Belzoni's collection expedition and, 31–37, 40–45; British Museum acquisition of, 24, 26–27, 29, 65; early removal attempts, 30–31; excavation of and removal of, from site, 24, 35–37, *38–39*, 40; guidebook descriptions of, 51, 52–55, 288 n.

93; Jabarti's account of collection and, 73, 290–91 n. 3; museum installation of, 25, 45–46; Noeden's study of, 51–52; provenance records of, 26–27, 62–63; relocation of, to Egyptian Sculpture Gallery, 55, *56*, 57; Shelley's "Ozymandias" and, 67–71; transport of, from excavation site, 24, 26, 43–45; in travel accounts, 30, 35

Memnonium, 24, 29–30. *See also* Memnon head

Merenre, 253–55

Merton, Thomas, 203, 204

Meskell, Lynn, 15

Metropolitan Museum of Art, 176, 183

Miller, Edward, 50

Misr al-Fatat (Young Egypt party), 126, 157

Misriyya (Egyptianism), 247–48

Mitchell, Timothy, 3, 15, 137–38

modern Egypt, Egyptians. *See* Egypt, modern; Egyptians, modern

monotheism, 129; Akhenaton's heresy, 146; Pharaonic religion characterized as, 144–46, 148

Montagu House, 6–7, 50, 59

Moser, Stephanie, 9

Moses-Pharaoh confrontation, 76–77, 263–64, 291 n. 7, 291 n. 8, 292 n. 11

Mountnorris, Lord, 31, 47

movies, 21, 276

Mubarak, 'Ali, 125, 136–42, 151, 164, 273, 295 n. 44

Mubarak, Hosni, 237, 276

Mukhtar, Mahmoud, 227–28, 230; *Nahdat Misr*, 228–33

mummies: in British Museum, 50; export trade of, 91, 290 n. 123; in Mahfouz's work, 241; mummy fictions and, 19, 222–24

Murad, Mahmud, 215

Musa, Salama, 155–56, 243, 268

museums: attitudes of, about Egyptian antiquities, 96; development of, as public institution, 5, 9, 47, 287 n. 79; Egyptian description of, 102; Egyptian Museum, Cairo, 176, 198, 208–9, 241; first Antiqakhana, 117, 118–20, 124; second Antiqakhana, 126–29, 135, 154; Tutankhamen tomb discovery and, 176. See also British Museum; exhibition; Louvre Museum

Muslim Brotherhood, 237, 238, 245–49, 261, 272

Muslim culture: Muslim rule of Egypt viewed as decline, 112–15, 132, 141; views of Pharaonic Egypt and, 21, 73–74, 84–85, 124. See also Islam; Islamism; literature, Arabo-Islamic

Mustafa, Ibrahim, 154–55

al-Mutanabbi, 81

Mutran, Khalil, 215, 230

al-Nahda (the Awakening), 20, 126, 178, 268; interest in Pharaonic past and, 271, 272; Islamist responses to, 237–38, 240–41, 260, 261; literature of, 155, 277; post-Nahda Pharaonism and, 234–39

Nahdat Misr: Le Réveil de L'Égypte, 228–33

al-Nahhas, Mustafa, 230

Najib, Ahmad, 143, 151–52

Napoléon, 97. See also Bonaparte savants

Nasim, Muhammad Tawfiq, 207

Nasser, Gamal Abdel, 238, 258, 261

national allegory, 269–70. See also literary allegory

nationalism. See Egyptian nationalism, nationalist themes

nationalist themes: in Mahfouz, 243–44, 250, 251, 257–60; in Pharaonic literature, 156, 161, 216, 218, 220–21; in popular literature, 222–24

National Repository, 5

Neoplatonism, 21

new-age paganism, 21

Nietzsche, Friedrich, 261

Nikrotis, 253

1919 revolution, 177, 199–200, 257; in Hakim's 'Awdat al-ruh, 159–62; Nahdat Misr commemorative sculpture and, 227–33

Noeden, G. H., 51–52

nomadic peoples and cultures, 130–31, 259; in Mahfouz, 250, 251, 256, 257–59

Norden, Frederick Lewis, 30

obelisks, 21

objectivity, objectification. See artifaction; power, control, and subject-object opposition

opera, 21

Orientalism, 101, 103, 128

Osiris myth, 126, 161, 163, 300 n. 81

Ottoman Empire, rule, 66, 126, 199; anti-Turkish sentiment in Mahfouz and, 244, 259; Belzoni's interactions with Ottoman officials and, 32–33, 35–36, 37, 41, 42–43, 44, 66

Ozymandias, 29

paganism: al-Jahiliyya, 144, 234, 238, 240, 248–49, 260, 266–67, 272; Muslim attitudes toward, 73–74, 78–79, 248. See also iconoclasm; idols, idolatry; Pharaonic religion; polytheism

Palestine, Palestinian conflicts, 246–47

pan-Arabism, 163, 164, 244

Parthenon friezes. *See* Elgin marbles

Passover, 21

patriotism (Egyptian), 133, 136, 149–50, 161–62, 164, 247; Banna on Egyptianism, 247–48; domestic tourism and, 154–55, 156, 158–59, 299 n. 64. *See also* Egyptian nationalism, nationalist themes; *watan*

pedagogy and museum exhibition, 3–4, 5–6, 47, 287 n. 79. *See also* Pharaonist pedagogy

Petrie, William Matthews Flinders, 9, 178–79, 183

Pettigrew, Thomas "Mummy," 21

Pharaoh figures, 277; in classical Arabo-Islamic tradition, 22, 74, 75, 76–78, 291 n. 7, 291 n. 8, 292 n. 11; in Mahfouz, 250, 251–52, 253–54, 255–57, 258; Moses-Pharaoh confrontation story and, 76–77, 263–64, 291 n. 7, 291 n. 8, 292 n. 11; Pharaoh as tyrant, 166, 169–71, 239, 264–66, 268; Pharaonic curse and retribution themes, 222–23; Qutb's analysis of Pharaoh, 265–66; Tutankhamen in literature, 216–24

Pharaonic antiquities: in classical Arabo-Islamic tradition, 73–75, 78–86, 271–72, 291 n. 4; destruction and defacement of, 87–89, 91, 98–99, 100, 108–11, 116–17, 295 n. 44; as Egyptian patrimony, 134–36; European viewers' relations to, 1–5; measurement of, 52, 85, 138; as universal patrimony, 103, 109, 112–13, 140. *See also* aesthetic values; artifaction; artifact owner-

ship, control; artifacts; exhibition; historical interpretation

Pharaonic Egypt: continuity of, with modern Egypt, 14, 101, 124, 133–36, 149, 161–62, 276; imperialism of, 98, 148–49; Muslim views of, 21, 73–74, 124; range of modern images of, 21–22; technology and, 84–85, 113–14

Pharaonic religion: Akhenaton's heresy, 146; Arabo-Islamic views of, 73–74, 124, 248–49; attempts at reconciliation of, with Islam, 128–29, 144–46, 148; Egyptian textbook account of, 145–46; Osiris myth, 126, 161, 163, 300 n. 81

Pharaonic sites: as habitation sites, 40–41, 91, 107, 281 n. 30; Roberts's lithographs of, 104–8, *105, 106*

Pharaonism, 14–15, 18, 20, 164–65, 268, 273–75; Egyptian nationalism and, 14–15, 126, 156, 164–65, 244, 273, 274; as elite movement, 18, 126, 155; emergence of, 124–26, 132; influence of, on later intellectuals, 234–35; Islamist responses to, 235, 238, 240–41, 248–49, 275; Mahfouz and, 234–35; modern echoes of, 275–77; Mukhtar's *Nahdat Misr* sculpture, 227–33; after the *Nahda*, 234–39; political, 125, 126, 177, 239, 274–75; as secularism, 239, 276; Tutankhamen tomb discovery and, 177–78, 211–16; visual imagery of, in print, 211–13. *See also* literary Pharaonism; Pharaonist pedagogy; Qutb, Sayyid

Pharaonist pedagogy, 125, 142–55, 164–65, 235–36, 238, 241; attempts at reconciliation of, with Pharaonic

Pharaonist pedagogy (*cont.*)
religion with Islam, 128–29, 144–
46, 148; Bulaq museum mission
and, 127; in contemporary Egypt,
275–76; motivations for learning
and, 143–44, 149, 150, 154, 156;
Pharaonic expansionism and,
148–49; Pharaonic history in textbooks and, 144–45, 145–46, 148;
School of Ancient Language and,
142–43, 144, 145; tourism as, 143,
151–52, 154–55, 276–77
photography, of Tutankhamen tomb
excavations and discovery, 183–84,
185, 186
place, territory, and Egyptian identity,
nationalism, 125, 133–36, 139–40,
141, 149–50, 164, 244, 247–48,
297–98 n. 20
Pococke, Richard, 30, 68
political control and acquisitions and
collecting, 9–10, 65–66. *See also*
colonialism
political themes in Mahfouz, 250,
251–52, 255–60. *See also* nationalist themes
polytheism: Islamic views of,
73–74, 248; Pharaonic polytheism
minimized, 144–46, 148. *See also*
Pharaonic religion
popular culture: in contemporary
Egypt, 276; impact of Tutankhamen tomb discovery on, 178, 180,
196, 211–16; in Pharaonic Egypt,
19, 21–22, 179, 222–24, 308–9 n. 1
power, control, and subject-object
opposition, 2, 3–4. *See also* artifact
ownership, control; political control and acquisitions and collecting
preservation. *See* conservation,
preservation

press: coverage of Tutankhamen tomb
excavations, 180, 191, 192–93,
196–97, 200, 203–4; Pharaonic imagery in popular press, 211–13, 276
progress. *See* development
publicity issues, of Tutankhamen
tomb discovery, 192–98, 203–4
Pyramids of Giza, 308–9 n. 1; Arabo-
Islamic views and accounts of, 78,
79–80, 81, 83, 84–86, 123, 138; attempts to enter or demolish, 87–88;
historical interpretation of, 122–23;
Mubarak's account of, 138–39; as
Pharaonic iconography, 211

Quibell, James Edward, 203, 204
Qur'an, Qur'anic interpretation,
263–64, 307–8 n. 49; Pharaoh figure in, 75, 76–78, 291 n. 7, 291 n. 8,
292 n. 11; quotations from, 76, 77,
248–49, 293 n. 32; Qutb's exegeses
on, 234, 238, 261–68; ruins and
monuments in, 78–79, 80, 90, 135;
wonder and marvel in, 294 n. 34
Qutb, Sayyid, 234, 237–38, 240,
260–68, 272, 275; on Mahfouz'
Kifah Tiba, 234–37

race: Afrocentric views of Egyptian
antiquity and, 12–13, 17; in Mahfouz' *Kifah Tiba*, 258–60; racialized
aesthetic analysis and, 53
Ramses II (the Great), 29, 53, 95, 97,
98, 279 n. 1,
Ram'sis (journal), 146, 148
Reid, Donald, 118, 120, 142, 145, 298
n. 36
religion, popular, and Pharaonic religious practices, objects, and sites,
91. *See also* Pharaonic religion;
*and under names of other specific
religious traditions*

representation, 1–3, 68–69, 71, 137.
See also exhibition
resurrection themes, 126, 132, 141,
144, 150–51, 163, 164–65; in
mummy fictions, 224; *Nahdat Misr*
sculpture and, 229, 230–31; in
Pharaonic literature, 126, 155, 158,
160–61, 163, 218
Riegl, Alois, 34
Roberts, David, portrayals of Egyptians, 104–8, *105, 106*
Robertson, Richard, 10
romanticism, 34–35
Rosetta Stone, 76, 91, 93, 284 n. 25
Rosicrucianism, 21
Royal Academy of Surgeons, 50
ruins: as aesthetic experience, 34–35,
40; in Arabo-Islamic literature,
21–22, 78–86, 89, 293 n. 31; in
Shawqi's poetry, 218–19. *See also*
Pharaonic sites; *and under names
of specific sites*

Sabaeans, Baghdadi on, 87
Sacy, Silvestre de, 93, 118, 121
Sadat, Anwar, 276, 277
Said, Edward, 23, 101
Sa'id Pasha, 126–27
Salah al-Din, 88
Salt, Henry, 29, 31, 32, 40, 58, 60, 61,
285 n. 37; reception of Memnon
head and, 46–47
sanam. See idols, idolatry
Sanu', Ya'qub, 22, 166, *167*, 168–69,
300–301 n. 2
Sappho, 253, 307 n. 29
al-Sayyid, Ahmad Lutfi, 142, 148–51,
199, 211, 213
School of Ancient Language, 142–43,
144, 145
schools. *See* Pharaonist pedagogy

science: in Egyptology, 8, 16, 62, 115,
178–79; Pharaonic Egyptian and
Muslim views of, 84–85. *See also*
technology
Scotto, Dr., 33
secularism, 200, 238, 239, 275; Pharaonic themes as symbols of, 239,
276; Qutb's break with and analyses
of, 237–38, 240–41, 260–63,
266–67. See also *al-Nahda*
security issues of Tutankhamen tomb
discovery, 188–89
Sells, Michael, 293 n. 31
separation: of archaeological sites
from modern context, 15, 41,
68–69; representation and exhibition and, 1–4
Seqenenre', 241, 257
Serres, Michel, 273
Seti I tomb exhibit, 287 n. 75
shame discourse, themes, 126, 144,
150, 155, 156, 164–65
Shamsi, 'Ali, *194*
Shawqi, Ahmad, 22, 170–71, 215, 230;
Tutankhamen poetry and, 216–22
Sheik Ibrahim. *See* Burckhardt, John
Lewis
Shelley, Percy Bysshe, 26; "Ozymandias," 29, 67–71
Shifra, 138
Silberman, Neil Asher, 14
slavery themes, meanings, 257–58,
265–66
Smirke, Robert, 55
Smith, Charles D., 297–98 n. 20
Smith, Horace, 26, 68
Smith, Joseph, 21
Société Archéologique, 121
Society of Muslim Brothers. *See* Muslim Brotherhood
Soliman, Abdel Hamid, *194*

Sommer, Doris, 308 n. 56
Sphinx: defacement of, 295 n. 44; in *Nahdat Misr* sculpture, 228, 229, 230, 233
Sphinx-Tutankhamen vignette, 222–23
stewardship, foreign intervention justified as, 112–14. *See also* conservation, preservation
Strabo, 29
Suez Canal, 136
Sufi tradition, Pharaoh and Pharaonic monuments in, 80, 291 n. 8
al-Suyuti, Jalal al-Din, 79

ta'ajjub (wonder, marvel), 82–83, 85, 294 n. 34
tadhkir, 78–79, 292 n. 15
Tagher, Jacques, 14
al-Tahtawi, Rifa'a Rafi', 118, 121–24, 125, 129, 211, 273; emergence of Egyptian identity and, 133–34, 141; as historiographer, 129–32, 133–34
Tawfiq, 154, 166, 168, 169
Teachers' College, 143, 154–55, 245
technology: modern Egyptian, 113–14; Pharaonic, 84–85, 113–14
territory, territorial nationalism. *See* place, territory, and Egyptian identity, nationalism
Thebes: Belzoni on, 33, 34; Roberts's Temple of Amun lithograph, 104, 105, 107. *See also* Memnonium
theft: accusations of, against Carter and Carnarvon, 208, 221–22; antiquities acquisition viewed as, 63, 64–65, 123; tomb raiding and security, 91, 188–89
"Third World Literature in the Era of Multinational Capitalism" (Jameson), 268–71

Thomas Cook Company, 154–55, 156
Thomsen, Christian Jürgensen, 8, 9
timelessness, 240, 272; as theme in Shawqi's poetry, 216, 218, 219, 220
timthal vs. *sanam*, 146, 298 n. 43
tomb raiding, 91; Tutankhamen tomb security and, 188–89. *See also* destruction, defacement of monuments
Tottenham, Paul, 195
tourism in Egypt: domestic, 126, 143, 151–56, 157–59, 276–77, 299 n. 64; foreign, 40–41, 96, 151–52, 276–77; public access to Tutankhamen's tomb, 190–98, 204–6, 208. *See also* travel narratives
Townley, Charles, 48
Townley Gallery, 6–7, 48–49. *See also* Egyptian Sculpture Room, Townley Gallery
travel narratives: Arabo-Islamic (*'aja'ib*), 82–84, 293–94 n. 33; European, 29–30, 33–34, 35, 68, 71, 94, 181–83; modern Egyptian, 182. *See also* tourism in Egypt
"Treatise on the Pyramids" (Suyuti), 79
Trinity, 87
Tutankhamen-Sphinx vignette, 222–23
Tutankhamen tomb discovery, excavations, 20, 172–226, 273; as aesthetic experience, 172–73, 181–83, 190; artifaction of tomb objects and, 174–77, 187, 189–90; benefits of, claimed by Egypt, 172; curse rumors and, 222; Egyptian reaction to, 192; excavation management tensions and, 176; impact of, on popular culture, 178, 180, 196, 211–16, 222–24; literature inspired by, 181, 215–24; objectification of artifacts and, 183–87; ownership

of artifacts, 200–201, 202, 208–10;
Pharaonism and, 177–78, 211–16;
photographs of, 183–84, *185*, 186;
political and legal context of, 177,
181, 199–210; preservation and
security issues of, 187–89, 191;
press coverage of, 180, 191, 192–93,
196–97, 200, 203–4; property
rights issues of, 200–201; public access issues of, 190–98, 204–6, 208;
significance of, 177–78, 224–26;
as spectacle, 193, 195–96, 197. *See
also* Carter, Howard
tyranny themes, 166, 169–71, 239,
262, 264–66, 268

Umma party, 199
United States, Qutb in, 237–38,
260–61
U.S. Consul. *See* Gliddon, George
'Urabi, Ahmad, 168
'Urabist revolt, 168, 169, 300–301 n. 2

Valley of the Kings, Belzoni at, 44
von Hees, Syrinx, 293–94 n. 33

Wafd Party, Wafdist politics, 126,
153, 177, 244, 251, 275; Carter
excavations and, 205–6; emergence
and early successes of, 199–200;
Muslim Brotherhood and, 246, 247;
Nahdat Misr and, 230, 231–32,
233. *See also* Egyptian nationalism,
nationalist themes

warnings (*tadhkir*), 78–79, 292 n. 15
Wasif, Wisa, 228
watan (homeland), 133–34, 135–36,
139–40, 297 n. 20. *See also* patriotism; place, territory, and Egyptian
identity, nationalism
Westmacott, Richard, 51, 55
Wilkinson, John Gardner, 119, 146, 148
Winckelmann, Johann, 48
women: in 1919 revolution, 200; peasant woman of *Nahdat Misr*, 228,
229, 230–31, 233
wonder themes, rhetoric: in Carter's
account of Tutankhamen tomb
discovery, 172–73, 181–83, 225;
in classical Arabic literature,
(*ta'ajjub*), 82–83, 85, 294 n. 34
World War I, 199, 201

Yakan, 'Adli, *207*, 228
al-Yamani, 'Umara, 123
Young, Thomas, 93
Young Egypt party, 126, 157
Young Men's Muslim Association, 246
Yusuf Kamal, 227

Zaghloul, Sa'd, 199, 200, 205–6, 208,
212, 244, 251
al-Zarkashi, Abu 'Abdallah Badr al-Din,
292 n. 15, 294 n. 34
Zaydan, Girgy, 244, 245

ELLIOTT COLLA

IS AN ASSOCIATE PROFESSOR OF

COMPARATIVE LITERATURE

AT BROWN UNIVERSITY.

Library of Congress
Cataloging-in-Publication Data

Colla, Elliott
Conflicted antiquities : Egyptology, Egyptomania,
Egyptian modernity / Elliott Colla.
p. cm.
Includes bibliographical references and index.
ISBN-13: 978-0-8223-3975-5 (cloth : alk. paper)
ISBN-13: 978-0-8223-3992-2 (pbk. : alk. paper)
1. Egyptology. 2. Egypt—Antiquities.
3. Nationalism—Egypt—History.
4. Egypt—Civilization—1798– I. Title.
DT60.C634 2007
932.0072—dc22
2007032514